W9-DFW-409

CAPITALISM AND CLASS STRUGGLE IN THE USSR

*To the memory of my mother, Jean Fernandez (1938-93),
who taught me the importance of struggle.*

Capitalism and Class Struggle in the USSR
A Marxist Theory

NEIL C. FERNANDEZ

Ashgate

Aldershot • Brookfield USA • Singapore • Sydney

HC
335
.F43
1997

Published by
Ashgate Publishing Ltd
Gower House
Croft Road
Aldershot
Hants GU11 3HR
England

Ashgate Publishing Company
Old Post Road
Brookfield
Vermont 05036
USA

British Library Cataloguing in Publication Data

Fernandez, Neil C.
    Capitalism and class struggle in the USSR : a Marxist
    theory. - (Avebury series in philosophy)
    1. Capitalism - Soviet Union 2. Philosophy, Marxist
    I. Title
    335.4'01

Library of Congress Catalog Card Number: 97-74510

ISBN 1 84014 186 7

Printed in Great Britain by The Ipswich Book Company, Suffolk.

Contents

List of Figures

List of Tables

Acknowledgements

The doctoral research from which this book grew was supervised by Hillel Ticktin, whose solidarity and encouragement were unfaltering; the difference in our views on transition and partyism was no impediment. John Crump made many useful suggestions, several of which I have acted on. Niels Turnbull helped with the final proof-reading. Warm thanks too to Dexter Dias, Roger Evans, Lorraine Hewitt, Kapil Juj, and Sîon Whellens.

I should like to express special gratitude to Hilde Hambro, who read numerous drafts of every chapter. She was a constant source of immense support throughout the entire period of research. Our son Arran helped spur the completion of the work.

Introduction

AIMS

Of the considerable number of Marxist and Marx-influenced works on the USSR, many have criticised the Soviet system as being either capitalist or based on class exploitation in a new guise. At the same time, however, there has been a great paucity of profound analyses of what Marx himself would have considered the most important factor in the history of the country: namely, the class struggle. The first aim of this work is to place an understanding of this factor at the centre of a critical theory.

The second aim, related to the first, is to broaden the scope of the Autonomist Marxist critique. No other Marxist school has focused so unfalteringly on the centrality of class antagonism; and yet until now no Autonomist writer has ever really theorised the conditions of class struggle in the world's largest country. This failing has been all the more glaring given that the 'hidden' — or rather, until the end of the 1980s, the largely 'unrepresented' — character of the workers' struggle, which most commentators agree has involved a widespread 'refusal of work,' would seem *prima facie* to make the USSR the country most clearly conforming to the Autonomist model. We do not, of course, aim simply to transfer insights which were primarily developed in criticism of Keynesianism to a context where Keynesianism has not been employed. But in emphasising the necessarily antagonistic nature of any class struggle, we do seek to identify the real political-economic importance of this struggle in all its profundity. In this sense, the work is intended as a contribution to the Autonomist-influenced field of critique in which important contributions were made earlier in the 1990s by Lebowitz (1992) and Shortall (1994).

In order to achieve these aims it is necessary to have some kind of overall theory of the nature of the Soviet system. But if such a theory's clarity and coherence must be grounded above all in its explanatory and analytical value in relation to the class struggle, it is still the case that a study of working class struggle alone provides an insufficient basis for an understanding of the nature of the social formation. Our third aim is thus to reach an understanding of the underlying logic of the mode of production in the USSR and of the specifically Soviet political-economic forms. Hence the work is also a contribution to the area of critique in which notable works have appeared in the present decade by Ticktin (1991) and Chattopadhyay (1994).

In the course of this book we attempt to show that the political economy of the USSR is fundamentally capitalist in nature; and in considering it in a critical and theoretical fashion we find the Marxist critique of capital and the Autonomist Marxist understanding of class struggle to be tools of very substantial utility. It is also argued that previous considerations of the USSR, both 'Marxist' and sovietological, do not offer a critique of the production relations of an adequately profound kind; and that even those Marxist writings which come closest to one are weakened by the insufficiency of their attention to the necessarily classist and antagonistic basis of those relations. Thus we hope not only to provide a framework for a more profound theoretical understanding of the nature of Soviet production relations than has hitherto been available; but also to demonstrate in what way the production relations in the USSR have been racked throughout the Soviet period by the irreducible struggle between the proletariat and capital. In both areas the examination of the contradictions of the Soviet economic system has led to the drawing of important and original conclusions.

Insofar as further empirical work could be done, however, in attempting to explain Soviet economic functioning in greater detail in terms of the manifestation of the underlying relations described here, the present work will hopefully point the way to further endeavours in what Marx referred to as the "reproduction of the concrete situation." (1903, p.208).

THE THEORETICAL APPROACH ADOPTED

In Chapter 1 we present our main theoretical concepts. Describing the overall theoretical orientation as communist, we present two ideas as fundamental. These are, first, that the basic stuff of history is class struggle; and second, that the essence of class struggle is class antagonism. References are made to the work of Marx; and Marxist theoretical positions are summarised which might be denoted as anti-Statist, Autonomist, and world-revolutionary, and described as anti-elitist, anti-ideological, and struggle-based. In order to emphasise the radical nature of the approach, and specifically of the view taken of autonomous working class struggle, we outline positions on leftism, trade unionism, and so on, as they have been developed in western Europe. Other writers who have adopted a similar approach (Negri, Cleaver, Pannekoek, Debord) are also referred to, but restrictions of time and space have meant that there is no discussion of opposing views, such as those espoused by empiricists or functionalists, democrats or Leninists. Nor do we deal at length with apparent weaknesses in the various communist works quoted.

It should be noted that this is a theoretical work. In other words, rather than the unearthing, collection, presentation, and analysis of a mass of empirical data, it has involved the development of an understanding centred around concepts of categories which, though real, are abstract. The work will, it is hoped, prove accessible to readers other than those closely acquainted with the workings of the Soviet 'administrative command system,' but inevitably there will be places where those more familiar with Soviet economic reality will find it easier to grasp the concrete significance of what is being argued. Thus there are no highly-detailed descriptions here of the practical operation of gross output targets; nor of the functioning of the other success indicators; nor of the weight of the ministries and *glavki*; nor indeed of the role of the ratchet principle (*planirovanie ot dostignutogo*), the plan revision process, passive money, full employment, norms, storming, plan fulfilment bonuses, or wage levelling. We have sought instead to theorise the political-economic basis which underlies these realities, and to give meaning in this context to the dynamic of class struggle: to focus on the wood, not the trees. For those among the less familiar with the USSR who are motivated to increase their 'background' knowledge, the following sources can be recommended, especially those marked with a (*): on the Soviet Economy, *Berliner 1957, Kaser 1970, Nove 1980b, A. Smith 1983, Lane 1985a, *Rutland 1985, Hewett 1988, and Åslund 1989; on the more specific topic of Soviet Economic Development, Hutchings 1982, Munting 1982, *Nove 1982 and Rutland 1985; on Soviet History, the 'textbooks' by Kochan and Abraham 1983, *Hosking 1985, and Dziewanowski 1989; and on Soviet Politics, *McCauley 1981, Lane 1985b, Hill and Frank 1986, G. Smith 1992, and Ponton 1994. To readers who are less than familiar with the categories and terminology of Marxist critique, meanwhile, we would recommend the following sources: Parts 1-2 of Volume 1 of Marx's *Capital* (1867, pp.125-280), Rubin 1928, Barrot 1972, Kay 1975 (pp.13-72) and *1979, and Cleaver 1979 (pp.71-173).

The field of knowledge in which the work is situated is that of the theoretical critique of political economy. To paraphrase a well-known passage from Marx (1903, pp.205-06), it might be said that when examining the USSR from the standpoint of the critique of political economy the proper thing to do may seem to be to start with the characteristics of concrete conditions such as industrial development, success indicators, and shortage. But in fact the methodological requirement is not so straightforwardly empirical, and the basis of the critique must on the contrary be the explanation of the "few decisive abstract, general relations" the movement of which *lies behind* the concrete historical developments. The present work is a contribution precisely to the theoretical understanding of these 'general relations.'

It does not, then, belong in the field of economics. It is not a 'case study' of

> how men and society *choose*, with or without the use of money, to employ *scarce* productive resources, which could have alternative uses, to produce various commodities over time and distribute them for consumption (Samuelson 1967, p.5),

nor of how supplies are distributed upon the stark assumption that they must necessarily be scarce in any "community" whatsoever. (Bergson 1964, p.3). In short, we do not assume that as soon as human beings no longer produce, either individually or in small groups, everything that they themselves wish to consume, exchange and scarcity must necessarily figure as permanent and natural features of the landscape. (Begg, Fischer, and Dornbusch 1987, p.2). On the contrary, we are interested in developing a 'root-and-branch' theoretical *critique* of a set of production relations: that is, of a set of human, social relations. (See Perlman 1968). And, as Rubin puts it, some production relations among the members of a given society presuppose the existence of others, whereas the latter relations do not necessarily imply the existence of the former. (1928, pp.31-32).

To take some examples: the commodity is of course a form of the product, and its existence is dependent on the relation known as 'social production.' But in the absence of the social relation known as exchange the result of social production would take a form other than that of the commodity. People could conceivably produce socially without making the distribution of product X from person or group A to person or group B dependent upon the transfer from B to A of control or 'disposal rights' over a given quantity of product Y. Indeed humans could not only do so socially, we could do so across the entire planet. Similarly, constant capital is a form taken by the material means of production, and those material means are themselves a product of 'accumulated labour.' But in the absence of capitalism the material means of production would take a form other than that of capital. Indeed there is nothing in the physical nature of a tool or a warehouse which makes it even a commodity, let alone which gives it a role in the cyclical expansion of the socialised product of wage-labour.

It is undeniably the case, of course, that numerous means of production do exist which it would be very hard to envisage outside of an exploitative mode of production. People unsubjected to forced labour would have no reason, for example, to spend time on 'dehumanising' production lines, in 'dehumanising' offices, or breathing in dust from cement or coal. But it is not the thing which determines the relation. (See Marx 1939, p.303). Rather, even the world's worst workplaces are not just iron, fast-moving conveyor belts, chemical and physical hazards, and heat: they are places where proletarians find themselves socially constrained to labour, to engage in social production. And the relations which determine the construction of means of production, along with those which determine the introduction of forms of discipline, are dependent upon — and contributory to the functioning of — underlying relations which are not only social but socially-determined and therefore destructible. Thus if people free from exploitation decide to get rid of offices, mines, and cement works altogether, this will not be because these means of production necessarily constitute capital owing to their physical characteristics, but rather because they could find no non-capitalist, non-exploitative, non-anti-social use for them. Until they were actually razed or diverted, they would still possess their physical characteristics, but they would no longer be capital. They would not be capital because no-one would be carrying out forced labour, either in those places or anywhere else. And if people further decide, as they probably will, that they want to build and use not only tools and warehouses but also machines and robots, these machines and robots will not be capital either, although they will take the form of material means of production and accumulated labour. To take the third case, even if a building currently used as a shoe-making plant, say, continues to be used for the same physical purpose in a non-exploitative society which it formerly served under capitalism, it too will be very far from being capital. Indeed it will no longer even be a 'factory' in the usual sense of the word, since it will no longer be a separate 'enterprise,' an area of social production socialised only indirectly via the nexus of commodity competition.

All of this becomes quite clear as soon as one has access to properly worked-out concepts of social production, the commodity, and capital, and an understanding of the possibility of communism. These, however, are precisely what the economists do not have, and it is no exaggeration to state that their approach depends literally on ruling them out right from the start. In a very well-known textbook, the 'positive economist' Lipsey can thus write in so many words that "the things...produced by the factors of production are called *commodities*"; and that "all those man-made aids to further production, such as tools, machinery and factories[,]...economists call *capital*." (1989, p.3). One merely wonders at the fundamental submission to the existing order of things which such formulations evince, in the same way that one would have little to say to someone who averred that a tree was something from which to lynch black people; or, to take one of Marx's examples, that a chair with four legs and a velvet cover must necessarily be used as a throne. (1933, p.997). In presenting themselves as 'disinterested' experts specialising in the objective functioning of the social 'machine' — as social scientists — economists are essentially among the high priests of modern capitalism. The critic can only reiterate, in passing economics by, that the aim of achieving a global generalisation of social relations other than those of exchange is not just feasible; it has actually been consciously striven for by numerous people and movements throughout various ages of exploitation. The science of economics does not simply fail to recognise these facts; it holds that to speak in this way at all is *by definition* to enter the realm of the stupid and the nonsensical. (See Buick and Crump 1986, pp.130-32).

Moreover, in no way is political economy free from this fundamental weakness. It does, of course, aim to study underlying relations — even those which pertain between classes — but the viewpoint from which it attempts to do so is precisely that which establishes the basis for the more empirical discipline of economics. (A. Smith 1776, Ricardo 1817). Smith, for example, observing that the development of the productive forces in the late 18th century depended on the "propensity to truck, barter and exchange one thing for another," does note, albeit in passing, that a question might reasonably be raised as to the origins of this "propensity." But the possible answers he suggests are, first, that it might be a matter of "human nature," and second, that it might be a necessary consequence of "the faculties of reason and speech." (1776, pp.117-18). In his *General Theory* (1936) the 'anti-classicist' Keynes follows a similar line, although in his case the attempt to 'justify' capitalism is more explicit. Thus he states his 'personal belief' that not only are there "valuable human activities" — he fails to specify which ones — "which require the motive of money-making and the environment of private wealth-ownership for their full fruition"; but there are also

> dangerous human proclivities [which] can be canalised into comparatively harmless channels by the existence of opportunities for money-making and private wealth, [and] which, if they cannot be satisfied in this way, may find their outlet in cruelty, the reckless pursuit of personal power and authority, and other forms of self-aggrandisement. (p.374)

In reality, both Smith and Keynes are indulging in little more than mystificatory waffle. Capitalism is not here because people in general are making the most of their mental and verbal and moral faculties; nor because if it were abolished the few who currently control it would become any more anti-social than they already are. The mode of production based on the profit-making of the few and the wage-labour of the many has been at least as blood-drenched as many of the slave societies of ancient times, and indeed it surpasses them all in terms of the extent and intensiveness of human alienation. Political economy does not simply assume this mode of production to be an inevitable result of the way humanity has 'progressed' — seen as a proposition, this is actually more celebratory than logically meaningful — but to be inescapable in the future too. In terms of the underlying relations, the message is simple: what is, must be, and should be, for all time — only ever more technologically equipped. O'Brien in

Nineteen Eighty-Four speaks from the same viewpoint when he offers the memorable image of "a boot stamping on a human face — for ever." (Orwell 1949, p. 230).

Doubtless some readers will feel that we are over-stating the case. Does the 'classical' Mill not attempt to give 'socialism' — or at least its 'workability' — a fair hearing? (1848, pp.253-69). Does the 'neo-Keynesian' Galbraith not actually advocate some form of it? (1974, pp.274-85). Surely these are two examples of political economists, or of 'macroeconomists,' who are less completely pro-capitalist than, say, Smith and Keynes? In response to such objections we would simply point to two of Mill's definitions: of wealth as "all useful or agreeable things which possess exchangeable value" (1848, p.11); and of capital as the "accumulated stock of the produce of labour." (p.68). To criticise exchangeability would still appear to be to criticise wealth; and to criticise capital to criticise the very existence of means of production other than land. And we will simply mention, without need for comment, the assertion by Galbraith, one-time president of the American Economic Association, that the American arms sector is 'socialist' in all but name. (1974, pp.283-85).

The standpoint of the *critique* of political economy is entirely opposed to that of political economy and economics. First, since the division of labour everywhere is social and not 'natural,' the fact that the organisation of labour could take a social form other than the existing one is held to be extremely important. The existing form is not a necessary result of advanced socialisation; and indeed this is what the radical critic must first understand in order to be a radical critic at all. As Shortall puts it, "human labour is not biologically determined": hence "any human individual has the potential, at least in principle, to perform any type of human labour." (1994, p.208). Second, it is understood that privative appropriation — the taking of control over resources in a way that deprives other people — is not 'natural' either. Third, once scarcity is understood as a result of privative appropriation it is grasped for what it really is: a *social* relation.

At this point both economics and privative appropriation appear in their true colours: the first as simply the science of scarcity's organisation; the second as preventive of the real possibility of a mode of production founded on *active human community*. (See Marx 1932, pp.90-97). This does not mean that it is methodologically wrong to conceive of scarcity as a form of distribution of the productive resources, nor of course to study its ramifications and organisation. The fallacy lies in holding that the social distribution of productive resources necessarily implies scarcity. In fact, since social production does not have to rest upon privative appropriation, it could take another form entirely: the form of abundance. (Kay and Mott 1982, pp.27-29).

Moreover, not only does the prevalence of scarcity depend upon the non-realisation of the possibility of communism; but the necessary existence of a tendency towards the realisation of this possibility, given that the alienation of humanity cannot be total, implies that so long as the communist tendency does not come to fruition scarcity must needs be *enforced.* This, in fact, is what is implied when scarcity is described as not being 'natural' in any way at all. Capitalism, then, or any other exploitative class society, involves the interaction of forms of production, distribution, and consumption which are also forms of the prevention of communism. And this is no mere side issue. Once it is understood, classes can be defined theoretically in the way that they define themselves in practice: not simply in terms of the 'factors of production,' but in terms of relations which are both antagonistic and eradicable.

THE NATURE OF SOVIET SOCIETY

In Chapters 2-3 we consider the question of the type of society which existed in the USSR. Taking the 'null hypothesis' regarding the production relations existing after the clear failure of a wartime revolutionary proletarian movement to be that they remained capitalist, we show that such a hypothesis is fully compatible both with Soviet reality and with the fundamental tenets of Marxian theory. We do not, though, in these two chapters, consider the role of the class struggle. Instead, enacting what Shortall would call a 'provisional closure' (1994), we close off the issue of class subjectivity in order to focus on the nature of the Soviet system as an objective reality.

In order to theorise the mode of production which existed in the USSR as capitalist, it is first necessary, of course, to be quite clear on what capitalism actually is. At the same time, if capitalism can take 'classical,' Soviet, and other forms, one would expect a Marxist theory of Soviet capitalism not simply to reproduce the Marxist critique of capitalism as a whole, but rather to enhance it. One would certainly mistrust any mere 'application' of a theory whose exposition was based on earlier developments in England (Marx 1867), Germany (Hilferding 1910), the United States (Braverman 1974), or elsewhere.

Before developing this line of thought, however, we first consider the various theories of Soviet capitalism which have been advanced so far. (Chapter 2). (Limitations of space have meant that the numerous 'non-capitalist' theories are not considered at this stage). In analysing and criticising them, we look first for whether or not they show the capitalist nature of the USSR in such a way as to reinforce and enhance Marx's critique of capitalism in general; and second, for whether or not they really contribute to a profound understanding of the specifically Soviet forms of economic bureaucracy. In short, we look for how they deal with the following two questions: why should the USSR be called capitalist? and how is it specific? We deal with the weaknesses of each theory individually, but in general we find that the grounding of each in Marx's critique of capital as self-expanding value is either inadequate or non-existent, and that the specific critique of Soviet bureaucracy is either untheoretical or else severely misinformed.

It may seem that it is putting the cart before the horse somewhat to criticise various previous 'capitalist' theories of the USSR prior to presenting an understanding of Marx's critique of capitalism in general, but the reason lies in the unfeasibility of presenting a theory of Soviet capitalism as in any way separate from the critique of capitalism as a whole. Since we have felt it best to expound the new theory only after having criticised earlier theories, and since any Marxist theory of the capitalist nature of the Soviet social formation must not only shed light on the USSR but must also enhance the overall critique, we have left the formulation of a critique of capitalism in general until the first part of Chapter 3. The categories of exchange-value, commodity, wage-labour, production for profit, value, abstract labour, surplus value, and capitalist money are gone through in sequence, and particular stress is laid on generalised exchange and the drive for growth. The central organising concept of the Marxist understanding of the capitalist system is described as being that of the M-C-M′ cycle.

Given the unsatisfactory nature of previous theories, we have consequently had to develop a theory of Soviet capitalism which is entirely new. (Chapter 3, second part). Soviet relations of consumption, distribution, and production are discussed in detail and are shown to take forms based upon generalised exchange; the form of labour is shown to be wage-labour; and a need for profitable growth is shown to have been intrinsic to the Soviet economic system. We then discuss how the functions of the M-C-M′ cycle are fulfilled in a manner specific to the Soviet context. The most important new concepts developed are those of bureaucratic/*blat* exchange-value and bureaucratic/*blat* money.

Readers should bear in mind at this stage that what we do not do is to start with a model of 'typical' capitalism defined as the capitalism which prevails (or prevailed) in, say, Britain or Germany or the United States — or the 'West' as a whole — and then proceed to argue that the USSR is also capitalist because it shares many of these countries' main characteristics. As with similar arguments regarding China, Cuba, India, Iran, or Japan, this would be a clear case of pandering to bourgeois thought. Certainly, capitalism can be and is more advanced in some areas than in others, but the areas where it is more advanced are not necessarily those where it developed earlier. Even if they were, in fact, that would still not mean that the production of surplus value would have a 'centre' of purity or typicality. We would propose, therefore, that a critic could quite reasonably begin an enquiry into the nature of capitalism in general by looking at how it developed in the USSR — or indeed in any other country. (And let us note in passing that in the 21st century she will indeed have cause to pay special attention to the forms of capitalist development in China and Japan). Of course it is true that some of the capitalist functions which were achieved in the USSR principally bureaucratically are often achieved elsewhere via the market — the construction of much working class housing, or of car or cigarette factories, for example — but it must also be realised that this statement can be turned around. That is, many of the functions fulfilled for capitalism in western countries by the market are in fact the self-same functions which behind the Iron and Bamboo Curtains are (or were) fulfilled for capitalism bureaucratically.

Behind the various methods and functions, it is argued, the overall 'function' of capital remains one: namely, its own accumulation, the cyclical accumulation of value. But an understanding of what capital achieves — a matter of class oppression and its own profitable circulation — by differing means in various areas, is in no way simply an intellectual complexification of revolutionary theoretical critique, any more than an understanding of capital's development in a given area over a period of time could reasonably be called an extravagance. On the contrary, it is practically and theoretically indispensable from a world-revolutionary point of view.

More concretely and specifically, whichever location the critic decides to take as her starting-point, she can hardly expect to construct an adequate understanding of capitalist world society except on the basis of a firm understanding of the variety of different forms which can be and are taken by capitalist *money*. Thus the critique given here of capitalist money in the USSR is most certainly offered as a contribution to the critique of capitalism as a whole; and in this sense it is intended to mark a point of departure.

Important questions which are not considered include the origins of the Soviet economic system as well as what might be termed the 'Russian question': namely, the elements of social continuity which have apparently been evident in certain aspects of life in Russia for centuries. These are questions which have often been related to that of the multilinearity or unilinearity of the succession of modes of production. (See Wittfogel 1957, Melotti 1972, Zimin 1977, Barbaria 1980, Shanin 1983; also Marx 1856a and Marx and Engels 1843-95). In light of the theory of Soviet capitalism argued here, though, it would now seem necessary to broaden the scope of research in this area. Not only must various developments within a single mode of production, capitalism, be considered in relation to the contradictions of preceding societies — a point which has been argued very effectively by Goldner (1991) — but the relative efficiency and inefficiency of various types of capitalist 'system' must be studied in terms of their relationship to various types of proletarian struggle as well as to contradictions within world capitalist society as a whole. It is hoped that this complex three-sided theoretical task will eventually be tackled in depth.

THE CLASS STRUGGLE

If the USSR should rightly be understood as capitalist, then of course, according to the ideas given in Chapter 1, one would expect the Autonomist critique — to some extent at least — to be of a certain explanatory value in relation to both the history of the system and its eventual crisis and downfall. Indeed, one would not expect to be able to reach a satisfactory theory of the nature of the system without understanding the forms which have been taken by the class struggle. Having moved from the 'world in general' (Chapter 1) to the fundamental nature of Soviet society (Chapters 2-3), we therefore concentrate in Chapters 4-7 upon the significance of class struggle in the region. The 'provisional closure' of Chapters 2-3 is removed. Having narrowed down the topic of consideration, we are able to consider a broader literature.

In Chapter 4 we consider the 'sovietological' theories: that is, theories presented within the field of Soviet Studies but outwith the area of 'Marxist critique.' We begin by scrutinising the most influential (political and economic) theories of the nature of the system to see what they have to offer, if anything, concerning the nature of working class struggle. It is probably necessary to state, though, that in considering sovietological views of the Soviet economy we do not attempt to cover exhaustively the entire literature on its various characteristics and problems — from the problem of technological introduction to the prevalence of poor quality output, from the effectiveness or lack of effectiveness of various kinds of targets to the role of plan fulfilment bonuses, from consumer shortages and excessive savings to the hoarding of supplies and the weight and relative efficiency of the military sector. Since the suggestion that most sovietological work has been focused elsewhere than on the class struggle is not in any way controversial, there is no need to cover this material at great length. Little purpose would be served in identifying all kinds of passing references to the workers purely in order to demonstrate that either they appear parenthetically or else their conditions and behaviour are simply 'noted' on lists of social facts. Instead, after choosing as illustration a number of influential works focused upon three well-known concepts (technological development, success indicators, and the constraints of shortage), we show how they do not provide an adequate basis for the formulation of a meaningful theoretical understanding of class struggle.

Nor do we criticise in detail the full gamut of all the sovietological analyses of various characteristics of workers' conditions either inside or outside the workplace, from the details of hiring to the role of closed enterprises, from the composition of expenditure to the role of the *propiska* and various types of convict labour, from the rise of the *sovkhozy* to the role of technical training. Instead, after showing how a range of descriptive work falls short of providing a basis for understanding even the category of class struggle, we proceed to look at three conceptions developed within sovietology: those of the 'incorporated worker,' the 'social compact,' and the 'historic compromise.' If not particularly influential in terms of 'general theory,' these nonetheless involve considerations of the class relation which suggest certain (albeit bourgeois) views of the nature of the political-economic system.

Next for consideration are the various 'Marxist' theories. Given that according to the positions outlined in Chapter 1 it is apparent that most of those who have endeavoured or claimed to write from a Marxist perspective have in fact failed to do so, a clear distinction is made between their theories and those of the few theorists who are held to have done so in reality. Chapter 5 is thus devoted to a critical review of the various theories we have labelled 'Marxist.' These are the theories which, while using Marxian terminology, have nevertheless neglected to consider the working class as a subversive force independent of representation, and consequently defend, in one way or another, the use of force over the working class. Related to this omission there is also the well-known view, wrongly considered to be Marx's, that during the period of 'revolutionary transition' relations such as money, the market, and wage-labour will actually be compatible with socialism (communism). It is clear that these include the various Leninist theories. Categorising them according to the three main theories of the nature of the USSR — the 'degenerated workers' state,' 'capitalism,' and the 'mode of production *sui generis'* — we scour them, as we have already scoured their 'sovietological' rivals, for what they have to say about working class struggle. In particular, we look at how working class struggle is understood to relate to the nature of the system.

In Chapter 6 we consider from a similar standpoint the existing *Marxist* theories of Dunayevskaya and James, Castoriadis (in one period), and Ticktin and the *Critique* school. In all of these theories working class conditions and resistance play a much more important role than they do in the theories criticised in Chapter 5. Dunayevskaya and James and Ticktin are all, of course, supporters of some kind of Leninist vanguardism, and they and Castoriadis are believers in some kind of 'transitional society'; and thus there are major contradictions in their work. But if we do not wish to brush the latter aspects of their work under the carpet, in the present context it is the former aspect which interests us most. The latter aspects have certainly played their part in causing what weaknesses there are in their consideration of class struggle, but it is most relevant here for these weaknesses to be considered as limits on the corresponding strengths. Paying special attention to Ticktin's theory, we show it to be suggestive of an Autonomist understanding of class relations even as it remains confined within faulty concepts of capitalist decline and non-capitalist 'exceptionalism' — and we recognise this for the major theoretical achievement that it is. Chattopadhyay's theory is also considered in this section. Although closer to a communist viewpoint than the others insofar as he insists uncompromisingly on the nature of communism (socialism) as a society without money and wages, unlike them he admittedly fails to take the power of the workers into much account. But his consideration of issues that the other 'capitalist' theorists miss, based on his specific theory of Soviet capitalism, is nonetheless of relevance to the class struggle. A main concern at this stage is to encourage a preliminary understanding of the explanatory power which one could expect of a methodological prioritisation of class antagonism.

This is the first time that these theories of the nature of the USSR have been systematically criticised in terms of what they say about the working class and its struggle.

It is worth stating, however, what we do not cover. Thus we give no consideration to what the official 'Communist' ideologies have said on the issue. These we view as fundamentally conservative — either of the international standing of one of the world's established regimes (the USSR, China, Yugoslavia, etc.), or of the parliamentary standing of certain western political parties — when not literally reactionary in the sense of harking back to the (actually wholly capitalist) 'geopolitical bipolarities' of the 1940s and 1950s. If they are (or were) thus necessarily apologetic — of present, past, or both — rather than critical, then in the very Marxian terms to which they themselves superficially appeal they have to be understood as being propagandistic rather than theoretical. Of course sovietological studies fall similarly under the heading of capitalist ideology, and are similarly commissioned by capitalist authorities, and in no way do we mean to suggest that in comparison with them the ideologies of the 'Communist' Parties are even more distant from revolutionary critique — or yet that they are 'madder.' (It is hardly less mad to defend capitalism in general whilst claiming to oppose the underlying 'society' of the USSR, or indeed to affect a full 'objectivity,' than it is to claim to oppose capitalism in general whilst defending that 'society.') It is simply that, since these parties are — at one and the same time — both explicitly defensive of Soviet political economy (or its roots) and pseudo-oppositional to capital, rather than pseudo-objective in the fashion of much of sovietology (particularly liberal sovietology), they would have to be criticised in a different way. In order to go beyond just saying that they are mad, one would not be able to avoid looking at why, subjectively, they say what they say — for example, that the working class is the dominant class and that the USSR knows no class contradictions of an antagonistic nature; or, conversely, that 'class struggle' becomes more intense under 'socialism' than under 'capitalism.' And to study such political 'Lysenkoisms' is not one of the aims of the present book.

Second, nor do we consider in this context the works of Soviet social scientists. If it would be a mistake to deny their interest, nonetheless the main aim from a revolutionary viewpoint would be to show how they appear not as 'objective' analyses or theories, but rather as constituting a necessary field for policy debates on one side of the class antagonism. In other words, since the proletarian pole of this socially-determinant antagonism is understood as being identical to working class autonomy, all consideration of 'what official policy should be,' however 'objective,' and perhaps even especially when 'radical' or 'progressive,' would be explained as serving the material interests of the exploitative society. This point has already been amply demonstrated by Arnot (1988) with reference to various Soviet academicians. More specifically, Arnot shows how the utility of the "traditional Stalinist view of political economy" declined from at the latest the 1960s on, and how a revised, 'functionalist' sociology was fostered instead until it became able to provide serious "policy responses to management problems." (p.23). In Chapter 7 we do consider the most 'strategic' of the relevant policy advice delivered by Soviet social science in the 1980s, and find that it definitely supports our basic conclusions; but there undoubtedly remains considerable scope — for someone more inclined to undertake the nitty-gritty of the 'critique of sociology' — to research this material in greater depth and decode it in finer detail.

We come in Chapter 7 to construct a view of the relationship between class struggle and the nature of the system. The structure of this chapter is similar to that of Chapter 3. In the first section we present a theoretical understanding of the class struggle under capitalism in general. The antagonism between the working class and capital is identified at each stage of the capital and labour-power circuits: investment and sale, production and reproduction. We also discuss the antagonism with reference to capitalist growth, paying special attention to the categories of productivity and labour intensity, absolute and relative turnover, and the workers' struggle for higher wages and less work. Specific references are made to works by Kay and Negri.

In the second section we proceed to construct a view of the importance and radicality of working class struggle in the concrete case of the USSR. This bears a number of original aspects. Building upon the theory of Soviet capitalism developed in Chapter 3, we attempt to avoid the weaknesses of previous theories criticised in Chapters 4-6. In discussing the control exercised by Soviet capital over its own circuit, over socialised production and reproduction, we emphasise throughout the inherent and fundamental class opposition to this control. In particular we look at the extraction of absolute and relative surplus value. In a Soviet context this is a topic which only Chattopadhyay has dealt with before (1994); and in relation to class antagonism it is dealt with here for the first time.

The view is reached that whilst capitalist domination in the USSR did enter the period of relative surplus value extraction, and both wages and productivity rose, the form of growth — involving the systemic prioritisation of material investment and 'gross output' — was based merely on increasing productivity, and not also on labour intensification (accelerated turnover). At the root of this lay the fact that the rulers made substantial concessions to the workers' struggle for *less hard work*, especially in terms of product quality. This ensured that the capitalist subsumption of labour, although 'real' rather than simply 'formal,' was not only inefficient but eventually chronically so. Owing to the workers' successful resistance to hard work Soviet capital was not 'unwilling' but rather unable to institutionalise a dynamic of labour intensification. With brief reference to analyses made by Gorbachev, Aganbegian, and especially Zaslavskaia, it is shown that this understanding is fully consistent with the views expressed by these important strategists during the 'pre-crisis' period of the late 1980s.

After summarising our understanding of the specific forms of both class struggle and the development of capital in the USSR, we then propose a basis for understanding the nature of the present economic crisis in the region.

1 A Communist Approach

In this chapter we present the theory and concepts which underlie and inform the work as a whole. Since the nature of the USSR is considered in context below (Chapter 3), as is the class struggle within its borders (Chapter 7), the current chapter is confined to considerations deemed to be the most over-arching. Core ideas are introduced according to their usage within a radical tendency which is most usefully described as 'theoretical communism.' As will become clear, this tendency's thought has been greatly influenced by the school of Autonomist Marxism (especially Negri), from which in particular it takes its strong insistence on the fundamental importance of antagonistic class polarity.[1] But at the same time it is both eclectic and fundamentally critical — highly critical, in fact, of some of Autonomism's weaknesses.[2] Influences in the present century have also included council communism (especially Pannekoek), the Situationist International (especially Debord), and the writings of the French theoretician Barrot.[3]

The most important concepts are given in **bold** when they first appear in the main text.

CLASS STRUGGLE AND COMMUNISM

It is convenient to clarify the theoretical starting-point with reference to Marx's conception of the **class struggle** and **communism.**

First, it is taken as axiomatic that "the history of all hitherto existing societies is the history of class struggles." (Marx and Engels 1848, p.67). In any society which is not communist — that is, in any society founded upon exploitation, in any class society — there is held to be a necessary struggle between the exploiters and the exploited. In the most general terms possible, the underlying categories which relate to this struggle are those of the **surplus product** and the **control over its extraction**. The surplus itself is defined as that part of the social product which, rather than going to fulfil the needs of the producers, is appropriated instead by the exploiters. In other words, it is a category defined by the exploitation by one social group of the productive activity of another. And clearly the extraction of this surplus must be subject to some sort of control.

It is further understood that the extraction of the surplus product is a process which differs from one kind of exploitation to another. And since it is the existence of the surplus product which determines the existence of exploitation in the first place, it can only be the form of this extraction which determines the nature of the specific exploitative relationship. As Marx puts it:

> the specific economic form in which unpaid surplus labour is pumped out of the direct producers determines the relationship of domination and servitude, as this grows directly out of production itself and reacts back on it in turn as a determinant. On this is based the entire configuration of the economic community arising from the actual relations of production. (1894, p.927)

The form of extraction of surplus labour has a double aspect. Not only is there the material thing being extracted, the objective surplus product; there is also the process itself, the raw exploitation of thinking, feeling, productive human beings. Thus the nature of the overall set of social production relations, or mode of production, can best be defined by two categories which form a pair. These are, first, the form taken by the surplus product; and second, the form of control which is exercised over its extraction, over the labour which produces it. In determining the nature of the mode of production, these two categories must also determine the overall conditions in which the struggle unfolds between the exploiters and the exploited.[4]

Given the unified nature of the specifically capitalist mode of exploitation, under which the exploited have no control even over the production of goods which they themselves consume, it is held that the class struggle under capitalism is an antagonism which expresses itself across the entire society. (Marx and Engels 1848, pp.33-35). Indeed, the struggle of those exploited by capitalism antagonises not only the control of production narrowly considered but also the entire logic of the reigning society.

In terms of the critique of this capitalist mode of exploitation, the methodological implications of the insistence on the centrality of class struggle are taken from Marx's *Grundrisse* as read by Negri. In the latter's words,

> materialism and dialectics have given us totality and difference as well as the structural link which subjectively unites them. But that is not enough. It remains insufficient as long as this structure, this totality is not internally split, as long as we do not succeed in grasping not the structural (capitalist) subjectivity but the subjectivities which dialectically constitute the structure (the two classes in struggle). (1979, p.44)

In other words, Autonomist theory hypostatises neither the 'contradictions of capital,' nor the laws of crisis, but the class struggle. Hence the theory's

'voluntarism,' which has led Negri to describe the methodology as being that of the 'point of view,' as opposed to that of the 'totality.' (1984, pp.56-58).
The understanding gained by applying this methodology

> does not in any way become transcendent in relation to the formation and development of the [two] subjects. The method of the 'point of view' works on the traces, symptoms and experiences of rupture and recomposition of the subjects. It reconstructs the general framework without losing sight of the subjects' singularity: it is more a forced movement ahead from the reality of class relations than a theoretical mastery over them. The analytical materialism of this advance is no less rigorous than in the method of the totality; but the specifically political dimension appears with a freshness that the latter often fails to express. (pp.56-57)[5]

Explaining the approach, Cleaver writes that

> In the class war, as in conventional military encounters, one must begin with the closest study of one's own forces, that is, the structure of working class power. Without an understanding of one's own power, the ebb and flow of the battle lines can appear as an endless process driven only by the enemy's unilateral self-activity. When the enemy regroups or restructures, as capital is doing in the present crisis, its actions must be grasped in terms of the defeat of prior tactics or strategies by our forces — not simply as another clever move. That an analysis of enemy strategy is necessary is obvious. The essential point is that an adequate understanding of that strategy can be obtained only by grasping it in relation to our own strengths and weaknesses...
>
> It serves little purpose to study the structures of capitalist domination unless they are recognized as strategies that capital must struggle to impose. (1979, pp.42-43)

It is not necessary to hold that there is a 'crisis of capitalism,' or even that one was evident in the 1970s, to adopt this approach.

The contradiction between the two sides of the class struggle is thus understood as being 'antagonistic' rather than 'dialectical' in the usual sense. Such a conception is derived from the materialist view that the essentially *anti-capitalist* content of working class struggle is its tendency to disrupt the rational, 'integrative' functioning of exploitation. Rather than theorising a 'dialectical' relation between capital and labour, therefore, Autonomist theory grasps the respective natures of the poles of capitalism's fundamental class contradiction according to what it is that actually makes them contradictory poles: that is, not their interpenetration within an 'entity,' conceived philosophically in terms of 'necessary mediation,' but their

antagonism.[6] "Outside of antagonism, not only is there no movement, but the categories do not even exist." (Negri 1979, p.9).

The Autonomist approach can be clarified in terms of the distinction between the working class in itself and the working class for itself.

> The working class in itself is constituted of all those who are forced to sell their labor-power to capital and thus to be labor-power. It is a definition based purely on a common set of characteristics within capital. The working class for itself (or working class as working class, defined politically) exists only when it asserts its autonomy as a class through its unity in struggle against its role as labor-power. (Negri 1979, p.74)

Defining the latter category in different words in the *Grundrisse*, Marx writes that

> the opposite of capital cannot itself be a particular commodity [*i.e. not even labour-power*—NCF], for as such it would form no opposition to capital, since the substance of capital is itself use value; it is not this or that commodity, but all commodities. The communal substance of all commodities, i.e. their substance not as material stuff, as physical character, but their communal substance as *commodities* and hence *exchange values*, is this, that they are *objectified labour*, labour which is still objectifying itself, *labour* as subjectivity. (pp.271-72)

But whereas Marx defines this labour as *productive* labour (pp. 272-73, 304-05), as "that which produces capital," Negri, stressing the general social level of the function of value, holds that it is no longer possible to distinguish between productive labour and that which is reproductive. Whether or not Marx's "heavily reductive definition" is attributable to the "noxious effect of the limits of the workers' movement," as Negri asserts (1979, pp.63-65, 182-84), it is Negri's position which is relied upon.

In this connection it is useful to compare the Autonomist position with that developed by Castoriadis, since in going 'beyond Marx' both emphasise that the evolution of capitalist society is a product of the antagonistic thrusts and parries of two main class subjects. (Castoriadis 1960-61). Like the Autonomists, Castoriadis also insists (p.264) on the important and historically 'formative' role of the "*implicit, informal*, daily and hidden struggle at the point of production," and rejects the idea that since 1945 a crisis of capitalism could conceivably result from the operation of 'objective laws' or dialectical contradictions. (1958, p.240). The two theories differ greatly, however, in their understanding of the relationship between working class and labour-power. In Castoriadis's terms, the "extraction of 'use-value from labour-power'...is a process of bitter struggle in which, half the time, so to speak, the capitalists are the losers." (1960-61, p.248). Formal enterprise organisation conflicts with informal enterprise organisation (1958, pp.170-72), and capitalist bureaucratisation with an autonomous struggle tending to push towards a 'transitional society' where work would be managed directly by the workers.[7] Outside of production, meanwhile, the class struggle either no longer expresses itself at all, or else does so only in a "truncated and distorted way." (1960-61, p.229). The Autonomist view of the class-for-itself is completely different. Autonomous struggle is not the struggle of 'labour-power' against its transformation into a capitalist use-value; rather, it is the emergence within social labour-power of the working class as a separate subject.[8] It is the movement of need. More generally, it is the *non-exploitative assertion of needs and desires*, and the appropriation of resources to fulfil them; and hence it operates not only in the workplace but also on the terrain of the 'social wage' and looting.[9] As 'proletarian self-valorisation' — a somewhat ill-chosen term — it relates to use-value, rather than simply to labour-power. This does not mean that Negri is right to view it as the struggle to acquire whatever is thought to have a use (1979, p.137)[10]; nor should it detract from the fact that it tends towards a seizure and non-exploitative use of the material means of production, towards a new organisation of labour. Simply, as Negri himself has shown (1971), it subverts the enterprise-form and work (forced labour) in general. (See also Echanges et Mouvement 1979; Negri 1978, chap.4; and Zerzan 1974). And in doing so it embodies the possibility of the *abolition* of work and its replacement by what Kay and Mott call the "direct unity of needs and capacities" (1982, p.29). (See also Black 1985).

In theoretical terms the categories of 'working class in itself' and 'working class for itself' are brought together again within the category of **class composition**. For Negri this is defined as

> that combination of political and material characteristics — both historical and physical — which makes up: (a) on the one hand, the historically given structure of labour-power, in all its manifestations, as produced by a given level of productive forces and relations; and (b) on the other hand, the working class as a determinate level of solidification of needs and desires, as a dynamic subject, an antagonistic force, tending towards its own independent identity in historical-political terms. (1982, p.209)

The class composition of the working class is determined by the class struggle.

As yet, there are no Autonomist studies of the history of the USSR,[11] so an example of the application of this approach is perhaps best provided by Negri's work on Keynesianism. (1968). In the beginning, Negri argues, Keynesianism appeared as a response by capital to workers' success in making wages 'sticky downwards.' By tying wage increases to productivity increases, the bourgeoisie attempted to harness working class struggle as a sort of motor of economic development.

> With Keynes, capitalist science takes a remarkable leap forward: it recognises the working class as an autonomous moment within capital. With his theory of effective demand, Keynes introduces into political economy the political notion of a balance of power between classes in struggle. (p.28)

Working class struggle, however, was able to subvert the Keynesian strategy by setting in motion a mobility in the labour market, and by means of the process whereby "the mass worker [of large factories] ... spread the infection of his subjective behaviour into the fabric of proletarian society [i.e. outside the world of work]." (1982, p.211).[12] Capital's response this time was both political, as evidenced by the Italian repression which began in 1979 (Red Notes 1981), and directly economic, as demonstrated by the increasing parcellisation of industrial tasks, the growth of part-time and precarious work, and the rise in unemployment, sickness, and homelessness fuelled and institutionalised by the 'Thatcherite' free-market offensive. It would, no doubt, be going too far to suggest that the growing disaffection with the law and the party system, as exemplified by the eruption of a major riot in London in 1990 (the biggest in Britain for over a century), and a full-scale insurrection in Los Angeles in 1992 (ditto for the US), heralded a new counter-offensive by the working class. But both sets of events did influence macroeconomic policy: in the UK, by helping force the abolition of the poll tax, and in the US by forcing the government to spend more on the inner cities. In the American case, time will tell whether or not this means higher spending on inner city wages, either individual or social. Meanwhile the ongoing 'third industrial revolution,' associated not only with information technology but also with genetic engineering, involves a ruling class strategy of altering the terrain of battle in ways which have yet to be fully theorised.[13]

The methodology is clear. The complexity of historical change and continuity is examined not in terms of the internal contradictions of capitalism, nor those of its administration, but in terms of the antagonism between two subjects: on the one hand, capital's dialectic, which seeks to harness working class potential to the yoke of capitalist development; on the other, **working class subjectivity**, which certainly pushes for higher wages, but whose logic is separate, non-dialectical and 'autonomous.' Since this antagonism is understood as being permanent within capitalist society, the view that the working class is essentially passive is consequently written off as 'myth.' (Gorman 1990).

The second plank of our theoretical approach concerns the relation between class struggle and communism. Here the understanding is taken from that which Marx expressed when discussing what was new in his work:

> What I did that was new was to demonstrate: 1) that the *existence of classes* is merely *linked to particular historical phases in the development of production*; 2) that class struggle necessarily leads to the *dictatorship of the proletariat*; 3) that this dictatorship itself only constitutes the transition to the *abolition of all classes* and to a classless society. (1852b, p.64)

This classless society is understood as a world human community in which "the free development of each [would be] the condition for the free development of all." (Marx and Engels 1848, p.87). As the young Marx puts it succinctly, it is the

> complete return of man to himself as a *social* (i.e. human) being — a return accomplished consciously and embracing the entire wealth of previous development.... [It is] the *genuine* resolution of the conflict between man and nature, between man and man, ...between the individual and the species. (1932, p.20)

In such a society the foundations of capitalism (wage-labour, commodity economy and money) would no longer exist: private property would have been abolished, along with nations, the State, classes, and all forms of exploitation. The means of achieving this goal are seen as those of **social revolution**. Carried out by the international working class, this revolution would enforce what Blanqui and Marx referred to as the **dictatorship of the proletariat**: the power of the formerly dispossessed, and all who join them, to bring non-exploitative social relations to complete victory against exploitative social relations and those who defend them. Finally, the forces currently working for such a revolution are defined not as ideas, but as those of "the real movement which abolishes the present state of things," the "old mole" undermining capitalist domination in the here and now. (Marx and Engels 1846, p.47; Marx 1856b, p.300).

This much would seem familiar. The ideologies and practice of opponents of communism, however, often employed in the name of communism itself — a phenomenon Marx and Engels observed as early as 1848 [sec. 3]) — suggest that further clarification is required.

Communism[14] implies the elimination of work in favour of a "new type of free activity." (SI 1963, p.102; see also Marx and Engels 1846, pp.85 and 220, and SI 1961, p.64). As the group L'Insecurité Sociale has put it:

> As communism is the creation of new social relationships between people which would bring about a quite different human activity, it must be understood that production would not be what it is today without money. If we can, for want of a

better term, still speak of production to express the process by which a part of human activity would be devoted to reproducing existence and in which would be expressed the human ability to create, to innovate and to transform, the disappearance of exploitation and the abolition of money would mean that this production would not involve the subjection of people to it since it would be they who would decide its aims, its means and its conditions. It would therefore be an expression of their humanity and would not strip them of other dimensions (love, play, dreaming, etc.). (1984, p.11)

Moreover,

Along with the disappearance of commercial value would disappear the division of the human being into a producer and a consumer. In communist society, consumption would not be opposed to production since there would be no contradiction between being concerned with oneself and concerning oneself with someone else.... Unless this was imposed by the nature of a product, people would no longer need to hurry all the time as they would no longer be constrained by the necessity to produce commodities. The "consumer" would not be able to blame the "producer" for what he or she did by invoking the money that had been paid since none would be given in exchange, but simply to criticise from the inside, not from the outside. What would be at issue would be their common effort. (p.13)

It should perhaps be added that this is not a novel vision.

Such a goal is seen as incompatible with all conceptions of a transitional society. (See Buick 1975). The creation of communism is accepted as being something processual, but is identified with the direct **communisation** of social relations, rather than with the onset of a stage accessible only after a transition through 'socialism.' (See the journal *La Banquise*, and L'Insecurité Sociale 1984). The "transition to the *abolition of all classes*" is thus understood in very straightforward fashion: it is the process of replacing capitalist or other exploitative social relations with communist ones. In Negri's well-chosen words,

it is not the transition that reveals itself (and eliminates itself) in the form of communism, but rather it is communism that takes the form of the transition. (1979, p.153) (italics original)

It is recognised, of course, that the controllers of capital will not give up the means of production, and hence their command over labour-power, peacefully. On the contrary, they will make maximum use of their most important weapon: the capitalist State. Being an obstacle of an essentially military nature, this can only be destroyed by military means. To enable the spread of non-exploitative, non-monetary social relations it will therefore be necessary to wage class war against the State on a world level. And the organisation of the revolutionary side in this war is what we define as the dictatorship of the proletariat.

This, however, does not imply that the social revolution is dependent upon a prior 'political' revolution understood as the appropriation of 'political power.' One cannot deduce from the need for anti-State action that there must also be a process of 'political transition' which must first reach completion before the process of social change can begin. For even while means are being employed which will not exist after the victory — that is, violent means — the achievements of the revolutionaries are *always in essence social*. In short, the liberated area grows. Some sort of centralised organisation will be necessary, certainly — for constructive reasons as much as destructive ones — but there is no point in calling it a 'state' because there is no intervening 'political' period *between* the revolution and communism. Being above all social, the revolution *is* the transition: it *is* the communisation process. The periodisation is therefore as follows: first, for a short time, there is the organisation of violent action to destroy whatever obstacles cannot be destroyed in any other way; next, this violence comes to an end. Constructive aims are pursued, and other obstacles tackled and removed, both during the war and afterwards.

The difference between revolutionary transition and the establishment of a new political regime or a new kind of State can also be understood in terms of the non-institutionalisation of revolutionary struggle. Since the revolution would cease to be a revolution were it to institutionalise its relationship with its enemies, or to seek to do so, the dictatorship of the proletariat cannot but be anti-Statist. (Pannekoek 1912, pp.119-36; Debord 1967, para. 179).[15] It seeks not to rule over its enemies, but to destroy them. Of course this does not mean that some of its former enemies cannot become friends; but what it does mean is that the power of the self-abolishing proletariat necessarily involves the intensive and extensive *spread* of communist social relations.[16] That is its whole point. Here, as Pannekoek puts it, "sword and trowel are one." (1947-49, p.107).

In relation to the construction of the new society, the further point can be made that communism is conceived of as Marx understood it in 1844, that is, as undifferentiated into phases, rather than as he described it in 1875, as consisting of a "first phase" where distribution would be according to work.[17] (Marx 1832, pp.87-101; Marx 1875; Crump 1975). Of course it seems likely that for a time immediately following the victory in the revolutionary war some goods might have to be rationed. And it is even more likely that extensive rationing would have been necessary during the war itself. But since people would not be competing with each other to get hold of things they needed or wanted, the basis of this rationed distribution and consumption would not be privative appropriation. Similarly, since the production of important things would be an issue for everybody, collectively and subjectively, nor would the basis of production be private labour. Thus the use of rationing by social revolutionaries, either during the war or in its aftermath, would not keep the new social relations at an identifiably 'lower stage.' Indeed we would go further and state that even long after monetary relations and the State had disappeared globally there might occasionally arise circumstances when the inhabitants of a communist civilisation might make use of rationing, and in doing so they would not be putting the overall social relations in any danger. The reason for this is that neither during the transition nor during the subsequent unchallenged reign of communist social relations would the type of 'scarcity' which might lead people to organise rationing be comparable to the *enforced social relation* of scarcity formerly associated with commodity exchange and the concomitant atomisation of individuals. (See Fernandez 1984, p.19). Rather than being a problem for the individual, it would be a problem for the community.

In rejecting the theory of stages we are not arguing that communist civilisation, once victorious, would become static. Communist society would indeed *advance*, both in the negative sense of solving the remaining problems inherited from the old society; and in the positive sense of changing and exploring the natural environment and developing human needs and potential. But the point regarding distribution is essentially the same as the point we have made regarding the overthrow of the State: communist organisation does not organise that which is not communist.

Finally, we have asserted that the forces already at the proletariat's disposal are understood as constituting a social tendency which is inherently antagonistic to capital. In accordance with materialist methodology, therefore, the insistence on **proletarian autonomy** excludes any idea that the class by itself is incapable of developing revolutionary consciousness. If the proletariat is capable of overthrowing capital by intensifying its struggle, then *ipso facto* it is capable of achieving the required consciousness. No overlap is imagined between this communist conception on one hand, and that of a Kautskyist-Leninist 'injection' of consciousness on the other. (Lenin 1902, p.98; see also Barrot 1977). The essence of proletarian autonomy is understood to be non-exploitative human need — the only kind of fully *human* need — and its manifestation is understood as necessarily tendential towards the full realisation of communism.[18]

AGAINST INCORPORATION

On the basis of the above understanding, critics have also made use of further concepts of a more specific kind. In the main these have been developed in relation to capitalism in the West, but in order to illustrate the radicality of the view taken of class antagonism, we shall list some of them here. They cannot, of course, be applied automatically to non-western capitalism, but they will nonetheless help to illustrate the meaning of the insistence on proletarian autonomy. Those chosen can be grouped under two headings: capitalist politics, and the incorporation of struggle.

Capitalist Politics

One of the tendency's major tenets is that the autonomous proletarian movement grows in strength the more independent it is of the political 'spectrum,' indeed, the more hostile it is towards its constituent parts. Thus there is the concept of **capitalist politics**, understood as comprising the entire tableau from extreme right to extreme left.[19] The struggles which the participants in such politics are engaged in are seen as revolving fundamentally around the management of the capitalist State and economy.

Debord has further explained how

> the historical moment when Bolshevism triumphed *for itself* in Russia and when social-democracy fought victoriously *for the old world* marks the inauguration of a state of affairs which is at the heart of the domination of the modern spectacle: the representation of the working class radically opposes itself to the working class. (1967, para.100)

In the past century this representation has often been associated with the non-communist idea that changes in the existing society — such as an increased dose of nationalisation, participation, welfare expenditure, social mobility, or 'planning' — would amount to the creation of a new one. Specific terminology is therefore needed to denote those sections of the capitalist political spectrum which propagandise about the need for 'socialism' and 'communism' and aim to build a base in the working class. These are divided as follows.[20]

The left, in loose usage, is taken to denote all such sections lumped together. More strictly, it denotes those which, being more moderate, do not seek disorder. Thus in western Europe the left includes mainstream 'Socialist' Parties — to the extent that they still present themselves as 'socialist' — and, with a similar rider, the former 'Communist' Parties too. The French Socialist Party, whose members sang the Internationale at party occasions, is considered to to have been on the left until the mid-1980s, as was the British Labour Party until the mid-1990s, whereas the British Liberal Democratic Party is not. Part of the Scottish National Party is also positioned as left-wing: namely, that which presents its nationalistic and pro-independence ideology as being pro-working class. The nominally analogous British National Party would not be described as left-wing, since its brand of nationalism is racist first and foremost.

Extreme left and **leftist** (from the French, *gauchiste*) are the terms used to designate groupings which are more extreme than the left. The changes they seek to implement often involve violence and usually a significant change in the legal system. Whereas Trotskyists stress nationalisation, anarchosyndicalists stress the power of unions in industry, and 'Red Greens' the need for a comprehensive environmental policy. Much of the energy of these groups is (or was) spent on denouncing the 'official' left as insufficiently representative of the working class, or as 'treacherous', with the implication that working class people should switch their support away from the politicians of the left to the politicians of the extreme left. Correspondingly, most parts of the extreme left have a Leninist conception of the division between 'political' and 'economic' struggles, and adopt a 'substitutionist' position on class consciousness.[21]

The term **ultra-leftist** is used to describe those sections whose ideas are more radical than those of the left, the Leninists and the anarchosyndicalists, but who are nonetheless loath to reject ideas and forms of activity which conflict with the communist project. For example, they might oppose each and every force which would substitute itself for the working class, but still support some sort of self-managed capitalist economy. (See, for example, the advocacy of wage equalisation in Castoriadis 1957, pp.126-27 and Solidarity 1961, p. 11.) Or they might even understand the need to abolish wage-labour, but still propagandise in such a way as to encourage workers to put their hopes in some force other than proletarian autonomy: a supposed economic crisis, for example (see *Révolution Sociale*), or an ostensibly 'cure-all' organisational *form* such as the workers' council. Ultra-leftists are usually active in criticising the left and extreme left, and in encouraging workers to organise. They are distinct from the extreme left in that they do not retrospectively 'support' past counterrevolutions, such as the Bolshevik one in Russia or the Republican one in Spain. And unlike most leftists they do not support any of the world's nationalist 'liberation movements.'

Another political term which needs to be mentioned is **democracy**. Democracy is understood as involving a form of relationship between the capitalist State and capitalist civil society such as that established by bourgeois political revolution.

> In democracy, man does not exist for the sake of law, but the law exists for the sake of man. (Marx 1843a, p.88)

In criticising Bauer's project of political emancipation, Marx explains:

> The rights of man as *such* are distinguished from the rights of the citizen. Who is this man who is distinct from the citizen? None other than the *member of*

civil society. Why [in the New Hampshire constitution] is the member of civil society simply called 'man', and why are his rights called the rights of man? How can we explain this fact? By the relationship of the political state to civil society, by the nature of political emancipation.

The first point we should note is that the so-called *rights of man,* as distinct from the *rights of the citizen,* are quite simply the rights of the *member of civil society,* i.e. of egoistic man, of man separated from other men and from the community. (1843b, pp.228-29)

Marx focuses on one particular right of man in order to illuminate the whole:

the right of man to freedom is not based on the association of man with man but rather on the separation of man from man. It is the *right* of this separation....

...The practical application of the right of man to freedom is the right of man to private property....

...[This individual freedom], together with this application of it, forms the foundation of civil society. It leads each man to see in other men not the *realisation* but the *limitation* of his own freedom. (pp.229-30)

'Security' in this sense is thus

the supreme concept of civil society, the concept of *police,* the concept that the whole of society is there only to guarantee each of its members the conservation of his person, his rights and his property....

But in fact

...Not one of the so-called rights of man goes beyond egoistic man, man as a member of civil society, namely an individual withdrawn into himself, his private interest and his private desires and separated from the community. In the rights of man it is not man who appears as a species-being; on the contrary, species-life itself, society, appears as a framework extraneous to the individuals, as a limitation of their original independence. The only bond which holds them together is natural necessity, need and private interest, the conservation of their property and their egoistic persons. (p.230)

Democracy, then, is a political form, a Statist form, which involves not just a specific relationship between the State and civil society, but also a corresponding ideology of that relationship. Everyone who is a member of civil society — otherwise known as the 'people', the 'public,' the 'country,' or the 'nation' — and capitalist democracy intends this to mean virtually everyone who lives on the territory claimed by a given State, or at least everyone who is adequately accessible to the means by which that State spreads its ideology, and who is not a 'foreigner' — is also portrayed in some sense as a 'member' of that State, or in other words as a 'citizen.' In other words: whatever a person owns, whatever his economic status, whether he lives in a hostel for the homeless, a council house, or a castle, whether he is a worker, a major share-holder in a large company, or the head of the civil service, whether he lives on welfare payments or off of a private income, he is an 'equal,' a person with equal political rights. One of his main rights, of course, is his right to vote. The circumstances in which he can be deprived of this right are extremely exceptional — if he is reclassified as a foreigner or a minor, for example, or if he is confined to a mental institution — and even then the deprivation is not irrevocable. In a well-functioning democracy, almost everyone will be allowed to keep their right to vote throughout their lifetime, precisely because it is a main plank of the State's ideology that the State simply *recognises* everyone's 'entitlement' to take part in the political 'life of the community.' Similarly, everyone is assumed to possess a formal and equal legal personality, which they are at full liberty to exercise howsoever they wish according to the rules of the State's judicial system. At the core of democratic ideology there lies the public and even ritual emphasis of formal equality.

It is further evident that political democracy is closely bound up with the less political *civil* rights — or 'civil liberties' — associated with bourgeois life, such as the right to one's own business in both senses of the term. In general, people actually have a right to do whatever they please so long as they act within the law. Of course they are sometimes granted other kinds of 'right' too, such as the right to receive social security payments. But since these kinds of right do not carry anything like an illusion of 'inalienability' — as any claimant knows — they are not among the rights we are discussing, and are perhaps better classified as special kinds of wage payments. Depending on the relation of forces in the class struggle, these latter rights can be removed under democracy, or indeed they can be granted under fascism. More relevant is the fact that the civil rights associated with political democracy necessarily imply the right of the State to function — and the underlying functions of the State are, first, to embody the organised might of the ruling class, and second, to represent the supposed 'general interest' of a false, cross-class, usually national, 'community.' Civil rights necessarily come together with the 'equal' duty of submission to this might and this representation. And like political rights they are ideally independent of who someone is and what their relationship is to other people and the means of production.

But what is really defended by the ideology of civil liberty at a deeper level is precisely what comes after the 'whethers' and 'whatevers' listed above, precisely that which civil rights present themselves as being independent of:

namely, the existing economic relations, the social production relations which determine the nature of the society. The real subtext to the ideology that people in a certain country are 'free' states that workers and employers are actually in the same game (buying and selling); that no-one, however rich he might be, has any rights that someone else does not; that no-one is obliged to sell something he owns at the price someone offers him instead of keeping hold of it, or to buy something he has expressed an interest in and been quoted a price for; that everyone can in principle buy whatever they want as long as they have enough money and the owner is willing to sell it to them; or, in short, that everyone's pound or franc is worth the same, that 'money has no smell.' Not by accident did the famous French 'Declaration of Rights' of 1789 recognise the rights of property as natural, inalienable, sacred, and inviolable. (See Cobban 1963, p.164). When the electoral property qualification gives way to universal suffrage, these economic rights become a 'given,' something which is held to be 'self-evident': that is, not necessary to justify. Everyone can own money and property, and in advanced countries virtually everyone does. No market is fully 'free,' of course, but many are often apparently 'fair' according to their own rules. Gangsters must purchase their weapons; and membership of bourgeois and petty-bourgeois networks can be bought, one way or another. Money does 'talk' — anyone's money. In reality, of course, this does nothing whatsoever to reduce the inequality inherent in the exclusion of the vast majority from control over the means of production; in the exchange of labour-power for the wage; in the exploitation of the labour-power thus purchased; in the dictatorship of the ruling class, the controllers of capital. But unlike the democracy of ancient times, modern democracy helps conceal this by subsuming the exploited into civil society: and at the same time it rests upon that subsumption. Democracy can therefore be said to achieve its fullest expression under capitalism (ICG 1987); and democratic ideology, in the sense in which it incorporates the ideology of civil liberty, to be an adequate form—a tendentially schizophrenogenic form—of advanced capitalist false consciousness.

The Incorporation of Struggle

The concepts given in the preceding section were those denoting the relations of representative capitalist politics. The ones listed in this section relate to the dynamics of class struggle.

Proletarian autonomy has been described as something separate from, and antagonistic to, the logic of capital. Since this logic is understood as one of harnessing working class potential, it follows that the advancement of autonomy implies resistance to the imposition of mediated, 'negotiated,' institutionalised forms of struggle. Conceptual tools are therefore required in order to be able to understand the meaning of **incorporation**.

It is necessary to begin by emphasising that workers' autonomy is a reality, and that to see it as purely interstitial within a context of incorporation would be to adopt the viewpoint of capital — or rather, the viewpoint which capital would like to be able to have. As Negri puts it, then, it

> seems...fundamental to consider the totality of the process of proletarian self-valorisation as *alternative* to, and radically *different* from, the totality of the process of capitalist production and reproduction. I realise that I am exaggerating the position, and oversimplifying its complexity. But I also know that this 'intensive road,' this radical break with the totality of capitalist development, is a fundamental experience of the movement as it stands today.
>
> *Today the process of constituting class independence is first and foremost a process of separation....*
>
> ...Working class self-valorisation is first and foremost *de*-structuration of the enemy totality, taken to a point of exclusivity in the self-recognition of the class's collective independence. (1978, p.97)

Incorporation must thus be seen as part of this enemy totality.

This can be clarified with reference to the contribution of the council communists. Thus Pannekoek, in a major controversy with Kautsky in 1912, gave his view that

> The proletariat's organisation — its most important source of strength — must not be confused with the present-day form of its organisations and associations, where it is shaped by conditions within the framework of the still vigorous bourgeois order. *The nature of this organisation is something spiritual* — no less than the whole transformation of the proletarian mentality. It may well be that the ruling class...succeeds in destroying the workers' organisations; but, for all that, the workers will remain as they were.... The same spirit, compounded of discipline, cooperation, solidarity, the habit of organised action, will live in them more vividly than ever, and will create new forms of intervention. (1911-12)

What Pannekoek was theorising — to put it in modern language — was the relation between the power of the autonomous working class and the type of organisation within which it invested its hopes. His view was that if struggle intensified, workers would intervene in new ways, independently of both parliament and the **trade unions**. (See Bricianer 1969, chap. 3). The whole process would be a development of their autonomy, their collective 'self-activity.' In Germany in 1918, new forms of organisation indeed appeared — action committees, factory organisations, and workers' and soldiers' *councils (Raten)* — in what was a forceful revolutionary movement opposed to both social democracy and trade unionism. The fast-forming 'council communist' tendency, however, did not simply adopt Pannekoek's earlier insights: they nuanced their position in the light of experience. Thus Rühle and his comrades denounced the official workers' councils after a week, identifying them as a brake on the movement. Whilst continuing to advocate the council *form*, they launched a struggle to create new councils that fought directly for the dictatorship of the proletariat. (Authier and Barrot 1976, p.83). In 1920 Pannekoek spoke for the tendency as a whole when he wrote of the need for proletarian autonomy to mature in *opposition* to incorporative forms of organisation. (1920, pp.111-16).[22] In itself no particular form provided an answer to incorporation, since what was most important was the basis of subversion: namely, the workers' self-organised and antagonistic advancement from their existing position of power. But the trade union form could not be made other than a form of incorporation.

Even under 'normal' conditions, when there is no revolutionary movement, the contradiction does not disappear between, on one side, trade unionism, and on the other, workers' autonomy and its need for development. As Brendel explains:

> From the very first day of their existence unions have had the task of mediating between capitalists and workers, mediating...in order to extinguish the flames of conflict between the two parties, not to kindle the fire by pouring oil into it, mediating in order to stabilize the antagonistic relationship of workers and capitalists, not to destroy it.... Not a single union would ever have been accepted for a single day by any capitalist or employers' association if it had not shown its capacity of operating a combination of defending and integrating workers, or, to be more precise, of integrating them into the capitalist system by defending them to a certain extent and with regard to specific problems. On the other hand not a single union would ever have been accepted for a single day by any worker or group of workers if it had not defended them to a certain extent and with regard to specific problems. That's what mediation means. (1992, p.30)

The trade union is seen as the form *par excellence* of the *'encadrement'* of workers' struggle. (See GOC 1929, Zerzan 1974, Echanges et Mouvement 1977, and Wildcat 1986 and 1992). More concretely, it is defined as a large, permanent organisation of workers in a specific branch or sector, disposing of a permanent apparatus and functioning both to 'represent' workers' interests in negotiations with the aim of maintaining a firm and fast *modus vivendi* between workers and management; and to regulate strike action — and prevent it from becoming out of control — when there is no other alternative. In practice this means opposing the dynamic whereby workers reject the whole project of a *modus vivendi* and fight for their own class interests without regard to what is viable from the point of view of the economy. But regardless of what views the workers may hold, reject this project is precisely what their struggle must do — tendentially in extreme fashion, always in some fashion and to some extent.

Another way of looking at trade unions involves recognising that they seek to monopolise through representation not only the apparent enforcement of workers' interests within a specific part of the capitalist economy, but also, on that basis, the communication with workers elsewhere. In practice this means defending the structure and logic of the economy which workers' power necessarily tends to disrupt and undermine. Based on and reinforcing both the divisions within the working class, and its 'integration' within the economy, the trade union form is understood to be obligatorily defensive of a society founded on wage-labour, and hostile to the advancement of working class subjectivity.

Two further concepts have been found to be particularly useful in the communist consideration of the barriers to the development of autonomous struggle. The first is that of **workers' democracy**. This is understood both as an ideology concerning the advancement of struggle, and as a form of organisation. It is defined in terms of three characteristics. First, there is the application of the principle according to which, wherever possible, decision must follow discussion and precede action. Second, the minority must always submit to the decision of the majority. Third, each worker involved in a struggle must have an equal say, regardless of level of interest, involvement, or commitment. (ICG 1987). Workers' democracy has been described as "the application of democratic parliamentarian rules at the heart of the proletarian 'mass' organs (assemblies, unions, councils,....)." (p.52). Although rarely seen in its purest form — where strikers, for example, would respect the other workers' 'right' to strike-break — even in other forms it restrains the advancing dynamic by tending to dissolve the offensive community of struggle into an institutionalised collection of atomised individuals, tied together by means of 'rights.'

The second concept is that of **self-management**, understood as a system wherein as many economic decisions as possible are taken at enterprise level. Behind the retention of the enterprise form, there lies all that it entails: privative appropriation, exchange, and — if we ignore 'mutualist' utopias of simple commodity production — *capitalism*. (Négation [1974?]; Sabatier 1977, pp.27-28). One type of self-management requires specific mention: namely, **workers' management**, or the management of an enterprise by its workers. (This is to be differentiated from **workers' control**, or the right of workers to inspect the books and be consulted on matters of policy). (Brinton 1970, i-xv). Workers' management is seen as a debureaucratised form of capitalist economy, a sort of fantastic 'reconciliation' of workers' interests with those of enterprise capital.

MARXISM AND 'MARXISM'

It is readily apparent that the overall theoretical orientation outlined above has been greatly conditioned by a sympathetic reading of Marx. We certainly consider it to be in close accordance with Marx's basic attitude towards the role of the class struggle in history, the self-assertion of the proletarian class in particular, and the tendency towards communism. As is made clear in the first part of Chapter 3 below, it also relies heavily upon Marx's historical and materialist critique of capitalist political economy. (1867, 1885, etc.). In these terms, it is evidently Marxist.

At the same time, it cannot usefully be described as 'orthodox Marxist,' since it neither relies upon, nor follows on from, the political and theoretical positions developed within the various traditions associated with the Second and Third Internationals.[23] It is, on the contrary, highly 'heterodox.' Being neither social-democratic nor Leninist, it is the product rather of a wholly separate 'heritage' associated notably with the council communists, the Situationists, and the Autonomists.

The adoption of such an orientation implies a position regarding both social democracy and Leninism which is not only 'different,' but also antagonistic. In short, both of these other sets of positions are perceived not simply as being oblivious to proletarian autonomy in theory, but as expressing social interests and aspirations which are radically opposed to it in practice. Social democracy and Leninism — alongside, for that matter, anarchism[24] — are understood to be but parts, in both theory and practice, of the widespread 'representation of the working class' which arose in the late 19th century and which has wholly opposed itself to working class autonomous practice (or power). (See Debord 1967, para.100). It follows that whereas the approach described above, along with the theoretical positions of the three movements on which it has drawn, can usefully be characterised as *communist*, the positions of 'orthodox Marxism,' of social democracy and Leninism, cannot be so characterised.

The matter then remains of the use of the term *Marxist*. Two points in particular should be clear in relation to this. First, the theories produced by the application of various 'orthodox Marxist' approaches are perceived to have been wholly out of line with the theoretical approach, the practical orientation, and the revolutionary intent displayed by Marx himself from the 1840s on. As Debord has described,

> Marx's theory is fundamentally beyond scientific thought, and it preserves scientific thought only by superseding it; what is in question is an understanding of struggle, and not of law. (1967, para.81)

This is true even if it was the "deterministic-scientific *facet*" [emphasis added] in Marx's own thought which

> was precisely the gap through which the process of 'ideologization' penetrated, during Marx's own lifetime, into the theoretical heritage left to the workers' movement. (para.84)

Recently this view has been developed highly successfully by Shortall, who demonstrates how the 'closure' within *Capital*, which Marx enacted in order to focus upon capital as an objective and positive system outside of class subjectivity, is essentially provisional in nature. And since it is provisional, even this scientific analysis necessarily points 'beyond itself' to a unitary communist critique. (1994).

Second, the communist insistence on proletarian autonomy and subjectivity, on the power disposed of by the working class, while describable as Marxist, cannot be reconciled with any sort of epistemology which argues the 'correctness' of a position with reference mainly or solely to an exegesis of the works of Marx. We have no intention here of arguing in depth that any position is 'true' to Marx, with all its rivals being 'false.' To argue thus would imply not only making a full-scale analysis, in the light of various historical developments, of many of the numerous interpretations of Marx's positions (and, crucially, their material roots: see Goldner 1991); but also making a detailed critique of certain of Marx's positions themselves. These are not among the aims of the present work.

As a consequence, we have found it possible, and indeed useful, to have more leeway with the term *Marxist* than with the term *communist*. When used in inverted commas (Chapter 5), the former term thus denotes the various positions which are straightforwardly social-democratic or Leninist; when used without them, it denotes those positions which might not necessarily be communist — these are considered in the first section of Chapter 6 — but which have been developed outside of the mainstream of 'orthodox Marxism' in such a way as to underline, however weakly or strongly and with whatever reservations, the autonomous power of the workers as a category independent of representation. (These we consider in the second part of that chapter).[25] The term *communist*, meanwhile, without inverted commas, will be used to denote the principles outlined above and influenced by the three specific tendencies mentioned.

Since all the theories and positions considered are assessed according to the same criteria, the *a priori* nature of this classification will not constitute a hindrance to the precision of the critique. Indeed, providing as it does a reminder of the underlying theoretical and critical orientation we have described in this first chapter, it will on the contrary prove of clarificatory significance in the chapters to follow.

SUMMARY

A theoretical approach has been defined in which the most important organising ideas are as follows. First, in the words of the *Communist Manifesto*, the history of all existing societies is seen as a history of class struggle. Second, this struggle is understood not merely as an objective 'conflict of interests,' but as an antagonism in the literal sense: that is, as an irreducible contest between class subjects or subjectivities. Third, the fundamental 'tendency' of proletarian struggle, understood to express truly human need, is seen as being towards a revolution which would bring about communism on a world scale. Fourth, and in accordance with the ideas put forward by Marx and the Situationists, communism is understood to be a society without money, commodities, the

---

SURPLUS PRODUCT

CONTROL OVER THE SURPLUS PRODUCT

CAPITALIST POLITICS   INCORPORATION

left, extreme left   *trade unions*

ultra-left   *workers' democracy*

democracy   *self-management*

CLASS STRUGGLE

CLASS COMPOSITION

ANTAGONISM   COMMUNISM

SUBJECTIVITY   SOCIAL REVOLUTION/COMMUNISATION

AUTONOMY   DICTATORSHIP OF THE PROLETARIAT

Figure 1.1   Main Concepts Introduced in Chapter 1

State, wage-labour, and exploitation, wherein work would be eliminated in favour of a new type of productive activity.

As an example of the application of a communist approach, we have outlined further concepts on a less abstract level in relation to the West. Capitalist politics, described as a struggle to manage the capitalist State and economy, is taken to include the entire spectrum from extreme right to extreme left. Democracy, or the rights of the member of civil society to citizenship, is a political form which expresses in profound fashion the capitalist principles of separation and atomisation.

Finally, proletarian autonomy is defined negatively as subversion, as the negation of capital's tendency to incorporate workers' struggle. Concepts relevant to this incorporation include *trade unionism*, which expresses incorporation both into the national economy as a whole and into one of its sectors or branches or enterprises; *workers' democracy*, which consists of an adoption of bourgeois 'parliamentary' attitudes by workers in struggle; and *self-management*, which binds workers to the enterprise-form and therethrough to the market. (See Figure 1.1).

Notes

1 This insistence is especially manifest in Negri's discussion of Marx's *Grundrisse* (1979), first published in English in 1984.

2 See the criticisms made in Notes 13 and 21 below. A full critique of the Autonomist *oeuvre* would only be feasible, of course, in the context of an overall consideration of the development not only of revolutionary theory but also of autonomous class practice. This would demand both a knowledge of Italian and another book.

3 Important works and collections of works include: Pannekoek 1912, 1920, 1934, and 1947-49, Rühle 1924 (council communist); *SI Anthology* 1953-71, Debord 1967 (Situationist); Negri 1967-83, 1973-74, 1978 and 1979, Cleaver 1979, Kay 1975 and 1979a (Autonomist); Barrot and Martin 1972-74, and Barrot 1979. Journals include: *A Communist Effort* (London); *Aufheben* (Brighton,*); *La Banquise* (Paris); *Communist Headache* (Sheffield,*); *L'Insecurité Sociale* (Paris); *Internationale Situationniste* (Paris); *Midnight Notes* (New York,*); *Proletarian Gob* (Reading,*); *Radical Chains* (London,*); *Wildcat* [in German] (Karlsrühe,*); *Wildcat* [in English, unconnected with the above] (London,*); *Workers' Playtime* (London); and *Zerowork* (New York). (* = current). A detailed history of much of the communist theoretical tendency is given in La Banquise 1983; also useful are the essays on various tendencies in Rubel and Crump 1987.

4 Under capitalism the surplus takes a value form and the control over its extraction takes the form of the wages system, to which we return in Chapter 3.

5 A confusion could arise here around the concept of the 'political.' Rather than using it in its etymologically correct meaning, to refer to the State, Negri and the other Autonomists use it to denote social subjectivity and struggle.

6 The term 'antagonism' is sometimes misused to denote simply a conflict of interests. (See for example Szelenyi 1979). Here it is used in its proper meaning of an active conflict

between subjects (from the Greek αντι, against, and αγωνιστης, combatant, actor).

7   For Castoriadis the "central problem of socialism" is "in short, the question of the management and goals of work." (1960-61, p.302; see also 1957). Behind this view lies the belief that the current separation between production and consumption will continue to exist under 'socialism.' The Situationist International criticised such conceptions for abandoning "the very core of the revolutionary project, which is nothing less than the suppression of work in the ordinary sense (as well as the suppression of the proletariat) and of all the justifications of previous forms of work." (1963, p.102). See also Négation 1974. In the 1980s communist journal *La Banquise* a distinction is emphasised between *travail* and *activité*, with the former term denoting work and the latter labour, either forced or free. (La Banquise 1986). (See also the piece from L'Insecurité Sociale 1984 quoted in the main text). The connotations of 'activity' are highly relevant and in some ways clearer than those evoked by the English terms 'labour' or even 'free labour.' However, the recognition that communism is based on activity and not work must now be distinguished from the subjectivist — and usually individualist — expression of opposition to work/labour (as a supposed whole) from the standpoint of 'radical subjectivity' or 'play.' (See for example Vaneigem 1967). Our own understanding of communism rests on the firm insistence that the overthrow of the alienation of labour necessarily brings to victory the movement towards 'realised human nature'; and, equally fundamentally, on the insistence that this movement, while not yet victorious, necessarily takes a class form.

8   "The working class is defined by its struggle against capital and not by its productive function" (Zerowork 1975, p.3). This refers, of course, to the class-for-itself.

9   Seen from the point of view of capital, groups of dispossessed people undoubtedly exist who are outside of the employed workforce but who are still 'working class' in the sense that they are worth being paid (directly or indirectly) for being 'productive' (actually or potentially). These include non-employed dependants of employed workers who help to reproduce another person's labour-power both physically and psychologically (for example, housewives); those whose capacity to sell their labour-power is expected to appear in the future (for example, workers' children, the employable unemployed and sick, and many refugees); and the nurturers of those who are likely to develop such a capacity (for example, unemployed mothers receiving welfare, or grandmothers looking after children whose parents are out at work) — three groups which overlap in various ways both with each other and with the employed working class. The relative sizes of the different groups is evidently subject to considerable variation, but in the Soviet context we would cite as an example the immense amount of work done by single (widowed) grandmothers in caring for future workers, an economic fact very closely related to the low level or non-existence of official unemployment. In addition, even those retired workers and permanently unemployed people who do not fall into any of the above categories — for example, some unemployable single mothers whose children have grown up, and some of the unemployable disabled — often play a role in the psychological reproduction of employed labour-power; and in this sense they too can be 'productive.' From an oppositional point of view, we would stress that whilst some of these permanently unemployed people may not technically belong to the *working* class, they are nonetheless dispossessed of both the means of production and their own labour-power — even if capital can find no use for it — and can and do struggle for their needs in such a way as to participate in the struggle of a broader class: the proletariat. The extent to which they are allowed some kind of access to means of consumption — via

'social wage' or contributory pension — is determined precisely through such struggle in all its complexity, particularities, divisions and disorganisation; its organisation and subjective unity (successfully restricted by capital to a local level, and evidently subject to numerous mediations); and, to a not completely negligible degree, its existence as a global totality. Recognition of these facts will facilitate an understanding of how in an exploitative society even the operation of the category of human need depends on social, class struggle. More precisely, it operates not only in struggle but also through struggle.

10   Negri's exact words are that "use-value is for the proletariat an immediate revindication and immediate practice of power." (p.137).

11   For an Autonomist-influenced view of class struggle in the USSR, see Chapter 7 below. For a brief comment on Negri's marginal comments on the struggles in Eastern Europe, see the first footnote in Chapter 6.

12   One could, of course, criticise this statement by observing that the extra-workplace struggles of working class women, for example, were hardly 'spread' to them by male mass workers. But the main point is that in the course of struggle a single class broadened the area of its strength.

13   It should be noted that Autonomist Marxism, whilst it understood very well the relationship between class struggle and the crisis of Keynesianism, has more or less collapsed in its efforts to understand the changes of the 1980s and 1990s. Either it has fallen into a kind of post-Frankfurt school concentration upon 'difference,' focusing on 'culture' in a way formerly associated with various left-wing intellectuals from Gramsci to Bahro, albeit with the more modern terminology of 'plurality,' 'multipolarity,' and 'information' (see for example, Guattari and Negri 1985, Negri 1990, and Witheford 1994); or else it has theorised the supposedly subversive nature of the politics of single-issue campaigns (see Cleaver 1989), thereby tending to block off its escape routes from subcultural anti-imperialist leftism. (For the rudiments of a much more useful and classist discussion of the information revolution and present changes, see Tillium 1994).

14   While some communists (for example, Rubel and Crump 1987) use the words 'socialism' and 'communism' interchangeably, we have followed the majority in preferring to use the latter word exclusively.

15   See also Ryan's discussion of Negri's work on the State form (1977) which has yet to be translated into English. "Law is the form of relation between the organization and command of exploitation.... There is no proletarian law. Therefore, in the transition to communism, law founded on antagonism will become extinct. The State of law will no longer be possible." (Ryan 1993, p.210, referring to Negri 1977).

16   Thus from this point of view the concept of the *defence* of the revolution is meaningless.

17   In the *Critique of the Gotha Programme* (1875) Marx jots down a few thoughts on the transition from capitalism to communism. Whilst recognising that the decisive factor is the transformation of the underlying social relations, he states that "corresponding" to this social transformation there must also be a "transition in the political sphere." During this time there is still a 'state,' but this state can "only take the form of a *revolutionary dictatorship of the proletariat*." (p.355). The bourgeois State will have been destroyed; and since the purpose of the new state is to help abolish money, wages, and classes, it too ceases to exist at the moment of these relations' final disappearance. In fact, it is in its nature to wither away from the moment it is set up. Even after it has disappeared, though, the new communist society is still 'stamped with birth-marks' from the society out of which it has emerged. Social development, in other words — and one should note that Marx does not

portray the 'means of production' as determinant — is insufficient to allow the free distribution of everything according to need. In this 'first stage' of the stateless, moneyless, classless society, it is thought, some kind of rationing would be unavoidable, and Marx makes the suggestion that this would best be organised according to labour-time vouchers. Only once people have freed themselves from "subjugation ... to the division of labour," and only once the "all-round development of individuals [had] increased their productive powers," can the "more advanced phase then begin," and rationing be dispensed with. (pp.346-47).

This view, espoused consistently by Buick (1975, 1978) and Chattopadhyay (1994, pp.116-18) — although Buick disagrees about labour-time vouchers and argues that the 'political transition period' will be very short (1975, p.70) — is somewhat different from our own. At the same time, however, it is radically opposed to the usual leftist view on the 'economics of transition.' Thus the latter holds that money, the State, wages, and classes would still exist in a "transitional society," the basis of which would supposedly be the "hybrid combination" [*sic*] of commodity production and "non-capitalist economic planning" (E. Mandel 1974, p.10): or more simply, nationalisation. Trotsky even writes that the transition from capitalism to socialism in the USSR must actually mean the "extraordinary extension" of commodity relations. (1936, p.67). Marx's view of 1875 is equally opposed to the Leninist view of the 'politics of transition.' In generalised form this states that in each country the 'transitional' economy, complete with money, commodities, and wages, would be administered by a 'socialist' national government (or a "socialist state") — supposedly until the material means of production were sufficiently developed for it to cease to exist. (Trotsky 1936, pp.45-56). Whilst Marx, though, found no use for any concept of a 'socialist state,' the gap between Marx and Leninism is considerably greater than might be inferred even from this. See, for example, Lenin's assertion in *The State and Revolution* that "under communism there remains for a time not only bourgeois right, but even the *bourgeois* state, without the bourgeoisie!" (1917b, p.94, emphasis added). On a practical level, this corresponded to the Bolsheviks' inheritance of the State apparatus formerly wielded by Tsarism and the Provisional Government. On a theoretical level, it is not only anti-communist, if the term *communist* is to retain any meaning at all; it is also an extreme distortion even of Marx's later position.

Although rarely expressed openly, the idea underlying the Leninist theory of 'transition' is that even under 'socialism' the workers — assumed still to be a distinct class! — will not be particularly inclined to produce. Thus they will have to be subjected — by their own 'representatives' — to a combination of economic incentives and political (that is, State-mediated) discipline. At this point one can see how reformism, substitutionism, and the belief that the working class on its own is incapable of reaching a revolutionary consciousness and making a social revolution, form a single whole.

18   Or as Marx puts it, "when the proletariat proclaims the *dissolution of the existing world order*, it is only declaring the secret of its own existence." (1844, p.256).

19   The following definitions are not completely rigorous. Given that the usage of such tems as 'left' and 'extreme left' is based on these tendencies' self-description, however, and given that the ideas which demarcate the communist tendency have been detailed above, such definitions are not necessary in the present context.

20   Communist usage of the terms 'left,' 'extreme left' and 'ultra-left' in these meanings was developed in western Europe, particularly in France. Even in this region, though, these politics have undergone a major decline, as the intra-capitalist struggle between left and

right has fallen in importance on the general basis of a victory of the right. Many former left-wing parties, such as the British Labour Party, have actually joined the right.

21   It is worth pointing out in this context that some communists have argued, with substantial justification, that the Autonomists did not, in practice, break effectively with leftism even at the peak of their influence in the 1970s. (Insurrezione 1984). Specifically, neither political vanguardism nor national liberationism were ever put properly into question. Despite its pathbreaking theoretical contribution, Autonomism cannot therefore be seen as part of the communist tendency in the same way as groups and journals of an anti-vanguardist and anti-nationalist orientation.

We would suggest in partial explanation that although Autonomist Marxism always had the strength of being commendably 'up-to-date' and indeed forward-looking, it also had the weakness of being unable, even in the 1970s, fully to compensate for its lack of a fruitful encounter with earlier communist theoretical contributions, particularly those of the council communists and the Situationists. Bologna, for example, in discussing in a comparative context the workers' councils movement of 1918 in Germany, fails altogether to consider the practical (and armed) force of the council communist workers' organisations which arose as part of that movement. (1972). Despite his useful concentration on class composition, especially in the United States, his omission to consider the ideas and experience of European council communism can then reinforce his assumption that Russian Bolshevism was still some kind of a proletarian manifestation even as late as the civil war. (pp.90-91). Such views in turn reinforce the failure to reach a full rejection of partyism.

Moreover, Autonomist Marxism, unlike Situationist theory, has little or no concept of false consciousness. But a theoretical understanding of the fact that the working class necessarily holds power which is tendentially disruptive of the realisation of capitalist imperatives, so long as it remains untied to a full understanding of *means of integration*, can quite feasibly allow a movement from the original 'workerism' (*operaismo*) of the 1960s towards a positive appraisal of various kinds of accommodation, or at least to an abdication from the need to criticise them wholesale. The idea of global communist revolution can then be shifted towards a concept of the 'permanent' contestational occupation of a militant or sub-cultural 'area of autonomy,' corresponding in effect to a form of self-management. (See Insurrezione 1984).

Such a concept does not appear to be completely contradictory to the idea of Autonomist Marxism as it is understood by Cleaver, who coined the term. In outlining what it covers, he lists the following areas of interest (or points recognised):

    1. the autonomy of the working class vis-à-vis capital, 2. the autonomy of workers vis-à-vis their official organizations, e.g., trade unions or parties, [and] 3. the autonomy of various sectors of the class from each other, e.g., that of blacks from whites, women from men, etc. (1997, p.1)

We would argue that from a communist point of view it is Point 1 that is essential, and that whilst this directly implies Point 2, it does not imply Point 3, with which it actually conflicts. This is because the concept of the autonomy of a 'sector' of the class can only go against the understanding that it is class struggle as a globality that *determines* class.

It has also been possible to ignore or obscure the relevance of Point 2. The case of the early 'workerist' theorist Tronti, who in 1967 decided to espouse the 'really-existing workers' politics' of the Communist Party of Italy — which in the late 1970s became a main force in the Italian judicial repression of the principally Autonomist-influenced radical movement (see Red Notes 1979) — was admittedly exceptional. More recently, though, Lebowitz has been able, while elaborating a largely Autonomist theory of the primacy of class struggle, to maintain a more orthodox view of the trade unions as the "critical organising centre of the working class" and the State as a 'mediator of labour' which is apparently independent of capital. (1992, pp.149-51).

22   Pannekoek's view that any future capitalist collapse would have as its essential ingredient the "will to revolution of the proletariat" (1934, pp.78-79) should serve as a caveat against over-estimating the originality of Autonomism.

23   The International Workingmen's Association, or First International, did not formulate an agreed ideology of any comparable type.

24   On social democracy, see for example Pannekoek 1919 and 1920; on Bolshevism, Voline 1947 or Brinton 1970; on the conflict between proletarian autonomy and the anarchist union the National Confederation of Labour (CNT) during the Spanish civil war, Seidman 1988, pp.1-14.

25   Chattopadhyay's work does not fall easily into any of these three categories. Adopting a viewpoint which is neither social-democrat nor Leninist, he undoubtedly understands the need for working class self-liberation. (1994, p.148). Moreover, unlike Dunayevskaya and James, Castoriadis, and Ticktin, he rejects the concept of a 'transitional society' (pp.116-18) — albeit on the basis of Marx's *Critique of the Gotha Programme* (see Note 17 above). But he does not bring working class struggle into his theory of Soviet capitalism — or at least not explicitly — and theorises in a highly 'objectivist' fashion. Most important in the present context, however, is the fact that his critique of Soviet capitalism's historical development raises questions which seem all but to cry out for a 'classist' resolution. For this reason we have considered his work in the second section of Chapter 6. As with the example of Autonomism, which stresses workers' autonomy but bears the weaknesses referred to in the notes above — and as indeed with the critique of the USSR advanced by Ticktin, which emphasises workers' power without focusing explicitly on class antagonism — this will hopefully serve as good illustration of the need to be wary of over-tidy, dogmatic classifications.

2 Soviet Capitalism: A Critique of Existing Theories

In this chapter we look at the various theories which depict the Soviet system as capitalist. Critical consideration is given first to the numerous theories of 'state capitalism,' and then to the other 'capitalist' theories. In analysing and criticising each theory, we ask two main questions: why is the USSR perceived to be capitalist? And how is it perceived to be specific?

The view that Soviet society was capitalist has been held by a large number of writers from various political tendencies, including — in alphabetical order — anarchism, council communism, 'impossibilism,' many types of Leninism (including Bordigism, Maoism, and a number arising out of Trotskyism), libertarian socialism, Marxist-Humanism, Menshevism, the Situationist International, and social democracy.[1] If the very disparity of these tendencies raises significant problems in classifying the theories they have produced, we have found the most straightforward solution to be one which has rarely, if ever, been applied before. This is to classify them according to the simple presence or absence of an idea, however conceived, of 'state capitalism.' Present in the works of the Socialist Party of Great Britain, Rühle and the later council communists, Buick and Crump, Wildt, Dunayevskaya and James, Munis, Cliff, Bettelheim, and Sapir, this concept is quite absent in those of Gorter, Castoriadis, Bordiga, and Chattopadhyay.

The 'state capitalist' theories are discussed in the following order. First, we take the earliest theories, developed in the aftermath of the Bolshevik seizure of power: namely, the theory of the Socialist Party of Great Britain and the more developed theories of Rühle and the council communists. We then look at a more recent work by Buick and Crump which draws on both of these sources, as well as a little-known contribution by Wildt. All of these theories stress that neither the changes of government in 1917, nor the zigzags of economic policy thereafter, in any way led to the abolition of workers' exploitation.

Next we consider the theories produced by those writers who were originally of the Trotskyist view that the USSR was a 'workers' state,' but who later rejected it in favour of the view that under Stalinism this was no longer the case. These theories, produced by Dunayevskaya and James, Munis, and Cliff, were developed in the 1940s: around the time, that is, that the USSR began to receive military assistance first from the United Kingdom and then from the United States, proceeding to defeat Germany and become a major imperialist power. Criticism is made not of Bolshevism, but of Stalinism, established ostensibly in the course of a 'counterrevolution' in the late 1920s.

We then consider the alternative Leninist theory crafted by Bettelheim, who stresses above all the changes which took place in the years following the death of Stalin in 1953. If Chavance has de-emphasised these changes, and Sapir has more recently argued that capitalism has predominated since before 1917, both theorists base themselves chiefly on Bettelheim's view of the capitalist nature of the Soviet system.

Of the 'capitalist but not state capitalist' theories we deal first with the early council communist view constructed by Gorter, and then with the somewhat lengthier anti-Leninist work produced in the 1950s by Castoriadis. Next we consider the theoretical work of the left-Leninist Bordiga, and finally the recent work by Chattopadhyay. Notably, all of these theorists hold the view that capitalism was never abolished.

At this juncture it is worth mentioning, though, that this is not the only way the various theories might be sorted. Another sensible system would involve concentrating on the extent to which the development of the USSR is understood to have differed from the development of 'traditional' or 'classical' capitalism in the West. According to this second system, it would then appear that at one end of 'state capitalist' thinking there is Cliff, who holds that in the USSR there were neither commodities nor wage-labourers, but that even so the country was capitalist, owing to the internal effects of military competition with the West; and at the other end there are those such as the Socialist Party of Great Britain, for whom Soviet 'state capitalism' is little more than state ownership, as well as Buick and Crump, who refer to the existence throughout the Soviet period of a *market* — albeit an unfree one — wherein prices were ultimately determined by value. In between these two positions would stand Bettelheim, who sees the 'plan' as being a sort of transmission mechanism for the logic of the market; and Dunayevskaya and James, who write of capitalist profit but avoid falling into the trap of identifying it with its apparent forms.

A similar division is evident in the camp rejecting 'state capitalism.' Thus Castoriadis begins by making a major distinction between 'private capitalism' and 'bureaucratic capitalism'; and even once he decides that 'bureaucratic capitalism' prevails in the West as well as in the USSR, he still perceives a major structural difference between the two areas, with 'bureaucratic capitalism' being 'fragmented' in the former and 'total' in the latter. Bordiga, on the other hand, even more so than Gorter in the first half of the 1920s, takes the view that any differences are quite unimportant: given that 'mercantilism' is dominant in the USSR just as it is elsewhere, he sees no need to add a supplementary adjective to the basic characterisation as 'capitalist.' Between the two ends of the spectrum stands Chattopadhyay, who, whilst emphasising the sameness of the underlying

| | | STATE CAPITALIST? | |
		YES	NO
	FUNDAMENTALLY	Cliff	
		Wildt	Castoriadis
		Munis	
		Johnson-Forest	*[Present Theory — see Chap.3]*
DIFFERS FROM THE WEST		Bettelheim/Sapir /Chavance	
		Rühle/GIK	Chattopadhyay
		Buick & Crump	
		SPGB	
			Gorter
	HARDLY		Bordiga

Figure 2.1 Theories of Soviet Capitalism

categories, nonetheless points to major differences concerning the importance of technological change to the extraction of surplus value.

Since in every case one is dealing primarily with qualitative analyses, any attempt to give precedence below to the second method of classification would prove needlessly confusing, not to say inelegant; but the display given in Figure 2.1 will nonetheless serve to demonstrate the relevant axes of variety in the group of theories considered.

'STATE CAPITALISM'[2]

The Socialist Party of Great Britain's Theory[3]

Consistently emphasising the nature of socialism as a wageless and moneyless society, in the years following 1917 the SPGB lays particular stress on the fact that it is not seriously possible to view Soviet conditions as socialist. In short, "capitalism has always existed in post-revolutionary Russia and the working class there has never had political power." (1967, p.27).

In an endeavour to explain why it was that no socialist transformation came about, they then point to the backwardness of the productive forces (1918, pp.13-14), Lenin's explicit support for capitalist development (1920, pp.20-21; see Lenin 1917a, 1918b, and 1918-23), and the role played by private enterprise in both town and countryside under the New Economic Policy (NEP). (SPGB 1924, p.32). Whilst these points are interesting, however, they are not offered as a full theoretical demonstration of the capitalist nature of Soviet (urban) society, and it is perhaps worth pointing out that if they were they would be inadequate. Thus the first argument would fall straightaway since it would depend primarily upon two dogmatic assumptions: namely, that capitalism can only be succeeded by socialism, and that socialism is impossible without an industrial society. Clearly it is impossible to derive these tenets either from Marx's basic categories or from empirical reality. The second point, meanwhile, relates only to *part* of the urban economy, and at most to the political ideas and overall aims of Lenin's government; and the third can explain neither the role of the state sector nor the development of the economy after the 'Great Leap Forward.'[4]

In this early period the SPGB's theory of 'state capitalism' remains rudimentary, and they use the term — as Lenin does — primarily to describe the regulation and supervision of 'private' trade by the State. (1918). Allied to this conception there is the idea of a capitalist "road" along which the Bolshevik government is seen as being in "retreat." (1920, p.21). By 1924 the SPGB goes as far as to argue that the country already stands "halfway on the road to capitalism." (p.35). The implicit view here is that after 1917 there were at least some non-capitalist (and non-pre-capitalist) elements operating in the economy at a fundamental level, presumably associated with regulators other than market competition. Since, however, the SPGB eventually comes to adopt another view this is never argued out in full or reinforced theoretically at any great depth.

By the late 1920s the SPGB begins to oppose the concept of 'state' capitalism to that of 'private' capitalism (1928, p.40), with the implication that the former is not simply a form of regulation of the latter. Even after this, however, the old idea continues to exert an influence, and the resultant theoretical perspective is therefore highly confused. On one hand, there is an emphasis on the fundamentally capitalist relations — commodity production, wage-labour, profit, and capital — which underlie even the "extremely centralised" system of economic control under Stalin (see 1967, p.33); on the other there is a revealingly 'over-determined' interest — relating to the very same period — in such matters as the role of concessions granted to foreign companies (1930), the importance of interest-bearing government bonds, and the rise of Soviet rouble millionaires (SPC 1948, pp.45-46).

To understand the SPGB's theory of 'state capitalism,' it is first necessary to follow their argument as to why the USSR is capitalist. This is so, in their view, because all the essential features of capitalism continue to exist: namely, the class monopoly of the means of production; the wages system; great inequalities of wealth and income; State coercion against the workers; the production of commodities for profit; and arms production, nationalism, and war. (1967, pp.13-14). Endeavouring to theorise more precisely, they focus on four features in particular: the class monopoly of the means of production, commodity production, wage-labour, and the accumulation of capital. (p.27). Correctly, from a Marxist standpoint, they then point out that commodity production itself is not a sufficient condition for capitalism: there must also be categories of wage-labour and profit.

Unfortunately, though, their usage of the words 'profit' and 'capital' remains extremely loose, suggesting little more than the extraction and reinvestment of a surplus product.

> In Russia the means of production are used to exploit wage-labour for a surplus. In other words they function as capital. (p.29)

This may be formally true, since wage-labour plus accumulation as the aim of production do indeed imply capital; but there is nonetheless a gaping hole in the theory. As 'orthodox Marxists' the SPGB must certainly believe that Soviet profits derive from the production of *surplus value*, but they make no attempt to show how this might be the case. To do this, of course, would first of all mean showing how value actually functions other than through the market, particularly in the producer goods sector. (Or, alternatively, one might argue that the apparently non-market forms were in fact forms of the market). Since, however, the SPGB's concepts of profit and 'capital' remain detached from the Marxist concept of value, they must necessarily be judged inadequate. It may be possible to deduce from the SPGB's writings that the Soviet system really was capitalist, but it is not possible to gain an understanding of how the various capitalist categories actually worked.

Their residual concept of 'state capitalism' is highly patchy, and sometimes seems to boil down to little more than the idea of state ownership. (1943, p.85; 1967, p.29). Elsewhere, reference is made to ministerial target-setting under Stalin.

> The State directed what should be produced; the factory managers merely had to carry out these orders. The State also fixed the prices at which goods were to be

sold to the consumer. As in all systems of rationing (which this State-directed system resembled) a black market appeared. Industrial agents or 'pushers' made a living by getting scarce supplies for a price. Indeed they became an essential part of the system. (1967, p.33)

The reference to rationing here would seem only to obscure the fact that, whilst it might have been possible in 1940s Britain, say, to buy bread 'off ration,' and in Stalin's USSR to procure industrial raw materials for cash or favours, it was not possible in the latter to buy, say, machine-building plants or car factories for roubles. This impossibility was as much an "essential part of the system" as was the operation of industrial *tolkachi* — as indeed the SPGB recognise in this extract. But to such systemically necessary and apparently *non-market* aspects they give no more than passing attention. As a consequence, their theory is weak because they do not *theorise* any significant differences between the USSR and the West.

Council Communist Theories[5]

Among those who saw the USSR as capitalist in the 1920s were also the council communists: anti-parliamentary Marxists whose theoreticians included Pannekoek, Gorter, Mattick, Rühle, and, for a time — albeit somewhat belatedly — Korsch.[6] After 1920-21, once the facts about Russian conditions had become clear in western Europe, the council communists forthrightly condemned not only the despotism of the Bolshevik political system but also the capitalist economic conditions it policed and defended.[7] At first, during the NEP (1921-28), the majority emphasised the role of market competition and the capitalist peasantry (see below, section 2.1 on Gorter), and only a minority theorised 'state capitalism'; but by the mid-1930s the 'state capitalist' position had become one of the tendency's principal tenets.

Rühle's Theory[8]

The origins of the council communist theory of 'state capitalism' lie with Rühle, who in a major work of 1924 comes to understand the internal economic role of the Soviet State in terms of capitalist development on a world scale. Whilst keeping to the view that in the capitalist economy "the market is the centre," Rühle thus attributes substantial significance to growing State authoritarianism and administrative centralisation, not as purely Soviet developments, but rather as aspects of a general tendency throughout the capitalist world. In this view, it is precisely the "centralism" of the capitalist *economy*, expressed through the market, which determines the changes in the political organisation of the State.

One can undoubtedly criticise Rühle for being confused, in that he fails to trace convincingly the interactions between the economic 'centrality' of the market and the political 'centralism' of the State, preferring simply to aver that the latter 'corresponds' to the former. (1924, pp.19-22). He can hardly be said to deal with the full complexities of Soviet economic bureaucracy. But at the same time, in describing "nationalisation without socialisation" — or, as the Bolsheviks called it, 'War Communism' — as tending maximally towards a "large-scale tightly centrally-run state capitalism" (p.15), Rühle undoubtedly provides the germs of a more advanced critique.

In 1931 Rühle published pseudonymously a much fuller theory which remains remarkably little known. In *The World Crisis, or Towards State Capitalism*, he first shows that capitalism has undergone a tremendous process of cartelisation and monopolisation, evident in the consumer retail sector as much as much as in coal, electrical technology, or steel. (pp.90-119). Economic power in Europe now rests in very few hands indeed. (pp.105-06). He then points to the parallel and long-term growth in State subsidies. (pp.120-49). When economic crisis appears, each capitalist government's need to subsidise becomes particularly acute; and as a result, capitalist domination employs ever greater levels of State intervention and indeed planning. It is no longer a paradox that early subsidies were given especially readily to concerns which lay outside the monopolies, and which indeed the monopolies threatened. Monopolisation and intervention are simply twin aspects of the concentration of the productive forces. Looking specifically at the Germany of the time, Rühle correctly predicts that the State and the economy will increasingly overlap and intermesh. (p.178). In this view, State involvement eventually reaches such a level as to constitute a fundamental change; and even if 'State capitalism' neither permanently solves capitalism's problems, nor fundamentally alters its nature, it nonetheless represents a genuinely new stage of capitalist domination.

It is in this context that Rühle sees the USSR. Here, though, rather than being a consequence of the 'over-ripeness' of a capitalism racked by crisis, State capitalism emerges instead from far more primitive forms of capitalist evolution. In Russia,

> the planned economy was introduced before the free capitalist economy had reached its full fruition, before its life-cycle had led it to senility. In concrete terms, it amounted to a premature birth, rendered possible by specific historical circumstances. (pp.179-80)

In Rühle's view, not only did the world war destroy Russian 'feudalism'; it then also "devoured" a bourgeoisie which was unable to make peace. Following the collapse of the war effort, many capitalist concerns, despite being officially subject to increased 'supervision' (*kontrol'*), lapsed into a state of utter chaos, or even complete inactivity. They ended up being nationalised. In quick succession, the banks, the merchant navy, foreign trade, and whole industries were taken into State hands: the "form of property" was changed. During NEP, the State then kept control of at least the commanding heights of industry, and set about laying the foundations of the organised State capitalist system which was later to undergo such rapid expansion. (p.192).

Different in origin to western European developments, the subsequent industrial, agricultural, and infrastructural upheavals launched by the Soviet State at the end of the 1920s are also of a different significance in their effect. (pp.207-09). State disposal of the means of production allows the revolutionisation of technique in all the main sectors; and moreover, millions of new workers are made available for such development to exploit. Whereas in western Europe there is hunger, misery, and the threat of total ruin, in the USSR besides hunger and want there is also a great leap forward, growth, and a new future. There is no crisis. Capitalist 'planning' in the USSR has evidently nothing whatsoever to do with socialism, but nonetheless it consititutes a movement quite distinct from those occurring in Germany and elsewhere. Whereas in western Europe the declining "free capitalist" economy seeks to move beyond the stage of cartels and monopolies so as to save itself by means of State planning, in the USSR State planning started at "the bottom of the ladder" (p.209), rubbished the inheritance of feudalism, and now makes use of the conquests of the free capitalist economy in its own autonomous self-expansion. Since sooner or later the lines of development must cross, it is the East which shows the West the light of 'salvation' and not *vice versa*. Rühle later describes the Bolshevik State as a model for Nazism and fascism. (1939, p.6).[9]

It is, however, only State capitalism that western Europe tends to copy, not its specific Soviet manifestation. Whereas western Europe will see either the 'usurpation' of the private economy by the State, or else the establishment over the State of a strict control by private firms (1931, pp.229-40), Soviet capitalism follows an altogether different route. In considering this route in his final chapter, though, Rühle loses much of his earlier clarity. Without providing adequate theoretical support, he thus avers that whilst the measures advocated in the *Communist Manifesto* (Marx and Engels 1848, pp.59-60) have been "almost completely realised," in terms of the manner of their realisation there are still "survivals of capitalism." (Rühle 1931, pp.227-29). It is, of course, straightaway apparent here that Rühle fails to appraise the rather more radical position on the State which Marx later expressed in the aftermath of the Paris Commune. (See Marx 1871, pp.206-12, and, for clarification, the first draft, 1934, pp.246-52). More than this, though, the question of the "manner of realisation" of measures advocated in 1848 is really a non-question. Either capitalism survives or it does not survive: the implied division between two dimensions of change, non-capitalist and capitalist, would seem to make little sense and at any rate is not coherently argued out.

Such carelessness only increases. Explaining Soviet 'State capitalism' Rühle mentions in addition to economic backwardness the suppression "in principle" both of private property in the means of production and of class antagonism. (1931, p.227-29). In this view, though, if the high level of planning and the widespread "tendency towards co-operation" will be useful in the future, they are of little importance today. State capitalism in the USSR "tends towards" and prepares the road for socialism; it is even the most mature form of a "transition towards socialism" (*sic*). But it is not socialism. Indeed it is completely opposed to socialism. It is capitalism. The wage remains the price of labour-power, not an "aliquot-part" of the social product.[10] The production process adapts itself to market requirements, not to needs. And the value of the currency remains set according to the gold rate, not according to "collectivist accountability." The leadership of the State, meanwhile, is authoritarian, bureaucratic, and dictatorial; and there are no real councils expressing the collective will of the masses, no associations of free and equal producers. All these factors constitute what Rühle calls "capitalist atavisms."

It would seem, of course, rather an under-statement to describe such relations as wage-labour as mere "survivals" of capitalism, sloppy to refer thus to the market, and simply rhetorical even to use the phrase 'capitalist atavisms' at all. (As yet, capitalism does not date back to a distant ancestral past). Moreover, having avoided referring to the original wartime dislocation of 1917-21 as a 'crisis,' and preferring for unexplained reasons to explain the 'Soviet route' with reference instead to an untheorised category of 'co-operation,' Rühle fails to show how the tendency towards such co-operation is actually manifested. Correspondingly, he neglects to explain in what way mere 'atavisms' might permit substantial capitalist growth. His view of the actual Soviet production relations consequently remains fuzzy and poorly theorised.

Councilist Theory[11]

The 'councilists' of the 1930s soon rejected the view that Soviet developments were only one expression of a movement towards state capitalism which operated globally. In the *Theses on Bolshevism* (1934) — an important landmark in the maturation of the councilist tendency[12] — the Group of International Communists (GIK) give correspondingly much greater consideration to the USSR as a specific case. They thus begin by pointing to Russia's intermediate situation between the industrialised area of western Europe and North America and the colonial, agricultural regions of eastern Asia. They show how, before 1917, the Russian economy combined an antiquated and feudal agriculture with a capitalist industrial sector which was relatively far more advanced. Russian industry had not only been 'engrafted' onto the country by the Tsarist State; it also, in its own sphere, preserved many feudal features, such as the binding of many workers to the village and their accommodation in barracks while in the towns. Since the workers were largely 'unfree,' Russian industry was organised upon the basis of "capitalist serfdom." Elements of feudal agriculture and capitalist industry interpenetrated. (pp.5-6).

The "economic tasks" of the Russian revolution became those of commodifying agriculture and facilitating the unrestricted creation of a class of really 'free labourers' for exploitation in industry. In other words, they were the tasks of the bourgeois revolution. As in the western countries, this meant overthrowing the nobility. Since, however, Russian absolutism in the 20th century differed considerably from, say, French absolutism three centuries before, the contradictions were not identical. The bourgeoisie in Russia had become anti-revolutionary even before the tasks had been accomplished, and the revolution therefore had to be carried out against it. (p.8).

As the bourgeoisie gradually threw in its lot with reaction, it was left to elements among the petty bourgeoisie, schooled in western ideas and organised Jacobinically, to take its place in the struggle against Tsarism. In time these forces assumed the leadership of the peasantry, which was revolutionary but politically weak; and of the working class, which may have developed an "independent class policy" in 1917 but nonetheless remained socially weak in the country as a whole. The revolutionary petty-bourgeois intelligentsia found its vanguard first in the broader Russian social democracy, and then, more specifically, in the Bolshevik party under Lenin. (pp.9-10).

Although the Bolshevik leadership had originally aimed to collaborate with liberal employers and priests (p.13), once in government it was forced by working class pressure to undertake the full nationalisation of the enterprises. The capitalist economy was not simply appropriated by the State, which had played such a large role in building it up; it was now administered directly by the State bureaucracy. Bolshevik 'socialism' was nothing but "state-organized capitalism." (p.21).

The GIK's analysis of Soviet conditions once the Bolsheviks are fully established in power, however, is considerably less impressive. With scant argumentation, they thus assert that whereas

> the proletariat, enchained with the methods of compulsory membership in the trade
> unions and the terrorism of the Tcheka, formed the basis of the bolshevistic

bureaucratically conducted state economy [,...] the peasantry concealed and still conceals in its ranks the private capitalist tendencies of that economy. (pp.24-25)

Tossed back and forth between the "two tendencies," the Soviet State attempts to 'master' them, but only at the expense of increasing the contradictions: it 'overtensions' the forces of the workers and peasants. By now the analysis appears mainly rhetorical, and the language is both confused and confusing: there is no clear definition of what the first 'tendency' actually is.

The previous rigour vanishes.

The inner character of the Russian economy is determined by the following circumstances: it rests on the foundation of commodity production; it is conducted according to the viewpoints of capitalist profitability; it reveals a decidedly capitalist system of wages and speed-up; it has carried the refinements of capitalist rationalisation to the utmost limits. Bolshevist economy is state production with capitalist methods. (p.25)

All of these assertions may well be true, but four years after the onset of collectivisation the commodity nature of the product undoubtedly requires to be argued out in full. And if the goal of production is presented as being profitability, this has to be shown unambiguously to be the case, since after the onset of breakneck industrialisation such an idea clearly goes against *prima facie* impressions. Instead of showing that the surplus product takes a value form, though, the GIK simply assumes that it does and ploughs on regardless. Further assertions that the surplus value is "pocketed" by the State by means of the "bureaucratic, parasitical apparatus as a whole," and that part of that value is then passed on to the peasantry (pp.25-26), albeit original, fail to compensate for the lack of theoretical foundation. This becomes even clearer once it is realised that the nationalisations and mass proletarianisation which put an end to NEP were, in terms of accumulation, a major economic success.

Buick and Crump's Theory

Building upon insights from both the above sources, Buick and Crump also take the view that capitalism was never abolished. Not only do they thus avoid giving a Leninist explanation of the 'degeneration' of proletarian revolution due to 'isolation'[13]; in fact they go further and argue that the revolution that did occur was a state capitalist one. They then proceed to analyse the Soviet system in terms of a 'state capitalist market.'

Like the SPGB and the council communists, but unlike Cliff (see below), Buick and Crump see the USSR as capitalist because of what it was like internally. They consequently begin their exposition in what seems an eminently sensible fashion:

> To say that state capitalism is a variety of capitalism may be a tautology, but it brings out the need to be clear on what capitalism is before embarking on any discussion of what state capitalism might be. (1986, p.1)

Capitalism they define as a class society with six essential characteristics: generalised commodity production, where nearly all wealth is produced for sale on the market; investment of capital in production with a view to obtaining a monetary profit; wage-labour; regulation of production by the market via a competitive struggle for profit; accumulation of capital; and a single world economy.

In their discussion of state capitalist revolution, they explain (pp.46-47) how capitalist revolutions are not always carried out by the bourgeoisie. Thus in Japan the revolution of 1868 was led by samurai, but was "no less capitalist in its effects than the French Revolution of 1789, [for]...both...succeeded in creating an environment in which commodity production and wage labour could develop further." (p.46; see also Crump 1983, pp.3-19). Countries particularly susceptible to state capitalist revolution tended to be those which were backward, "unable to accumulate sufficient capital rapidly and hence to modernise at an acceptable rate," and under either "the threat or the actuality of foreign domination." (1986, p.45). In the Russian context, Buick and Crump also mention (p.47) the important role the Tsarist State played in industry prior to 1917, a role which hindered the emergence of a revolutionary bourgeoisie.

Their theory concerning the *specific* nature of state capitalism is contained in a chapter on "The Capitalist Dynamic of State Capitalist Economies." (pp.67-101). The model they develop has seven main features (p.72): state ownership of the principal means of production; generalised wage-labour; generalised use of money and monetary calculation; a free market for consumer goods; a market for producer goods that is closely monitored and 'directed' by the State; widespread 'planning', in the form of State allocation, target-setting, price-fixing and direction of capital flows between sectors; and a sizeable black market.

Since it cannot seriously be denied that accumulation was the basic motive of Soviet production, even despite the stagnation which began under Brezhnev and led in 1990 to officially-recognised negative growth, the core of Buick and Crump's argument that the USSR was capitalist relates to two subjects in particular: wage-labour and the market. If it can be shown that these were the fundamental bases of the Soviet economic system, then their particular 'capitalist' argument will prevail.

Buick and Crump argue for the existence of a Soviet labour market (and hence, wage-labour) by stressing (p.75) that "enterprises have always retained a degree of independence," and that this has been especially manifest in the sphere of adjusting wages and working conditions. Even the draconian restrictions on labour mobility introduced in certain periods, such as between 1940 and 1956, when it was illegal to change jobs without permission, have always proved unenforceable in the long term. Annual labour turnover was 38% in 1956, the year the ban was removed, and fell only to about 20% by the early 1980s (p.76), a level that clearly cannot be dismissed as unimportant.[14] One can assume that most of the workers who changed their jobs, as an 'average' worker might do once every five years, did so because they wanted to. Moreover, in the late Brezhnev period almost all hiring took place either at the factory gates or at the labour exchange. (Sapir 1984, p.61; see also Lane 1987, p.59, and Marnie 1990, pp.4-5). So, with whatever limitations, and there were many, labour was to a substantial degree 'free.' It is worth anchoring this point with reference to Marx, who devoted a chapter of *Capital* to the sale and purchase of labour-power. For him, labour-power could appear on the market as a commodity only if the worker really possessed it, that is, if he disposed of it as a "free proprietor." The wage-labourer is the possessor of his labour-capacity, and "hence of his person." (1867, p.271). It is thus clear that labour turnover and competition to employ workers provide a strong argument for the existence of wage-labour in the USSR. (We disregard here the question of the concentration camps, where labour was not at all free: the present context is that of work in the rest of the economy alone).

Although there is little problem in identifying a consumer market — in food, clothing, and so on (Buick and Crump 1986, p.80) — problems arise when they endeavour to show the existence of an inter-enterprise goods market. Thus first they mention that Soviet planning was based on guesswork, approximation and often just "wishful statements of intent" (in other words, as Ticktin has shown [1973a and 1991c, pp.116-29], it was not real planning[15]); and then they state their approval of the Maoist Bettelheim's argument that Soviet planning was in fact no more than the planning of market transactions. (p.82). (On Bettelheim, see below, 1.8). In other words, "the 'plan' does not abolish exchange relations between enterprises, but merely attempts — not too successfully — to quantify the exchanges in advance." (p.83). Physical inflows of equipment are simply balanced by corresponding outflows of money. On the one hand, they seem to be saying, there was no (successful) planning, or at least not much, but instead there was competition between enterprises; on the other, even if there *had* been planning, it would still have been the market that was being planned.

Their attempt to square this circle undermines their entire theory of the state capitalist market. In answering the anticipated objection that buying and selling between Soviet enterprises was a purely *formal* matter, since enterprises were prevented from dealing with each other independently and directly, they naturally arrive at the question of *price*. Recalling that although commodities do not normally sell at their value even in "private capitalism," it is still value that "ultimately determines prices," they then accept that

> if, in the state capitalist countries, exchange between enterprises occurred at prices which were established entirely arbitrarily by the state, the case for seeing this as genuine commodity exchange would be weakened. Yet what, in fact, ultimately determines state capitalist prices is once again value....The process of extracting surplus value can be accomplished efficiently only when suitable indicators for measuring value exist, in the form of money prices which take into account the law of value. Certainly state capitalist prices do not directly reflect value, but...this is not the case in private capitalism either....[The] refracting effect of planning modifies but does not cancel the commodity status of the means of production in state capitalism. (pp.83-84)

A consideration of basic Soviet economics will make their main mistake clear. In general, producer prices did not reflect considerations of monetary (rouble) profit to any great extent; and in any case, the main indicator was hardly ever rouble profit but almost always gross output. It might be argued with reference to the above extract from Buick and Crump that the process of extracting surplus value was therefore inefficient, since rouble prices simply did not *adequately* take into account the law of value. But the reality was that producer prices, not being determined principally by the drive for maximum rouble profit, did not reflect the law of *value* in the usual way: instead, they reflected "the preference of the centre or whoever [had] most control in fixing the price at any one time." Moreover, "changes in price in the producer goods sector [had] only secondary effects, since the physical target [was] all important." (Ticktin 1976, p.26). In other words, rouble price did not play the all-important important mediating role in the producer goods sector: neither its formation, nor its effects, were prime determinants in decisions as to output, distribution or use.

In making this point, Ticktin speaks of the need to analyse "the blend of force, administration, self-interest and price." (p.27). Rather than taking this approach, Buick and Crump do not begin with empirical reality: instead, their argument concerning the 'state capitalist market' seems to be that since the USSR is capitalist, prices 'must' reflect value. We would suggest that this confusion of function with form stems from an over-eagerness to compare the USSR to the countries ruled by the bourgeoisie.

Wildt's Theory

In some ways Wildt's theory can likewise be placed within a political area quite close to that of council communism. Having as his main aim the unification of a political theory of totalitarianism with a political-economic theory of 'state capitalism,' he cites with approval the council communist insistence on the "counter-revolutionary historical function of Bolshevism" and the "transformation of capitalism as a whole promoted by fascism and Stalinism." (1979, p.45-47; see also pp37-38). After outlining an original framework for an understanding of 'state capitalism,' he then attempts to make use of that framework in the development of a non-liberal theory of totalitarianism.

It is Wildt's overall approach to Soviet 'state capitalism' which is relevant here. Wildt may not study the Soviet economy in any great depth, but even so his work is useful in that he describes explicitly a certain critical attitude towards the applicability of Marx's categories.

> It is argued that one can speak of capitalism only in a market economy, i.e. an economy with a division of labor and independently producing economic units that relate to one another through competition in the marketplace.... Of course, Marx occasionally says that market competition is a necessary condition for 'capital.' But Marx's and Engels's discussions of the abolition of 'private production' or of 'capital as private property' in stock companies, trusts, and cooperative factories, are not entirely applicable, since these forms of organization, as well as partial nationalization, government contracts, etc., do not abolish the market economy. If market competition were to be part of the definition of capitalism, it is unlikely that Marx was really all that concerned with distinguishing the 'inner nature' of capitalism from these phenomena. (p.43)

The translation here could doubtless be improved, but Wildt's point is that if Marx had seen the market economy as the one capitalist economic form which underlay all the others, he surely would have said so more often when actually analysing them.

In itself, such an abstract assertion is not very interesting, since even taken as a whole Marx's work is evidently incapable of providing *all that is needed* for a theoretical critique of modern capitalism either within the USSR or without. Capitalist forms continue to develop historically: history does not stop. But that is something of which Wildt is not unaware, as his next point shows. He writes as follows:

> As for the systematic description of capital, a dialectical 'development' can be interpreted so radically that in the course of development the categories with which the description begins [commodities and money] are not just critically relativized, specific, and completed, but abolished. (pp.43-44)

Above all, he puts the emphasis on the most fundamental definition of capital itself: namely, as "a disjointed movement of the self-exploitation of value." ('Self-expansion' might be a better translation). In Wildt's reading of Marx,

> disjointedness and self-exploitation are more central...than commodity and money, and are followed by the definitions of the 'domination of reified labor over living labor'.... Accordingly, what is decisive for capitalism is not that the products of labor take the form of commodities, but the structural pressure for accumulation, which is realized through the exploitation of the commodity 'labor power.' Whether this compulsion for accumulation is the result of market competition or otherwise is secondary. (p.44)

There are many things wrong with this view. For instance, it is impossible to sustain a concept of value in the absence of a concept of exchange-value; and goods which possess an exchange-value are by definition commodities. Second, Wildt does not define what it was that Soviet workers were paid in return for selling their labour-power which was non-monetary in nature. (In the conventional view, of course, wage-labour is *by definition* bought with money). Third, one might add that whatever a commodity is exchanged for, including if that commodity is labour-power or the contents of the wage-packet, must surely itself be a commodity. Wildt's concepts of value without commodities and of wage-labour without money are *prima facie* insupportable, and at any rate are very poorly-founded.

As will become clear in Chapter 3, however, the most useful critique one can make is that the concept of 'disjointedness' is left completely undeveloped. If capital is defined as disjointed, then one must be able to define further at least two functional elements within it whose interrelation is disjointed in nature. It is, indeed, precisely as such elements that Marx presents money and the commodity in *Capital*. Wildt, however, fails to consider in any concrete fashion the form which Soviet capital's disjointedness may actually have taken. The only non-market form which he does present, namely the totalitarian state machine, remains not only singular and 'undisjointed,' but also essentially political rather than political-economic. (pp.55-57).

It must be acknowledged that Wildt shows courage and imagination in daring to develop Marx's conception 'beyond Marx.' However, his argument that capitalism exists in the USSR remains at bottom that of the SPGB: namely, that capitalism reigns wherever there is a "structural pressure for accumulation...realized through the exploitation of the commodity 'labour-power'." (p.44) His originality lies in the view that this is so even when other commodities and money are absent. Unfortunately, though, since he offers no alternative definition of *capital* to Marx's formula M-C-M´ (see Chapter 3 below), his use of the term 'capitalism' actually explains very little.[16]

The Johnson-Forest Tendency's Theory

Another view of Soviet 'state capitalism' was put forward by James and Dunayevskaya, who lent their respective pseudonyms of J. R. Johnson and F. Forest to a tendency which emerged within American Trotskyism in 1941 and lasted for ten years.[17] Although later to follow widely divergent trajectories, they would both always keep to the original 'state capitalist' view upon whose development they cooperated.

The tendency's main theoretical work on the USSR was published by Dunayevskaya in the form of two series of articles appearing between 1942 and 1947. In the first series, she describes two phenomena in particular: first, the significant growth of Department One (means of production) relative to Department Two (means of consumption); and second, the related fall in working class living-standards since the start of the first Five Year Plan in 1928. (1942-43, pp.329 and 18). At this time, Dunayevskaya does not present these two factors as adequate proof of the continued operation of the law of value, but later she not only does this, but she also asserts quite incorrectly that she has already done so in the earlier work. (1946-47[18], p.313). Since, however, it is quite easy to draw up models of non-capitalist societies where these factors are also present — as they are, for example, in the model 'bureaucratic collectivisms' of Shachtman (1940-61) and Rizzi (1939)[19] — Dunayevskaya undoubtedly stands on very weak ground. A more precise application of Marx's method would show that before theorising the 'law of value' one must first show the existence of value itself (and its form, exchangeability), rather than just its effects. (See Marx 1859, 1867).

In comparison, Dunayevskaya's more specific work on the mechanics of value accumulation is considerably stronger. If at first she simply describes the turnover tax and the official profit motive as being accumulation's two 'handmaidens' (1942-43, p.19), in the second series she concentrates much more usefully upon the various categories which Marx saw as necessary ingredients of capitalism. Taking first of all the category of *profit*, she begins by dealing with the official Soviet position that the USSR is not capitalist because there is no systemic equalisation of the profit-rate. Ostensibly, "capital does not migrate where it is most profitable, but where the state directs it." Dunayevskaya demolishes this argument by explaining that profit does not at all

> have the same meaning in Russia as it does in classical capitalism. The light industries show greater profit not because of the greater productivity of labor, but because of the state-imposed turn-over tax which gives an entirely fictitious 'profit' to that industry. In reality, it is merely the medium through which the state, not the industry, siphons off anything 'extra' it gave the worker by means of wages. It could not do the same things through the channel of heavy industry because the workers do not eat its products. That is why this 'profit' attracts neither capital nor the individual agents of capital.

She continues:

> Precisely because the *words*, profit and loss, have assumed a different meaning, the individual agents of capital do not go to the most 'profitable' enterprises, even as capital itself does not. *For the very same reason* that the opposite was characteristic of classic capitalism: The individual agent's share of surplus value is greater in heavy industry. The salary of the director of a billion-dollar trust depends, not on whether the trust shows a profit or not, but basically upon the magnitude of the capital that he manages. (1946-47, p.314)

What 'state capitalism' has changed, in this view, is the "mode of appropriation" by the agents of capital of their respective shares of the global surplus value. Dunayevskaya points out that at no time in the history of capitalism has the agent of capital realised directly the surplus value extracted in his particular factory: instead, he has only participated in the distribution of surplus value

> to the extent that his individual capital was able to exert pressure on this aggregate capital. This pressure in Russia is exerted, not through competition, but state planning. (p.314)

What is impressive here is that Dunayevskaya does not try to defend the view that what the Soviet State says is 'profit' actually is profit. She prefers instead to undertake a functional analysis of the cycle of capital accumulation as it really takes place, regardless of what things are called. In doing so, she finds that rouble profit can qualify only as 'profit,' or 'fictitious profit,' and that the mechanism of distribution of surplus value is quite distinct from that which operates under classical capitalism. These are highly significant theoretical achievements.

Unfortunately, though, Dunayevskaya does not provide adequate answers to the questions her work raises. First and foremost, if rouble profit is only 'profit,' then what form does *profit*, without the inverted commas, actually take? Second, in what way do individual capitals exert pressure on aggregate capital? Since the very idea of pressure by parts upon the whole implies some sort of competition, the view that such pressure is exerted by means of state *planning* would appear to represent a mere reinterpetation of the official position.

A similar criticism can also be made of Dunayevskaya's discussion of Soviet money, which she sees as the means through which prices and wages are equated in the supply and demand for consumption goods. (p.315). In Department Two at least, as long as profit is interpreted as meaning 'more money' — and Dunayevskaya does not reject this conventional interpretation — there would seem to be no reason to distinguish between profit and 'profit' so long as a similar distinction is not drawn between money and 'money.' In other words, if money is unambiguous, then profit should be so too. To put the same point differently: if profit is not what it seems, then nor is money. Admittedly, Dunayevskaya considers money only in the context of consumer goods, but rather than providing a defence this in fact only makes the inadequacy of her consideration of money more apparent. It was, of course, crucial to Marx's critique of capitalist political economy that money be understood to be divided between the two Departments. (1885, pp.474-78).

Despite these weaknesses, however, the Johnson-Forest Tendency undoubtedly deserves credit for endeavouring to nuance its theory of state capitalism with a consideration of the empirically operative reality of the capitalist category of surplus value. It can only be regretted, therefore, that in considering the nature of Soviet capitalism in a subsequent book on 'state capitalism' James focuses merely on the tendency towards the personification of capital by bureaucrats, and on the intensified exploitation of the workers (1950); and fails even to reiterate, let alone make more profound, the points derived earlier from the application of a 'categorial' approach. The similarly disappointing work later published by Dunayevskaya as a 'Marxist-Humanist' philosopher (1958, chap. 13), in which she largely restricts her attention to a recounting of nuts-and-bolts data about purges, camps, and Stakhanovism, demonstrates that neither of the Tendency's leaders was able to break the theoretical impasse any more than the other.[20]

Munis's Theory[21]

Emerging from Trotskyism around the same time, Munis takes similar care to consider the USSR in terms of some of the categories presented by Marx in Volumes 1 and 2 of *Capital*. In his case, though, the categories understood to be the most crucial are not profit and money, but rather the various portions of the overall social product.

According to Marx, of course, the social product under capitalism can be divided into three parts: constant capital c, variable capital v, and surplus value s. (See for example Marx 1867). These specifically capitalist forms can be expressed in relation to more general terms, applicable not only to capitalism but to any society which produces in excess of the immediate needs of the producers. Thus constant capital is simply the form taken under capitalism by the material means of production, both fixed and circulating; variable capital is the capitalist form of the portion of the product which meets the socially-determined consumption needs of the producers; and surplus value is the capitalist form of the surplus product. Munis's argument is that in the USSR each of these portions takes a recognisably capitalist form, hence so does the mode of production.

Munis makes this argument by first offering a model of 'planning', which he seems to see as an adequate definition of communism. (1946, p.15). Using c, v, and s somewhat confusingly to denote the more general terms, he then argues that whereas under capitalism surplus value is appropriated by and in the interests of a specific social stratum (*catégorie*), which then splits it into investment and consumption portions, in a planned society the capitalisation [*sic*] of s is now governed solely by the needs of consumption (that is, by v). If on one hand the surplus now passes wholly and directly into new means of production, and is no longer split into two parts, on the other hand the very expansion of the means of production is itself directed solely towards the enlargement of consumption. "The fulcrum of [the] c-v-s [relation] passes fully from s to v." (p.16).[22]

Munis then assumes that in the years following 1917 Soviet Russia was "in the first stage of the society of transition." He admits that some strata still benefited from surplus value, even if the only example he gives is that of the non-party technicians.[23] But since, in his view, "v, the working population, was in possession of the instruments of labour, and disposed of the distribution of s," the state of affairs was qualitatively wholly different from the "systematic exploitation of surplus value practised by the Stalinist bureaucracy." (p.18; see also Munis 1975, chap. 1).

Under Stalinism, s is not in the hands of "society"; it is in the hands of a particular stratum or category. In short, s is once again the fulcrum of production. In line with the establishment of domination by the bureaucracy, the surplus adopts anew its former character as surplus value. Looking then at the actual material composition of s, Munis focuses especially on military production and the luxury consumption of the elite "privileged caste." Military production he sees as especially important, occuring as it does in the sole interest of the bureaucracy, insofar as the latter does not seek 'world revolution.' Meanwhile, whilst it might be possible to imagine that all of s could be ploughed into c even in a 'society of transition,' one could not conceive of the development of production in such a society permitting the uninterrupted growth of c for 10 or 20 years without a consequent growth in the consumption of v. (1946, pp.18-19). In actual fact, the intelligentsia's living-standards have soared as those of the working class have plummeted.

It would perhaps be too easy to criticise Munis's view of Soviet conditions following 1917. Thus he conceptualises surplus value without capitalism; assumes without argument that production occurred for a time on the basis of a "society of transition"; inadequately nuances the term 'bureaucracy'; draws the figure of 10-20 years seemingly out of thin air; and remains implicitly burdened with the insupportable Trotskyist view that the adoption in 1925 of the ideology of 'socialism in one country' constituted a major turning-point.[24] At the same time, however, he does effectively show what he is principally aiming to show: namely, that the fulcrum of social production in the USSR is the extraction of a surplus s; and that controlling the extraction and reinvestment of s there stands a particular social group which exploits the workers.

The point is that this is not enough to prove the existence of surplus value. As Marx was well aware, surplus labour (and hence the surplus product) "has an antagonistic form" just as much in the slave system as in capitalism. There too, its "obverse side is pure idleness on the part of one section of society." (1894, p.958). The rulers of capitalism do, of course, unlike the Pharoahs, dictate the systematic expansion of production, rather than simply consuming or squandering the surplus they appropriate. But it is quite possible in principle to imagine modernised slave-owners doing the same. Unfortunately for Munis, for the surplus product to take the form of surplus value there must be more than the predominance, in the absence of 'transitionality,' of expanded reproduction wherein a portion of s is necessarily reinvested into c under the control of a specific group. This is because it is impossible to grasp the essence of the category of surplus value without reference to the category of value, which in capitalism is inextricably bound up with that of wage-labour, and depends fundamentally upon the generalisation of the relation of exchange-value. (See Marx 1867, parts 3-5, and Rubin 1928). It is difficult to see how exchange value might operate if, as Munis claims, the ruling stratum "dictates wages and prices outside of all competition." (1975, p.28).[25] Munis's insistence that the USSR is not transitional to socialism, which might be deemed self-evident, is no compensation for the inadequacy of his attempt to demonstrate that it is capitalist while eschewing any reference to these categories.

Cliff's Theory[26]

Sharing the view held by the other Leninist former Trotskyists that what is usually known as the 'October revolution' of the Bolsheviks led to the formation of a "workers' state under Lenin and Trotsky (1917-23)," which was defeated in the later 1920s by means of a gradual counterrevolution (1955, p.181), Cliff differs with them by stating explicitly that viewed in isolation from *world* capitalism the USSR knew no real exchange of commodities.

His first argument is that this is so because "the ownership of all the enterprises is vested in one body, the state"; his second, given in the following paragraph, begins with the "direct connection between the enterprises through the medium of the state," which "controls production in nearly all of them," and he uses this as a basis from which to conclude that prices no longer have the "unique significance of being the expression of the social character of labour." (p.203). The reader is thus left confused as to why exactly Soviet goods are not commodities: is the reason to do with ownership, or is it derived from control? And if control is the key, then it hardly makes sense for Cliff to refer in the same section to the "almost complete plan of the division of the total labour time," when earlier he has denied that planning exists at all,

> [if] by the term 'planned economy' we understand an economy in which all component elements are adjusted and regulated into a single rhythm, ... [and] in which foresight prevails in the making of economic decisions" (p.83)

So what kind of control is there? When denouncing "bureaucratic mismanagement" (p.83) Cliff focuses on the absence of planning, but when dealing with deeper issues of the "Russian economy and the Marxian law of value" he falls back on the legal category of state ownership and the unelaborated one of "regulation" (p.205) by government rather than through the price system. In the process, he omits to bring into his discussion whatever existed in the USSR in place of planning.

From such a fragmented and confused discussion Cliff moves on to state (p.206) that "there is one thing in Russia that appears on the surface to fulfil the requirements of a commodity: labour-power," before describing how this is an illusion, since there is only one employer: the State. Once again, an important question, namely that concerning the existence or non-existence of wage-labour, is answered without reference to the contradictions within a system that is not planning but which is still a form of control over the extraction of the surplus product, namely, over labour. Such matters appear in Cliff's argument only to show up the inefficiencies of Stalinist "mismanagement."

Cliff is forced to conclude — or rather, assert — that "the division of labour is planned," but that it would nonetheless be "absolutely arbitrary" if "Russia" did not have to compete with other countries. (p.209). This competition is primarily military, but military use-values, "while being an end, still remain a means," serving the end of victory in the competition. (p.211). He then argues that production in "traditional" capitalist countries has also become determined by the production of military use-values. Relations of exchange between arms manufacturers and governments have become "purely formal," since the "state does not offer another commodity in exchange for arms." (p.212). (Why such countries are still capitalist he omits to explain). In other words, there are use-values and there is competition, but the basis of capitalist economy is no longer commodity exchange: instead, there is the arms race.[27] Rather than conceiving of the arms race as a *product* of capitalist contradictions, we are asked to agree that it is the arms race which *makes* the society capitalist. One can only wonder as to the type of contortions Cliff might have got into if Soviet military competition had been with China alone!

Cliff's position appears untenable when it is remembered that whatever capitalism may or may not entail, what it *is* is a mode of production, defined by a certain type of social production relations. If the USSR is capitalist simply because it produces weaponry to compete with those countries that themselves would have been capitalist even without such competition, then one might as well say the same about tribes whose production is directed to the provision of tomahawks in the fight against colonialism.[28] By arguing purely from the existence of an arms race, Cliff is forced to take the view (pp.159-61) that Soviet 'state capitalism' is "a partial negation of capitalism," or, in other words, although he never says so explicitly, that the USSR is somehow less capitalist than the West.[29] His term 'state capitalist' might easily be replaced by the term 'limitedly capitalist,' or even 'not-quite-so capitalist.' Since he has a minimal grasp of the categories by means of which capital can be defined, his work is of little use to investigators of the real society and class struggle in the USSR.

Bettelheim's Theory

Bettelheim's 'state capitalist' thesis is in some ways at the other end of the Leninist spectrum from Cliff's. Rather than focusing on international relations, he grounds his argument (1970, p.85) on the existence of a 'double separation': of the workers from the means of production, and of the enterprises from each other. Given the capitalist nature of the enterprise-form, he argues, there must be a continuous struggle in the 'transition period' to 'revolutionise' the enterprises in the sense of working to abolish them. Without this struggle — which for Bettelheim means without the necessary type of ruling party and 'ideological revolution' [*sic*] — the 'representatives' of the workers, the state and the party come to identify themselves with enterprise managers rather than with the workers; and the 'plan,' instead of exercising a dominance over the enterprise-form, becomes an "instrument of the 'duplication' of commodity relations." (pp.89-93).[30] Ultimately, then, for Bettelheim the ruling party was not adequately ideologically correct and representative of the 'masses': as a consequence, the separation between enterprises came into its own and capitalism was re-established.

In a slightly later work (1971, p.59) he argues that the existence of wages — upon which he does not elaborate — combined with the separation between the State and the masses, meant that Soviet workers suffered both capitalist production relations and the rule of a state bourgeoisie. The State's 'separation' from the masses he blames on the absence of a ruling party with a 'proletarian character' and a 'mass line,' a party embodying a 'proletarian ideology.' (p.64). His Maoist prioritisation of politics is self-evident. Since Bettelheim always assumes that throughout the Stalin era the USSR was 'transitional' between capitalism and socialism, for him the workers only began to be exploited after Stalin's death. This conclusion is remarkably unconvincing.

Bettelheim's theory fails for two reasons. First, despite his useful insistence on the 'double separation,' his argument for the capitalist nature of the Soviet economy ultimately depends on an identification of capitalist commodity relations with the market, with competition and assessment in terms of *currency* (as normally understood); and more specifically with the disposal of enterprises by their possessors so as to gain similarly expressible profits. (For an opposing view, see Chapter 3 below). Second, he imagines that such a system was predominant in the USSR. In other words, he vastly overestimates the autonomy of the enterprises, and takes almost at face-value the official propaganda about the role of rouble levers, price formation and 'profit' targets. (For this he is adequately criticised elsewhere [Ticktin 1976]). He fails to tackle the nature of bureaucratic dependence as a fundamental characteristic of the system, and is therefore unable to get to the roots of capitalist competition in its bureaucratic form. In his case the reason for this appears to be primarily political: rather than analysing the nature of bureaucratic relations as they were established under Lenin and Stalin — indeed, with influences which go back further still — he concentrates above all on the post-Stalin period and fails to draw a distinction between 'capitalist restoration' and what was merely a process of liberal reform.

Later work from the same theoretical viewpoint has been carried out by Chavance, whose main originality lies in his attempt to develop a deeper view of the contradictoriness of Soviet price formation. He thus writes (1980, p.193) that since full and effective price-setting by the State would necessitate that the planning authorities be informed of the realisable values of each unit of production, it must be impossible in practice. It follows that there must be some kind of unplanned compensation for the deviation of prices from values. This acknowledgement, however, allows Chavance to supersede Bettelheim's analysis only superficially, for it does not lead him to go beyond the latter's original assumption that purchase cost and price are one and the same thing.[31] In fact, all he means to point out is that the sum of prices is necessarily equivalent to the sum of values, from which it follows that prices which are less than values are balanced out by those which are greater. (1980, pp.191-96; see also 1989, pp.67-77). This is hardly a theoretical breakthrough. Like Bettelheim, Chavance bases his analysis primarily on a critique of the *written* 'political economy' of the Soviet authorities (that is, their ideology), and hence he necessarily fails to deal with the concrete forms which this 'compensation' takes. He has no concept either of *blat* or of capitalist bureaucracy.

Sapir's Theory

Another theorist influenced by Bettelheim is Sapir. If Chavance is vaguer than Bettelheim concerning the beginning of capitalist dominance in the USSR, Sapir is willing to suggest, albeit without argument, that it was first established during the rise of Stalin in the mid-1920s. (1980, pp.20-21 and 31-32).

At this time, however, he uses the term 'state capitalism' as little more than a label, and is most intent on arguing that the USSR and its satellites are heading for a severe economic crisis. (1980). His view of such a crisis is straightforward: it is a product of the economic system's structural problems in coping with the changes required to move from a period of extensive accumulation to one of intensive accumulation. (pp. 64-65 and 284). But although he is evidently thinking about the accumulation of the productive forces in the form of capital, the attention he gives to the term 'capital' is minimal.

More recently Sapir has developed concepts of the USSR which owe much to the French 'regulation school.'[32] He begins by analysing the economic effects of *mobilisation* in both Germany and Russia during the first world war, pointing to constants such as the central fixing of prices, the receipt of profits according to the volume of production, and the de-emphasis on the production of consumer goods. In Russia these effects were largely overseen by the War Industries Committees set up by the employers in 1915. Similar developments were later instituted by the new government during the civil war, and then by the ruling faction led by Stalin which imposed warlike conditions at the end of the 1920s. (1990, pp.23-33).

Sapir proceeds to develop his concepts. In his current view, then, whenever mobilisation is limited in scale it produces negative feedback: it appears as a deviation from the usual system. But when it leads as far as a full-scale war economy, it produces instead positive feedback. It itself becomes the system. When it is further generalised under Stalinism to the whole of industry "with the aim of inducing a radical tranformation in the country's mode of growth," what results is a fully *mobilised economy* of which the war economy was a mere prototype. (pp.36-39).

This mobilised economy is still a commodity economy, but it is not a 'commercial' economy, since "the validation of production is no longer effected through the sale (or non-sale) of the goods concerned."

> As a constraint, this validation no longer rests directly upon the producer. [*i.e. upon the enterprise directors*—NCF]. It is the organism which replaces the commercial system which also, at the end of each period, notices that such-and-such products have remained unused and such-and-such demands unmet. For this organism, this translates into a need for finance (which it reports to the fiscal agency); for the economy, it translates into a disequilibrium between supply and demand. The constraint is still present, but operates at the level of the society as a whole. (p.39)

The "principle of non-commerciality" is systematised.

Sapir discusses his underlying reasons for ascribing a capitalist nature to the Soviet 'mobilised economy' in the following terms:

> [To reach a definition of capitalism which is analytically operational,] it would be perfectly conceivable to work from the apparent functioning of economies which are already widely known to be capitalist.... Criteria such as the nature of property or the forms of adjustment, or the existence of unemployment or a stockmarket, are quite admissible. With such a definition, though, we should see the number of capitalist economies wither away miserably. And why not? But it would then be necessary to invent new systems, with their own laws, to account for all the economies which had thereby become non-capitalist. (p.20)

Although it would, of course, be possible to do precisely this, perhaps leaving the definitions of some of the 'other systems' to other scholars, Sapir proceeds to write that

> we therefore need a definition which will allow us to distinguish between, on one hand, the logic of a system, and on the other, those forms which stem from the

specificities constituting each society's individuality, or from procedural conditions confined to a particular historical period. (p.21)[33]

In fact, though, as Sapir readily avers, the definition he chooses remains that of Bettelheim. Since there is a labour market, there is wage-labour;[34] and since roubles play an important role in the economy and the ideology of planning does not quite correspond to reality, there is a commodity economy. (pp.14-17). The workers are separated from the means of production, and the enterprises are separated from each other. (Sapir 1989, p.10).

The insufficiency of these points as an explanation of the basis of capitalism is evidenced by Sapir's discussion of the form which the 'non-commercial' system actually takes. He thus explains that in the USSR there are theoretically two money circuits. On one hand, there is 'scriptural money' (credit instruments or scrip), which circulates among enterprises; on the other, there is 'fiduciary money' (paper money or current deposits in fiat form). Whereas the first kind is merely a passive means of account, the second is active and also functions as a means of exchange and a store of value. Households have access only to the second type. In practice, the two types are not 'watertight,' since every purchase by an enterprise creates some fiduciary money and every sale destroys some. It is therefore impossible to distinguish between roubles destined to stay 'scriptural' and roubles destined to become active. (1990, pp.78-79). What is noticeable here is that Sapir does not theorise money itself, of which presumably scriptural money and fiduciary money are simply the forms. And in particular, he does not theorise money as a form of capital.[35]

A similar omission is evident when he considers the purchase of labour-power. Since the USSR is not just one large enterprise, he reasons, both goods and labour-power must be bought locally. Moreover, they must also be sold, which implies money as a means of account, a means of exchange, and a store of value. (p.19). This may indeed be the case, but there is no firm identification here of the existence of what Marx saw as money *in its capitalist form*: namely, money as the "absolute form of existence of exchange value"; as the general representative of wealth which takes the form of exchange value (1867, p.234, and 1939, pp.203-12; see also Rosdolsky 1968, chap.8); and crucially, as the form in which value must appear if it is to accrue a surplus. (Marx 1867, pp.247-69). Bereft of concepts of generalised exchangeability, value, and surplus value, Sapir writes of money as a "store of value" when what he really means is a means of deferred payment, or a hoard.

One should certainly note that he attempts to employ concepts which explain capitalist functioning in the USSR but which do not detract from its specificity. But his western-style model of 'firms and households' hardly lends itself to being applied to those Soviet enterprises which supply only producer goods to the

State. (From a Marxist point of view it might be added, of course, that this model fails to explain the functioning of 'classical' free-market capitalism too).[36] When the terms 'supply' and 'demand' are applied in a critique of capitalist political economy, they should not be equated with 'production' and 'perceived requirement': they relate directly to the role of active money as the basis of the capitalist system. It is not enough simply to show that not all 'passive money' stays passive. His distinction between scrip and fiat money is intelligent, but he makes no attempt to theorise any over-arching form; and as a result he fails to explain how and why it is that the Soviet system has the pursuit of more money — that is, the drive for profit, for more capital — as its *foundation*. But this is precisely what has to be shown if the system is rightly to be called capitalist. (See Chapter 3 below).

Sapir's idea of capitalism appears as separate not only from any concepts of capital and value but also from any idea of money as the generalised representative of exchange-value. The purpose which it serves in his work is therefore limited. At the same time, concentrating as he does on rouble accounting he is unable to produce a sufficiently discerning analysis of the theoretical significance of other forms such as gross output targets and economic bureaucracy.

'CAPITALISM' BUT NOT 'STATE CAPITALISM'

Gorter's Theory

The first theory of Soviet capitalism not to label Soviet Russia 'state capitalist' was defended by the Communist Workers' Party of Germany (KAPD)[37] and the Fourth (Communist Workers') International (CWI).[38] Espoused by the majority of the left communists of the early 1920s, it rested above all on the thesis of 'dual revolution.' Thus in the view put forward in the CWI's *Manifesto*, written by Gorter in 1921, not only did the Bolshevik ascendance to power depend on the peasantry as well as on the workers, but in fact two revolutions took place which could be distinguished one from the other. Whereas in the towns the revolution was 'socialist,' and the proletariat had taken the economy from the bourgeoisie, in the countryside the revolution was bourgeois and capitalist, since the peasants had become petty landowners *en masse*. It was "the bourgeoisie in the shape of the peasants" which now ran the economy. In the towns the change had been from capitalism to socialism; in the country, from feudalism to capitalism. (1921, p.1). The desires and interests of the peasants, who constituted the vast majority, came increasingly to dictate government economic policy in all areas, including industry and trade. The culmination was the introduction of NEP in March 1921, under which grain requisitions were replaced by a tax in kind (and soon by a tax in money), most of light industry was denationalised, and private trade and small-scale manufacturing were officially encouraged. In Gorter's terms, capitalist wage-slavery was then 'reintroduced' in the towns. (p.7).[39]

If Gorter stresses the actual conditions of exploitation under NEP, and correctly underlines as an important factor the capitalisation of agriculture, he unfortunately fails to provide a theory which could explain the exploitative conditions either of 'War Communism' (1918-21) or of the Stalinist industrialisation period which came later. The reason for this is straightforward: while he criticises bureaucracy (pp.3-4), he neglects to consider either its origins or its role in the economy.

This major weakness in his critique is also apparent in a text he published in 1923. By this time he has updated the thesis of 'dual revolution' in favour of the view that the 'Russian revolution' was of "double character," partly proletarian but "in most of its features bourgeois-democratic." Even in the first period (1917-21) the measures introduced by the Bolsheviks are now understood to have had "to a large extent, a bourgeois character." (1923, p.2). Gorter still describes the nationalisation of industry and some of the measures of 'War Communism' (1918-21) as being "proletarian and communistic"; but now, having denounced the Bolshevik aims of national self-determination and peace with foreign capitalist powers as "bourgeois-capitalist," he explains how "the bureaucratic despotism of the leaders was also bourgeois-capitalist." He continues:

> In leader-dictatorship lies the kernel of the bourgeois capitalist revolution....
>
> The party dictatorship was in its origin bourgeois capitalist. It began through the power of the peasants, the non-proletarian class. A party dictatorship could overpower and lead the peasant class in Russia. A proletarian class dictatorship could not do this, for a dictatorship of the proletarian class will always aspire to pure Communism. (pp.4-6)[40]

Unfortunately, though, Gorter does not look too closely at the relationship between the party dictatorship and the urban workers prior to NEP; and fails to show exactly how a government based on the principles he describes — or, indeed, any government — might be capable of introducing communistic changes of *any* sort.[41] Ultimately, the only differences he points to between the conditions of "rising capitalism" (p.3) in Russia and Asia and the conditions of fully-established capitalism elsewhere are those which concern the peasantry. In the light of subsequent history, his failure to draw a convincing theoretical connection between the force of the peasantry, supposedly determinant, and the specific authoritarianism of the Bolsheviks towards the workers can rightly be called glaring.

Castoriadis's Theory[42]

The first 'capitalist' theorist to eschew any concept of 'state capitalism' but at the same time to theorise economic forms which were specifically Soviet was the libertarian theorist Castoriadis, who to an even greater extent than Rühle sees the USSR as the most administratively 'advanced' capitalist country. Where Rühle, however, focuses on the role of the State, Castoriadis stresses above all the role and contradictions of *bureaucracy*. In this view increasing bureaucratisation is a necessary tendency of modern capitalism in general — indeed, it is capitalism's very essence. (1960-61, p.282). The USSR then appears as the country furthest along the bureaucratic path.

Although nowadays, of course, it is impossible to defend a view of the USSR or its successors as more capitalistically advanced than, for example, their creditor countries, nonetheless there remain in Castoriadis's theory two elements of great utility and significance. The first, which we shall discuss below in Chapter 6, is his insistence on the permanent struggle waged by the Soviet workers against the bureaucracy. The second is his original understanding that not only do Soviet capitalist forms differ from free-market and 'monopolistic' forms, but they are also irreducible to forms such as state ownership or state control.

A major problem with Castoriadis's work, though, is that he never states precisely what elements have to be present in a country for it to be capitalist, so as then to show how it is that the USSR fits all the requirements. Thus even though he discusses, in the context of imperialism, the differences between competitive capitalism, monopoly capitalism, and bureaucratic capitalism (1954, pp.258-61), he does so without actually defining the term 'capitalism' which figures in all three concepts.

In fact all we have in way of a demonstration that the USSR is capitalist is a collection of disparate statements scattered through a number of articles. First, it seems that for capitalism to exist there must also exist a class of proletarians. Clearly few doubt that such a condition is present in the USSR. Second, in Castoriadis's view, those who exploit the proletariat must control both production and accumulation. In the Soviet context he sees such exploiters as forming a 'bureaucratic class' exercising

> sovereign control over how the total social product will be used. It does this first of all by determining how the total social product will be distributed among wages and surplus value (at the same time that it tries to dictate to the workers the lowest wages possible and to extract from them the greatest amount of labor possible), next by determining how this surplus value will be distributed between its own unproductive

consumption and new investments, and finally by determining how these investments will be distributed among the various sectors of production. (1955, 293-94)

Unless, however, one's definition of 'modern capitalism' is a purely empirical one — such as 'whatever the capitalism of Marx's day has turned into' — Castoriadis's formulation remains unconvincing. Certainly in the USSR there do exist those who exploit the producers, control production, decide investment priorities, and try their utmost to determine and limit the share of the social product paid in wages; but if we bear in mind that it is theoretically possible for a non-capitalist social formation to replace capitalism for a time in one area or another (or indeed in the whole world), such exploitation does not *of itself* necessarily imply capitalism. The key term in the piece cited is *surplus value*, and a sceptic would be perfectly justified in pointing out that Castoriadis gives neither a rigorous definition nor an explanation of why he holds such a form to exist in the USSR.

Castoriadis's confusion on the issue of value is all too evident. Thus even when he still self-identifies as Marxist, he fails to follow the concept of capitalism back through *capital* to *value*, despite the fact that an understanding of capital as self-expanding value is famously crucial to Marx's entire critique of political economy. (Marx 1867, chap. 6 and app.; see also Rubin 1928). Instead, the nearest he comes to focusing on the form of value — namely, exchangeability — is when he describes how Soviet 'planning' is 'as chaotic as the market.' This is so, he explains, not because the USSR is capitalist, but because it is bureaucratic. (1956, p.63). Conflict within the bureaucracy — Castoriadis declines to write 'competition' — is described not as something which actually makes the system work, on the basis that without competition there can be no generalised exchangeability and hence no value, but merely as "a basic sociological given in a regime organized along the lines of a 'civil service.'" (p.63).

The notion of 'bureaucratic capitalism' in Castoriadis's sense fails to satisfy. Thus even while asserting (p.76) that the Soviet 'regime' is "simply another form of the capitalist system of rule in which the bureaucracy has taken the place of private employers," Castoriadis writes in the very same text that the essence of 'bureaucratic planning,'

> like that of capitalist production [*sic*], lies in an effort to reduce the direct producers to the role of pure and simple executants of received orders, orders formulated by a particular stratum that pursues its own interests. (p.62)

From here it is only a short step to rejecting Marx's view of what constitutes capitalism's most fundamental contradiction, namely that which exists between the proletariat and *capital*. Neglecting to theorise the crucial importance of value, exchangeability, and exchange, Castoriadis eventually ends up replacing this contradiction with one which Marxism understands as far less 'basic,' namely that which sets 'order-givers' against 'order-takers.' (1960-1, pp.258-59; 1964, p.6). Theorising 'bureaucratic capitalism' in relation to the capitalist 'fragmentation' which preceded it, he writes that

> this fragmentation [i.e. the division of production into independently managed units] has nothing essentially capitalistic about it. From the point of view of the system itself, such an arrangement is just as absurd as the independent management of various workshops in a large factory would be. The logic of capitalism is to treat the whole of society as one immense, *integrated enterprise* [emphasis added]. Far from revealing the essence of the system, the problems it encounters as long as this integration has not been fully realized serve only to mask it. (1964, p.282)

By this time the concepts of exchange, value, and the adoption by things of a commodity form have vanished entirely. Denying that fragmentation constitutes part of the basis of capitalism, and unable to postulate forms of fragmentation other than that of independently managed enterprises, Castoriadis cannot back up his theory of Soviet capitalism on Marxist grounds, and soon rejects Marxism explicitly. (1964, 1964-65).[43]

Bordiga's Theory[44]

Bordiga too rejects the idea that the USSR was 'state capitalist,' and refers to it instead simply as 'capitalist.' In response to Stalin's *Economic Problems of Socialism in the USSR* (1952) he argues that the system of commodity production — unlike in pre-capitalist societies when it was purely marginal — is not merely incompatible with socialism, but also inseparable from capitalism. (1952, pp.11-12). Thus when Stalin accepts that commodity production exists in the USSR, he is in fact admitting the capitalist nature of the country over which he rules. Far from capitalism being absent because wage-labour is absent, on the contrary it is wage-labour itself which must have led the mass of commodities to appear in the first place.

The major problem here is that in wanting to criticise Stalin's pamphlet Bordiga is led to accept the assertions which the former presents as facts.[45] If there is no disagreement between the two men as to the existence in the USSR of a 'system of commodity production,' more importantly there is no dispute as to the meaning of the term itself: both men use it solely to denote the production of things for sale on the market for roubles. Moreover, Bordiga accepts Stalin's false — or at least, irrelevantly legalistic — assertion that collective-farm output belongs wholly to the collective farms (Stalin 1952, p.19), whereas in fact compulsory procurement remained in force, at least for part of production.[46] Correctly pointing out that Soviet workers sell their labour-power in order to earn wages to buy goods, he then refers to the fact that they spend a greater proportion of their wages on agricultural products than that spent by their American counterparts.[47] Hence, he argues, the USSR is further from 'full state capitalism' than the US, since in both countries it is industry rather than agriculture which falls under the greatest State control. If the strength of Bordiga's work lies in the emphasis he puts on the *spread* of capitalism and monetary economy throughout the countryside — and on the massive expansion of the proletariat in formerly pre-capitalist areas such as Central Asia (Bordiga 1952, p.27) — this example of his argumentation typifies his chronic *over-concentration* on agriculture, and on the collective farm in particular. In arguing *from* agriculture *to* the rest of the economy — as opposed to focusing on control over labour, surplus product, and accumulation — he follows Stalin in avoiding a real discussion of bureaucracy. Since for Bordiga (1956-57, p.340) bureaucracy is wholly dependent upon "monetary accountability and the commodity budget-system," it is of little interest as an empirical reality: far more important (p.324) are the successive "unstable and spineless forms of social kolkhozianism."[48]

Problems follow when he looks at industry. Accepting that "the large enterprises belong to the State," he adds that

> they are subject, however, to monetary accountability, and they have to show profitability in money terms — that is, a credit margin, a profit — if the law of value is to be respected as regards both raw material prices and wages (outgoings, costs), and the prices of goods sent out (income). (p.40)

As we have pointed out above, though, this is incorrect: in fact, gross output targets were far more important than rouble profit targets. As Kontorovich has shown (1988), the first attempt to increase the significance of the latter, made in 1965 as one of the Kosygin reforms, failed dismally owing to a basic 'organic' conflict with the 'efficiency' of the system. Bordiga's view that the "key to the entire system" is the accumulation of roubles by the State (1956-57, p.320), even when allied to an understanding of money as part of the capital cycle, points to a very weak grasp of Soviet economic reality.

Turning his attention to the process of investment, Bordiga is further led to draw a distinction between enterprises and the State in such a way as to avoid reaching an adequate understanding of the latter. Thus he asserts that

industrial enterprises have their own budget and carry out an internal investment —
which figures in the plan but not in the income and expenditure of the State as
entrepreneur, operator and investor. (p.216)

Reading in official Soviet sources that a substantial proportion of construction
work is farmed out to 'special organisations' by 'allocation of contracts,' Bordiga
decides that since contracts can only occur between parties with different
interests, the organisations receiving the contracts are not themselves part of the
State bureaucracy. In such cases, the State itself lacks the 'courage' to be an
'economic operator,' and simply hands over money-capital to other organisations
to distribute among the enterprises. This form of capital distribution Bordiga
sees (pp.232-33) as expanding after the introduction of the *sovnarkhozy* reforms
in 1957.

Whilst unlike Cliff he rightly points to the competition which is a necessary
feature of a value-based society, Bordiga neglects to mention the basic
characteristics of the 'organisations' to which he refers. Directed by the appointees
of Party committees, and not disposing of anything even approaching 'inalienable'
rights over resources — either in terms of directors' individual rights or on
a collective level — these organisations cannot seriously be considered as
anything other than part of the State. Bordiga is clear that it is rather easy for them
to get hold of funding — or in our terms, that the part of the State which gives it
to them does not usually control them either by exercising a despotic power over
their purse-strings or by simply reflecting the logic of the market. He omits,
however, to give proper consideration to the bureaucratic *blat*-ridden
considerations which do exist; and moreover, he fails to grasp that such
considerations also govern the exchanges which take place lower down. He is
simply mistaken to view such exchanges as primarily determined by considerations
of rouble profit.[49]

Chattopadhyay's Theory

In a more recent analysis of the capitalist nature of Soviet production
Chattopadhyay similarly avoids describing it as 'state capitalist.'

Beginning like Buick and Crump by presenting an understanding of what
capitalism essentially is, he focuses above all on the category of the separation
of the workers from the means of production. Thus

there is no reason to think ... that Western capitalism, as it appears on the surface at
a particular epoch, is the unique form of the capitalist mode of production, and that

any economy (or society) that does not manifest similar phenomenal characteristics cannot be considered capitalist. On the contrary, whatever be the different forms of manifestation of an economy, if the latter is based on the laborers' separation from the conditions of labor, necessarily rendering labor wage labor, then the economy in question is capitalist. (1994, p.6)

Relying on Volume 1 of *Capital*, he explains this separation in terms of the worker's "double freedom": on one hand, the worker is free *to* sell his labour-power, free from feudal-type bondage; on the other, he is free *of* the means of production, and *must* therefore sell his labour-power, which is all he has in the way of a productive force, to ensure his own survival. (See Marx 1867, pp.272-73).

Capitalism, though, is more than this, and Chattopadhyay identifies as additional defining features the existence of generalised commodity production and the extraction of surplus value. But even these, he proceeds to show, are determined by the relation of wage-labour. More specifically, he quotes Marx as stating that the adoption by labour-power of a commodity form allows commodity production to become generalised; and that the relation of surplus value presupposes the existence of wage-labour. (1994, pp.16-17; Marx 1885, p.196 and 1894, pp.1019-20). As if in avoidance of a charge of reductionism, he then summarises the relationship between wage-labour, generalised commodity production, and capitalist production — the production of surplus value — as one of "reciprocal implication ... a kind of tri-symmetric relation." (Chattopadhyay 1994, pp.17-18). On the basis of this relationship which defines its essence, capital exists as a "social totality": in other words, as a matter of total surplus value, or, more simply, as the rule of a class. At this fundamental level it takes the form of private property (class property) as a matter of definition. At the level of its 'second,' juridical existence, however, which Chattopadhyay sees as constituted by the legally recognised capitalist property forms, these forms can and do vary. (pp.21-22). The rise of forms of directly social capital distinct from classical individual capital, such as share capital and State capital, is thus explained in terms of specific forms of property within class property, which apparently do not present the critic with any great theoretical problem. (pp.22-28).

In considering the USSR, Chattopadhyay refers to well-known features of the regime, such as the power of the Politburo and the role of the nomenklatura system, to demonstrate that workers are indeed free of the means of production in the evident sense that they do not control them. (pp.49-50).[50] And with reference to the issuing of job contracts at enterprise level and the high rate of labour turnover he further shows that they are also free to sell their labour-power. (p.52). Subjected to class domination, they are not bonded to individual units of

production, and as a consequence they are constrained to sell their labour-power:
to work as wage-labourers.

Endeavouring next to demonstrate the existence in the USSR of the
commodity form, Chattopadhyay states that

> the products of labor taking commodity or *value form* and thence appearing as
> *exchange values* is independent of the question of *how* their prices are actually
> determined — "administratively," or by the (spontaneous) "market forces."

Moreover,

> the exchange of the products of human labor in commodity form is not invariably
> related to the existence of juridically *separate properties* in the means of production.
> For the existence of the commodity form of these products it is enough that they are
> exchanged as products of "private [that is, non-directly social] labors executed
> independently of one another" [Marx 1867, p.165][51], in other words, that the total
> social labor be fragmented in reciprocally autonomous units of production,
> independently of the specific (juridical) form of the latter's ownership.
> (Chattopadhyay 1994, p.53)

Thus in relation to the commodity or non-commodity form of the product, neither
the precise mechanisms of price formation nor the juridical property forms are
of prime importance. Rather, since

> it is sufficient that the total social labor be fragmented in reciprocally autonomous
> units of production [,]... the juridical act of the Soviet state resulting in a (quasi)
> single ownership in the means of production and the institution of central planning
> could not overstep the reality of *reciprocal (organizational) separation* of the units
> of production relating to one another through exchange in *money-commodity form*."
> (p.53)

Leaving aside the enterprise-level hiring of labour-power, which has already
been covered, the argument thus boils down to the existence of autonomous
production units (enterprises or associations of enterprises) exchanging goods
for roubles and roubles for goods.

In demonstration of the 'reciprocal autonomy' of the units of production
Chattopadhyay points to the retention by the enterprises of part of their sales
income; and cites in support of the argument a Soviet economist's pronunciation
in 1959 that it is this retention which serves as the basis of the *"money-commodity
relations between State enterprises."* Somewhat incongruously, given what he
has already stated about juridicality, he also mentions the fact that State

enterprises enjoy a legal personality. Since it is well-known, though, that Soviet enterprises buy from their suppliers, sell to their customers, and even borrow money from their bankers (pp.54-55), he views the matter of their reciprocal autonomy — and hence of the generalisation of commodity economy — as requiring little further in the way of empirical demonstration.

He proceeds to criticise the "received idea" that Soviet money — or much of it — was 'passive,' and that there were two mutually water-tight systems of circulation, "cash and non-cash." (See our critique of Sapir above). Even the widespread existence of 'scriptural' money, he argues, does nothing to make the economy any less capitalist, since this form of money, no less than cash, is clearly a form of the "general equivalent for all commodities." Soviet economists are again quoted to the effect that the turnover of scrip-type money and the circulation of cash were not at all separated by the Great Wall of China: money in one form could be and was converted into money in the other. (p.55). More important at an underlying level was the generalisation of inter-enterprise monetary exchange: the fact that money itself played a generalised role.

If we can agree with the thrust of what Chattopadhyay has written on the separation of the workers from the means of production, however — see our discussion of Buick and Crump's work above — we would nonetheless point to a fundamental methodological flaw in his theorisation of the existence in the USSR of generalised commodity exchange and generalised monetary economy. In principle, of course, he does not argue that the existence of wage-labour allows the commodity exchange of *products* to become generalised; rather, he notes correctly that it allows commodity exchange *tout court* to become generalised, insofar as it is now not just things which adopt a commodity form, but human labour-power itself. (p.17).[52] But even if he is not mistaken in identifying wage-labour as "*the* determining characteristic of capitalism," it is not enough — indeed it verges on the sophistic — to depict the "fragmentation" of social capital into competitive units as a simple product of the fact that workers are separated not from total capital but "only in relation to *individual* capitals." (p.112). Of course capitalism's separation of the workers from the means of production and the competitive interrelation of capitals are related,[53] but if one wishes in a Soviet context to demonstrate the fragmentation empirically, in opposition to those who deny the existence there of capitalist competition, one should surely show what forms the competition actually takes in areas of the economy other than the purchase and sale of labour-power: namely, in the production and distribution of material things.[54] Above all, one needs to show how it is generalised. But for all his correct insistence that forms taken by capitalist relations in the USSR do not necessarily have to be the same as those which prevail in western countries — a formal insistence which is absent in the work of Bordiga — this he signally fails to do. Indeed, his empirical argument for the existence of such competition reduces to little more than the observation that when enterprise A delivers goods to enterprise B, the directors of B pay roubles to the directors of A in return. Since this does not explain how the decision to distribute is actually reached under conditions where rouble profit targets are considerably less determinant than gross output targets, it can hardly in itself serve to demonstrate how considerations of exchange can dominate the sphere of distribution in a generalised way.

In addition to explaining the basis of the making of decisions to supply finished goods, a successful demonstration of the existence of generalised commodity production would also explain the making of decisions affecting the distribution of the means of production among those who controlled them. In this area it is a fact that not only are Soviet directors appointed bureaucratically, but being subject to ministerial authority as well as belonging to the Party's nomenklatura, they are in no way able to sell their enterprises at will, and invest the proceeds; nor can they use their enterprise's income in whatever way they wish: to purchase other enterprises, for example. The enterprise directors and ministerial bureaucrats clearly distribute their control over the means of production in a different fashion from that which is familiar, say, to majority shareholders of western firms. Hence one cannot successfully use the formal entries in company books, along with juridical appearances, as a basis for understanding the generalisation of commodity exchange at this level either.

Chattopadhyay does eventually recognise that

> for competition of capitals to exist ... all that is required is the functional fragmentation of STC [social total capital] into reciprocally isolated units of production exchanging products of wage labor (p.129)

and points out that

> those who deny the existence of competition of capitals in the Soviet economy seem to be considering certain historically determined forms of competition, as they appear in the so-called classical capitalist society, as identical with competition (of capitals) as such (pp.129-30)

It is therefore unfortunate that he does not build on this formal recognition to develop a deeper view of the economic forms in which this functional fragmentation and competition appeared in the USSR. Rather, in his first chapter he describes State capital as another form of 'directly social capital' alongside share capital, "logically" but not necessarily "chronologically" subsequent to it (p.27); and in a later chapter he refers to State capital outright as capital's "highest form," albeit still only "logically." (p.111). In this connection he also states that

> once given the concept itself [of state capital], the essential elements for constructing the basis of the relevant analysis could easily be gathered from his [Marx's] discussion of the first form [share capital], just as he himself bases the latter on his analysis of the initial property-function separation of capital. (p.31, n.25)

In his own analysis of actual Soviet economic functioning from such a standpoint, however, he hardly does more than to observe that Soviet capital, being 'statist,' is 'directly social' (p.110); and to assume that individual capital takes the form of the enterprise, the latter being both a 'unit of production' and a 'hiring unit.' (p.54). He does not bring the two aspects together, and thus the concept of social capital is left floating.[55]

In referring to the generalised role of money, he again implies that considerations of rouble-denominated profit maximisation are predominant in the determination of distribution. (pp.54-56). In response to this we need only note that it is simply not the case that the distributional role played by capitalist money is fulfilled in a straightforward way by the over-arching drive of every capital to increase its rouble holdings and its stock of rouble-evaluated assets — even if we include under this rubric the ministries and ministerial departments as well as the enterprises. Thus the step from an understanding of the generalised *payment* of roubles to an understanding of the generalised functional *role* of money, and of how that role is fulfilled, which Chattopadhyay assumes to be almost self-evident, is in fact nothing of the kind.

The category of surplus value also receives inadequate treatment.

> In the Soviet economy, the existence of (free) wage labor producing commodities in reciprocally autonomous units of production naturally ensured the production of surplus value. The realization of surplus value in the Soviet economy had its own specificities conditioned by the (quasi) single juridical ownership over the social total capital as well as by the economy's specific mode of capital accumulation. (p.58)

But what were those specificities? In relation to the role of the State in the realisation process Chattopadhyay covers familiar aspects of the Soviet economy such as the role of the turnover tax on consumer goods; the importance of preferential pricing — more specifically, the practice of keeping industrial prices low; and the centrally-set objective of 'catching up and surpassing' the more advanced economies. He also notes the decreasing overall quantitative importance of turnover tax relative to formal profit. (pp.58-59). But like Bordiga he shows little interest in discussing the specificity of the bureaucratic system through which the surplus value is distributed for reinvestment. And eventually his lack of grasp of the significance of generalised competition leads him to explain the drive for such accumulation simply in terms of the overcoming of international backwardness: a position which he accepts is largely similar to that of the non-Marxist 'development' theorists Nove and Gerschenkron. (pp.132-33). (See especially Gerschenkron 1962). Despite his wishes, this cannot reasonably be said to explain the drive as a matter internal to the Soviet economy. Moreover, there is an obvious contradiction between the idea of backwardness and the idea of State capital as capital's highest form, which the attempted de-historicisation of 'logic' does not redeem.

In relation to the specificity of the mode of capitalist accumulation, however — in other words the mode of subsumption of labour by capital — his analysis is much more substantial. (1994, pp.61-82). The fact that this issue has not been addressed before in connection with the USSR demonstrates perhaps most starkly the extent to which previous theories are inadequate; but Chattopadhyay undoubtedly deserves credit for being the first to consider it at all. Since, though, it is not possible to separate it, even on a purely theoretical level, from the issue of the specific historical development of the class relation, we must leave for a later chapter our own critique of this aspect of his work. For the moment we simply note that it does not rescue the theory from all the weaknesses which flow from his incomplete theoretical grasp of the category of generalised capitalist competition, and from his inadequate empirical grasp of the reality of Soviet economic organisation.

SUMMARY

It will be understood that a Marxist theory of Soviet capitalism can be argued successfully only if it is grounded very solidly in relation to one or other set of Marxian categories. In addition, one must then judge whether or not it explains empirical Soviet reality with sufficient accuracy. In order to construct a theory which meets both these criteria, we shall in the following chapter give much more rigorous definitions than we have been able to hint at above of what in our view are the crucial categories. In the present chapter, though, we have been concerned rather with contributing negatively to the construction of an adequate theory by scratching away at the weakest points of the positions argued up to now by other theorists. We shall now summarise the failings of the various theories considered.

It is evident that some theories must be deemed to have fallen at the first hurdle. Thus if Cliff's concentration on externalities involves an unemphasised but ultimately extremely weak redefinition of capitalism in terms of use-values, Castoriadis's theory of bureaucracy — which has the merit of de-emphasising legal State ownership — similarly fails to give real weight to a characterisation of the mode of production in the USSR as *capitalist*. Both theorists avoid outlining precisely what is involved in *capital*, and thereby fail to come at all close to giving a coherent theoretical account of what it might mean for the Soviet economy to be based upon its accumulation.

Gorter and the early council communists, meanwhile, along with the SPGB, make use somewhat more insistently of Marxian categories such as those of profit and wages. But they do so in such a way as to avoid giving the necessary consideration to the role of *value*, upon which Marx based his entire theory of capitalism. (See Marx 1867 chap.1-3, 1939; and Rubin 1928). Their lack of explanation of this apparent theoretical weakness corresponds, we would argue, to a desire to exaggerate the similarities between the USSR and the 'classical' capitalism of the free market.

Writing slightly later, the councilists admittedly lay greater stress on the economic role of the State, but even they fail to focus with sufficient clarity upon the actual value-related functioning of bureaucracy. Meanwhile Rühle, who theorises the *difference* between Stalinism and western forms in terms of an over-arching theory of a global tendency, somewhat surprisingly bases his analysis of the former upon a concept of 'co-operation' which remains highly vague. Like the earlier council communists, these theorists too are unable to provide adequate theoretical tools for the analysis of Soviet political economy after the end of the 1920s.

Munis, on the other hand, does make a valiant attempt to base his theory on a profound consideration of categories, but unfortunately he chooses the wrong set in that he shows only that the aim of Soviet production is the accumulation of a surplus in the interests of the exploiters. He fails to show that the surplus takes a capitalist form (surplus value). Sapir, less interested in the political-economic significance of the surplus in the first place, similarly fails to theorise either value or capital. Thus his consideration of Soviet money remains theoretically unarmed.

Dunayevskaya and James point the way to a solution of the problem, by suggesting that profit must not automatically be reduced to what appears to be profit; but equally unfortunately they avoid developing the point. Wildt, meanwhile, attempts to cut through the *forms* of capital altogether, so as to get to its essence, but ends up with a concept of capital which is deprived of any nuance or substantial meaning.

Buick and Crump undoubtedly give an elegant presentation, in that they move from a category-based definition of capitalism to an elaboration of the concept of 'state capitalism' — but fall quite badly at the second hurdle, in that they wildly over-estimate the extent of rouble-based competition in the producer goods sector. Cruder examples of the same type of mistake appear in the works of Bettelheim, Chavance, and, among those who do not write of 'state capitalism,' Bordiga and Chattopadhyay. If Bettelheim's approach is based upon an ideology of the contradictions of 'transition,' like Chavance's and Bordiga's it depends chiefly upon an 'immanent' critique of Soviet official propaganda. Neither this nor Chattopadhyay's frequent reference back to the prevalence of wage-labour can compensate for a poor empirical grasp of the predominant forms of competition. Although self-consistent, these models remain far removed from reality.

The various theories have been shown to share one overriding failing. That is this: in arguing that the Soviet social formation is capitalist, they do not demonstrate the existence of *capital* as the dominant political-economic category.

Notes

1   If it is impossible to give a full bibliography here of all the texts wherein the USSR has ever been called capitalist, it is nonetheless worth mentioning that in regard to the relations and mode of production many works give mere descriptions or analytical rudiments, and cannot be said to contain fully-fledged theories. Bauer ('Austro-Marxist'/social democrat) and Mattick (council communist), for example, even as they use the term 'state capitalist,' both also describe Soviet society as 'socialist': 'despotic socialist' and 'state socialist' respectively. (Bauer 1920; Mattick 1969, pp.251-53). This idea would seem completely insupportable in terms of the very Marxian categorial approach they seek to apply, and in the absence of a prior explanation of an alternative approach it can only mystify. Meanwhile Negri (Autonomist) redefines socialism, as opposed to communism, as a kind of planned capital accumulation structured according to forms of State coercion and amounting to a form of backward capitalism. But in a few brief sentences he does not refer to the USSR directly. Indeed he does little more than to call for a substantial analysis which would provide a "composite image of the development of the societies based on the exploitation of wage-labour" and suggest "various alternative shapes that this model may assume." (1986, p.180). He does not himself assume the task.

In the period after 1917 the term 'state capitalism' was applied to Soviet Russia by a number of writers both from Russian Menshevism and from orthodox social democracy abroad. As Jerome and Buick show, though (1967), the main reason that writers from these two tendencies mention 'state capitalism' is that they see Russia as being too 'backward' for socialism. Not recognising the theoretical possibility of the existence of any modern large-scale society other than capitalism or socialism, they reason that since bureaucratic nationalisation could not bring socialism, nor can it have abolished capitalism. The undemocratic nature of the political system is further cited as evidence that there is not even a 'transition' towards socialism. (Kautsky 1919, Iugov 1929).

For the Mensheviks the term 'state capitalism' refers to little more than the State restrictions on 'private' capitalist enterprise, primarily under NEP. (Iugov 1929, p.336; see also Brovkin 1987, p.79-86). Since it is not used to bolster any overall political-economic critique of capitalism, which is still taken to mean essentially the 'private sector,' the term 'state-restricted capitalism' might equally well be used. The subjective attitude corresponding to this view is as follows: whilst in the political sphere the Mensheviks denounce repression, in the economic sphere they level their criticisms merely at the limitations on capitalist freedom, not at capitalism itself. (See Wolin 1974, and Brovkin 1987). Even the Menshevik left, which eventually joined the 'Austro-Marxist' Bauer in seeing Stalin's economic reforms as generally positive, never breaks with this view. The various factions adopt different positions on the expansion of the economic role of the State after 1928, but there is widespread agreement among them all that from then on capitalism exists only peripherally, if at all. (Iugov 1929; and see Wolin 1974, pp.325-33).

The exception here is Iurevskii, who in an empirically wide-ranging critique insists on calling Soviet society 'state-capitalist.' (1932, pp.143-56). (It is worth noting in parenthesis that we have been unable to discover his real identity, and our regarding him as a Menshevik is based on circumstantial evidence alone). Referring not to the 'private sector' but to the systemically necessary "widest possible capital accumulation by the state" (p.145), he then describes the operation of "primitive capitalist accumulation within a state-capitalist framework." But he explains his choice of the term 'capitalist' only in passing, simply by citing the severity of the exploitation of the workers and the State control of accumulation. (p.145).

In 1919 the social democrat Kautsky also refers for a time to the existence in Soviet Russia of capitalism, which he sees as subject to an ongoing 'resuscitation.' Seeing the working class as necessarily unready and inadequately self-disciplined and intelligent to institute socialism, he describes how the government had to become increasingly despotic in order to protect its position. This involved the permitted growth of corrupt "private capitalism" and the merger of State and capitalist bureaucracies into a single system. (1919, pp.201-02). "Industrial capitalism, from being a private system, has now become a State capitalism." (p.202). Unfortunately, though, Kautsky does not define the term 'state capitalism,' nor does he justify his view that capitalism temporarily left the picture.

In his book on Bolshevism in 1930 (q.v.) Kautsky no longer calls the USSR capitalist, and three years later he states specifically that "of course, capitalism has been destroyed." (1933, p.207). By this time he takes the view that Soviet society involved a new kind of exploitative and despotic "state economy." This view was shared by the 'Austro-Marxist' Hilferding. (1940).

A third political area within which various people used the term 'state capitalism' with reference to Soviet conditions was that of Bolshevism itself. Owing, though, to their social base and their support for the regime and the party, neither Lenin (1918-23) nor the 'constitutional' Bolshevik oppositionists who focused upon 'state capitalism' — namely the confusingly-named 'Left Communists' (1918) and the later 'Zinoviev' Opposition (1925-26) — merit consideration here. (See Introduction; on the politics of these groups, see Osinskii 1918, *Theses of the Left Communists* 1918, and Zinoviev 1925; see also Daniels 1960, chaps. 3 and 11, and L'Insecurité Sociale 1982). As works by Schapiro (1955) and Daniels (1960) make clear, an oppositional attitude towards Bolshevik party rule as such was quite as absent for these factions as it was for the more numerous Bolshevik groupings which chose not to emphasise 'state capitalism,' such as the early Democratic Centralists (1919-20), the Workers' Opposition (1920-21), the Left Opposition (1923-24), the United (or Left) Opposition (1926-27), and the Right Opposition (1928-29). (See *Theses of the Democratic Centralists* 1921, Kollontai 1921, *Platform of the*

Forty-Six 1923, *Platform of the Left Opposition* 1927, and Bukharin 1928; see also Service 1979).

This leaves us with a number of other factions which emerged within the Bolshevik party but which later broke with it, rejecting the Party of Lenin and Stalin to call for proletarian struggle against the system and against the Party itself. These factions evidently form a quite distinct fourth category. Perhaps best known is the Workers' Group around Miasnikov, founded in 1921 by elements who rejected the Workers' Opposition's support for the suppression of Kronstadt, and who were clandestine from the following year. Its manifesto, though, published in 1923, stops short of calling the country capitalist: it merely makes the suggestion that the NEP might in the future become "transformed into the New Exploitation of the Proletariat." (1923, p.48). Nonetheless, the Workers' Group seems to have had a strong connection, to say the very least, with the Group of Revolutionary Left-Wing Communists of Russia, a faction which founded the Communist Workers' Party of Russia in 1922 and rallied to the positions of the Communist Workers' International (CWI). (See Workers' Dreadnought 1922a and 1922b.) The CWI emphatically did see Soviet Russia as capitalist (not state capitalist) and we consider its positions in the main text below.

Another faction was the Workers' Truth group inspired by Bogdanov, which stated explicitly in its Appeal of 1922 that the NEP heralded the "rebirth of normal capitalistic relations." This group held that the State and economic bureaucracy had become a new bourgeoisie standing alongside the NEPmen. Moreover, the Communist Party "has become the ruling party, the party of the organisers and directors of the governmental apparatus and economic life." (1922, p.148). But it did not take the theoretical critique of Soviet capitalism any deeper than that. Like the Workers' Group, Workers' Truth was destroyed by the security authorities in the aftermath of the strike wave of August 1923. (See Daniels 1960, p.210).

Some of the Democratic Centralists, a group which was originally a very moderate and 'loyal' opposition very much to the right of the Workers' Opposition, also eventually came round to a 'state capitalist' view. Their precise history is rather interesting. After calling in 1926 for the formation of a new party — a position which placed them far to the left of, say, Trotsky — in 1928 the group did not react to the first Five Year Plan in any consistent fashion. Many 'Decists' 'capitulated' to Stalinism, while others responded in traditional Leninist language by referring to the transformation of the USSR into a "petty bourgeois State." (See Ciliga 1938-50, p.276). It seems that only later, in jail in the early 1930s, did various 'Decist' factions then manage to reject Leninism altogether and criticise Soviet conditions comprehensively as 'state capitalist.' V. Smirnov, for example, came to argue that Lenin had always been an "agent of the intelligentsia," and that the entire world was tending towards State capitalism under a ruling bureaucracy. (See Ciliga 1938-50, Book 3, chap. 9). But any documents written by the revolutionary prisoners who held such a position, or indeed by the uncompromising 'Miasnikovists' of the same time, have yet to come to light.

Anarchists have also adopted a 'state capitalist' position, and constitute a fifth group. Thus Berkman (1922, pp.29-32) writes of a mixture of 'private capitalism' and 'state capitalism,' even as he does little to develop a theory of the latter beyond pointing to the fact that the State oppresses the workers within the economic sphere as well as outside it. E. Goldman's work is even less theoretically useful. She may describe (1925) the despotic, exploitative, and anti-socialist characteristics of Bolshevik rule, but her central notions remain the highly vague ones of the conflicting ideas of liberty and authority. Ultimately, neither Berkman nor Goldman add much that was not already present in their respective journals. (Berkman 1925, Goldman 1931).

Those anarchists who were involved for longer and immersed in greater depth in the revolutionary movement in Russia have produced accounts which are more valuable and less impressionistic, but they too have omitted to give profound theoretical consideration to the nature of Soviet society. Maksimov provides a lengthy and well-sourced account of the Bolshevik counterrevolution and terror, but writes of 'state capitalism' only in passing (1940, pp.62-63 and 329), in reference to Lenin's belief in its necessity. Colourfully but without materialist explanation, he refers to the State as the "sole capitalist,...monarch,...teacher, landowner, policeman, philosopher, [and] priest." (pp.325-26). Voline, meanwhile, who undoubtedly has a more nuanced view of the production relations of the post-counterrevolutionary period (1947, pp.353-408), also refers to 'state capitalism.' (pp.389, 391, 402). Bound by the mistaken belief, though, that Soviet industrialisation is only a pretence (pp.402-05), he fails to relate the concept to the relations and contradictions of actual capitalist profit-making.

In the sense that they did not withdraw the term 'state capitalism' at the onset of Stalin's 'Great Leap Forward,' anarchists have undoubtedly proved loyal to it. On a theoretical level, though, anarchist writers on Soviet Russia have shown but two things: first, that just as in 'private capitalism' the workers remain exploited; and second, that the Soviet system of exploitation is completely opposed to revolutionary liberation. The term 'state capitalism' serves only to underline these basic insights, not to aid their development.

Works by Ciliga (independent communist) and Debord (Situationist) also deserve mention. Ciliga's extremely well-observed revolutionary autobiography covering the years up to 1935 is critically very rich and not at all ideological (1938-50), despite his earlier support for Bolshevism and his subsequent support for Croatian nationalism. (Bourrinet 1992b). He describes the early stages of the civil war as marking the victory of State capitalism (Ciliga 1938-50, p.284); the NEP as an alliance of State capitalism and private capitalism against socialism, serving the interests of the bureaucrats and the upper layers of the village in opposition to those of the workers and the rural poor (1938, p.15); and the first Five-Year Plan as the bureaucracy's assault on its former allies. (1938-50, p.287). But he does not offer a profound work of theory.

Debord's magnum opus, on the other hand, is such a work, but in the few pages he devotes to the USSR the focus is chiefly on economic underdevelopment, the lunatic mendacity associated with the reigning bureaucratic ideology, and the relationship between the two. (1967, paras. 102-11). Thus he describes a "totalitarian bureaucracy...caught between its need for rationality and its rejection of the rational," whose very "existence as a class" depends on its maintaining an ideological monopoly. Owing to the ideology with which it is encumbered, this bureaucracy is unable to rival the bourgeoisie in the production of 'commodity abundance,' and therefore stands revealed as capitalism's "poor relation"; or, as it is also described, as "inferior to capitalism in industrial production." (paras. 108 and 110). If this is somewhat confusing, elsewhere the Situationists make it clear that in their view there are "two capitalisms — private-bourgeois [and] state-bureaucratic." (1969, p.264).

The nearest the Situationists come to a theory of the specific political economy of Soviet production is in a text on the events of 1966-67 in China. Here they argue that like its Chinese counterpart the Soviet bureaucracy — the "ruling class of bureaucratic state-capitalism" — is necessarily centralised "due to its mode of appropriation of the economy since it must draw from itself the hierarchical guarantee to all participation in its collective appropriation of the social surplus production." But when they proceed to state that "the summit of the bureaucracy has to remain fixed, for in it lies the entire legitimacy of the system" (1967, p.186), there remains evident an over-concentration upon the importance of the regime's ideology — as well as a hint of Weberianism absent from their critique of capitalism under the bourgeoisie.

Secondary works include Jerome and Buick 1967; Bellis 1979, chaps. 4-6; CWO 1982; and, less useful, Kelly 1985.

2   Since our aim here is to consider the various 'state capitalist' theories of the USSR, we shall not be dealing with those aspects of the 'state capitalist' literature which relate solely to perceived developments in (or from) 'classical' capitalism, or to the question of the 'transition to socialism' (for example Bukharin 1915 and 1920, and Lenin 1918-23). Nor shall we consider the totally abstract model constructed by Pollock. (1941).

3   The political positions of the SPGB and its sister parties, often termed 'impossibilist,' involve an uncompromising rejection of the wages system, and hence of reformism; the belief that today's struggle for socialism depends primarily on workers' education and democratic organisation; and a belief in the necessity of using existing legislatures to establish socialism. If the first distinguishes them from the anti-revolutionary approach of the left, the second and especially the third separate them too from the revolutionary approach of the communists. For a discussion of 'impossibilist' positions, see Barltrop 1975, and Coleman 1987.

4   This is not to deny, of course, the major role played by the market under NEP. In 1923 two developments occurred which showed the macroeconomic nature of this role in particularly dramatic fashion. The first was the 'scissors crisis,' when the differential between industrial prices and agricultural prices soared to three times its pre-war level. Given that agriculture had recovered considerably more rapidly than industry from the dislocations of war between 1914 and 1921 (see Nove 1982, pp.93-96), such a movement of prices is precisely what should be expected from an elementary consideration of supply and demand. The second was the removal of the prohibition of alcohol which had been in force since 1914. As Carr has shown (1954, p.35n), since this took the form of a re-establishment of the State vodka monopoly, it vividly demonstrated the government's fiscal dependence on the indirect taxation of luxury goods.

5   The most valuable general works on council communism in English or French are Authier and Barrot 1976 and Bourrinet 1992a. Both are in French; no works of comparable quality exist in English. For an account of 'anti-parliamentary communism' in Britain, see Shipway 1988. More specific works include Bricianer 1969, Mattick 1939-67, and Socialist Reproduction/Revolutionary Perspectives 1974. Also of interest is Gombin 1978.

6   Korsch refers to the USSR as a capitalist State (1938) in an expanded article published in the council communist journal *Living Marxism* (Chicago). But he does not discuss the country's actual conditions.

7   Of course, the revolutionary Marxist view of Soviet Russia was also coloured by the latter's role in western Europe, where the Bolshevik-dominated 'Communist' International tried to bounce those who considered themselves communists into sustained militation within parliaments and trade unions, and eventually insisted on the formation of national 'united fronts.' In May 1920 the West-European Bureau of the Comintern was shut down by

Moscow, and in June Lenin published *Left-Wing Communism: An Infantile Disorder*. In 1921, pro-Bolshevik forces fused in Germany with the bulk of the Independent Social-Democratic Party (USPD), a more 'orthodox' and much larger faction of social democracy. All these developments were clearly in keeping with Soviet diplomacy: trade treaties were secured with both Britain and Germany the same year. Also in 1921, Krassin criticised the British miners' strike for interfering with Bolshevik trading needs. (Shipway 1988, p.27). Indeed, when MI5 eventually needed evidence of Bolshevik 'revolutionary internationalism,' they had to forge it in the form of the 'Zinoviev letter.' (See West 1981, pp.60-62). Military co-operation with Germany began in 1922, and possibly even earlier. (See Sutton 1968, chap. 15). (For a discussion of the impact of Bolshevik foreign policy on the left communist critique, see Authier and Barrot 1976, pp.130-43 and 175-88. See also Lenin 1920; McCauley 1981, p.62; and the Comintern's *Theses, Resolutions and Manifestos* [1919-22]).

8   A leading member of the International Communists of Germany (IKD), an extremist group to the left of Liebknecht and Luxemburg's Spartacus League, Rühle was later a leader of the East Saxony section of the council communist KAPD (see below, note 37). From 1921 he was involved in the General Workers' League of Germany (Unified Organisation) (AAUD-E), also council communist, which rejected the party form and insisted on the workplace as the basis of council communist organisation. On the development of his thought, see Socialist Reproduction/Revolutionary Perspectives 1974, and Authier and Barrot 1976, chap. 14.

9   Rühle would eventually also use the phrase 'world fascism.' (1940).

10   Perhaps surprisingly, neither Rühle nor the 'councilists' rejected the 'orthodox Marxist' view of lower and higher stages of communism. (See GIK 1930). Rühle's failure to question this view only adds to his confusion.

11   Councilism can be defined as 'anti-vanguardist,' anti-party council communism, stressing above all the forms of workers' self-organisation. (For elements of a critique, see Barrot 1973 and Shipway 1987, pp.118-24). Growing from the positions defended by the Group of International Communists in the Netherlands (1927-40), it won adherents in the United States, Scandinavia, France, and elsewhere, and proved overall to be the most abiding current of council communism. Ceasing to be a properly international 'milieu' with the second world war, it decomposed in the Netherlands only in the 1970s. (Bourrinet 1992a, pp.153-284). By this time, of course, the term 'councilism' had adopted new shades of meaning, relating to the ideas of Castoriadis (1957) about the self-management of wage-labour, and to those of the Situationists (see Riesel 1969) about the organisation of communist revolution by mass assemblies and revokable delegates. The rise of these two tendencies, however, both of which also decomposed in the 1970s, was largely *sui generis*: hence their ideas on the USSR are considered separately elsewhere.

12   Apart from this document there is very little councilist material on the USSR of a similar theoretical level. In *Lenin as Philosopher* (1938), the only explanation Pannekoek gives of the capitalist nature of a system of production "directed by a state bureaucracy under the leadership of the Communist Party" is that "state officials...have the disposal over the product, hence over the surplus value." (p.75). I have already pointed out the inadequacy of this argument with reference to the SPGB. He later writes in *Workers' Councils* (1947-49) of the collective possession of the means of production by leading officials who exploit the workers and pay them wages, but fails to take the analysis any further than that. (Part 2, p.85). It is revealing that in a section on "The Foe" (Part 3)

he applies rigorous analysis to a number of national capitalist groupings, but fails to include in his sights the rulers of Soviet Russia. We would add that it may of course be true, as Gerber claims (1978, p.27), that the *Theses on Bolshevism* were really written by Pannekoek; but since he offers no support for this claim, we would opt at present to follow Bourrinet, who writes in a lengthy work on Dutch council communism that they were based on a document by Helmut Wagner, which was then revised by the GIK collectively. (1992, p.182).

13   They also avoid having to find reasons for the defeat of whatever radical movement there really was among Russian proletarians. It should be noted that one can agree with them that capitalism was never abolished while still affirming that Bolshevik power was only imposed in opposition to a proletarian revolutionary movement, albeit a weak one. (Voline 1947; [Jones] 1984, [Fernandez] 1985; and Wildcat 1986 and 1991).

14   As Sapir has shown (1984, p.60), job-hopping was far more frequent among younger workers. The annual rate of job-changing by workers aged 20 to 25 reached some 50-65%.

15   For a critical analysis of Ticktin's arguments, see Chapter 6 below.

16   For his part Meszaros does provide an alternative definition of capital. In his view, the "developed capital-relation, prevalent in the USSR as much as in the West," demands the existence of

>(1) the *separation* and *alienation* of the *objective conditions* of the labour process from labour itself;
>
>(2) the *superimposition* of such objectified and alienated conditions over the workers as a separate power exercising *command over labour*;
>
>(3) the *personification of capital as 'egotistic value'* — with its usurped subjectivity and pseudo-personality — pursuing its own *self-expansion*, with a *will* of its own...in the form of setting as its internalized aim the fulfilment of the expansionary imperatives of capital as such...; and
>
>(4) the equivalent *personification of labour* (i.e. the personification of the workers as 'Labour' destined to enter a contractual/economic or a politically regulated dependency relation with the historically prevailing type of capital), confining the subject-identity of this 'Labour' to its fragmentary productive functions — whether we think of the category of 'Labour' as wage labourer under capitalism or as the norm-fulfilling and over-fulfilling 'socialist worker' under the postcapitalist capital system, with the latter's own form of vertical and horizontal division of labour. (1995, p.617)

Capitalism, however, extends only over "that particular phase of capital production" where

>(1) *production for exchange* is all-pervasive...;
>
>(2) *labour-power*...is treated as a commodity;
>
>(3) the drive for *profit* is the fundamental regulatory force of production
>
>(4) the vital mechanism for the *extraction of surplus-value*, the radical separation of the means of production from the producers, assumes an *inherently economic form*;
>
>(5) the economically-extracted surplus-value is *privately appropriated* by the members of the capitalist class; and
>
>(6) following its own *economic imperative* of growth and expansion, capital production tends towards a *global integration*, through the intermediary of the world market... (1977, pp.912-13, quoted in Meszaros 1995, p.630)

In the USSR, apparently, whereas the conditions for the existence of *capital* did obtain, five of the six necessary for the existence of *capitalism* did not, and even number 4 existed only in a way that involved a form of regulation of the extraction of surplus labour which was 'political' rather than 'economic.' Hence the system was not capitalist.

It is instructive to look at what Meszaros thinks the USSR actually was — that is, 'post-capitalist' — and why. Thus he writes that

> the *political* mode of extracting surplus labour became necessary in the Soviet system precisely because it was structurally incompatible with the objective requirements of setting up and maintaining in operation a postrevolutionary labour market. This is what made it genuinely postcapitalist, in that the socioeconomic reproduction process could not be regulated in it by a clearly identifiable and effectively functioning *plurality of private capitals*. (1995, p.667)

The theorising is evidently extremely unclear. How can the establishment of a labour market be an 'objective requirement' in a so-called 'postrevolutionary' period? And to take the final sentence of this extract, what exactly was it, of what is purported to have been the case, that demonstrates that capitalism was non-existent? Was it the absence of a plurality of private capitals, or the lack of a 'clear identification' of such a plurality? Was it the 'ineffective functioning' of such a plurality; or was it the other-than-private nature of the capitals within it? Meszaros does not say. Moreover, the distinction which he draws between two forms of control over surplus extraction (economic and political) does not quite hide the fact that he refers to surplus *value* in relation to the first form but not the second. The implication — although that is all it remains — is surely that the Soviet surplus product took a form other than that of surplus value. But the idea of 'developed' capital without surplus value is absurd. We would also point out that Meszaros's convoluted style of expression hardly compensates for the absence of definition of terms such as 'economic,' 'political,' and 'private.'

At least one implication of the term 'post-capitalist', though, is somewhat clearer: namely, that capitalism was got rid of. And here we reach one of the main underlying ideas, which is that *capital* can be superseded only in the course of a period which begins once a 'revolution' has abolished *capitalism*. (See pp.604-05). During this period,

> capital maintains its — by no means unrestricted — rule...primarily through:
> (1) the material imperatives which circumscribe the possibilities of the totality of life-processes;
> (2) the inherited social division of labour which, notwithstanding its significant modifications, contradicts 'the development of free individualities';
> (3) the objective structure of the available production apparatus (including plant and machinery) and of the historically developed and restricted form of scientific knowledge...;and
> (4) the links and interconnections of the post-revolutionary societies with the global system of capitalism, whether these assume the form of a 'peaceful competition' (e.g. commercial and cultural exchange) or that of a potentially deadly opposition... (Meszaros 1977, p.913)

We will simply observe that whereas the first and third points are vague to the point of irrelevance, the second assumes some of what must be proved and the fourth is straightforwardly leftist.

The trend to be followed during this period is not predetermined. If it is to be towards the abolition of capital, then according to this view there will have to be "material and moral incentives" of an "egalitarian" kind, functioning under conditions which are not those of 'market socialism' but where instead people will "control what they are involved in." (1992, pp.981-82). For some reason there is still an "economic surplus," but the 'mode of regulating its production and allocation' is transformed. The "old state's protective functions vis-à-vis the capital system" are taken over, but at the same time there is a 'successful articulation' of the "autonomous and positive regulatory functions through which the associated producers can put to their chosen ends the fruits of their surplus-labour." (1995, pp.631-32). This articulation will be "*non-hierarchical.*" (p.635). (We note in passing that he does not say whether or not the 'incentives' he posits will take a monetary form. To his credit, when he discusses the nature of 'communal social relations' [pp.758-60] he does seem to assume money's non-existence, but he does not—in the half-million words of *Beyond Capital* — include any discussion of money's *abolition*). If, on the other hand, the politically-regulated extraction of surplus labour is controlled not by the associated producers, but rather by a political authority imposed on them, the trend will be quite different (see also pp.761-63) and capital will find a new personification. This is what it did in Soviet Russia in the form of State bureaucrats. (p.617). Notably, though, he does not explain how capital could ever continue to exist *without* a personification, when he has previously posited personification in one kind or another as one of its necessary conditions of existence, at least in its "developed" form. His consideration of the question of transition becomes even less convincing when, clearly building on the implicit assumption that a revolution abolished capitalism in Russia in 1917, he makes the curious statement that "Lenin could not envisage the possibility of an objective contradiction between the dictatorship of the proletariat and the proletariat itself." (p.633; see also 1985, pp.926-27).

Meszaros's view of more recent possibilities in the "post-revolutionary societies" (*sic*) of a Soviet type is far from radical. Thus he writes that

> positive developments...may be envisaged only if the system finds some way of achieving an effective institutionally underpinned *distribution of political power* (even if very limited in the first place) which does not represent a *danger to the prevailing mode of extracting surplus-labour* as such — although of necessity it would question the particular manifestations and excesses of surplus-extraction. In other words, 'decentralization,' 'diversification,' 'autonomy' and the like must be implemented in post-revolutionary societies as — in the first place — *political* principles, in order to be meaningful at all. (1977, p.914; see also Meszaros 1990, p.974)

The context is that of opposing the introduction of the market, but nonetheless this is hardly a communist alternative.

The understanding of Soviet capital on a more abstract level is similarly weak. In Chapter 3 we discuss the nature of the category of capital in some detail; but for the moment let us recall that capital in its modern (not pre-capitalist) form, as understood by Marx, is of course self-expanding value: that is, value which necessarily accrues surplus value. Second, value can only exist if production for exchange is generalised. Third, as we pointed out in relation to the position held by Wildt, the expansion of value requires that it take the alternating forms of the commodity and money. And fourth, the generalised rule of self-expanding value implies wage-labour. If Meszaros disagrees with any of these points, he does not say why. But unless they are shown to be false, his somewhat odd belief that the USSR, whilst being ruled by capital, did not meet the conditions necessary for capitalism, is punctured straightaway. This is particularly clear in relation to his omission to give adequate support to his view that there was no wage-labour. He accepts — with reference to Stalin's work of 1952 — that a 'quasi-market' existed through which labour-power was 'compensated' for the effort expended in production. But, he states, the defining characteristic of a labour market is not that the parties involved in it are "simply 'buyers and sellers.'" On the contrary, it is the operation of these parties as *"particular personifications* of the *structurally entrenched* but necessarily particularized capital-relation — i.e. *particular* personifications of both capital and labour — who enter into a contractual relationship of commercial transaction with one another." (p.667). Without saying anything about Soviet workers' wage-packets, he states that since the parties did not operate in this way in the USSR there was no labour market. Even in his own terms, however, it is not at all clear that they did not operate in this way. Thus in his very definition of the necessary conditions for capital's existence he writes:

> it is also important to stress here that it is not the bureaucrat who produces the perverse Soviet type capital system,...but, rather, the inherited and reconstituted postcapitalist form of capital gives rise to its own personification in the form of the bureaucrat, as the postcapitalist equivalent to the formerly economic-extraction-oriented capital system which had to give rise to the private capitalist...(p.617)

But is this not to say that Soviet bureaucrats *were* 'particular personifications' of capital? Later, Meszaros states that "capital's controlling functions" were vested "in the party as such, and not in particular individuals," and that party leaders were "genuine personifications of capital in their collective capacity only." (pp.668-69). But this would seem only to create further confusion. Given that each individual bureaucrat evidently did control something, how could he do so without personifying capital when it was surely precisely through exercising control functions that the bureaucracy as a 'collective' did personify capital? How could 'collective' control be exercised other than through individual bureaucrats? (Nor is the critique strengthened when Meszaros looks at the form of labour. See below, Chapter 5, note 12). Thus as well as offering insufficient support for his contention that there was no capitalism, he offers an incomplete theory of why there *was* capital.

17 James and Dunayevskaya began their collaboration as the leaders of the minority tendency (1941-47) within the Workers' Party in the United States, eventually ending their involvement in the Trotskyist movement in 1950. Their increasing and important recognition of the autonomous power of the workers then led both to formulate positions in opposition to traditional Leninist vanguardism. James co-operated for a time with longer-standing defenders of workers' autonomy working within council communism and the group Socialisme ou Barbarie, but eventually came to base his politics mainly upon anti-imperialist nationalism. Meanwhile, Dunayevskaya became the founding figure of idealist-Hegelian 'Marxist-Humanism.' It should perhaps be added that neither James nor Dunayevskaya ever arrived at explicit opposition to Leninism in its entirety.

After James and Dunayevskaya ended their co-operation in 1955, it soon became clear that no love was lost between them. It is thus doubly unfortunate that a satisfactory non-partisan analysis of the tendency's development has yet to appear in English. (But see Appendix to James, Lee, and Chaulieu 1958, and Dunayevskaya 1958-72.)

18 This work was in fact written in August 1943, not long after the publication of the first series.

19 Whether these models would be feasible in practice is quite another matter.

20 As we show below in Chapter 6, though, the theoretical impasse which they reached in their consideration of the nature of the system in the USSR did not prevent them from adding meaningfully to the understanding of the class struggle in that country.

21 The founder of the Spanish section of organised Trotskyism during the Spanish civil war, Munis (Grandizo) continued to be its leader once it was exiled to Mexico. Although his

'state capitalist' and non-defencist view of the USSR would eventually lead him to reject Trotskyism (see Munis 1975, pp.7 and 39-42), his sympathetic view of Bolshevism and his belief in the need for the leadership of the working class by a Leninist vanguard party remained heavily influenced by Trotsky. Correspondingly, Munis denies that the imposition of Stalinism represented primitive capitalist accumulation and "the beginning of a social era." (1975, p.28). One should have thought it self-evident, however, that the proletarianisation of scores of millions of peasants and the breakneck industrialisation and urbanisation (which have never been reversed) did indeed involve the move to a new way of life for the majority of the population. For a presentation of the politics of this tendency, see FOR 1965.

22   Munis's presentation of this train of thought as being the commonly acknowledged Marxian one is highly questionable, since at no time in his life did Marx himself write of a future 'society of transition' or 'transitional society.' (See Buick 1975). Furthermore, the young Marx states outright that communism will embody the "true resolution of the strife between freedom and necessity." (1844, p.90). In short, rather than 'freeing' work, communism abolishes it, as Marx and Engels also say explicitly. (1846, p.220). Such a revolutionary transformation can hardly be reconciled with the continued existence of a categorical gulf between 'immediate needs' and subjective requirements, or indeed with a division between the necessary product and the 'surplus,' between v and s. Admittedly, later, in Volume 3 of *Capital*, Marx suggests that the twin realms of freedom and necessity will not altogether be superseded, but even so his vision of communist society most definitely still centres upon the "development of human powers as an end in itself." (1894, p.959). This cannot be reduced to "planning for consumption." (Munis 1975, p.37).

23   The remuneration of experts in the 'transitional society' is a question of special interest to Leninists. Cliff, for example, in discussing the increase in differentials between experts and workers under Stalin, produces figures according to which no exploitative relationship exists when a specialist receives a salary a mere six times greater than the wage of an unskilled worker, but one does exist when the differential rises to 17. (1955, pp.67-81). Such matters are a complete non-issue for those who hold the view that the proletarian revolution — the same thing as transition — abolishes money, wage-labour, and privative appropriation. (See Chapter 1 above).

24   In fact, as the council communists and others showed, the Bolshevik government never sought world revolution, and was always principally concerned with the rescue, stability, and expansion of the national economy. (See note 7 above). Moreover, the adoption of the new ideology, strongly advocated by Bukharin as well as by Stalin, in no way brought an end to NEP. (See for example Nove 1982, pp.122-29). It can further be added that even on the purely ideological plane, the difference between Stalin's view and Lenin's was not great: Lenin too thought that a victory of 'socialism' was possible in a single country (1915, p.203) — albeit not in Russia.

25   For Munis, the struggle between different "clans" of the bureaucracy for the distribution of surplus value and the control of the State is something for the future. (1946, p.24).

26   Breaking with orthodox Trotskyism over the Soviet question in the 1940s, Cliff became a leading light in the British group the International Socialists, and then the top leader of the Socialist Workers' Party which replaced the IS in 1976. If the first contained certain tendencies which leant towards Luxemburgism, the second is more clearly substitutionist and Leninist. For an account of Cliff's political itinerary, see Callaghan 1984.

27   Drawing a clear relation of determination between the place of the USSR in world society and the nature of the internal social relations, Cliff manages to look at both, even if he

mistakes the direction of the determination. The 'world-system' theorist Wallerstein, however, simply assumes the USSR to be part of the 'capitalist world-economy' and then goes on to make assertions about Soviet conditions which are idealist, incoherent, or demonstrably false. In his view, the USSR was 'state capitalist' — a term he leaves undefined — because "the CPSU forgot the dialectical relationship between transformation within the Soviet Union and [the] evolution of the capitalist world-economy (of which it remained structurally a part)." (1975, p.240). It would thus seem that the CPSU "created a variant of state capitalism" because it had mistaken ideas. Elsewhere he holds that even as late as 1945 the 'unworkability' of a 'Leninist' road to socialism was impossible to appreciate. (1990, p.96). So the USSR would seem to have been destined to be part of the capitalist 'world-economy,' even if no-one could have known. This analysis is clearly incoherent. Moreover, whereas the first assertion is idealist, the second contains an empirical falsehood, since such movements as anarchism and council communism appreciated very rapidly the supposedly inappreciable.

There are many similar examples of such confusion in Wallerstein's view of the USSR. Thus even as he fits the country into a theory of the 'capitalist world-system,' he asserts that to try to create a "morphological category" for such "socialist states" [*sic*] is futile, since any morphology assumes, first, that the units to be described are the States, and second, that these States have (their own) modes of production. In fact, of course, however one labels a State, from a Marxist viewpoint paramount importance must always be given to modes of production. Moreover, to ascribe the label 'capitalist' to a single State can hardly be to deny that the capitalist mode of production might be global. Wallerstein proceeds to assert that any 'morphology' portraying the Soviet State as capitalist leads "almost immediately" to the view that the State is in some "transitional stage." (1982, pp.93-94). Actually, many theories of Soviet capitalism do not say this at all. But for Wallerstein the USSR's most important characteristic is its presence in the 'world-system,' and to theorise its production relations in any fashion is pointless. His own approach is consequently not as 'empirical' as he might wish, and his view of Soviet 'state capitalism' would seem to be based on pure belief.

28   In a different context, Marx was quite clear that non-capitalist economies did not become capitalist simply by trading with capitalist ones. (1885, pp.189-90).

29   This conclusion is approached even more closely by the 'world-system neo-Marxist' Chase-Dunn, who writes that "it may be a mistake" to over-emphasise the exploitative nature of class relations in 'state capitalist' countries. There is only one other aspect of his overall view of the nature of the USSR which differentiates it notably from Cliff's: that is, his inclusion among the internally influential considerations of foreign policy — alongside the arms race — of a reluctance to allow labour and capital exports. (1982, pp.34-38).

30   Bettelheim refuses to infer even the non-existence of 'socialism,' let alone the existence of capitalism, just from the simple existence of money, prices and the market, which he refers to as a mere "surface fact." (1969, pp.18-19.) Disregarding what we hold to be the capitalist nature of the USSR even under Lenin and Stalin, however, as well as the nominal character of its producer markets, it would seem quite straightforward that people creating a new and free society would have no reason to mimic the terminology of the commodity. But for those who have already crossed the hurdle of seeing a regime that incarcerated millions in concentration camps as even potentially 'socialist,' this is a relatively easy point to miss.

Missed it is, though, by Bland, who argues that the creation of a privileged stratum was achieved by an "opposition" within the CPSU, against the "minority" led by Stalin and

Beria. (1980, pp.i-xv, 72-91). This, he states, provided a basis for the "restoration" of capitalism and the emergence of a "fascist-type State of a new type" [*sic*] after the 1965 reforms. (p.312). In discussing the 'Leningrad affair' of 1949-50, which led to the execution of Gosplan chief Voznesensky, Bland praises Stalin's sterling defence of 'socialism' which supposedly culminated in the publication of his work on the *Economic Problems of Socialism in the USSR* in 1952. (pp.343-56). In particular, he quotes Stalin approvingly to the effect that the law of value can operate without being the 'regulator' of production. Together with his combination of support for Beria with a condemnation of Brezhnev's 'fascist' persecution of 'independent' trade unions, this is an example of what can only be called doublethink. Value can only *exist* if it regulates production. (Rubin 1928, pp.77-83). Bland's pro-Chinese (Liu Shao-Ch'i-ist rather than Maoist) and later pro-Albanian ideology exists at the extreme 'fundamentalist' fringe of Stalinism, and need not be considered further.

31   The Hong Kong 'left communist' L. L. Men , meanwhile, adds similarly little to Bettelheim's critique. Having asserted that at the 'point of departure' the 'content' of Soviet prices is totally insignificant, he first shows that the existence of price as a form implies private labour and private property. Focusing more closely on the separation between enterprises, he further observes that relations of private property exist among the people who "own" the means of production. Then, looking at the 'content,' he writes that

> prices in the 'socialist' countries are set by the state (as said, we are assuming a perfectly planned economy), but obviously, the state planners cannot set them arbitrarily, at will, without any basis whatsoever at all. Otherwise, the economy will be in complete chaos. What is this basis which governs the state planners' decisions within specific boundaries, i.e. which determines the prices? In Marxist analysis, only one thing and one thing alone can constitute this basis: the socially necessary labour congealed in products. (1986, pp.34-35)

In relation to the really-existing USSR after Stalin, this view is indistinguishable from Bettelheim's. The dogmatic nature of the argument is self-evident.

32   But he fails to account for the apparent change in his viewpoint. If in 1980 he focuses on the system's inability to institutionalise intensive accumulation, by the end of the decade he writes of a 'voluntaristic mode of regulation' which gives way to a 'consensual' one during de-Stalinisation. (1989, p.33; 1990, pp.128-29). This is quite a jump — but Sapir neither explains how the two views can be brought together nor explicitly rejects his earlier view. It would seem that the underlying basis of his theory of Soviet economic development, which was originally political-economic, has now become primarily political; and he explains the crisis of the mobilised economy (seen as a "metamode") chiefly in terms of international relations. (1990, pp.129-30).

33   Notable here is the very 'sociological' use of the term 'society' to mean 'country.' Apparently, then, capitalism would not be a society but rather a conglomeration of societies. This, of course, is a view separated by an unbridgeably wide gulf from Marx's. (See Marx and Engels 1848, Marx 1867, etc.).

34   Sapir was previously of the opinion that workers must sell their labour-power so long as production is not based on their free association. (1980, p.165). A glance at any pre-capitalist exploitative mode of production, such as serfdom or ancient slavery — or indeed colonial slavery — is sufficient to demonstrate the untenability of this position.

35   A hypothetical analogy from the 'advanced West' will serve to illustrate further the point of these criticisms. Imagine, then, that in an area earmarked for 'development' an enterprise

body allocates a grant to a local firm to cover the costs of building a car park. Although this grant evidently takes the form of a real financial account, it must still be spent in the specified way. Once the money is paid to the construction company, however, the new owner — whose identity may even have had to be specified before the grant was cleared in the first place — is qualitatively much freer in terms of what he can spend it on. This is certainly a good example of how scrip money turns into fiat money; but to offer the analysis as the basis of an understanding of the monetary circuit itself is in no way to avoid the trap of empiricism. What is missing at a general level from this sort of consideration is the theorisation of the overall 'context': namely, of the mode of social production and reproduction, and of the role of money within it. More specifically, it touches on but does not yet provide a critical theorisation of the circuit and accumulation of value. (See Chapters 3 and 7 below).

36   See Perlman's remarks on 'economics' as opposed to the critique of political economy. (1968, ix-xi).

37   The KAPD was founded in April 1920 by the large majority of members of the Communist Party of Germany (KPD) who rejected parliamentary and trade-unionist tactics, party substitutionism, and co-operation with social democracy, favouring instead workers' self-organisation and revolutionary action. See Authier and Barrot 1976, chaps. 10-14.

38   The CWI's affiliate in England was the Workers' Dreadnought group around S. Pankhurst, which joined in 1921.

39   In Scotland the Anti-Parliamentary Communist Federation (APCF) around Aldred reached positions which were very similar. This group first recognised the existence of capitalism in Russia in 1925, and proceeded the following year to describe the adoption of the NEP as the 'liquidation' of the revolution. (APCF 1925b, p.43, and 1926, p.113; see also idem, 1925a). Eventually in 1935 the APCF arrived at a 'councilist' position, publishing the *Theses on Bolshevism* under the title *The Bourgeois Role of Bolshevism*.

40   This represented a repudiation of the earlier left communist position that whereas party substitutionism was inapplicable as a revolutionary tactic in western Europe, it was nonetheless acceptable in Russia. (See Gorter 1920). With this development left communists became council communists.

41   Elements of communistic change introduced in Kronstadt were supported by the Left Socialist-Revolutionaries, Maximalists, and Anarchists, but bitterly opposed by the Bolsheviks. See Voline 1947, pp.456-63.

42   Although best known as the leading member of the political group Socialisme ou Barbarie [Socialism or Barbarism] (1949-65), Castoriadis wrote copiously on the USSR from the late 1940s until the 1980s, which was time enough to change and develop his views on a number of relevant issues. Of prime importance in the present context are those articles published between 1949, when he first referred to the USSR as capitalist, and 1961, when he brought out the final part of *Modern Capitalism and Revolution*. In addition, the summary he wrote in 1977 has also been useful. It is perhaps worth mentioning the distance which later separates him even from 'Marxism.' Thus in 1964 (p.146) he argues that the social world is "in every instance constituted and articulated as a function of...a system of significations...[which exist] in the mode of the...actual imaginary"; in the same year he makes his rejection of Marxism explicit. (1964-65). By 1972 he rejects even the concepts of exploitation and class (1973, pp.24-25), holding instead that the basic 'instituting' factor in society is the 'radical imaginary' 'incarnating' itself in various imaginary significations. (pp.30-31). Returning in the 1980s to matters Soviet, he

then develops a theory of 'stratocracy' (army rule). (1981a). Although he himself asserts a continuity with his earlier critique of Soviet bureaucracy (p.9), in our view this latest shift should be assessed together, first, with his now disproven belief in a substantial Soviet military superiority over NATO; and second, with his newly-found self-identification with "Greco-Western ('European')" tradition and society. (1981a and 1974-91 passim, especially 1981b and 1982b).

43   Castoriadis's views are adopted uncritically by Bradford. The latter manages, however, not only to approve Castoriadis's position on "total bureaucratic capitalism" (1992, p.11), but also to suggest in one and the same article — written in response to the USSR's demise — that the Soviet 'society' was also "bureaucratic collectivist." (p.7). In fact he proposes two further views as well: namely, third, that the USSR was "state socialist" (p.18); and fourth, that "the society created by marxism-leninism was a new hybrid of capitalism and the despotism of the ancient slave states — a kind of state capitalism, though certainly not the only kind, since private Western capitalism has also evolved into state capitalism." (p.16). Going further still, he adds that capital itself has "always been a hybrid, in its early stages most particularly a hybrid of mercantile industrialism and chattel slavery." But even this latter understanding (or non-understanding) of what capital is can hardly explain how the decomposition of Soviet "civilization" could amount simultaneously to a "triumph of capital" and an indication of the future demise of "global capitalism" and "global industrialism." (pp.19-20). Denunciation follows denunciation, the 'megamachine' enters as Leviathan, "human decency" as its opponent, but one looks in vain for a coherent critique. (For an excellent critique of 'primitivism' more generally, see Aufheben 1995).

44   Although of a certain influence in Belgium, France, and Italy, Bordiga's ideas remain little-known in the English-speaking world. 'Bordigism' can be described as a variety of Leninism to the left of Trotskyism, whose central organising concepts are the 'class party' and the 'invariant programme.' For an account of the development of this tendency and those related to it, see Bourrinet 1982.

45   For the sake of accuracy, it should also be mentioned that the first official admission that the law of value operated in Stalin's USSR came not in 1952, but in 1943. (Leontiev et al. 1943). This year did not merely see the dissolution of the Comintern and the recognition in Moscow by the 'Big Four' powers (China, the UK, the US, and the USSR) of the necessity of the establishment of "a general International Organisation." (Bentwich 1946, p.17). It also saw the first presence of Soviet observer-delegates at the meetings in the US on the creation of the post-war international monetary system — meetings which led to the signing of the Bretton Woods treaty the following July. (Millman 1995, p.76). When a translation of the Soviet article appeared in the September 1944 issue of the *American Economic Review*, the matter even made the front page of the *New York Times*. Noting that the Dumbarton Oaks conference — also attended by the 'Big Four' — lasted from August to October of the same year, we can and should speculate on the role the Soviet admission played in matters of foreign policy, and in Soviet-American diplomacy in particular.

46   After a limited drift towards privatisation during the second world war, government and party control was strengthened in 1946. For details on Soviet agriculture under late Stalinism, see for example Nove 1982, pp. 298-304.

47   Bordiga also states rather bizarrely (1952, p.13) that the enterprises which produce such goods as clothing and housing remain 'untouched' by the State. Although even Stalin does

not go this far, this could be taken as an exaggeration of the official Soviet position. See "The Nature of the Operation of the Law of Value in Socialist Economy," sub-chapter in Soviet Academy of Sciences 1957, pp.590-99.

48   Today's Bordigists still make the same mistake, holding that it is within "agriculture and the kolkhozian hybrid" that we find "the real nucleus of the reproduction of mercantile relations and the accumulation of capital." (ICP 1991, p.4).

49   Bordiga's view of the State funding of the Soviet construction industry might possibly be over-influenced by an understanding of the relations involved in such funding in Italy.

50   Rather than stating in simple fashion that the workers had no *control* over the means of production, Chattopadhyay actually refers less clearly to their "non-property." But the context of their "[exclusion] from all power starting at the highest economic level" is clearly that of social totality rather than juridicality. (p.50).

51   The attribution here has been altered to refer to the English translation of Marx's *Capital* published by Penguin in 1976. We have left unchanged the words actually quoted, which are Chattopadhyay's own translation from the original German.

52   Or, as we would put it, wage-labour does not simply provide the basis of generalised commodity production: rather, the reproduction of labour-power actually becomes an area within that production. (See Dalla Costa 1971 and Chapter 7 below).

53   This fact is crucial to a proper understanding of commodity fetishism and the categories of surplus value and capital. Chattopadhyay's reference to Marx's statement that objects of utility become commodities only because they are the products of labour of "private individuals who work independently of each other," however, which we have cited above, is taken somewhat out of context. Thus Marx states immediately afterwards that

> the sum total of the labour of all these private individuals forms the aggregate labour of society. Since the producers do not come into social contact until they exchange the products of their labour, the specific social characteristics of their private labours appear only within this exchange. In other words, the labour of the private individual manifests itself as an element of the total labour of society only through the relations which the act of exchange establishes between the products, and, through their mediation, between the producers. (1867,p.165)

It is important to realise that at this stage Marx is still assuming, for the sake of simplicity of presentation, that the producer and the owner-exchanger of the product are the same person: in other words, that the producer engages in labour purely with a view to exchanging the product. Once the consideration moves to the capitalist form of labour, wage-labour, where the worker is separated from the means of production and therefore also from the product, this assumption must necessarily be dropped. The relationship between private labour and the exchange of products is now different in nature from what it was in the previous (hypothetical and heuristic) case of generalised 'simple commodity production.' Now that the worker is permitted to work only when someone else believes he can acquire an exchangeable product, the categories of labour and commodity exchange might usefully be described as 'further apart' or subject to greater mediation; and so it becomes much easier to fall into the methodological trap of conceiving their relationship in a one-sided way. It should thus be stressed that whilst the gap between worker and product is now qualitatively much greater, since at no time is the product the worker's own, this does not mean that the socialisation of labour ceases to take the form of the exchange of products. And the form of this socialisation — which is what determines private labour as nonetheless social, albeit indirectly — is hardly a secondary or derived issue. For an admirably clear presentation of

Marx's critique of the "form of value" — that is, generalised exchangeability — see Rubin 1928, pp.107-23, especially pp.115-16.

54   In this context it is surely insufficient simply to quote a line from Marx's *Capital* to the effect that one can analyse competition scientifically only after first understanding the "inner nature of capital" (1867, p.433, cited in Chattopadhyay 1994, p.130), unless one proceeds actually to do so.

55   Thus one infers in some places that capital is 'socialised' owing to State ownership; and in others that it is 'socialised' by means of the exchange of products.

3 Soviet Bureaucratic Capitalism: A New Theory

In this chapter we give expanded Marxist definitions of the basic underlying categories of capitalism, and then show how they continued to exist in the USSR. In doing so we develop an original understanding of the capitalist nature of Soviet society; and more generally, we provide a framework for understanding capitalist formations wherein the function performed in bourgeois countries mainly by the market is performed in a way that is qualitatively more bureaucratic.

We begin the discussion of the nature of the USSR by stating clearly what it definitely was not. Since it is an obvious fact, then, that privative appropriation and exploitative production were not replaced with a society based upon collective happiness and goodwill (Babeuf and Buonarotti's *bonheur commun* — see Rose 1978, chaps. 13-15), where the "free development of each" was the condition for the "free development of all" (Marx and Engels 1848, p.61), it is self-evident that Soviet social relations were never communist.

It is further clear, however, that the fact that the social relations were not communist does not automatically imply that the country was capitalist. Thus according to Marx's theory, and indeed to the general principles of logic, there is nothing to prevent the theoretical possibility that a society might exist which is neither capitalist, nor 'pre-capitalist,' nor communist. Such a society might arise from a development somehow 'parallel' to capitalism, from the "common ruin of the contending classes" of capitalism,[1] or perhaps from an unforeseen and unforeseeable technological revolution. It should not be assumed at the outset that modern forms of exploitation differing substantially from 'classical' laissez-faire forms, and indeed from what has replaced those forms in their heartlands, must necessarily be capitalist themselves.

In this connection it is useful to recall a few facts about the character of Russian conditions of production prior to the first world war. In particular we would underline two main points. The first is that even at that time the conditions were not those of 'classical,' bourgeois, free-market capitalism. Thus a crucial role in the economy was played by the State, both in providing demand — primarily in heavy industry — and in supporting the credit system. Foreign investment was massive: directly in stocks; in shares, including bank shares; and in government and municipal bonds. Meanwhile, even as the urban economy was skewed towards large-scale heavy industry, substantial numbers of industrial workers belonged to *arteli*, either supporting families who remained in the villages or keeping their own plots to work on in the summer. In the countryside itself, subsistence production was widespread and most peasants remained in communes. (For an excellent account of the Russian economy in the post-emancipation period, see Milward and Saul 1977). But the second point is that behind these specifically Russian conditions we can identify a list of more fundamental features which in world history are quite familiar. Thus industry was organised on the basis of wage-labour and profitable growth; banking was advanced; and the countryside was increasingly subject to monetary relations. In short, it is not at all controversial to state that the predominant mode of production was precisely capitalism.

Regarding what happened after the first world war, there is thus a choice of two theses. The first is that of the 'abolition of capitalism.' This states that the peculiarity of Russian conditions — including, of course, political conditions — and of external conditions affecting Russia, caused the previously prevalent non-classical capitalism to be abolished in such a way that capitalism itself was abolished. Since this did not involve proletarian communist revolution, we should thus have to explain why it was that capitalism was abolished in a way that was totally different from the ways that had been envisaged and discussed up to that time. The second, alternative thesis is that of the 'non-classical development' of capitalism in a country where, in a certain fashion at least, some of the existing capitalist forms were already non-classical. It is this thesis which we will endeavour to support below. Although we do not now have to argue that industrialisation continued on the basis of a wholly new society even if the most evident changes it brought about (virtually everyone having a job and watching television), along with many of its principal products (nuclear power, computers, cars, weapons of mass destruction), are also apparent in, say, the United States, we still need to argue in a theoretical fashion. The problem now becomes that of discovering whether or not we can demonstrate the viability of this thesis without becoming tied up in too many theoretical knots.

Before we undertake this task we need to understand, though, exactly what kind of assertion is made when a country is adjudged to be capitalist. For the Marxist, then, to call the USSR a capitalist country is to make a statement about the relationship between a set of real social production relations on one hand and Marx's theory of capitalism on the other. Such a statement clearly says something about both the former and the latter. It implies many things. First, it means that the interests of the exploited inside and outside the USSR/CIS are fundamentally identical: higher wages, unity in struggle, and, ultimately, the revolutionary destruction of existing society. Second, Marx's theory of capitalism becomes of theoretical use for those who wish to undertake a radical critique of Soviet society. And third, since Marx knew nothing of the USSR, its critique by today's communists must involve certain interpretations of Marx's theory that were not made explicit by Marx himself. Indeed, the critique of the USSR as a capitalist formation — just like the critique of industrial monopolies and arms production, post-war nationalisation and the 'welfare State,' and late-century privatisation and the 'information revolution' — should be expected not simply to draw upon the overall Marxist critique of capitalism, but rather to enhance it.

Thus the fact that Marx's *Capital* cannot be applied lock, stock and barrel to the USSR does not invalidate the 'capitalist' theory of the USSR right from the start. In his preface to the first volume, Marx writes that

> what I have to examine in this work is the capitalist mode of production, and the relations of production and forms of intercourse that correspond to it. Until now, their *locus classicus* has been England. This is the reason why England is used as the main illustration of the theoretical developments I make. (1867, p.90)

His use of the phrase "until now" should be noted. What he conceived himself as doing in writing *Capital* was not to write a book for all time, but to construct a theory of capital in general as seen through the lens of what were then (in 1867) its forms in the most advanced country, that of 'classical' capitalism. If, more than a century later, we are seeking for a definition of what to include under the heading of capitalism, we should therefore be looking for relations which do not necessarily appear in 'classical' forms, but also in 'non-classical' forms. The theory of Soviet capitalism thus clears the first hurdle: it is not absurd. It would be quite wrong to infer that the major differences between the USSR and the bourgeois countries allow us to assume without proof the non-capitalist nature of the former.[2]

At the same time, it is equally wrong to go too far in the opposite direction, and to reduce or abstractify Marx's definition of capitalist relations to such a degree that the categories with which the description of capital begins, namely, the commodity and money, "are not just critically relativized, specific, and completed, but abolished." This is what Wildt does, and even if he is right (1979, p.44) to view capital as a "disjointed movement of the self-exploitation [or self-expansion] of value, for which commodities and money are mere forms," he is wrong to rule the commodity and money out of his definition entirely. As we shall argue below, if capital is, as Wildt says, necessarily 'disjointed,' then one must be able to identify two theoretically and practically distinct categories within it, namely those which Marx labels C and M. Otherwise the concept of 'disjointedness' has no meaning. And once the underlying categorial analysis of

Marx's *Capital* is ignored as too 'specific,' the concept of 'capital' itself becomes at best purely mystical and at worst superfluous.

DEFINING CAPITALISM

Our starting-point is thus the same as Buick and Crump's: namely, the consideration of what capitalism essentially is. The definition of capitalism which we shall begin with has three main elements, and it is convenient to deal with them here in the following order: the *commodity* (hence *exchange-value*), *wage-labour* (hence the *proletariat*), and generalised *production for profit* on the basis of generalised exchange (hence profitable growth). We then deal at length with the further underlying categories of value, abstract labour, and the value (or capital) forms of the commodity and money.[3]

Commodities, Wage-Labour, and Production for Profit

Commodities are goods which are bought and sold. On one hand, they are useful things which satisfy human needs, and hence have a utility or *use-value*. On the other, since they are exchanged, they must also have a value in exchange, or an *exchange-value*. At this level, they are only useful to their possessor insofar as they can be exchanged for something else: in themselves they are quite useless. Or, in Marx's words, "the exchange relation of commodities is characterised precisely by its abstraction from their use-values." (1867, p.27).

Since commodities have only existed for a tiny fraction of human existence, it is necessary to stress what lies behind purchase and sale. First, there must be an absence of concrete community, of communism, where everything would belong to everybody. In its place, there is private property, a state corresponding to the process of *privative appropriation*, where constituent parts of the world's wealth are appropriated in such a way as to deprive or impoverish those excluded from such appropriation.[4]

Second, if things are appropriated privatively, then by the very fact of appropriation their utility must have been "mediated through labour." This does not mean that they are necessarily movable and solid 'objects'; still less does it mean that they must be manufactured. Indeed, pure oxygen, or space on the beach, once privatively appropriated and made saleable, are just as much commodities as are tables or telescopes. But if something's utility has not been so 'mediated,' as is the case with unenclosed virgin soil, for example, then it cannot have been made into private property. (Marx 1867, p.131). The "essence of private property" can only be labour, described by Marx as an "expression of human activity within alienation." (1932, p.114). In short, by dint of being private property, commodities must necessarily be the *products of labour*.

Third, the categories of purchase and sale are but aspects of the single category of exchange. This implies the existence of *economy*, definable as the organisation and social reproduction of scarcity. Human relations are mediated not only by the interrelation of objects, but also, more generally, by the very exchangeability and socially reproduced scarcity — themselves human relations — which underlie the exchange process.

But however "mystical" the character of the commodity may be (as Marx puts it: 1867, p.164), no understanding will yet be able to provide us with an adequate definition of capitalism. This is because commodities, while they are necessary for the existence of capitalism, are not yet sufficient for that existence, as is best shown by the fact that they existed many centuries before capitalism was born. Indeed there is nothing in the definition of commodity exchange which does not apply equally to goods which are bartered, or to those exchanged by merchants enriching themselves merely by buying cheap and selling dear. Capitalism is more than this, and was established only when commodity logic became generalised and, in becoming generalised, made a major historical step forward by taking over *production*.

There are two main aspects of this change. First, human productive power itself becomes a commodity. There is thus the expansion of a class of men and women who own no productive assets apart from their creative capacity: namely, their ability to work, or 'labour-power.' In the case of expropriated peasants or dispossessed artisans, the productive resources they once had are taken away from them. In the case of freed slaves and serfs, what was formerly the direct utility, from their own viewpoint, of a portion of their labour-time is removed. (Marx 1939, p.419). Those with any of these pasts are consequently forced to sell their capacity to work, demand permitting, in order to be able to buy back the conditions of survival. The ability to create, produce, and enjoy productive adventure is alienated, crushed into an abstract common denominator by being sold in return for a wage-packet. In Marx's words, the worker's

> life-activity is for him only a means to enable him to exist. He works in order to live. He does not even reckon labour as part of his life, it is rather a sacrifice of his life...The product of his activity is not the object of his activity. (1847, p.19)

Qualitative dispossession, or poverty, corresponding to the separation between enjoyment of the environment and its productive transformation, becomes absolute once productive activity takes the form of *wage-labour*. The adoption by human labour of such a form, as Marx makes clear, is absolutely crucial to capitalism. In his words,

> *capital presupposes wage labour; wage labour presupposes capital. They reciprocally condition the existence of each other; they reciprocally bring forth each other.* (p.33) (emphasis original)

The second aspect which characterises the emergence of capitalism and distinguishes it from previous societies is the generalised establishment of production on the basis of an intention to sell. Since this involves the generalisation of exchange, and therefore of competition, it also implies the generalisation of *production for profit*. This is not so simply by reason of the greed of those who control the means of production, but also on pain of their losing out to competitors. Thus the accumulation of exchange-value becomes the motive of production in a generalised way. This means not only that there must necessarily be profitable growth — and indeed capitalism without profit-based material accumulation would be like fire without burning — but also, more generally, that there must be a constant and profitable technical development of the forces of production. In the course of this, capital moves from merely subordinating the labour process to transforming it and its actual conditions. (Marx 1933, pp.1023-25 and 1034-38).

Bearing in mind that wage-labour is the exchange of labour-power for the wage, we are now able to compress the above into a 'nutshell' definition of capitalism. This is as follows: capitalism is a mode of production which does not simply *allow* exchange and growth, but which is *founded* upon exchange as a general form and growth as an underlying drive.

Value, Abstract Labour, and Capitalist Money

It is necessary now to explain the significance of generalised exchange and necessary growth for the determination of the other main categories of capitalism.

Value

In the first place, the development of production dominated by exchange — and by the drive for the accumulation of exchange-value — means that the production of each commodity tends to influence and be affected by the production of virtually all other commodities. As exchange relations become generalised, exchange-dominated interconnectedness grows. And since labour-power itself is a commodity, a corresponding increase must also occur in the social division of labour. As a result, workers become increasingly connected with each other through their labour, even if they themselves do not determine the conditions of their interconnectedness as free and conscious agents. Human interconnectedness is determined instead by the exchange of products.

It is in order to explain the implications of this that Marx is led to base his entire theory of capitalism upon a rigorous understanding of that which all commodities have in common, and of which their various exchange-values are merely expressions: namely, that which is defined as *value*. He was not, of course, the first to identify human labour as being the single universal component of all commodities, and hence the substance of value; nor was he the first to insist on socialised labour as the only possible basis on which exchange-value can become generalised.[5] But he was the first to concentrate theoretically on the qualitative aspect of value, and thereby to criticise the basis of generalised exchange in such a way as to inform a root-and-branch theoretical critique of both wage-labour and the capitalist forms of the commodity and money. Whereas Ricardo proposes an 'embodied labour' theory of value, wherein the value of a commodity is explained as being proportional to the specific quantity of labour engaged in its production (1817, pp.9-51), Marx thus emphasises the overall social importance of the *generalisation* of exchange relations, including the relation of wage-labour. Since these relations cannot be assumed to be a 'natural' feature of 'advanced' human society — of the advanced socialisation of production — there is a need to explain the social categories that underlie not just their existence, but precisely their generalisation and their domination of production. These are the fundamental targets of the Marxian 'labour theory of value.'

This, then, is the level of the fundamental significance of the category of *abstract labour*. (1867, pp.140-54; for a useful commentary, see Rubin 1928, pp.107-23). In short, the interconnectedness of capitalist society is determined by the exchange and exchangeability of products; the exchange-values of products express their values; and the category of value is dependent upon the form of labour which is socialised and 'equalised' exclusively through the generalised exchange of its products. In terms of Marx's famous coat,

by equating for example, the coat as a thing of value to the linen, we equate the labour embedded in the coat with the labour embedded in the linen. Now it is true that the tailoring which makes the coat is concrete labour of a different sort from the weaving which makes the linen. But the act of equating tailoring with weaving reduces the former in fact to what is really equal in the two kinds of labour, to the characteristic they have in common of being human labour. This is a roundabout way of saying that weaving, too, in so far as it weaves value, has nothing to distinguish it from tailoring, and consequently, is abstract human labour. It is only the expression of equivalence between different sorts of commodities which brings to view the specific character of value-creating labour, by actually reducing the different kinds of labour embedded in the different kinds of commodity to their common quality of being human labour in general. (1867, p.142)

Thus labour is indeed social; but rather than being social directly it is social only indirectly, or abstractly, or reifiedly. Production is not controlled by the associated producers. Workers work together, and what they produce is socially determined; but the terrain on which they are brought together and made to work, rather than being determined by their own needs, is determined by the requirement on the part of the controllers of capital to ensure the expanded production of exchange-value in an environment of generalised exchange. Labour which is thus alienated can be defined as taking the form of 'abstract' social labour; and the commodity which embodies a portion of such labour correspondingly takes the form not just of exchange-value but also, more generally, of value. Abstract labour and value are no more than the forms taken by wage-labour and exchange-value when exchange has become generalised.

An understanding of the nature of capitalist commodities and capitalist production thus depends on an understanding of the inseparable relationship between the categories of abstract labour and value. And hence, as long as we bear in mind that the labour we are discussing is wage-labour, abstract labour, we might equally well describe the critique as being focused around a *value theory of labour*. As Rubin puts it, value

is not a property of things but a social form acquired by things due to the fact that people enter into determined production relations with each other through things. (1928. p.69)

Such a brief summary has the merit of emphasising the essentially qualitative nature of our method, by pointing up the nature of abstract labour as labour which produces value.

There now arises the quantitative question: *how much* value is produced? More to the point, what does 'how much value?' actually mean? Given that we know that only a single component is present in all commodities, namely labour, this reduces to the question: what does 'how much labour?' actually mean? We might, of course, seek to answer this question by formulating a definition according to which an hour of skilled labour counts for more than an hour of unskilled labour: the labour of a watchmaker for more than the labour of an office cleaner. This is undoubtedly how things actually seem from the point of view of the individual controllers of capital, regardless of the form taken by the capital under their control: a project, an enterprise, a shareholding, a nationalised firm, or whatever. But in fact to take this road is to take our eye off the ball, for the category of value depends on the *generalisation* of exchange and on the category of *abstract* labour (labour in the abstract), and neither of these two categories appear to be of any weight at all in any answer based on the idea that some types of labour are 'intrinsically' more valuable than others. We can only conclude that the question of 'how much value?' should be answered in terms which are much more simple, and we thus arrive at the view that the quantity of value can only be determined by the total number of hours worked, regardless of the specific type and characteristics of the labour expended.

No sooner have we reached this point, however, than objections immediately present themselves. What if a worker twiddles his thumbs all afternoon — surely we do not mean to suggest that hours spent like this can actually contribute to the value of the product? Indeed we do not, and we must therefore introduce the qualification that the labour-time referred to is in fact the *average* labour-time. Clearly what is 'average' in this sense is determined by the class struggle, not only within the workplace but also in the wider society. But for the moment, since we are endeavouring to consider capitalist production as an 'objective' system, this does not stand in the way of the development of the critique.

Another objection rests on the fact that technological change can and does bring about circumstances where the amount of commodities of a given type produced by a given amount of labour-time increases. Of course the new technology is itself a product of abstract labour and therefore injects its own value into the product, but the point of the objection is that the labour-time necessary for the production of a commodity is liable to change. If one firm employs new technology and another employs old technology, our critique would thus seem to lead us to the conclusion that two commodities could have identical exchange-values and use-values but nonetheless contain different quantities of value. This is not, however, the case; and as the individual controller of capital would be likely to agree, what really happens is that the value of the commodities still being produced with the old technology decreases. (Marx 1867, p.318). Thus although the value of the product does not cease to be determined by the average quantity of labour-time, we must make the clarification that what we are referring to is the quantity of labour-time which is *necessary*. Since the context is precisely that of socialised production and socialised labour in their capitalist forms, we can further define this labour-time as that which is 'socially necessary' from the point of view of capital.[6] Thus what happens in the plants using the old technology is that the quantity of socially necessary time worked, considered per individual commodity, falls. And of course the means of social 'necessitation' — and once again we exclude considerations of class struggle — is the same as the means of 'averaging': namely, the generalisation of exchange.

In the second place, generalised exchange can only dominate production if value is able to take a form which is abstracted from specific products: namely, on one hand, from specific exchange-values, including those of specific forces of production, and on the other, from use-value in general. To understand why this is so it is useful to try to imagine a system based on generalised exchange where money was unknown: that is, a system of generalised barter. Clearly in such a system "a mass of swaps would be necessary before one obtained the desired article in exchange." (Marx 1885, p.215). Someone wanting a swimsuit, for example, might first find themselves constrained to exchange a table for a sack of potatoes. The point now is that for all sorts of possible reasons — delay in organising a new swap, for example — she might eventually decide to cook the potatoes and eat them, thereby destroying their exchangeability. Since she would have known all along that she might find reason to do this, the initial act of exchange would have been determined not simply by considerations of exchange-value but also by those of use-value. More generally, the strength of the ties which bonded an object's exchangeability to its use-value would make the process of obtaining the 'desired article' extremely cumbersome; and whilst one might posit exchange relations as striving to dominate the entire process of circulation, they would in actual fact find themselves restricted by cords of use-value at every step of the way. In practice such a system — which has not been actualised — would be insufficient to allow exchange to achieve full generalisation.[7]

We therefore see that the generalisation of exchange depends upon the functional existence of a *general equivalent*.[8] In an early stage of the development of exchange this can, of course, take the form of cattle or shells or any specially chosen material commodity, but historically the commodity owners experience a growing need for the spread of a simpler form. This form, the money-form, is general insofar as it represents pure exchangeability: in itself it has no use-value.[9] The principle — although later we shall see it to be modified in practice — is simple: anything can be exchanged for money, and anything else can be bought with the money acquired. Money is the form which enables commodities to compete with each other in a generalised way; it mediates their exchange; and it functions as a special commodity of its own type which allows the social averaging and generalised abstraction that define the categories of abstract labour and value in the first place. Money is "the bond of all bonds" (Marx 1932, pp.122-23); it "represents the form of social relations; it represents, sanctions and organises them." (Negri 1979, p.23).

Value Growth

On the basis of this understanding of value and money our next concern is to deepen our understanding of growth in its specifically capitalist form. We know, of course, that value is what is produced by abstract labour; and that from the viewpoint of the controllers of production the aim of production is the production of value: or, more precisely, of additional value. But what we must now ask is how the production of new value — that is, the growth of value — actually occurs.

It would appear that we are faced straightaway with a major theoretical problem. Given that labour-power and the means of production are themselves commodities, and must therefore have their own value, what can it actually mean to say that labour *produces* value? Surely if labour has its own value then all it does is to inject that value into the product, alongside the value drawn from the accumulated labour embodied in the means of production? And if this is so, then is the creation of new value not simply impossible? Another way to make this point is to argue that since value is determined by average socially-necessary labour-time, then the value of, say, forty hours of (concrete) labour can only properly be defined as being, on average, forty hours of (abstract) labour-time. We would appear to be left with a near-tautology.

This line of reasoning is unsound, however, insofar as it is based on an inadequate definition of concepts. Thus the controllers of capital do not in fact purchase the workers' labour: what they do is to exploit it, which is quite a different matter. Indeed, since it only exists as a process of exertion or 'expenditure' the workers never actually possess it and are therefore in no position to sell it in the first place. In terms of bourgeois economics, it is not a stock but a flow. A crucial distinction must therefore be made between labour and the *ability* to labour, where the former is the expenditure of the latter. Closer examination shows that it is the latter which is bought and sold, rather than labour itself, which is rather the use which the controllers of capital derive from what they have bought. And the value of this ability, of labour-*power*, is far less problematic. As Marx puts it, it

> is determined, as in the case of every other commodity, by the labour-time necessary for the production, and consequently also the reproduction, of this specific article. (Marx 1867, p.274)

We thus arrive at the categories of *necessary labour-time*, or the socially-averaged portion of the working day which is spent producing the goods consumed by proletarians, bought with wages, and which in being consumed reproduce the workers' labour-power; and, on the other hand, the remaining portion of labour-time, or *surplus labour-time*, which the environment of capitalist domination forces proletarians to give to the controllers of capital for free. Since we are not comparing these periods for each individual worker, but rather assuming a context of generalised social averaging by means of exchange, we see that the surplus produced in the hours of unpaid labour must itself take a value form. And since this value does not replenish existing value — either in the form of the abilities of the producers or in the form of the material means of production — it can only be the newly-created value whose production we are endeavouring to explain. As the form of surplus determined by generalised exchange — in the sense that includes the exchange of labour-power for the wage — the category of surplus value brings us close to an understanding of the very essence of capitalism.

There is, however, one remaining gap in our understanding of the growth of value. In effect, we have considered only a single 'moment' of production, wherein new value is produced. If this new value were simply consumed by the controllers of capital — as 'revenue' — then clearly it would cease to exist once they had consumed it. Since the controllers of capital, unlike workers, are not productive, their consumption does not help in the reproduction of labour-power. Surplus value would certainly have been produced, but value would grow only fleetingly before shrinking back to its original magnitude. This type of growth is not the actual growth of a more lasting kind which capitalist competition necessitates once it becomes generalised. To understand this latter growth in value terms we must therefore look not at a single moment of production, but rather at the entire cycle of production and accumulation.

The process by which growth becomes realised is not, then, the production of surplus value, although that is of course a necessary requirement; rather, it is the *reinvestment* of surplus value. What we must now consider is how that reinvestment can come about: its functional prerequisites in addition to surplus value production. In relation to the underlying drive for profitable growth — a drive determined by the category of generalised exchange, but not reducible to it — we see immediately that what is indispensable is *money*. This is not a different category of money from the one we have considered above as a 'general equivalent,' but the function it fulfils is no longer simply the permitting of generalised exchange: it now has the additional function of permitting growth on that basis. In other words, it does not simply permit the existence of the category of value; it also permits the expansion of value from one production cycle to the next. The capitalist role of money can now be understood at a deeper level. It is not necessary merely to allow self-expanding value — which is how we define *capital* — to be assessable and accumulable by its controllers. It is necessary too — crucially so in terms of the underlying growth drive — to allow it to be *investible*. It is thus in the nature of capital, and not just of value, that it is able to appear not only in the form of commodities, but also in the form of a general equivalent: namely, as money. (See especially Marx 1867, pp.247-57). In Volume 2 of *Capital* Marx presents this point as follows.

> As money capital, [capital] exists in a state in which it can perform monetary functions, in the present case the functions of general means of purchase and payment.... [But] money capital does not possess this capacity because it capital, but because it is money.
>
> On the other hand, the capital value in its monetary state can perform only monetary functions, and no others. *What makes these into functions of capital is their specific role in the movement of capital,* hence also the relationship between the stage in which they appear and the other stages of the capital circuit. In the present case, for instance, money is converted into commodities [that is, means of production and labour-power — NCF] which in their combination constitute the natural form of productive capital; this form therefore already bears latently within it, as its possibility, the result of the capitalist production process. (1885, p.112) (emphasis added)

Thus those who control the extraction of the portion of the product in excess of what is bought with wages — who in fact, since the extraction of a surplus in a value form is the basis of the capitalist mode of production, also control production *tout court* — require the generalisation of a *means* by which profits can first be assessed and then reinvested so as to generate more profits as efficiently as possible. They need to be able to answer such questions as these: was our last investment profitable? How profitable? Would such-and-such a future investment be likely to be profitable? How profitable? If they could not answer such questions they could hardly control capital in any viable way.[10] Thus the money form of capital is not simply the medium of generalised exchange: it is also the form that all value must adopt in order to expand. As a generalised form it might be described as determining a 'language' — enforced by the armed power of the law — which facilitates the exploiters' reinvestment of surplus value according to their own best interests. Its main locus of existence is outside of the production process but within the social production *cycle*, the accumulation cycle, the growth of value. The predominance of the capitalist mode of production thus requires that not only the commodity but also money adopt a specifically capitalist form.

It is instructive at this point to recall that money, just like the commodity, existed prior to capitalism. As Marx points out in the famous "Introduction" to his *Contribution to the Critique of Political Economy* (1903),[11] it is older even than banks and wages. But it is precisely one of those categories which,

> despite their validity — precisely because of their abstractness — for all epochs, are nevertheless, in the specific character of this abstraction, themselves likewise a product of historic relations, and possess their full validity only for and within these relations. (p.105)

Aware, then, that historical theoretical critique must be more than just a linear tracing of specific categories through time, Marx stresses that

> in all forms of society there is one specific kind of production which predominates over the rest, whose relations thus assign rank and influence to the others. It is a general illumination which bathes all the other colours and modifies their particularity. It is a particular ether which determines the specific gravity of every being which has materialized within it.

It follows that in formulating a theoretical critique of capitalism it would be quite

> unfeasible and wrong to let the economic categories follow one another in the same sequence as that in which they were historically decisive. Their sequence is determined, rather, by their relation to one another in modern bourgeois society, which is precisely the opposite of that which seems to be their natural order or which corresponds to historical development. (p.107)

And in capitalist society, the predominant 'kind of production' is the production *and realisation* of additional or surplus value: or, in other words, of capital. Money is not just money: it is capitalist money.[12]

The reason for quoting these passages is to show that the theorisation of money can easily reach a dead-end if the wrong kind of meaning is ascribed to the fact that Marx starts *Capital* with a critique of the commodity and only later moves to a critique of money. (1867, chaps.1-3). After all, it is not in dispute that when money first appeared on the scene its main function was to expedite efficient barter; nor that, even much later, it was still both a means of circulation (a medium of exchange) and an 'ideal' measure of value (real or imaginary gold, for example). (pp.188-90). Since Marx does not begin by discussing money, and since money itself, in a certain sense, is even now a special kind of commodity, it might be argued that even in capitalist society the commodity is more 'basic' than money. In other words, it might be suggested that the adoption of a value form by money is no more than a special case of the adoption of a value form by the commodity, and hence needs little additional explanation.

It therefore needs to be emphasised especially strongly that once the theory becomes a general critique of capitalist society, money is understood to join the commodity as a second form of a more general category, the category of *capital*. It is this latter category which is determinant of the entire nature of capitalist society and of its various political-economic categories. Considering the circuit of capital as a whole, Marx thus writes that

> all the premises of the process appear as its result, as premises produced by the process itself. Each moment appears as a point of departure, of transit, and of return. (1885, p.180)

In short, capital is neither a form of the commodity nor a form of money: rather, the capitalist commodity-form and the capitalist money-form are themselves moments of capital, of self-expanding value. And it is in this context that Marx writes in the *Grundrisse* of money's "third attribute," which "presupposes the first two and constitutes their unity." (1939, pp.216). It is not simply the general form of access to resources, a "precondition of circulation as well as its result." (p.217). It is the "*direct* object, aim and product of general labour." (p.224). It is the "material representative of general wealth" and indeed the "general form of wealth." (p.221).[13]

It is at this overall and general level that the specifically capitalist function of capitalist money is best understood: capital's drive to enlarge itself appears as the drive on the part of each of its controllers to enlarge the capital under their control; and this determines the adoption not just by each portion of capital, but by wealth in general, of a monetary form. In particular what must be grasped is the interaction of the categories of the capitalist commodity and capitalist money in the framework not simply of productive capital, but of the entire cyclical production relation of which this is a necessary moment. In this context the letter 'C' is used to denote not the category of the 'simple' commodity, but rather that of the productive forces as commodity. Under this heading are counted not only the material means or objective conditions of production (namely, instruments of production plus raw materials, or fixed plus circulating capital), but also the subjective conditions of labour (namely, purchased labour-power 'expressing itself purposively'). (Marx 1933, pp.979-81). The capitalist commodity can thus be defined as the form of capital which necessarily embodies a concrete use-value. (And we stress again that this includes labour-power). Correspondingly, its categorial counterpart, capitalist money, or 'M', can certainly be described negatively as the form of capital which has no use-value at all apart from its exchangeability. But that is not yet a definition. Whilst definable classically as a means of circulation, a medium of exchange,[14] and a measure of value, money is best defined critically in direct relation to the cycle of capital. It is *the mediating form which capital necessarily adopts to allow its drive for expansion to dominate its investment.*[15] In other words, it is a necessary component of what Marx saw as the "general formula for capital": M-C-M´, or money-commodity-more money. (1867, chap. 4). If, as Marx puts it,

> capital is, as we have seen, M-C-M[´], i.e. value valorizing itself, value that gives birth to value (1933, p.1060)

then money is essentially *a form of capital corresponding to a function.* This function involves the representation of wealth, but that is still an inadequate definition. The specific capitalist function is that of the determination of profitability (and the assessment of hypothetical future profitability) in a sphere outside of the immediate relations of production so as to ensure (considerations of working class struggle aside[16]) that productive investment decisions can continue to be made in accordance with the systemic logic of value expansion, manifesting itself as the drive for profit maximisation.

It should now be clear that the aim of capitalist production cannot be defined merely as the accumulation of money by its controllers. Nor can it be defined as their accumulation of the productive forces. Rather, and more simply, it is the accumulation of capital and the growth of capital's dominion over the productive forces both material and human. It might be said that capital is its own aim.

Our fuller definition of capitalism can be summarised as follows. First, products must be *commodities*, presupposing both privative appropriation and exchange. In other words, they must have exchange-value as well as use-value. Second, labour-power must also be a commodity. In other words, human production must take the form of *wage-labour*, which implies the existence both of a dispossessed class and of those who exploit it. And third, as exchange and the drive for *profitable production* (that is, the accumulation of exchange-value) become generalised, the self-expanding exchange-value which is now self-expanding value, or capital, requires the generalisation of a form in which it can exist apart from that of the commodity and outside of the immediate process of production. The extraction of surplus value and the *accumulation of capital* thus require, as both functional prerequisite and result, the existence of *capitalist money*.

BUREAUCRATIC CAPITALISM IN THE USSR

The issue now becomes: did these categories exist or were they absent in the USSR? Taking them in turn, we shall argue that they did exist, and that consequently the USSR was a capitalist country. The main theoretical advance will concern the nature of capitalist money and the rejection of the confusion caused by its identification with its currency-denominated forms.

Bureaucratic Exchange-Value

The question as to whether or not there were commodities in the USSR should be dealt with in relation to three areas which for analytical purposes can be set out as follows: consumption, distribution, and production.[17]

Consumption

Taking first the sphere of consumption, it is readily apparent that there were many, many goods which the vast majority of the population could only receive in exchange for roubles and kopeks. It is well known, of course, that people used various sorts of connections and information networks to find out when and where certain goods were on offer, to establish a place in the queue or to queue-jump, and to arrange barter deals; but it is hardly disputable that if a worker received rouble notes in his pay-packet and had to give some of them away each day in return for bread, then that bread took the form of a commodity. This would be so regardless of any effects which State subsidies may have had on its price or the shortage of potential substitutes on the level of demand. Similar statements can be made in relation to other goods and services, from apples and armchairs to toys and train tickets. It is equally well known that such 'consumer items' as domestic heating bills were considerably cheaper relative to, say, cars, than they are in a country such as the United Kingdom; but this too is hardly a relevant issue when we are endeavouring to focus upon the overall form of the social consumption relation. Of slightly more relevance is the fact that quite a large number of urban workers grew at least some of their food on individual allotments (*uchastki*); but even in this connection it has to be added that *in toto* this form of gardening was hardly of great political-economic importance. The fact of the matter is that even when goods were on ration proletarians either paid cash or went without.[18] Thus it is not seriously deniable that the basic relationship was one of purchase and sale. Some, including many rich western travellers to the USSR, may have perceived roubles as being 'worthless,' but this was not the reality lived by the Soviet working class. The restricted availability, even to those proletarians who had saved up enough roubles, of some of the consumer goods available on advanced western high streets is not the point; nor are the special shops for the elite. The point is that in the overwhelming majority of cases, goods passed from retailer to consumer only on condition that roubles passed from consumer to retailer; and in no way was this condition a mere formality.

Distribution

The second area to be considered is that of the distribution of materials and goods prior to end-user consumption. As well as the movement of materials and semi-finished goods from one productive enterprise to another, this also includes the wholesale distribution of finished goods from enterprises to warehouses.

Producer Goods   Concentrating first on the movement of producer goods, we see that the crucial point which needs to be addressed is not that prices were fixed bureaucratically, but that unlike in the retail part of the wage goods sector they did not determine the flow of goods.[19] A crude comparative model would be as follows: a worker without cash would not be able to take a loaf of bread from a shop unless she stole it; but an enterprise director with the requisite combination of official seniority and unofficial influence and connections could ensure the delivery of the supplies he needed and then leave the corresponding flow of bank holdings to be adjusted accordingly with minimal fuss. (Since legal considerations are not paramount, we are not especially interested here in whether the exercise of influence is legal or 'para-legal'; or, if it is 'para-legal,' to what extent it is really determined by official rank). Of course such a model of distribution remains rudimentary, since it cannot account for phenomena such as dysfunctional inflation (A. Smith 1983, pp.106-15) and the black market (Parry 1966, Grossman 1977, Katsenelinboigen 1977, O'Hearn 1981, Simis 1982[20]), which indicate that even in this area considerations of rouble price did play some sort of a role, and the functioning of roubles as 'active money' was not altogether non-existent; but it does serve as an adequate starting-point for the centring of attention on the type of decision-making which predominated in this particular area of the economic system.

It is hardly controversial to note that decisions as to the actual delivery of industrial supplies, as differentiated from paper intentions, were subject to two main formative influences. The first of these was, of course, the enterprise 'plan.' Rather than delving into the intricacies of the relations between enterprise management, industrial ministries and their *glavki* (departments), the dedicated planning authorities, the Politburo, and the Central Committee's economics departments, we are concerned above all to emphasise the role of the plan and the nature of its formulation in terms of the overall social production relations. In this connection the most salient point is that there was never a completely hard and fast item called the 'plan,' according to which all enterprises obtained and supplied a range of goods in strict accordance with a set of instructions passed to them at the beginning of each period. Even if the principal summary documents of the national Plan took the form of laws passed by the Supreme Soviet, in practice "as soon as the process of confirming individual plans [was] completed an extensive process of adjusting plans immediately [began]." (Wilhelm 1979, p.270). The various parts of each plan were then subject to a process of substantial and repeated revision. And since even current operational plans were very rarely drafted on time, for present purposes we can describe the plan revision process as effectively continuous.

As a result, the details of the process of supply were not determined simply by the successive requirements of the fulfilment of long-term planned contracts. In actuality, repeated changes in formal plans, together with the consequent late communication of relevant instructions, meant that in the course of each year the supply allocation organs had constantly to try to cope with endemic disequilibria and misallocations. This they did by issuing instructions according to pragmatic expediency. (See for example Nove 1980b, pp.43-45). The process of supply was highly disorganised.

It is known, of course, that supply plans were calculated according to underlying considerations of 'material balance,' which stipulated that inputs were to be matched with outputs rather than specifying every last detail of each receiving enterprise's exact requirements. But even in this more general context the constraints on information processing led the drawing up of balances to be completed for aggregate categories of goods rather than for specific products. (Rutland 1985, p.116).[21] Such a system was hardly able to erode the famous significance which gross output targets enjoyed within each enterprise; nor could it do much about the lack of an efficient system of incentives for the managers of one enterprise to be materially interested in meeting the full and detailed supply requirements of the managers of another. And so even the use of superficially sophisticated 'input-output' calculating techniques did not prevent the elements of 'planning' in the distribution of industrial supplies from operating in a highly mishmash and stop-go fashion.

The real role of the 'plan' in determining distribution decisions can be summarised as a matter, firstly, of bureaucratic bargaining during the plan revision process (that is, in effect, all the time); and secondly, of bureaucratic bargaining between enterprises and planning authorities to smooth over gaps (which is hardly even 'planning' with inverted commas.) And in fact, as Nove bluntly concludes, the main reason that complete chaos was avoided was that "most enterprises produce this year more or less the same things as they did last year." (1980b, p.45).

The other contributory factor in the determination of supply decisions was that which operated not simply in the interstices of even the most efficiently revised formal plan, but also with little or no reference to the planning authorities at all. This was the informal factor, defined by the unofficial links connecting enterprise managers both with each other and with various categories of suppliers. Usually these links were mediated by *tolkachi*, the much commented-upon roving representatives hired by enterprise managers to procure materials, parts, and equipment wherever they could and through whatever channels were necessary. As Berliner has described, by disposing of good connections with officials working in wholesale purchasing and allocation organs, and indeed in the supply departments of other enterprises, *tolkachi* played an indispensable role in ensuring the delivery of supplies to the enterprises for which they worked. (1957, chap.11).[22] Indeed a Gossnab *nariad* (supply chit) appears essentially to have been a 'hunting licence' granted to a manager setting out on the search for supplies. (See Rutland 1985, p.130). The American business theorist Weitzman has accurately likened the necessary 'brazenness' of such 'pushers' of an enterprise management's interests to the qualities expected of successful salesmen in the West. (1984, pp.36-37). Others might think of the role of 'fix-it men' in western public authorities, disposing of all the right connections in the relevant supply and maintenance departments, and able to ease the delivery of the required goods or a visit by the required service engineers. But analogies aside, the important role which such people played, their need of good personal connections, and their consummate skill in putting themselves forward and spotting openings, are well known.

The most important point to be grasped in relation to the *tolkachi* is that the kind of inter-enterprise relations which they mediated were in no way 'accidental' to the Soviet system of industrial distribution. Such relations were, rather, an inherent part of the system, for without the 'lubricating' role of the *tolkach* the administrative-command system would have faced insuperable difficulties in restarting production after each breakdown. (Rutland 1985, pp.128-33). Conversely, if the system had been replaced with one completely dominated by the drive for rouble profits, then Soviet suppliers would have been far less willing to hand over materials to a particular *tolkach* unless he or she could be relied upon to pay more than all the others who were trying to obtain the same materials. Hence the role of the *tolkach* would have been quite different from what it actually was in a system where the flow of roubles was not the main problem for either supplier or receiver.

But that is not all. Once we recall that the nature of Soviet 'planning' was inseparable from the twin processes of plan formulation and plan revision — which are also inseparable from each other — we notice that during these processes enterprise managers were themselves called upon to exercise bargaining skills which were highly redolent of those exercised by the *tolkachi*. (Berliner 1957, pp.224-27). The justification is thus all the greater for concluding that the distribution of producer goods in the USSR had a unified nature which was not reducible to aspects such as 'command' and 'administration.'

This is certainly not to deny the fact that there was a hierarchy; nor that information really was aggregated by Gosplan and Gossnab; nor that those who set targets and then handed them down from on high did indeed possess a degree of power; nor that an important role was played by the highly efficient prioritisation (*qua* prioritisation) of heavy industry, military production, and specific 'showcase' projects. But what we are arguing is that the characteristics of the distribution system, rather than constituting successes of 'planning,' are surely evidence of a playing out of political-economic determinations which were not themselves either planning or conducive to planning. In other words, the essence of the system was not the *successful achievement* of interconnected objectives set priorly and considered to represent the collective needs and desires of a social group (or of everyone). The fundamental nature of the distribution system was not what was superficially apparent at the level of its formal organisational environment. To put the same point differently: the political-economic role of the plan in determining the nature of the Soviet distribution process should not be understood on its own, but only in terms of an overall form of which it was one part, the role of plan revision was another part, and the role of the *tolkach* was a third part. It is necessary to understand that at bottom this overall form was one in which the process of *bargaining* was intrinsic. And the primacy of bargaining among those who benefited from privative appropriation clearly implies that the relations of distribution took the form of relations of exchange.

Consumer Goods Wholesaling   This last statement is equally applicable to the wholesale distribution of consumer goods, albeit in a slightly different way. The special characteristics of this category of distribution lie both in the role played by 'planning' and in the other mediating forms of competition. Thus as M. Goldman has observed in regard to plan revision,

> since consumers' goods are generally not used as components in the production of other goods, [...] feedback or readjustment of all material balances is usually not necessary in the allocation of consumers' goods. If wants are greater than supply, the frequent solution is to send the available goods where the need is most critical. (1963, p.57)

This evidently goes some way[23] to explaining why shortages were even more chronic in the consumer sector than elsewhere in the economy. On the other hand, though, after the end of the 1950s a substantial part was played in distribution by the bargaining which took place at wholesale fairs. As Skurski has shown, these fairs fell into two types. The first was the "contract" fair, designed to expedite the signing of contracts by pre-decided partners, as part of the planning process. The second was the "surplus goods" or "purchase and sale" fair, organised to help reduce unforeseen stock surpluses and deficits. This latter type functioned by allowing a high degree of competition among buyers and sellers, wherein the rouble played an 'active' mediating role. (Skurski 1970, pp.176-91; see also Goldman 1963, pp.198-200).

Given that in 1953 the wholesaling system was removed from the remit of the *glavki* of the various industrial ministries and placed instead under that of the Ministry of Trade, the holding of fairs of this second type is perhaps not especially surprising. (Skurski 1970, pp.162-66). Since the greater proportion of the cash receipts paid into Gosbank were deposited through the wholesale trade network, to a large extent there now arose an institutional as well as a functional differentiation between, on one hand, the receipt of new monies, and on the other, the transfer of monies between accounts held by industrial enterprises. And since the role of the rouble in retailing, as mentioned above, was real rather than merely nominal, it was now fitting that its role was to some degree enhanced in what was, in effect, the next stage of the economic circuit.

Production

We have not, however, yet reached the stage of grasping the full significance of these observations regarding resource distribution, and in order to do so it is now necessary to consider the third area, that of social production strictly defined. Whether the Soviet economy was fundamentally a commodity economy or whether in some subtle way it fell short of being one in the full sense, we need to pay special attention to this sphere in particular in order to achieve an understanding of the whole. In Marx's words,

> exchange is merely a moment mediating between production with its production-determined distribution on one side and consumption on the other, but in so far as the latter itself [consumption] appears as a moment of production, to that extent is exchange obviously also included as a moment within the latter [production].

And, as he continued:

> it is clear, firstly, that the exchange of *activities and abilities* which takes place within production itself belongs directly to production and essentially constitutes it. The same holds, secondly, for the exchange of *products*, in so far as that exchange is the means of finishing the product and making it fit for direct consumption. To that

extent, exchange is an act comprised within production itself. Thirdly, the so-called exchange between *dealers and dealers* is by its very organization entirely determined by production, as well as being itself a producing activity.... [emphasis added].

The conclusion we reach is not that production, distribution, exchange and consumption are identical, but that they all form the members of a totality, distinctions within a unity.... (1903, p.99)

We should, therefore, expect Soviet production to show at least some of the same characteristics as Soviet exchange-based distribution. But at the same time, in looking at production we shall be seeking to shed additional light on the nature of the entire political economy.

The question now becomes: did the Soviet productive forces and products take a commodity form? If they did, in what way did they do so? And what were the specific implications for the nature of an economic system which undoubtedly differed considerably from, say, one based on the drive for dollar profits? Clearly to answer this last question fully we shall have to discuss the overall nature of Soviet political economy, and this indeed is the subject of the present chapter as a whole. Since, however, we shall discuss the nature of labour and the nature of accumulation in other sections below, for the time being we can limit our attention to a consideration of the form of distribution of the instruments of production, and therefore — in fact inseparably — of the form of the product which the use of those instruments gave rise to.

The Means of Production   It is worth recalling at the outset that whatever form the appropriation of the productive forces in the USSR actually took, it was most definitely privative. Thus however fuzzy or broad or apparently tortuous the line might have been between low-level bureaucrats who were essentially wage-workers and low-level bureaucrats who disposed of a small degree of de facto control over the productive forces and other people's labour, it is quite clear that the workers were exploited by a social layer or conglomeration of social layers which stood above them and disposed of the material means of production. It evidently was not the workers who decided that a processing or manufacturing plant should be built; or where, when, and to what end; or what it should process or produce; or in what quantities, of what specifications, or at what speed. The material means of production were disposed of instead by those who exploited the labour of others and who were unproductive themselves. On one side, there was the relation of alienated labour; on the other, there was the control over the conditions under which that labour was expended. Equally evidently, whatever the rate might have been of workplace 'theft' — and whatever degree of institutional rivalry prevailed among senior officials of the three main 'pillars' of the State: the Party, the Army, and the KGB — the exploiters as a whole maintained considerable reserves of force to keep the material means of production under their control. The control over the means of production was protected from the workers by force.

The consideration of the distribution of the means of production among those who did control them can now be split into two parts. First, there is the question of the form which the control over the means of production actually took; and second, there is the question of how the control was distributed and redistributed among those who possessed it.

To answer the first question we must recognise that the occupations which involved varying degrees of control over the productive forces were themselves very varied in kind. Thus, on one hand, from very soon after the coup of October 1917 the principle which governed enterprise management in the State sector — and after the nationalisations and renationalisations which put an end to NEP this included the whole of industry — was the doctrine of 'one-man management' (*edinonachalie*).[24] According to this the pivotal role in operational management was assigned to the enterprise director, whose orders had to be obeyed by everyone beneath him. On the other hand, however, he clearly could not act in whichever way he chose. Firstly, he was answerable to higher-ups in the relevant industrial ministry and its relevant department (*glavk*). Secondly, through them he was also influenced by the decisions made by planning authorities. Thirdly, he was also subject, to some extent at least, to pressure from the secretary of the *partkom* (enterprise committee of the CPSU) and the secretary of the trade union, who himself would probably be a member of the *partkom*. And fourthly, even if the main line of command came down from the ministry, nonetheless enterprise directors were still members of the party's nomenklatura, appointed in practice by *raikom* or *obkom*.[25]

It is equally clear that enterprise directors, ministerial officials, planning officials, *obkom* secretaries, and so on, did not all exercise power in the same fashion. Thus enterprise directors would handle most of the day-to-day running of the enterprises and, crucially, they would be responsible for passing on the information required in the planning process; ministerial officials would try to wring maximum resources out of Gosplan, while simultaneously attempting to indulge in 'empire-building' by running their own supply organs for the enterprises under their remit (Nove 1980b, p.65); Gosplan officials would seek to set targets in accordance with strategic directives set by the Council of Ministers and the Politburo, and to police the plan-revision process; Gossnab officials would try to integrate the supply of ever-short materials; and *obkom* secretaries would exercise patronage in appointing the directors whom they favoured the most.[26]

But if the Soviet political economy had a nature at all then there must be some unifying characteristic running through all these types of exercise of power over the productive forces. And it turns out that there was. Thus, first, bureaucrats of all the types described above exercised power which amounted ultimately to power over the labour of the workers. Ministerial officials trying to exercise a degree of control over supplies, for example, or Gosplan officials trying to control, against considerable obstruction, the objectives of enterprise directors, could only be successful in any way at all so long as the workers were alienating their labour. This does not, of course, mean that the workers were completely passive, since evidently they were not. But the point for the moment is that bureaucratic competition among ministerial officials, Gosplan officials, and enterprise directors, was essentially a matter of the distribution and redistribution of power over the labour of the exploited and over the means of production which that labour made use of, and which indeed it produced.

Second, this power can be traced back in the opposite direction too, and it becomes clear that the power being distributed among the various exploitative officials was the very same power expropriated from the workers in the course of their labour. A ministerial official or a member of the Politburo might have thought that they had conjured some power out of thin air by achieving a dominant position in part of the economy, or by subduing competitors within, say, Gosplan, but in reality, of course, that could not be the case, since bureaucratic in-fighting alone does not increase the power of the economic bureaucracy — or, in a broader sense, the State — vis-à-vis the workers. The Soviet economic bureaucracy was a competitive apparatus in which exploiters fought among themselves for shares in the exercise of alienated power.

The third point is that it was not just accidentally competitive. Given that the workers were exploited, the only alternative forms of State economic system which might imaginably have been based upon a growth drive would have been as follows: one that was totally fragmented, with each controller — each enterprise director, say — having a precisely defined area of control, and communicating with other controllers only in cultural matters generally unconnected with the economy; one completely controlled from the top, where the supreme ruler knew everything he needed to know to formulate orders which denied everyone beneath him any scope for independence or bargaining; or, finally, one based on a fully co-operative collectivity among the rulers.

It is certainly true that autarkic tendencies did surface in various ways at various times in the Soviet economy. An enterprise director, for example, might choose a supplier enterprise located thousands of miles away because it came under the auspices of his own ministerial higher-ups. (Munting 1982, p.134). But this is of course competitive behaviour. Controllers and groups of controllers each possessed only a portion of alienated power, and it was in the nature of the socialised economy that they had to relate to each other in order to retain it: not even a ministry could achieve self-sufficiency. It is also true that there were despotic tendencies, and in a number of ways Stalin can be seen as the industrialising Tsar of the 20th century. But a system totally controlled from the top was always unfeasible. Like Nazism, Stalinism involved the exercise of 'arbitrary' power by hundred of thousands of petty dictators and inhuman 'men of the system,' rather than the omnipotence of an all-seeing dictator. Nor was full co-operative collectivity really a likely objective for those whose entire reason for existence as a group (or set of groups) was exploitative, and who had to defend their positions in the given competitive and hierarchical environment rather than spend time on searching for a wholly collective exploitative solution. Moreover they were continuously set against each other by the difficulty of obtaining accurate information either from the exploited or from their fellow exploiters. Competitiveness was self-reinforcing.

Thus it was in the nature of the system that it did not take any of these forms and instead was bureaucratic. In short, the *interconnectedness* of the economy — of the organisation of scarcity — determined the necessary existence of a *form of competition among those with alienated power.*

The same statement, of course, applies equally well to the economic systems of countries ruled by the bourgeoisie, but in such countries the general rule is the prevalence of a socially and legally enforced 'independence'-based medium for that competition, taking the form of the currency. In other words, a bourgeois with a fund of money can in principle set up shop trading whatever he likes, buy shares or indeed plant from anyone willing to sell them, and bequeathe his money to anyone he especially favours. These freedoms are not, of course, absolute. And there does exist a State bureaucracy which fulfils various functions for the good of the bourgeoisie as a whole, or for a section of it. But where this does not involve direct force over the working class it usually means either the ideological defence of the system of private property; the collective defrayment of bourgeois costs such as the reproduction of adequate numbers of workers or the investment in a transport infrastructure; or indeed the hiving off of tax receipts, or assets bought with such receipts, to favoured bourgeois groups distinct from the increasingly elusive 'national bourgeoisie.' Not only is the State's role in the economy crucially financial — setting interest rates, levying taxes, assigning contracts, borrowing and spending to meet costs — but the over-arching aim of State functioning is the amassing of capital in corporate hands in the alternating forms of means of production and financial accounts.

In the USSR, however, the mediation of competition was nowhere near as fluid (currency-based) as this, and for this reason the 'system' was founded mainly upon the importance of bureaucratic office and effective 'pull.' But this does not mean that these foundations ceased to be a form of such mediation. The functioning of the characteristic mix of manoeuvring, negotiation, bargaining, and bureaucratic diktat, then, was precisely the playing out of the necessary competition among individuals who disposed of alienated power over the productive forces: either close to the ground, as did the enterprise managers, or at one remove, as did the ministerial, Gosplan or *obkom* officials. The fact that it was impossible to draw a line between the official ('first,' 'white,' 'legal') economy and the unofficial ('second,' 'black,' 'illegal') economy (see Katsenelinboigen 1977) illustrates further how competition was the essence of the Soviet system.

The measure of control which each bureaucrat disposed of over the means of production was determined by his efficiency in this competition. Certainly, this competition did not operate in a market form; nor could bureaucrats pass on their portions of control to those whom they individually chose as their successors. Instead, control was passed on through a mixture of bureaucratic appointment and unofficial *blat* distribution, including via the inheritance of privilege and the 'education' system. But bourgeois forms such as market competition[27] and rights of inheritance are not our concern in the present context. We are interested in the underlying relation. The nature of a society is determined by the social production relations: not by a set of property laws, not even by those governing the details of inheritance. And since there was privative appropriation, and there was also competition among bureaucrats (post-holders) each of whom possessed a portion of control over the means of production (and hence over the extraction of the surplus product), then it is clear that this competition was itself neither more nor less than the *system wherein portions of such privatively-appropriated control were exchanged.* And anything exchanged (and mediated through labour) is by definition a commodity.

The Form of the Product   If the distribution of products was competitive then the fact that the distribution of control over the means of production was also competitive should come as no surprise. But the generalised environment of exchange which dominated Soviet production still requires further elucidation. In short, we need to consider what lay behind the *use* of the means of production to put out products. Why, in other words, were things produced?

One property of any Soviet product was that it had a use-value. Regardless of the 'relative' quality of Soviet consumer goods as assessed subjectively in relation to that of non-Soviet consumer goods, all things consumed had a use-value to their consumers as a matter of definition. The use-value of producer goods which were 'productively consumed' in the production of consumer goods is similarly straightforward. In fact, even producer goods consumed in, say, the space sector also had a use-value, since the people who commissioned space projects must have had, to some extent at least, a positive view of their utility (to themselves).[28] And anything with a utility conditioned by its physical characteristics is said to have a 'value in use,' or use-value. The problem with *wasted* use-value is beside the point.

The second aspect of Soviet products was that they had a 'value in exchange,' or exchange-value. To cover briefly the analysis given above: consumer goods were only valuable from the viewpoint of retail officials insofar as they could exchange them for roubles; wholesale goods were valuable to enterprise sales representatives insofar as they received in return either the goodwill of planning officials or a payment in roubles; wholesale goods were valuable to enterprise purchasing executives insofar as they could enhance their *blat* by reducing stoppage time and ensure a greater likelihood of nominal plan fulfilment; producer goods were valuable to *tolkachi* or enterprise directors or other officials insofar as by procuring them or achieving their planned allocation they could maintain or increase their *blat*; and plant and accumulated means of production were valuable to those who controlled them, whether at central ministerial level or from the office of the enterprise director, insofar as official bureaucratic influence and de facto 'pull' could be defended and increased. We can thus summarise by stating that there was another aspect of retail and wholesale consumer goods, goods to be processed, raw materials, and fixed investments which was just as apparent as the utility which they possessed by dint of their physical characteristics. This lay in the fact that those who controlled them could, by ceding their control to other economic agents, enhance their own control, or potential control, over other products or productive forces of a different type or at a later time. And here we have a textbook definition of exchange-value.

All products and productive forces can therefore be said to have had a dual nature which determined their production. On one hand, they were produced because they contained use-value. On the other — and this aspect was the dominant one — they were produced for exchange.

Labour-Power in the USSR: Its Purchase and Sale

The next issue is the question of whether or not labour took the form of wage-labour. In other words: was labour-power bought, or was it expropriated from each worker in some other way?

It is necessary to begin by noticing that there is a very strong apparence that workers did indeed sell their labour-power. Unlike in any previous society, virtually every producer had a 'job,' which meant that she had to work roughly the same hours every day under the supervision of others, make use of means of production controlled by others, and turn out a product for appropriation by others, in return for a wage-packet containing currency notes which she could then spend on things she needed to survive, such as food and clothing. As we have seen, this meant that the worker's consumption was mediated by exchange. Unlike the slave, therefore, she was not reduced to being merely a quasi-mechanical part of the means of production, the feeding and clothing of whom was taken care of by the master. Instead, by dint of being paid wages and being allowed the freedom to shop, she was permitted a certain degree of independence.

Those acquainted with Soviet reality are of course aware of the limitations on consumer choice. Given the endemic consumer shortages and the fact that things were usually snapped up as soon as they appeared, supermarket shelves were often bare. Often products such as toys could only be bought in one place in town. The rate of saving was quite high. Moreover, tenancies were hard to obtain, even if rents and domestic heating were cheap, at least relative to the ratios between wages and prices in western countries. And of course 'connections' were usually required to expedite the prompt purchasing of consumer durables such as cars. But these facts are beside the point, which is that the wage-packet given to the worker in return for her labour-power was real rather than purely nominal.

The onus is thus very much on those who deny the prevalence of wage-labour to prove their case. This, however, they have signally failed to do. Thus Cliff and Ticktin have both advanced arguments at the core of which lies the view that wage-labour was absent because there was no 'real' labour market. (Cliff 1955, pp.202-09; Ticktin 1991c, pp.83-84 and 102-04). In this view, workers were simply assigned placements by a single employer, the State. They had to work, and to work wherever they were told to. Even when they went shopping they received only what had been decided as appropriate for their consumption, in the appropriate amounts. Hence there was no competition for labour and therefore no unemployment. Since the rouble was essentially equivalent to company scrip, both wages and consumer prices functioned merely as a system of differential rationing.

Such an analysis is faulty from the very start. As we have shown above, there was a great deal of competition among the bureaucrats and enterprise directors exercising a degree of power over the productive forces. Indeed, it is quite impossible to consider properly the nature of the Soviet system unless this is recognised for what it was. Of course if one assumes that there was no competition and that 'state ownership' was 'monolithic,' then it does indeed follow that there was no competition for labour resources — but all one has done is to develop an assumption.[29] The non-existence of unemployment, meanwhile, would hardly show the absence of a labour market any more than the globalisation of just-in-time production would show the absence of a car market. And finally, the idea that workers were literally forced to work by 'non-economic' means represents a stretching of the facts, since the phenomenon of voluntary unemployment was not exactly unknown. (Lane 1987, pp.55-58).[30]

In describing above how the bureaucratic system was essentially a field in which portions of control over the productive forces were exchanged, we have concentrated on the control over the material means of production. But it is only necessary to reiterate the point that such control, or power, was derived from labour and essentially exercised over labour, to see that competition among bureaucrats must necessarily have involved competition for labour resources. And if, as seems apparent, workers really were independent of the material means of production and received their wages in return for selling their labour-power, then it follows that insofar as labour was really purchased there must have been a labour market.

There is abundant evidence to show that this deduction concorded with empirical reality. As Buick and Crump have pointed out (1986, pp.73-80) — relying upon the work of Chavance and Sapir — there was a substantial degree of worker-motivated labour turnover. (See the discussion of the works of each of these scholars in Chapter 2 above; see also Lane 1987, chap.3). Managers were actually led to collude with their workforces to secure bonuses in excess of centrally determined formal requirements. (Nove 1980b, pp.210-11; Rutland 1985, p.152). And quite aside from the implications of competition during the plan revision process, there was a notable level of direct competition for labour among individual local enterprises. Not only did enterprises advertise for labour, they also hired many workers at employment bureaux or at the proverbial factory gates. (Lane 1987, pp.50-54; Sapir 1984, p.61). The hoarding of labour, moreover, under conditions of microeconomic labour shortage, was a well-known feature of the economy. (See for example Kornai 1980a, p.256, and Hanson 1986). In reality, then, as Nove has noted, the "forces of supply and demand" were of considerable influence on "actual earnings." (1980b, pp.206-15). If earnings rose so that enterprise directors could tempt or keep workers, then this can only mean that labour-power was being bought.

Finally, it might be argued that even if labour-power was bought and sold, its exchange was nonetheless not 'general,' given the prevalence of the *propiska* (residence permit) system and a certain lack of congruence between official migration policy and the reality of population movement. (See Helgeson 1986). But even this argument will not hold. First, there is undoubtedly an element of class struggle here. A market in labour-power does not have to be absolutely 'free,' and the general rule is that capitalist rulers try to restrict 'unnecessary' workers' movements: both directly, by imposing border controls, and indirectly, by encouraging parochialism and nationalism. Similarly, they have always tried to assist movements which they have considered to be in their own interests. In both areas there is at least some opposition. Second, not only did *all* workers sell their labour-power, but *all* workers were connected to each other through the generalised exchange of the products of their labour as described above. The categories of labour-power and its sale were indeed 'general.' And third, every wage-packet contained roubles, which were acceptable in every shop in the country.

Since the distribution of labour-power, then, just as much as the distribution of the means of production and the distribution of the products of labour, was organised on the basis of generalised exchange, we are now able to state that the mode of production in the USSR was founded upon exchange as a general form.

Production for Profit

Finally, did the USSR know production for profit, and the categories associated with it, namely money and capital accumulation? This question, it seems, is best answered after being split into three parts. First, was the determinant aim of the Soviet economic system the production of a surplus? Second, if so, was the aim, at a more fundamental level, the *accumulation* of a surplus (that is, growth)? And third, if it was, did the surplus take the form of profit, i.e 'more money,' or 'ΔM'?

There can be little doubt that the first two questions should be answered in the affirmative. Even if the emphasis is put on military production, or on the various types of extensive growth which were most evident under Stalin and Khrushchev, it is clear that the aim of Soviet production was not the fulfilment of the needs of the direct producers, but rather production in excess of those needs, in fulfilment of the needs of the exploiters. More than this, it was always apparent that the underlying systemic aim was the development, both quantitative and technological, of the country's productive base. From Stalin's exhortation in 1931 (end backwardness or be crushed) to Khrushchev's speech in 1961 (bury the United States, economically) to Aganbegian's avowal in 1988 (increase overall growth rates, intensively), the official insistence was always on the continued expansion of the economy.

Perhaps the most convincing evidence that this insistence was thoroughly in keeping with the underlying political-economic reality, and therefore with the basis of the Soviet economic system, was the collapse of that system at the turn of the 1990s. Even before Gorbachev was ousted, virtually the whole of the elite — from Yeltsin to the putschists of 19 August 1991[31] — had been converted to the cause of market reform. From a Marxist viewpoint it is therefore self-evident, given that ideas do not determine the course of history, that the 'administrative-command' system was proving dysfunctional *in its own terms*. The system's rulers wanted to change it. By the end of 1990, once even the official rate of growth had fallen below zero (*Narodnoe Khoziaistvo* 1991, p.7; see also Schroeder 1991, p.3 and IMF 1992, p.93), and once the 'pre-crisis situation' which followed the 'times of stagnation' had itself given way to an 'open crisis' — to use the parlance of the Gorbachev period — the Soviet economic system was doomed.

Having shown above that the mode of production was founded upon generalised exchange, we are now able to add that it was also founded upon an underlying drive for growth. It follows that it was capitalism.

Value, Abstract Labour, and Bureaucratic Capitalist Money

The third question is more difficult to answer. Or rather, the implications of the answer are difficult to grasp. Where there is 1) generalised commodity exchange, of both producer and consumer goods, 2) wage-labour, and 3) the production of a surplus whose reinvestment into expanded production is crucial to the system — in other words, where there is capitalism — there must also be money: this is so because money was defined functionally, as the form of capital *by means of which* the controllers of the extraction of the surplus product gauge their returns and reinvest them so as to generate yet more returns. In Marx's words,

> it is impossible to abolish money itself so long as exchange value remains the social form of products. (1939, p.145)

And 'more money' means the same as 'profit'. Given, however, that in much of the economy — and most clearly of all in the producer goods sector — prices expressed in roubles did not fulfil what has been defined as the monetary function, identifying the form which money actually took becomes somewhat problematic.

As we have shown above, the category of capitalist money can only be grasped on the basis of an understanding of the category of capital, and this itself depends on the categories of exchange-value, value, abstract labour, and surplus value. It is therefore necessary to run briefly through these categories with respect to the USSR.

Exchange-value has been shown to be part of the nature of the Soviet product, insofar as those who controlled that product — either in the straightforward sense or in the sense of controlling productive forces — were interested in it in terms of a property which was quite distinct from, and abstracted from, its physical characteristics. This property was nothing other than its exchangeability, by dint of which its existing controllers could give up their present control and receive in return a degree of control over other products or productive forces in due course. To recognise this is by no means to stretch a definition, but rather to pinpoint in ordinary language exactly what exchangeability means. Thus we see that for any particular bureaucrat in the USSR it was not the physical characteristics of the products or productive forces under his control but rather their exchange-values which were his principal concern.

Since labour was socialised through the generalised exchange of privatively appropriated products, including of the labour-power commodity itself, it follows that the production of exchange-value in the USSR was also the production of *value*. Or, in other words, the labour exerted was *abstract labour* in the fullest sense of the term. Similarly, the accumulation of exchange-value by the controllers of the productive forces, on the basis of the exchange-based exploitation of labour, was also the *accumulation of value*; and another word for accumulating value is *capital*.

The issue now arises of what the accumulation of exchange-value — of value — actually amounted to. On one hand, of course, this is straightforward: successful bureaucrats were those who managed to extend their control over increasing portions of the overall social product. On the other, though, it is less so, since in order for exchange-value to be accumulated within a system of generalised exchange it must be able to take a form which is abstracted from the material product. And it is apparent that the only form able to play this role must necessarily have been symbolic. In short, it was whatever representation of *blat* or control which would be recognised by those with whom exchange took place. More simply, one might say that it was a category which unified unofficial *blat* with official influence or 'pull.' Thus if a ministerial bureaucrat, say, agreed to allow an enterprise director a certain quantity of supplies, he would actually be giving up something in addition to the actual supplies, since afterwards he would not, in general, be able to influence other enterprise directors or bureaucrats by claiming to have the power to order delivery of those same supplies. In return for this he might hope, for example, in expectation of making it easier for the given enterprise to meet its nominal targets, to increase his own influence in the ministry, relative to that of his colleagues, underlings, and superiors.[32] And as he increased his recognised influence, his real influence would increase too insofar as his recognised influence was continually invested into the real movement of concrete material goods and resources.

Above we have stressed repeatedly that the sum total of all the bureaucrats' and directors' control over the productive forces could not expand in a vacuum. It was not independent of the use of those productive forces: rather, it was exerted over the labour of waged workers and it derived from the expenditure of that labour. The point must now be made that the generalisation of exchange and exchangeability necessarily determined the 'generality' of a *form* of exchange-value. In other words, the recognition of bureaucratic influence and *blat* — and, in certain circumstances, *blat* was derived from the possession of large quantities of roubles (see Simis 1982) — was spread over the entire country. In view of the real and social interconnectedness of labour and distribution, this recognition should not be theorised as being split up into completely discrete areas of operation.

It is on the basis of this understanding of the categories of the political economy that we must now endeavour to identify in more detail the form of fulfilment of the monetary function. Since we are using Marxist categories in the consideration of a form of money which was assuredly quite different from western or Japanese currency — and indeed not reducible in any way even to the rouble — we must now return to Marx and subtract from his theory of money those characteristics which are possessed only by 'classical' capitalism, so as to leave behind what it is that applies to capitalism in general. As we should expect when attention is turned to the present era, this must also involve going 'beyond Marx.' Since, though, it is not our intention either to exegetise or to revise, we shall limit ourselves here to referring to those of Marx's thoughts on money which seem the most useful in the present context.

It is fundamental, then, that money has no independent existence. Thus in the *Grundrisse* Marx discusses money as a

> symbol [which] presupposes general recognition; it can only be a social symbol; it expresses, indeed, nothing more than a social relation. (1939, p.144)

Much of what was in the *Grundrisse*, of course, found its way into *Capital*. And as if to demonstrate that his use of such terminology was no accident, Marx goes further still in the chapter on money in Volume 1 of *Capital* (1867, pp.188-244), and makes a string of references to mysticism.[33]

> The name of a thing is entirely external to its nature. I know nothing of a man if I merely know his name is Jacob. In the same way, every trace of the money-relation disappears in the money-names pound, thaler, franc, ducat, etc: The confusion caused by attributing a hidden meaning to these cabalistic signs is made even greater by the fact that these money-names express both the values of commodities and, simultaneously, aliquot parts of a certain weight of metal which serves as the standard of money. (p.195)

If we disregard here the implicit reference to gold (which in the chapter under consideration Marx assumes to be identical with the money commodity), and attempt to unpack his reference to kabbalah, we see that Marx is in fact drawing an implicit analogy between money and God, or what might be called the monotheistic God-archetype as it is understood by kabbalists. His use of the concept of 'names' relates directly to the kabbalah, central to which is the idea of the *sephiroth*, conceived of as ten aspects of God in his capacity as Creator (Scholem 1971b, p.1104), and described as the "progressive manifestation of the Names of God." (Scholem 1971a, p.572). The especial importance which kabbalists ascribe to the understanding of sacred names (*Encyclopaedia Judaica*, pp.503-30, 538 and 570-638 passim) thus assists us in deciphering the point of Marx's metaphor. Just as understanding the system of Names helps kabbalists understand the nature of God, so an understanding of the system of currencies helps communist critics of existing society to understand the nature of money. But just as God is not equivalent to a list, sum, or even a system of Names, nor should money be reduced to a list, agglomeration, or even a system of currencies. It is hardly a great jump from Marx's work, then, to emphasise the crucial role played in the determination of the nature of money by its access to "general recognition," rather than its 'manifestation' in the form of a currency. Moving, it adopts forms in order to fulfil its function as one of the two states of capital; but whilst its adoption of forms is necessary, the specific characteristics of those forms, unlike those of the *sephiroth*, are not.

When dealing with 'really-existing' money in his own day — and we should recall that the main geographical focus of his analysis was England — Marx devotes several chapters of what became Volume 3 of *Capital* to the nature and role of *credit*. If it is impossible for those working in the Autonomist school to agree with Marx that

> [the credit system] is the abolition of the capitalist mode of production within the capitalist mode of production itself,...which presents itself *prima facie* as a mere point of transition to a new form of production (1894, p.569),

a critical understanding of credit is nonetheless found to be crucial to an understanding not just of money in general, but of 'really-existing' money. Among the functions of credit the equalisation of the rate of profit and the acceleration of circulation certainly feature very large (pp.566-67), but what we want to emphasise here is the nature of the relevant decision-making relations. With the development of the credit system money does not cease, of course, to be a "symbol presupposing general recognition": but what does occur is the growth of an entire structure, or system, wherein controllers of the extraction of the surplus product — more specifically, controllers of money and controllers of means of production — negotiate and agree upon *conditions* for the circulation and investment of large amounts of money. Of course bankers only lend money when they think they are assured of a monetary return, but above all we wish to focus on the type of bargaining involved. Bearing in mind the crude view which we are opposing — that capitalist bargaining always involves, necessarily and at every point, currency-mediated market relations — let us take the case in which such relations are perhaps as blatant as they can possibly be: namely, that of the direct placement of an investment banker onto a client company's board of directors. In such a case it is clear that the banker participates in a very straightforward fashion in making decisions designed to maximise the debtor company's profits. But even in this context we would emphasise that his initial appointment to a directorship must primarily have been a way of persuading the bank to lend more money, or longer-term, or at lower rates. Thus there is still a relationship between the company and the bank such that the company tries to borrow money on as favourable terms as possible and the bank tries to lend it according to its own independent assessment of likely risks and returns. Whilst of course the interests of company and bank overlap, they do not quite coincide, and it is inevitable that the company will massage information, seek goodwill, and indeed haggle, on a personal level. We do not wish to deny that in this example the end aim of all of the controllers of capital involved remains the amassment of value mensurable in currency terms; but it is still the case that the workings of capitalist competition make personal connections among exploiters and the underhandedness associated with such connections appear in such a way that considerations of currency do not dominate in *direct* fashion every little move, communication of information, deal, and decision that is made. Faced with otherwise equivalent reports on two rival companies, a banker might well lend to someone he knows best. At this level money, whose functions are necessarily derived from its role in the M-C-M′ cycle — the capitalist accumulation of productive forces and more generally the accumulation of capital — is thus inextricably bound up with personal connections and 'weight'. And since generally speaking the banker to whom we have been referring is most likely to be a salaried official rather than a part-owner of the bank, there is a second point which is even more illuminatory. Faced with two equivalent reports, then, a banking executive can hardly fail to be influenced by the knowledge that the chairman of one of the companies under consideration is actually a friend of one of his own superiors at the bank, and might therefore be able to help his own advance up the career ladder. This will, of course, mean a higher salary, but we arrive nonetheless at the general point that really-existing credit money is inevitably bound up with considerations of office, with bureaucracy.[34]

Such a recognition assists us enormously in identifying 'money as money' in the Soviet system, where, of course, economic bureaucracy was of considerably greater weight than it has been in the countries of 'classical' capitalism. We have argued at length above that Soviet economic bureaucracy was essentially a system wherein portions of control over labour-power, labour, the product, and the productive forces in general — portions taking the form of permission, clout and *blat* — were negotiated, exchanged, and, crucially, invested in production with the aim of accumulation. It was not simply a system wherein bureaucrats created posts and titles and then shuffled them around, without any bearing on labour, the exploitation of labour, and the growth of the social product. Bearing in mind Marx's warning to be wary of attributing too much significance to currencies, we should not, therefore, be afraid to look elsewhere than the rouble economy for the form taken by the money-relation, especially in the Soviet producer goods sector. Indeed, such a step is directly implied by Dunayevskaya's astute distinction between apparent Soviet 'profit' and the actual profit relation of the Soviet capital circuit. (See Chapter 2 above). If in western capitalism the credit system takes the form of a sphere of bargaining of which certain characteristics are inevitably bureaucratic, and which corresponds to a form of money (credit), then in the Soviet context it makes sense to see Soviet economic bureaucracy as corresponding to a form of money too, namely bureaucratic clout, influence, permission, and *blat*. The western-style overall domination by considerations of currency-denominated accumulation was absent, but the essential domination of capital underlying this was not: namely, by the cycle of accumulating value, taking the alternate forms of productive forces and *the representation of control over such forces manifested in portions which were necessarily and generally bargainable.* Once we see that in large-scale circulation money itself took a form which was principally bureaucratic, we have solved the riddle.[35] What in the West plays a certain role in mediating the rule of money-capital in its currency form, without being reducible to a 'case' of its taking that form, was thus in the USSR the principal form that money-capital actually took. The fact that power over the productive forces (pull) did not appear as different from its own representation (recognised pull) was merely an example of the false consciousness produced by the political economy: in the course of the actual cycle of the expanded reproduction of value, and more specifically the processes of bureaucratic bargaining and exchange — the specific forms of capitalist competition — the distinction and interplay between these two categories was crucial.

We wish to make it clear that in presenting this understanding we are not suggesting that capitalist money in the USSR was largely 'non-quantitative.' Since the nature of money-capital is determined by its fulfilment of a role functional to the *growth* of capital, clearly it must permit the controllers of capital to recognise whether or not their capital has grown. It must also allow them to recognise by how much it has grown. Both considerations are quantitative. But the key point is that a generalised basis for such assessment need not necessarily involve the assignment of a number to each 'result of production,' followed by the name of a currency. What is crucial is the generalised basis of quantitative comparison, not the 'numericality' of such a basis: that is, not the assignment of numbers and exact ratios to each individual result and comparison. The answer to the question 'How much profit?' might be 'A lot' or 'Not as much as last time' or 'Enough to curry as much favour as I expected' or 'Slightly less than my competitor got' or 'Not quite enough to allow me to have a new plant built, unless my competitor does much worse than before.' By aiding the exploiters in the making of subjective investment decisions the interconnectedness of such quantitative assessments — their shared 'language' — serves its function for the exploitative class as a whole: for self-expanding value as subject. Under market conditions the standardisation of numerical 'language' makes the general and quantitative nature of the basis of assessment immediately apparent, whereas money in the form of *blat*/bureaucratic office can often leave its own generalised, quantitatively-comparative nature somewhat more obscure. But in fact the basis is general and quantitative in both cases and in being so is functional to capital as subjectivity.

There is, perhaps, one last ditch which the defenders of a 'non-capitalist' position might wish to defend against this theory. This is the argument that as a "symbol presupposing general recognition," Soviet bureaucratic money was rather more 'fractured' than the pounds, dollars and yen which are moved around within the world credit system, to such an extent that the 'generality' of recognition as an equivalent should be put into question. Hence whereas in, say, the United States a million dollars might realistically be transferred from a current account to stocks in a South African goldmine, the portion of *blat* money held by the Kazakh Republic's Minister of Industrial Construction was not exchangeable in any realistic sense for anything at all even in the Moscow transport sector, let alone anything in South Africa.

Of course there are two objections here: the first relating to exchangeability within the USSR, the second relating to the question of 'world money.' Both, though, are in fact resolvable in quite simple terms. With reference to the first, we would cite Marx's statement in a seldom quoted footnote in Volume 1 of *Capital* that

> it is by no means self-evident that the form of direct and universal exchangeability is an antagonistic form, as inseparable from its opposite, the form of non-direct exchangeability, as the positivity of one pole of a magnet is from the negativity of the other pole.

As he continued,

> this has allowed the illusion to arise that all commodities can simultaneously be imprinted with the stamp of direct exchangeability, in the same way that it might be imagined that all Catholics can be popes. (1867, p.161, n.26)

He then describes how the literal and direct exchangeability of each commodity for all the others is simply the "philistine utopia" of Proudhon. The context of these remarks is the connection between the role of a specific commodity as a "direct and universal equivalent" and the non-direct exchangeability of all commodities in general; but we would reinterpret them to underline the fact that capitalism does not actually have to involve conditions wherein once commodity X has been exchanged for a sum of money Y, Y can then immediately be exchanged for any other commodity in the world. Only for those critics whose concept of capitalism has lost its moorings in the concrete could this appear to be so. In reality, not only is the money relation a mediation; but within that mediation there are more specific mediating relations which do not abolish the form and function of money as soon as they become bureaucratic. The Marxian critique of the capitalist commodity and capitalist money as forms of value rests upon the understanding of the indirect but real and generalised socialisation of alienated labour through generalised commodity exchange; not on the hypothetical possibility of literal exchangeability, at merely a single and undifferentiated remove, of any one thing for anything else.[36] Money as general equivalent is not simply a black hole into which a commodity's value can be injected in order later to be ejected, as if from a white hole, into a material good elsewhere. Rather, as what is now fundamentally *money-capital*, it has its own internal passageways, forms and rules which do not define its essence as a value form but which nonetheless must exist; and which exist with different characteristics according to specific sets of historical circumstances.

The second possible objection reduces to the isolation of the USSR from the world market. But this is hardly a substantial argument once the general critique of the internal conditions is accepted. One might well ask: if the capitalist world were divided into two separate halves, would they both stop being capitalist? To rely on this argument, one has first to assume that the development of capitalism in western countries — ultimately, western European countries — was not only 'classical,' but 'normal'; and that whatever there was in the USSR was 'peculiar' and would only have been capitalist if it had been fully conjoined to developments west of Prague. This would be a very biased and anti-empirical way to reach a theoretical critique of the history of capitalism. It is not at all based on a consideration of the internal contradictions of the political economy prevalent in the USSR.

In the final analysis, those who wish to maintain that the USSR was a non-capitalist formation will only be able to stress and stress again the fact that there was no individual ownership of enterprises, and that in important parts of the economy rouble holdings did not possess the characteristics of money as a form of capital. Accepting both of these points as true, we are arguing that in the capitalist world — which extends across the entire globe — such quantities of currency are not the only form that money can take. Instead, they are a specific type of legally-backed 'entitlement,' a form of exchange-value whose effective 'currency' depends on the specific organisation of the groups of exploiters controlling a specific territory, and in particular on the type of organisation of their internal competition. (See [Fernandez] 1989a, p.4). In the USSR this currency, in any active sense, was nil in much of the economy: but the crucial point is that other forms of 'recognised pull' could and did fulfil the same function as quantities of currency in countries ruled by the bourgeoisie.[37]

SOVIET CAPITALISM: ITS SPECIFICITY

In formulating a theoretical critique of the USSR we have attributed great weight to an understanding of the form taken by exchange relations among bureaucrats, and therefore we have not focused simply on 'state ownership,' a purely *legal* form. Consequently we would refrain from using the term 'state capitalism' to describe the nature of the system. Usually employed in contradistinction to 'private capitalism' this term has the additional fault of concealing the fact that privative appropriation always held full sway in the USSR, just as it has done elsewhere. On the other hand, though, since the economic system undoubtedly arose *sui generis*,[38] it certainly remains necessary to have a ready term to describe the USSR in the context of the history of world capitalism.[39]

Whilst we have rejected Buick and Crump's theory of the 'state capitalist market,' emphasising instead the bureaucratic features of the Soviet system and the absence of any 'active' role for the rouble in much of the producer sector, it does not follow that bureaucracy is a major feature of Soviet-type systems alone, and not of the countries ruled by the bourgeoisie. One theorist to point this out has been the 'self-managementist' Castoriadis, who uses the terms 'fragmented bureaucratic capitalism' and 'total bureaucratic capitalism' to describe the bourgeois and Soviet-type systems respectively. (1977, pp.15-16). His critique of bureaucracy, however, a form which he hypostatises, becomes resolutely non-Marxist, since he holds the libertarian view that the fundamental contradiction of capitalism is that which exists between the givers and takers of orders. Thus he arrives at a rather blunted critique of *bourgeois* political economy, which for the Marxist might be bureaucratic but is not *essentially* so in such a way that capital appears as a form which simply mediates bureaucratic rule. Indeed that is not even the case in the USSR. Moreover, libertarian anti-bureaucratism can easily lead to the view that, since the USSR was 'totally' bureaucratic, it must have represented a more 'advanced' form of domination than that of the bourgeoisie, and consequently should have been seen as the 'main enemy.' This indeed is the path along which

Castoriadis has travelled in recent years. (1981a).[40] Thus it is not possible for us to adopt his terminology either.

It would certainly be possible to refer to the system in which portions of *blat* money were exchanged, invested and accumulated as being a kind of bureaucratic market. But then of course the market in western economies is to a fair extent *blat*-mediated too, including at the top, without the role of the currency being reduced to that of the rouble in the USSR. The difference lies in the form of money. Wishing for a terminology which neither over-emphasises nor denies the major differences between the bourgeois and Soviet systems, and hoping to encourage critique rather than to discourage it with flashy neologisms, we would therefore suggest using the terms 'bourgeois' and 'market capitalist' to describe the economic systems where money capital takes the form of currency and, *faute de mieux*, 'bureaucratic capitalist' to describe the USSR.[41]

SUMMARY

In endeavouring to develop theoretically the 'capitalist' hypothesis, we have assumed throughout that the most logical basis on which to proceed is a consideration of fundamental categories of political economy. We have thus started by discussing the categories of the *commodity*, *wage-labour*, and *production for profit*. We then give a 'nutshell' definition of capitalism as a mode of production founded upon exchange as a general form and growth as an underlying drive.

Developing the analysis, we show how behind these realities lie the fundamental categories of value and abstract labour. Money is introduced as the general equivalent form of value. Once capital is shown to be a cycle of expanding value, taking the alternate forms of the capitalist commodity (C) and capitalist money (M), the latter term is then defined in relation to the capital cycle as a functional necessity.

We then argue that the first three categories continued to exist in the USSR, with perhaps the most controversial finding being the continued and generalised prevalence of exchange relations, and hence the commodity, in the producer goods sector. This is argued in the course of a lengthy analysis of the nature of the dominant relations of consumption, distribution, and production. After showing that the predominant form of exploitation of labour-power was founded upon its purchase, we then suggest that the systemic nature of a drive for growth was similarly evident. Hence the USSR was capitalist in nature.

Once the categories of value and abstract labour are identified, the theoretical task becomes one of identifying Soviet 'money as money.' This is approached by focusing above all on the function of the money form of capital: as the (generalised) means by which the controllers of the extraction of surplus value assess their returns and reinvest them. An argument is presented in which bureaucratic forms of permission, and, more generally, blat, are understood as fulfilling this function and therefore as constituting a form of money-capital other than the rouble.

Special emphasis is laid throughout on the necessarily competitive nature of Soviet economic bureaucracy. Since the term 'state capitalism' is seen to refer not to competitiveness but mainly to a legal form, it is rejected in favour of the term *bureaucratic capitalism*. This term is not, however, used to support a theory of 'modern bureaucracy' in general; rather, it is counterposed to the *bourgeois capitalism* or *market capitalism* which holds sway in areas where the basic form of money-capital is the currency.

It is argued that the Soviet political economy is founded upon wage-labour and upon bureaucratic forms of both exchange-value and money: and hence, given the systemic need for growth, on the accumulation of capital. In short, the USSR was a capitalist country which was especially bureaucratic, wherein money capital took forms which were largely bureaucratic rather than currency-based.

Notes

1   In the *Manifesto*, the quoted phrase is applied only to pre-capitalist societies (Marx and Engels 1848, p.33), but there is nothing that removes the theoretical possibility of its relevance at some time to capitalism too.
2   Our approach will be seen to be in clear contrast with that adopted by Ticktin, who writes that "in the case of the USSR, however, use value is all important." (1991c, p.11).
3   The best introduction to the underlying categories of capitalism is to be found in Parts 1-2 of Volume 1 of Marx's *Capital*. (1867, pp.125-280). Also useful are Rubin 1928, Kay 1975 (pp.13-72) and 1979, and Cleaver 1979 (pp.71-173).
4   In French the dependence of private property upon deprivation is linguistically self-evident, the adjective *privé* (private) being a past form of the verb *priver* (to deprive someone of something).
5   Nor indeed was he the first, even after the birth of the industrial era, to express a revolutionary communist opposition to commodities, money, and wage-labour. On the ideas of the Conspiracy for Equality in Paris in 1796, for example, see Buonarotti 1828 and the documents collected therewith, and Rose 1978, especially pp.185-204.
6   It should be remembered here that since capital is an 'inhuman' relation, socially necessary labour-time is equally well described as labour-time which is technologically necessary.
7   Marx refers in this context to the "philistine utopia ... depicted in the socialism of Proudhon." (1867, p.161, n.26).
8   It will be noticed that we are not theorising a distinction between 'general' and 'universal' equivalence. Thus in our terminology, exchange becomes generalised when it reaches the

point of being the sole form of distribution of any economic importance, and there exists "a circle of exchange, a totality of the same, in constant flux, over the entire surface of society." (Marx 1939, p.188). In this context we do not see Marx's distinction between the generality of value's relative form and the universality of its equivalent form as especially helpful. (1867. pp.157-63). The use of the concept of the 'universal' is perhaps not wrong *per se* — money is indeed 'universal' insofar as it is assumed, in principle, to be exchangeable even against something that does not yet exist — but it appears to us as too 'philosophical,' especially when it is distinguished from the concept of the 'general.' Rather than aiding in the formulation of a critique of the underlying categories of capitalism in such a way as to facilitate the critique of their historical movement over the past century — as expressed, for example, in the fluctuating importance of gold, the dollar, the IMF, and the rulers' need for war — the distinction would seem instead to be a hindrance, at least at this stage of the presentation.

9   What made gold and silver suitable as early general equivalents was not simply their rarity. It was also their near-absence of practical usefulness, combined with the fact that little or no use-value needs to be consumed in their maintenance, since they are non-bulky, not subject to rust, and — unlike mercury — neither poisonous nor liable to evaporate. (See Marx 1939, pp.174-80). Platinum (p.176) and palladium share these characteristics but appeared too late on the scene and are not as globally evident.

10   Money-capital necessarily concerns the controllers of capital as subjects, as *class*.

11   First published in 1903, this text was written in the notebooks now usually known as the *Grundrisse* (German for 'Outlines'), first published collectively in 1939.

12   The description of capitalist money as 'money as money' (Marx 1939, p.872) should not be over-used, since in the context of the idea that capitalist money is money's 'achieved form,' it carries more than a hint of the idea that the forms intrinsic in the capitalist mode of production are the 'necessary' developments of forms which existed in preceding modes. The inference can easily be drawn that the progress of capitalism was 'necessary' to provide the basis for the inauguration of communism. Although this is a statement that we would reject, it is not possible to discuss it in the present context.

13   In the famous 'missing sixth chapter' on "The Results of the Immediate Process of Production," Marx also states that money, which "from the standpoint of exchange-value" appears as "*real* wealth," appears when invested as opposed to the "*possibility* of wealth, i.e. labour-power." (1933, p.1015). Among other things this illustrates well just how 'inhuman' and 'mad' capitalism and its progress actually are. (First published in 1933, this text was originally written as a draft in one of the plans for Volume 1 of *Capital*. Since its publication in English in 1976 it has appeared as an appendix to that work).

14   The idea that circulation and exchange are identical is of course a capitalist mystification.

15   Camatte's observation that "surplus value can only exist if it is represented" is both accurate and useful. As he explains, if this were not the case, surplus value "would just be tied to a given process and would be of no consequence." There is also sense in his following statement that

> money has to be an undifferentiated totality where ΔK is not distinguishable from K, and also a differentiated totality where ΔK can present itself as different from K. (1980, p.10)

The weakness in this sentence, however, lies in the conceptualisation of money as a 'totality,' rather than — in this context — a form, sphere, state, or stage. This allows Camatte to confuse money with the totality of capital and eventually to arrive at the false or even meaningless view that once capital "becomes autonomous and escapes, it is nothing more than a representation." (p.12). This position is quite opposed to an understanding of capital as M-C-M´; and, as Guerre Sociale have shown (1977), it rests on little more than a "bowdlerisation" of Marx's critique of interest and 'fictive capital.'

16 From a working class point of view, of course, money does not appear as a form necessary for capital investment, but more simply as the form of the wage and the mediating form of the imposition of scarcity. "In exchange for his sold activity, the worker gets money.... With this money he can buy commodities, things, but he cannot buy back his activity.... He can sell his living activity for money, but he cannot buy his living activity for money." (Perlman 1969, p.5). Money must endure as long as capitalism. On the other hand, though, this does not mean that the quantity of money which is paid to the worker, or the quality or quantity of work which the worker does for a given wage, are not subject to contestation. But in the approach used here in relation to money the issue of class struggle, for reasons of clarity, has been 'foreclosed.' (See Shortall 1994, and Introduction above).

17 In what follows we have found Marx's "Introduction" to *A Contribution to A Critique of Political Economy* (1903) especially useful.

18 After being in force from 1916 to 1921, rationing was reintroduced in 1929-35 and 1941-47, and again in the late Gorbachev period. Except for a short time during the economic collapse marked by the civil war, all goods on ration have always borne a price. See Nove 1982, pp.87, 156-57, 202, 220, 249, and 308-10; see also Carr 1952, pp.233-36, and Rogger 1983, p.260.

19 As Rutland puts it, the question 'How do Soviet planners arrive at prices for their industrial goods?' is "not as crucial as it may first appear" since

few decisions are made on the basis of these prices. If the prices for a particular firm's goods are set too low it will turn in losses, but so long as it is fulfilling its plan targets for principal products no one will complain. (1985, p.127)

20 In chap. 5 Simis describes the role of cash bribery in industry; and in chap. 6 he describes black-market *production*. He points out, though (p.103), that "private industry in the Soviet Union does not manufacture machinery or automobiles...."

21 Rutland observes that whereas the total number of product plans was in excess of 60,000, the number of different types of product was over 10 million. (1985, p.116).

22 For an earlier reference to the role of "commercial travellers" in negotiating inter-enterprise deals, see Hubbard 1942, pp.5 and 239.

23 Goldman ignores the fact that the consumption of consumer goods is indeed productive, since it reproduces labour-power. But it is true that in the sphere of reproductive consumption — of foodstuffs, for example — there is more flexibility in terms of substitute goods.

24 In Lenin's words: "*Unquestioning subordination* to a single will is absolutely necessary for the success of processes organised on the pattern of large-scale machine industry." (1918a, p.35).

25 In preparing this brief description of Soviet economic management we have found the following sources invaluable: Berliner 1957, Nove 1980b and 1982, Lane 1985a, and Rutland 1985.

26 That this is a highly compacted model is amply illustrated by the sort of administrative changes which occurred throughout the Soviet period. Thus in the early years the Supreme Council of the National Economy (VSNKh) functioned as a kind of super-ministry; but in the late 1920s the powers of its *glavki* were handed to 'associations' (*ob´edineniia*) based

upon the State-sector wholesaling syndicates which had previously shared their function with the Nepmen. Then in the 1930s, as division and subdivision rapidly expanded the number of industrial ministries (commissariats), and the importance of the *ob'edinenie* faded from the scene, the role of Gosplan as a central coordinator rapidly increased. In Gosplan, however, the autonomy previously enjoyed by 'former Menshevik' economists was stamped out, and indeed every official's scope of operation was increasingly circumscribed by the GPU/NKVD, which spread fear and competition simultaneously. The head of Gosplan from 1938, Voznesensky, was arrested in 1949 and executed in 1950.

Then in 1957, once the security service's reign of terror was over, a proposal was made to re-establish an economic 'super-ministry.' Khrushchev responded to this by abolishing even the existing economic ministries (or most of them) and handing over most of their functions to newly-created regional economic councils (*sovnarkhozy*) subordinate to republican Councils of Ministers. This represented a move from division by industrial branch to division by region. Resultant autarkic tendencies were initially counterbalanced by an ascendant Gosplan, but then the latter organ itself had part of its plan-implementation function removed and given to a kind of central coordination of the *sovnarkhozy*.

Eventually in 1965 the branch ministries were reintroduced, albeit with much of their former role in organising supplies now taken over by Gossnab. But although the proclaimed aim was an increase in autonomy for the management of each enterprise, this proved impossible to achieve in the framework of existing relations between managers, ministries, and planning authorities: relations which included, for example, the ratchet effect, the shortage economy (or 'seller's market'), and the central setting of prices and gross output targets. Even the merging of enterprises in the 1970s into 'associations' or 'combines' — behind which lay the more specific aim of increasing managers' independence from ministries — failed to remove the weight of these factors. Such is the story of the development of Soviet economic management. (Hutchings 1982, Munting 1982, Nove 1982).

27   It is worth pointing out that Marx recognised unambiguously that capital accumulation could and sometimes did take place in a way not mediated by the market. (1905-10, pp.486-92). Whilst we do not argue here that he anticipated later developments under Lenin and Stalin, it is interesting nonetheless that his context, namely that of machine-building, industrial raw materials, and the communications infrastructure, is not wholly unsuggestive of the massive growth of Soviet heavy industry after 1929.

28   Indeed, even goods such as stockpiled nuclear weapons do not constitute an exception. Not only did they serve a purpose in preparation for an intensification of international competition, or in the maintenance of the existing competitive balance; but even those which were hypothetically never meant to be discharged at all would still have been either kept in good condition or left to go to ruin. In either case, we can speak of purposive consumption, albeit partial. And any product thought by its end-user to have any kind of utility is a product with a use-value. It does not matter that the use-value is subordinated to the need or drive to compete, or to snobbery, or to the tendency of bureaucrats to build empires: the important point is that the subjectively perceived utility of the product depends at least partially upon its physical characteristics. Similarly, if an unemployed person buys a suit solely because he needs it for a job interview, it still has a use-value, because

something that was not a suit would not be suitable. Use-value subordinated to exchange-value is still use-value.

This is a point obscured by Roland, for two reasons. First, in his model of capitalism he describes exchange-value as a "form of mediation" of use-value. (1989, pp.43-46). But, as Debord puts it:

> exchange value could arise only as an agent of use-value, but its victory by means of its own weapons created the conditions for its own domination. [...] Exchange value is the *condottiere* of use-value who ends up waging the war for himself. (1967, p.46)

In other words, since exchange-value is necessarily abstracted from use-value, its history is the history of the development of its opposition to use-value. (The translation here would better read "ends up waging war for himself.") Since exchange-value is *opposed* to use-value, it is not the capitalist form of 'instrumentality' as opposed to 'autotelicity' (Roland 1989, pp.25-26), for instrumentality can often be an aspect of use-value. Moreover, from capital's point of view it is actually use-value which is instrumental and the accumulation of exchange-value in its general form — that is, value — which is the main aim. Roland's position that the USSR knew exchange in the absence of exchange-value (pp.61-62), and his view that 'material remuneration' and incentives involve an "anthropological invariant" (p.149), serve to demonstrate further his insufficient grasp of the meaning of the concept of exchange.

Second, it makes little sense to hypostatise in the Soviet context a specific form of "mediation" defined as "indicator value" ("*valeur-indice*," or *pokazatel'naia stoimost'*). (pp.45-102). Once we recall that use-value is properly defined only in terms of the subjective consideration of a product's physical characteristics, we realise that "indicator value" is also so definable, and hence it cannot be opposed to the category of use-value in any fundamental way. If, for example, a car is produced simply so that an enterprise can put out a greater quantity of tonnes of steel — and let us disregard the fact that the reality would be extremely unlikely to be this stark, since in such a case it would no doubt be easiest to turn out a steel cube — then this is still a consideration of use-value, and in this sense we should have to agree with Ticktin (see Chapter 6 below) against Roland. The point of the present chapter is to look behind such considerations in terms of the control over the productive forces.

29   Cliff goes so far as to write that "in essence, the laws prevailing in the relations between the enterprises and between the labourers and the employer-state would be *no different* if Russia were one big factory managed from the centre, and if all the labourers received the goods they consumed directly, *in kind*" — a truly remarkable counter-factual avoidance of the issue. (1955, p.209). To be fair to Ticktin, it is necessary to accept that unlike Cliff he does consider the internal contradictions of Soviet economic administration. But he omits to look at competition in any profound fashion in the context of control over labour. His theorisation of production and labour in the USSR are criticised extensively in Chapter 6 below.

30   It is necessary to add a rider here to take into account the prohibition of voluntary labour turnover which was in effect from 1940. Like the system of labour allocation overseen by Bevin in the United Kingdom from 1941, however, this did not become entrenched as the basis of the distribution of labour. In practice it was eroded in the early 1950s and abolished in 1956, when labour turnover reached 38%. (Brown 1966, p.16; M. McAuley 1969, p.47). Moreover, the fact that labour-power is exchanged does not mean that it has to be exchanged on a free market, and even under a system of State direction there is still class tension over the wage. But this argument must not be taken too far; and if the (related) system of labour

camps had become the predominant form of expropriation of labour-power, or mode of production, then one would rightly speak of the prevalence of slavery rather than of wage-labour. (On labour camps, see for example Wheatcroft 1981).

31   In a press conference held by the putschists on the day they seized power, Acting President Gennadii Yanaev stated that "above all, we will direct our actions towards the stabilisation of the economy. We will not renounce reforms intended to move us in the direction of the market. We feel, however, that there will be a need to be more precise in defining and organising the management of our actions on a higher level." (*Pravda*, 20 August 1991, p.2).

32   Of course the real playing out of relationships would be somewhat more complicated than this, insofar as an increase in the influence of subordinates in one office, or contact network, relative to others of the same rank elsewhere could well increase their boss's influence relative to the influence of bosses elsewhere, and vice versa. The fact that subordinates were often 'protegés' should be understood precisely in such political-economic terms of competition and exchange.

33   The references are to kabbalah (1867, p.195), alchemy (pp.208 and 229), the Delphic temple (p.229), and the Holy Grail (p.230). In the previous chapter, referring to money as the universal equivalent, Marx has already quoted a piece from the biblical Book of Revelations concerning the "name of the beast, or the number of his name." (p.181). That he intends such references to be useful should be clear from the view of the commodity that he expresses in the very first chapter of *Capital*: namely, that "in order to find an analogy [to the commodity-form and the value-relation of the products of labour within which it appears] we must take flight into the misty realm of religion." (p.165).

34   In a western context these points are even more readily apparent in connection with the State sector, but we have chosen to focus on the non-State sector in order to stress the essence of the underlying relations.

35   In the theoretical presentation above, we have tried to anchor the argument as solidly as possible upon the fundamental concepts of privative appropriation, exchange, wage-labour, and surplus value. Chen Erjin takes a very different approach, ascribing major significance to concepts such as revisionism, historical necessity, and the division between the economic and the political; but nonetheless it is worth mentioning that one of his formulations in certain ways parallels our conclusions. Considering the system of "revisionism" which he sees as an actuality in the USSR and a possibility in China, he writes that

> Such ownership [by the bureaucrat-monopoly privileged class] forms an immensely *competitive system of capital accumulation* [emphasis added].... It is an enhanced, *privilegized* form of the private ownership system. For the bourgeoisie pools its capital for investment purposes, and derives profits in proportion to the amount of capital individually invested; exploitation is carried out through the capitalization of the means of production. But the bureaucrat-monopoly privileged class bands together for political purposes, and enriches itself through the sweat and toil of the people in proportion to the amount of *power* individually possessed; exploitation is carried out through the 'privilegization' of the concentration of power demanded by social production under public ownership, and through the subsequent *capitalization of privilege* [emphasis added]. (1979, p.72)

Even if Chen Erjin argues that "revisionism" is a quite different "mode of exploitation" from capitalism (p.85), this last concept of the capitalisation of privilege would seem quite compatible with our own understanding of Soviet *blat* as a form of money. Unfortunately, though, Chen Erjin's work is characterised by great theoretical imprecision: assuming that it is sensible to refer to the existence of capital accumulation in the absence of capitalism, he is clearly not in a position to develop this concept in any profound way. It might be said that he describes Soviet-type privilege as capital without paying attention to what capital actually is: self-expanding value. His concept of capitalisation, a term he applies to both East and West, is seemingly full of promise, but remains dismally underdeveloped.

But all the same, it must be noted that the concept of the capitalisation of privilege is still much more advanced than the vague view given by Horvat that in terms of 'the Marxian analysis of alienation' the concepts of 'money,' 'buying', and 'ownership' can be replaced in the context of the USSR with those of 'office,' 'doing,' and 'incumbency,' and the concept of 'commodity fetishism' with that of 'office fetishism.' (1982, p.96). Unlike Horvat, Chen Erjin does relate bureaucratic privilege to social production.

36 Of course there has never been such an uncontradictedly free market. To posit such a market as the essence of capitalism is to adopt a non-materialist attitude by disregarding the forms of appearance of actual exchangeability. Would James Goldsmith have been allowed to buy *The Times*?

37 In considering the changes which capitalism experienced during the economic crises beginning in the first world war we would thus emphasise the collapse of the rouble in 1917-18 and its eventual relatively viable replacement in large-scale capital circulation by a bureaucratic form at the end of the 1920s. And in the economic crisis evident throughout the 1990s, considered in relation to the changes which capitalism would have to undergo in order to escape the doldrums, we would stress above all the issue of convertibilisation. The rapid 'external' convertibilisation (of roubles for dollars and other 'hard' currencies) only points up the continuing need on the part of Russian capital for a widespread 'internal' convertibilisation (of currency, whether roubles or dollars, for means of production, and vice versa). We return to this point in Chapter 7.

38 Clearly capitalism, a mode of production which became global, and which is founded on wage-labour and the M-C-M´ cycle, can utilise a number of different systems of competition and control—ranging from apartheid to the republic of the ayatollahs, from the British old boy network to the Chinese triads, from the Ecuadoran military hierarchy to the German banking system, from Peronism to parliamentary committees. The precise characteristics of these systems depend upon the nature of past and present class and intra-class struggles, the role and importance of each area or power within world capitalist society, and factors inherited from pre-capitalist societies.

39 On the 'Russian question,' see the list of works mentioned in the *Introduction*.

40 Castoriadis eventually comes to open an article (1982a, p.17) with the following sentence: "Clearly [*sic*], stratocratic Russia's aim is the expansion of its empire and, ultimately, world domination." His position, which changed little even after Gorbachev came to power in 1985 (Castoriadis 1988), has led him to be viewed in some circles as a 'libertarian cold-warrior.' (A.D.1985.). In view of his eventual 'Europeanism' (see n.42 in Chapter 2 above), one might query the direction of the logical link he makes between the position that the USSR is the most advanced superpower and the position that it is the 'main enemy.'

41 Since these terms are political-economic rather than geographical, the future establishment of a currency as the principal form of Russian money capital — or indeed of a combination of currencies: the rouble, the dollar, and the deutschmark or euro, say — would thus mean that the economy would then be one of bourgeois market capitalism.

4 The Class Struggle: A Critique of Sovietological Theories

Since the social production relations in the USSR were exploitative, there must necessarily have been a fundamental and radical antagonism between the working class and the system. This antagonism is understood to have involved not just a conflict of 'interests,' or a 'contempt' for the elite's claim to represent the working class (see Ralis 1981), but continuous actual conflict. Thus it is held to be impossible to reach a full understanding of the nature of the system, whether or not that nature is held to be capitalist, in the absence of an understanding of the nature and forms of the class struggle.

But before focusing critically (Chapters 5-6) on the relevant works of those who define their approaches as Marxist, and before discussing the matter positively (Chapter 7) on the basis of the ideas presented in Chapters 1 and 3 above, we consider in the present chapter the relevant aspects of the 'mainstream' literature. In other words, we deal with the considerations of class struggle in the USSR offered by a selection of commentators adopting 'sovietological' approaches.[1]

In the first section we consider how the topic has been dealt with by the authors of influential 'political' theories about the nature of Soviet society (Inkeles and Bauer, Friedrich and Brzezinski, Skilling and Griffiths, Hough, and S. Cohen),[2] as well as by a number of those who have published influential works on the economy (the Birmingham school, Nove, and Kornai).[3] More precisely, we show how they have failed to relate to it. We then focus in the second section on the works of sovietologists who have dwelt at greater length upon the nature of the Soviet working class: either in specific contexts such as the workplace (Grancelli) or *perestroika* (Connor, and D. Mandel), or in a relatively broader relationship to the nature of the system (Lane and O'Dell, Pravda, and Zaslavsky).

GENERAL THEORIES

Politics: 'Totalitarianism' and Interest Groups

A consideration of the most influential theories will suffice to show that their authors have ascribed little importance to the role of class struggle. Working within the confines defined by 'political science,' they have preferred to focus on the decision-making process and the formulation of policy;[4] and consequently they have either ignored the subject or else approached it merely tangentially.

The view that it would be mistaken to attribute much importance to class conflict, since the form it took was not 'political,' is highly apparent even in the work of the sociological sovietologists Inkeles and Bauer. In their chapter on 'Social Class Cleavage' in *The Soviet Citizen* (1959), they thus suggest (p.304), given that the "salient social cleavage" was the one which operated between "party and non-party segments," that a treatment of class must necessarily be parenthetical. Indeed, after recognising that "workers and peasants [i.e. *kolkhozniks*] quite often [saw] themselves as sharing common interests *in opposition* to the nonmanual classes," and after showing how substantial numbers of émigré *intelligenty* and workers considered the others' class to be 'harmful' to their own, they remark that the responses to their investigators' questions may have given a false impression, since the "very wording might have aroused or excessively stimulated class consciousness." (pp.307 and 310-12).

Assuming, though, that the level of class hostility in the USSR was as high as that expressed verbally by their émigré informants, these early 'totalitarians' argue that even so it would not have been a critical problem for the system: firstly, since such sentiment was unlikely to find "a political channel for expression," and secondly, because of the restrictions on free discussion within the CPSU. In response to the anticipated objection that, denied formal political outlets, "class feeling" would then become all the more explosive in potential, "or at least a consistent major drag on organised, unified efforts in pursuit of the common political goals [*sic*] of the society," they give the view that it was in fact "much less intense than political sentiment, and much less likely to produce cleavage than the Communist vs. non-Communist dichotomy." (p.317). Backing this up with reference to comparable opinion studies showing similar levels of class feeling in the US, Inkeles and Bauer then state that they "no more expect the Soviet Union to cleave asunder along this 'fault plane' than the United States." Since in their approach they make no use of any concept of *exploitation*, or of resistance to it,[5] in making such an observation they are stating in effect that the social significance of class conflict was minimal.[6]

Writing slightly later, but putting a similar emphasis on the role of the CPSU, the more classically political-scientific 'totalitarians' Friedrich and Brzezinski concentrate above all on the absence of political rights. In their work *Totalitarian Dictatorship and Autocracy* (1961) they thus conclude the chapter on Soviet labour by giving the view that

> it seems very clear that labor has lost its freedom and independence, that its [*sic*] organizations have become bureaucratic agencies of the government, and that not only in his working hours, but in his leisure time as well the worker has become a cog in

the totalitarian centrally directed economy. To complete the paradox of his workers' paradise, any worker who fails to live up to the standards set by the regime is in danger of being made a slave in one of the many labor camps of the regime. (p.224)

In other words, the working class was 'totally' oppressed: it could not create independent organisations, and was therefore unable to struggle.[7] It is worth noting in this regard that a 'paradox' in this context is something that is contrary to received opinion. An 'over-determined' interest in debunking the supposed 'paradox' of the Soviet 'workers' paradise' — which was hardly a 'paradox' for the Soviet working class — leads to a concentration on the brutality of oppression, rather than on the contradictions of exploitation as a social production relation.[8]

In *Survival is Not Enough* (1984), Pipes, a leading successor to the 'totalitarians,' holds that the essential feature of the Soviet political system was "absolute rule by an oligarchy of Party officials who not only monopolize political authority but literally own their own countries and everything that lies within their own boundaries." (p.13). Since there is in fact nothing in his book about the Soviet workers apart from his view that they had poor living standards, it can be taken as read that he agrees with the original 'totalitarians' that the class struggle was non-existent or at least irrelevant to an understanding of the nature of the system.

The 'totalitarian' school began to decline in the 1960s owing to the rise of ideas about Soviet 'interest groups' after the onset of 'peaceful coexistence' and the end of the Cold War. In their edited volume *Interest Groups in Soviet Politics* (1971) Skilling and Griffiths thus focus their attention on the role and interplay of sectional interests within the elite. But their concern is exclusively with 'political interest groups' (pp.24-27), and so they too fail to deal at all with class conflict. Making what amounts to the same criticism, Ticktin remarks (1991c, p.7) that the 'interest groupers' "left unexplored the crucial question: How does the elite rule?"

The 'revisionist' Hough also focuses on 'interest groups' in order to develop the concept of 'institutional pluralism.' He thus rejects the idea that the USSR was, in essence, an 'ideological system' wherein the leadership sought to remould society on the basis of 'ideas and aspirations' (1972, pp.30-41),[9] and emphasises (1972, 1976) the post-Stalinist diffusion of decision-making power and the increased 'participation' of various groupings within the system. Unlike Skilling and Griffiths he does not restrict his attention to groupings within the elite. When he turns away from institutional matters, however, Hough simply describes the increasing willingness of the leadership to "listen to policy advice from 'society'," rather than conceiving of working class struggle as a real force. (1972, p.30). Although later he draws up a list of problems faced by policy-makers vis-à-vis the workers (1979, pp.368-72), he never reaches the point of theorising an overall *relationship* between the working class and the system. Instead, he prefers to give management-labour conflicts equal weight with problems arising between economic branches (p.373), on the grounds that for individual bodies and committees they are just as important.

Whereas Skilling, Griffiths and Hough base their rejection of the 'totalitarian' approach on a discussion of post-Stalinist changes, Cohen's attack is altogether more savage. In *Rethinking the Soviet Experience* (1985), he notes the politicisation of Anglo-American sovietology during the 'cold war' period, and explains (chap.1) how the polarisation of world politics probably ruled out any other development.[10]

A prominent figure in liberal sovietology, Cohen discusses the "sustained struggles between reformist and conservative groups inside the high political establishment," but accepts (pp.132-33) that "authentic reformism and conservatism are always social as well as political." Developing the point, he criticises the "untenable and persistent notion that the Soviet party-state officialdom is somehow remote and insulated from society and its outlooks." For him,

> Such a conception makes no sense in a country where the state employs almost every citizen and the party has 18 million adult members. In fact, there is every reason to think that virtually all the diverse trends in society,...from far right to far left and including those expressed by dissidents, also exist inside the political officialdom, however subterraneanly. (p.133)

But even if Cohen is aware of the inherent limitations of a concentration solely on the political, to the exclusion of the social and historical (p.24), he nonetheless assesses the importance of social trends in terms which remain essentially political (reformism, conservatism, left, right). Summarising his thesis, he states that

> the main obstacle to further reform...is not one or another generation, institution, elite, group, or leader, but the profound conservatism that seems to dominate almost all of them, from the family to the Politburo, from local authorities to the state *nachalstvo*. Put simply, the Soviet Union has become, both 'downstairs' in society and 'upstairs' in the political system, one of the most conservative countries in the world. Indeed, public opinion polls in recent years suggest that ordinary Soviet citizens — or at least the Slavic majority — are even more conservative than some segments of the ruling elite. (p.146)

Whilst it is, of course, possible for a Marxist to agree with this on an empirical level, it is not possible to share Cohen's 'point of view,' which leads him to assert that "to use the language of the official press, the antagonistic forces of 'innovation and tradition' have formed 'two poles' in Soviet politics, culture and society." (p.128). Whereas for Cohen the terms 'reformism' and 'conservatism' are "plain, historical and universal, as well as social and political" (p.129), and provide the key to an understanding of the basic conflict, for the Marxist all evidence on, for example, conservative trends in the working class or reformism in the elite is considered in very different terms. Two political tendencies each disposing of cross-class support cannot possibly be construed as polar opposites in any socially fundamental sense, since their opposition cannot be equated with — and indeed, fails even to express — the class contradictions of the social production relations.

Economics: Technical Development, Indicators, and Shortage

Numerous sovietological works have been published on Soviet economics, economic development, industry, and so on, but an equally brief consideration of some of the best-known will be sufficient to demonstrate that minimal theoretical attention has been paid even to the role and form of the relationship between the working class and the political-economic system, let alone to the nature of this relationship as a matter of class struggle.

An important place in the development of empiricist sovietology is occupied by the members of the 'Birmingham school.' In particular, these researchers have looked in detail at the technical level of various sectors of Soviet industry and at the pace and quality of industrial research, development, and innovation. (Amann, Cooper and Davies 1977, Amann and Cooper 1982, Amann and Cooper 1986). Their main finding is that there was a lag behind the West which was not being reduced.

On the whole this work is extremely empirical, but if there is a theoretical element within it of political-economic significance then it is perhaps most evident in Davies's early conclusion that

> important changes clearly need to be made in a planning system of the Soviet type, if it is to be flexible enough to allow for large-scale innovations and economic experiment at factory level; and if consumer demand is to find adequate expression in production planning. This does not, I believe, mean that a direct planning system is inappropriate for an advanced economy; but it does mean that the equation of direct planning with 'extreme centralisation' is a vulgarisation of the concept. (1958, p.327)

"Direct planning" is then defined as a system of planning in which growth is regulated by conscious aims "embodied" by a central authority and formulated on a basis of "realistic knowledge." In short, the implication is that growth was necessary but conceptual vulgarisation to some extent impeded it. Similarly, the implication of the later work is that technological development was also necessary, but was taking place only slowly and in a limited fashion. In regard to explanation, Amann states that "we do not yet know why Soviet technology is on the whole backward" (1978, p. 71), whereas Cooper briefly mentions the difficulty of introducing modern western management techniques in the face of "overriding departmental interests and the incessant pressure for output," and also the burdensome (cultural?) requirement that concepts developed abroad must first be 'sovietised.' (1982, pp.507-08 and 511).

If such essentially marginal comments at least show a recognition that a question exists as to why technological development was problematic, there is no recognition at all of the existence of more fundamental questions as to why growth and technological development were necessary in the first place. And since there is no conception of the existence of a surplus product, there can be no consideration of the category of exploitation, let alone class struggle. Thus even when Hanson comes to consider full employment he blames labour shortages simply on inefficient labour allocation, and inefficient labour allocation on the existence of the centrally-administered system, without considering how workers' "cynicism, apathy and larceny" might be causes as well as effects. (1986, p.105).

Other well-known sovietological works on the economy have been produced by Nove. (See especially Nove 1958a, 1980b, and 1982). As well as writing on a more historical level than the Birmingham school Nove has also written more theoretically, being the first person to introduce into sovietology the concept of the 'success indicator.' The usefulness of this concept cannot reasonably be contested, and indeed it is now part of the general background knowledge of the field. The importance of an understanding of the role of targets, whether for gross output, sales, productivity, quality, net output, or rouble profits, need not be repeated here. What needs to be stressed, though, is that in emphasising the category of the success indicator (*pokazatel'*), Nove is undoubtedly making a contribution to political economy.

Unfortunately, though, he does not make use of this contribution in such a way as to shed light upon a set of categories underlying and indeed constituting the political economy itself. Instead, what he does is to ask questions about the 'necessity' or otherwise of Stalinism in the context of an assumed necessity of economic growth or 'development.' Towards the end of his article "Was Stalin Really Necessary?", he writes that

> the serious problem for us is to see how far certain elements of Stalinism, in the sense of purposefully-applied social coercion, imposed by a party in the name of an

ideology, are likely or liable to accompany rapid economic development even in non-Communist countries.

And furthermore,

> unless we realize how complex are the problems which development brings, how irrelevant are many of our ideas to the practical possibilities open to statesmen in these countries, we may unconsciously drive them towards the road which led to Stalin. They cannot be satisfied with 'the pace of a tortoise.' (1962, pp.32-33)

Noting in passing the identification with 'western goals,' we notice that he takes as givens not only the existence of a national economy and a State, but also the categories of development and growth. Hence he is evidently unable to explain their basis: he does not contribute to the *critique* of political economy.

In similar fashion he *prefaces* a discussion of whether or not "Marxist 'class' analysis" can be applied to the USSR with the statement that

> few will disagree that the Soviet system has evolved into a hierarchical society within which status and power depends decisively on rank.
>
> Indeed, one could, without too much exaggeration, fit Soviet society into a 'universal civil and military service' model. (1975, p.616)[11]

Towards the end of the same text he states without qualification that Soviet society was indeed "*based* on a civil and military service." (original emphasis). Having adopted such a view he evidently disbars himself from analysing the class relations in political-economic terms: that is, in terms of the categories defining the relations of production. It follows that he cannot theorise the class struggle.

To some extent, though, such assumptions have been disregarded by the French 'Novian' theorist Roland, who has endeavoured to place the 'success indicator' at the centre of a much more profound political-economic analysis. (1989). Although not a Marxist in that he sees 'remuneration' and economy as anthropological 'invariants' and denies the possible existence of the category of abundance (pp.27-28 and 149), he is clearly influenced by Marx as well as by Nove when he theorises the existence of an important contradiction in the USSR between the category of use-value and the category of 'indicator value.' At the same time, however, he makes it clear that he is not arguing anything other than that

> the simple contradiction between use-value and indicator-value expresses in germinal form a large proportion [*porte en germe une grande partie*] of the

inherent contradictions of the Soviet mode of production. (Roland 1989, p.82)

And he goes on to say that what this means is simply that the contradictions of the mode of production appear "most starkly" when the analysis begins with the contradiction between use-value and indicator-value. (p.82).

We have criticised the concept of indicator-value in Chapter 3 above (Note 28), but now the point to be made is that it is part of a concept with which Roland describes the contradictory form of the product. It does not necessarily imply a concept of wage-labour. Indeed it is not Roland's view that the USSR was capitalist; and in his chapter on labour and the workers (pp.146-69) he simply states that the workers are subordinated and alienated, and does not discuss the form of the surplus product. Instead, he simply explains that the shortage economy corresponding to the inherent inefficiency of calculation by indicator-value necessarily leads to an endemic shortage of labour at enterprise level. In response to this state of affairs, a great premium is placed upon workers' marginal productivity, defined as their co-operation in ensuring nominal plan fulfilment as opposed to underfulfilment (the 'Micawber effect'). Marginal production is thus, generally speaking, highly 'labour-power elastic.' (pp.164-65). Consequently there is a tendency towards wage-levelling, as the low-paid are motivated by their less agreeable work to take more advantage of their own utility at the margin. Meanwhile, the "extra-economic means" of compulsion employed in the 1940s and early 1950s were bound to be of no long-term usefulness since their efficacity depended above all on "surprise."

On one hand, then, Roland does bring in workers' subjectivity, albeit vaguely, and albeit in terms of a 'natural' taking advantage of arhythmic production. On the other, he refers to the withering effectiveness of certain means of control as a 'natural' development dependent essentially on the regime's inability to ensure the "intrinsic moral motivation" of the "individual." (pp.161-67). Since the form of labour is not an issue which he tackles with the same kind of attention with which he theorises use-value and indicator-value, there is little discussion of the wage-form and no explicit reference to actual struggle, or even indeed to a conflict of interests.

The discussion of the shortage to which Roland refers has been associated especially with the Hungarian 'market socialist' economist Kornai, who has developed a theory of the so-called 'socialist' economies in which shortage appears as a major category. (See especially Kornai 1979, 1980a, and 1992, chaps. 11-12). The main features of this theory are the description of firm-level decision-making constrained by resource availability and 'vertical bureaucratic bargaining' rather than by demand, in an environment where budget constraints are 'soft' rather than 'hard.' (1980a, vol.2, pp.299-322; 1980b).[12] This work is certainly useful to a critique of the relations of distribution, but since Kornai's basic optic is the economist's one of 'firms and households' he pays but brief attention to the underlying form of the relationship between the workers and the overall political economy. Indeed the main question on which he concentrates in regard to the workers is the relationship between workers and 'employers,' by which he means enterprise managers. Thus he writes that

> the same can be said of bosses as of employees: the relative weights of the two opposing groups of motives vary according to the country, period, and individual concerned. But ultimately, it is typical of classical socialism for the bureaucratic interest of firm and factory managers to prevail. (1992, pp.220-21)

In relation to the allocation of labour and the setting of wages he considers two sets of factors. First, there are the bureaucratic factors, among which he counts the power of production managers to dictate tasks, the compulsory assignation to particular enterprises, the official "political propaganda activity in the workplace," and the connections which 'leaders of firms' enjoy with the local police. In summary, he states that "a firm becomes a cell of totalitarian power, not merely a scene of work." (pp.221-22). Secondly, in the specific context of wage-setting he mentions that there is considerable "bargaining between employed workers and their immediate superiors," which puts the worker in a position which is all the stronger according to the urgency of the assignment and the indispensability of the employee. Workers may 'convey their dissatisfaction' verbally or by 'withholding performance"; or they may leave a worse place of work for a better one. (1992, pp.225-26; see also 1980a, vol.2, p.401). But he does not state whether or not this has any political-economic effect other than the determination of wages at a higher level than would otherwise be the case. And even in this context he asserts that wage-setting remains "by and large" in the hands of bureaucracy. He thus omits to explain how the workers' position can be at all strong in the context of the firm's 'totalitarianism.' He is aware of wage drift as an empirical reality, but he does not give adequate meaning to his view that "how the average wage finally develops depends on the prevailing power relations." (1992, pp.225-27).

His conclusion is that the official ideology that labour — presumably he means labour-power — is not a commodity under "socialism" is invalid, at least in such a "strongly worded form." Market coordination does have a certain influence on labour allocation and wage-setting. On the other hand, the official assertion is true "insofar as the market influence is secondary" in relation to the influence of bureaucratic coordination. The analysis can thus be seen to be very far removed from a consideration of underlying political-economic categories such as the form of labour. Indeed the view of workers' struggle essentially reduces to the idea that to the extent that labour [sic] is sold, workers have some bargaining-power; but to the extent that it is not, they are subject to a form of oppression which is "graver" than market-based dependence. (1992, p.227).[13] This might easily be said about any society that is exploitative, but unfortunately Kornai gives no greater theorisation than this of the workers' actual position and struggle.

THE WORKING CLASS

Descriptive Studies

Thematic Studies: A Summary

Given the views of sovietology's leading theorists on the negligible importance of an understanding of the fundamental class relation underlying the nature of the political economy, it is perhaps not surprising that many of the sovietologists who have studied matters affecting the working class have ignored class struggle altogether. This is not only true of works by those such as Berliner (1957), Conquest (1967), and Schapiro and Godson (1981), who — by reason of their 'totalitarian' influence — are predisposed to conceive of the 'conflict' between the system and the working class as primarily one-way: it is also true of other studies. Thus Deutscher (1950) and Lowit (1971), in considering Soviet trade-unionism, fail altogether to consider workers' conflicts; as does Yanowitch in his study of inequality and management reform, despite describing conditions a Marxist would view as highly confrontational. (1977, 1985; see also his edited volume of 1982). Others have focused simply on various aspects of the 'function' of the official unions in mediation and policy formation. (Kahan and Ruble 1979, chaps. 4-7).

A number of authors have considered inequality without analysing either class conflict or even class itself.[14] Thus Matthews, who writes with considerable interest on numerous aspects of working class life (1972), fails in an explicitly 'illustrative' book (p. xvii) even to mention the empirical reality of class conflict either in the workplace or elsewhere. And when he considers the link between poverty and crime (1986, pp.109-12), he understands the former purely quantitatively, thereby ignoring questions of class altogether, to say nothing of the relationship between class and law. (1986, 1989). Connor adopts a similar approach when writing about deviance and inequality, considering class-based cultural 'bias' only in passing. (1972, pp.238-40; 1979a, pp.211-13 and 291-92). So does A. McAuley, who writes about "poverty, living-standards, and inequality," but not about class. (1979). Perhaps the most extreme position is occupied by

Kahan, who not only understands "economic differentiation" solely in terms of quantitative wage and income differentials (1979, pp.296-99), but denies the relevance of the term 'class' altogether. (pp.308-09).[15] Since without a concept of class it is hard to reach an understanding of how one society can have replaced another, for such theorists the need to refer in the Soviet context to a 'society' would seem equally encumbering.

This is not to say that some sovietologists have not studied various aspects of working class assertion. But those who have have usually done so in isolation from an overall understanding of society. Thus Roberts and Feingold (1958), Brown (1966), M. McAuley (1969), Ruble (1981), and Lampert (1986) each give consideration to working class pressure, but exclusively in terms of its formal structural mediations with the authorities, either with the unions or in the courts. Haynes and Semyonova (1979), meanwhile, assuming that the essence of opposition is to push towards social-democratic reform, devote most of their attention to the dissident minority and the miniscule 'independent trade unions' of the late 1970s. And whilst Ruble accepts that there may be a relationship, albeit 'indirect,' between workers' 'unofficial' activities and the official efforts to 'upgrade' union performance (1981), he unfortunately stops there and leaves the point theoretically undeveloped. In relation to "worker dissatisfaction" Gidwitz goes significantly further (1982), but even she limits her considerations to causes which are above all contingent: first, the "direct" ones, namely "actual working conditions" [*sic*], compensation, and "unsatisfactory labor-management relations brought about by party and state manipulation of the trade-union function" (pp.26-29); and second, the more "indirect" ones, such as the general "'quality of life' issues" relating to matters of health, morality, and rights. (pp.30-32). Seeing conflict as no more than a sum of disputes, she fails to theorise any sort of underlying cause relating to the workers' position as a class.

Recent analyses of labour relations under *perestroika*, whilst informative, have similarly tended to omit a more general theorisation of the nature of class and exploitation. (Friedgut and Siegelbaum 1990, Oxenstierna 1990, Rutland 1990, Aves 1992, Temkina 1992). Typically, Aves (1992) gives much empirical information on the institutional development of the labour movement between 1989 and 1991, but cannot be said to employ any approach of a *theoretical* kind. For him the conditions which the 'new' labour movement "grew out of and reflected" were nothing more than the disillusionment with socialist ideology, the difficulty under "authoritarian communism" of forming independent organisations, and the "unimportance of nationalism." (p.138). By listing these three negatives, he is clearly separating himself by a very great distance from the standpoint of materialism.

Even D. Mandel, who — from an explicitly left-wing point of view — has gone considerably further in emphasising workers' subjectivity, fails to achieve theoretical depth. Thus after running through some of the well-known characteristics of the relationship between workers and management — wage-levelling, labour shortage, and a relatively substantial social wage, as against poor conditions and frequent violations of labour law (1988, pp.139-43; 1989, pp.10-12) — he fails to put the elements together with any materially-based theoretical coherence. Instead, underlying his work there is the idea that worker-management relations were ultimately determined by something abstract called the 'system.' Workers enjoyed job security simply because there was a 'command economy'; and meanwhile they derived a certain bargaining power from a labour shortage created and maintained by the 'command system.' (1989, pp.10-11). (The inverted commas are Mandel's). Predictably, Mandel is led to underestimate the power that workers exercised in opposition to this system (see also Mandel 1988, p.148): not explicitly, because nowhere does he ask how substantial this power actually was; but implicitly, because by assuming the system as a sort of given, at least in the pre-Gorbachev period, he drastically overestimates its health. In stating that in return for their advantages workers "helped management meet plan objectives" (1989, p.12), Mandel misses the fundamental point demonstrated by Ticktin (1973a; 1991c, pp.116-29) and others (for example, Wilhelm 1979 and 1985, and Rutland 1985): namely, the Soviet economy was never successfully planned at all.

If the economy had been planned, of course, the question as to why it entered crisis would become even thornier. But progress might nonetheless be made if 'planning' theorists were to tackle this problem, especially in its aspects relating to labour relations. Mandel, however, fails to oblige.

> Some workers...only half-ironically refer to the last half of the Brezhnev era as their 'golden age' — because it was relatively easy then to reach a working agreement with management. But it is important to emphasize that the extreme development of this system was the direct consequence of the regime's refusal to reform the economy, a refusal dictated by the corporate interests of its bureaucratic base as well as by a more general fear of the popular forces a structural reform of the economy might unleash. (1989, p.12)

Any notion of a historical development of the class relation has been replaced here by the completely unsupported view that the central contradiction was that which operated between the tendencies for and against reform. We are thus left with the tautology that the system entered crisis because it resisted reform.

In looking at the movement for reform as it actually arose, Mandel consequently finds himself unable fully to cut through the official reformist propaganda. He may accept that the reform aims to "tighten things on the shopfloor," increase differentials, lower the social wage, and so on; but at the same time he asserts that

> another goal is to link the workers' well-being more closely to the performance of the enterprise,...to create a common motivation among managers and workers to discover and to release productive reserves, to increase individual and enterprise efficiency, and to produce quality goods that meet the needs of clients and consumers. (p.14)

Still standing on ground marked out the previous year (1988), Mandel goes so far as to approve of Gorbachev's avowal of support for this goal (1989, p.15) when others might take it for little more than 'participationist' managerial rhetoric. And whilst he eventually decides that the government has gradually abandoned "producers' self-management, originally a central part of its reform" (1990b, p.100), Mandel seems constantly anxious to relate the contradictions of labour market reform and labour conflict to the extent to which the authorities fail to live up to their word. (1989, 1990b). One can summarise his analysis by observing how it focuses above all upon the potential for realisation of Union-level economic and political reforms which are truly democratic. In this view, the 'essence' of the underlying anti-bureaucratic tendency of workers' self-assertion, were such a tendency to ripen, would manifest itself as follows. On one hand, initiative would flow 'upwards' from an independent movement of workers; on the other, the expression of that initiative would — at its most radical — involve the "coherent linking" of the interests of workers and managers with each other as well as with the "overall interests of society" (1989, p.35), in the context of a controlled and gradual expansion of market relations. (1990b, p.111). The difference between this aim and that of a capitalistic "monopolism based upon workers' self-management" would rest primarily on the placing of 'accent' upon "the collective power of the workers" rather than on the market mechanism which that power would supposedly make use of. (1990c, pp.143-49). Applied to specific struggles (1991a), Mandel's theory has no real explanatory value, and indeed appears as little more than a statement of political ideology.

Two Diachronic Descriptive Studies

Of the 'empiricist' work perhaps the most 'historical' extreme is occupied by Grancelli and Connor, whose works appear much more useful even in the absence of an overall view of society. Thus, even if Grancelli has collected most of his material prior to *perestroika*, he is fully aware (1988) that the conditions from which labour relations emerge are always none other than the material and contradictory labour relations of the previous era. Tracing such phenomena as absenteeism, turnover, theft, and poor productivity all the way through from Tsarism to the dawn of the Gorbachev period (pp.3-73), he looks at how they continued to manifest under a variety of management strategies. He consequently insists on studying trade-unionism in terms of the actual labour relations (pp.106-42), rather than — as is more usual — the other way around. But whilst his analysis undoubtedly provides a rich 'background' for the study of *perestroika*, its utility remains empirical rather than theoretical. Grancelli's empiricism might be described as 'diachronic' rather than 'synchronic': showing little interest in questions of class, he fails to study the *degree* to which the imperatives of systemic development are obstructed by workers' action. Having no theory of the nature and aims of social production as a whole, he fails to identify the *necessity* of this obstruction as a fact which translates to the immanent possibility of crisis.

Connor too attempts to focus on the role of the workers in historical fashion. After pointing out that throughout Soviet history workers were the objects of "tumultuous change," he recognises very early on that control, while "pervasive," was never total, and that in the long run there occurred "much autonomous development." (1991, p.8). Unfortunately, though, he fails to build on this idea with sufficient coherence, and the points he makes about the phenomena of wage drift, wage-levelling, rising aspirations, and increasing discontent during and after the Brezhnev period appear unanchored to any overall view of active historical process.

Although one of Connor's main preoccupations is to draw connections between 'autonomous development' and matters of class, his grasp of the former suffers greatly owing to his 'idealist' and sociological view of the latter. Thus all of the 'class characteristics' he looks for either relate primarily to consciousness (p.10; see also 1979b, pp.314-16) rather than to activity, resistance, or power; or else they derive from notions of collectivity and 'self-regulation' (1991, pp.41-42) which have little to do with any shared relationship, either objective or subjective, to the means and mode of production. The resultant effect on his work is severe. In making statements such as that over-qualification and 'unattractive jobs' provide "ample grounds for alienation," as does work which is hard, dirty, or boring (pp.167-68), Connor fails to escape the tautological, since people who are socially forced to engage in activities they find disagreeable are by definition 'alienated' both from the activities and from the enforcement. If alienation exists, Connor has done little more than to register its existence. His approach to workers' subjective action is similarly faulted, in that he considers a number of causes of discontent and a number of types of workers' resistance but remains unable to theorise what unites them. By looking at what workers thought so as to discover whether or not they formed a class, he misses the wider significance of what they did precisely *as* a class.[16] In these terms, their becoming more 'class-like' under Brezhnev and eventually a fully-fledged class by 1989 appears purely "accidental." (pp.316-18).

There is perhaps more theoretical substance to his analysis of 'negative control,' which he considers in terms of ease and mass of turnover, the structural microeconomic shortage of labour, and absenteeism correctly considered as "the 'recapture,' or theft, of time from the employer."

> Workers' 'negative control' practices certainly show some capacity to act, as workers, in opposition to what management does to impinge on workers' interests. (p.172)

Connor undoubtedly provides a great deal of empirical evidence to support this view. But nonetheless he omits completely to theorise the subjectivity whose existence as force one might have inferred from the very use of such terms as 'recapture.' Showing absenteeism as something "imposed" by awkward opening hours in the service sector and "abetted" by managerial laxity "in the area of 'unenforceable' rules" (p.172), Connor seems to forget that such a widespread practice represents a historical *choice*, on the part of tens of millions of workers, to *assert* their interests as workers. Choices are made, not imposed. Second, in relation to the workplace itself, whilst Connor accepts (p.197) that "workers' negative control practices" in general exerted pressure for 'easy' norms, higher wage bonuses, and lower differentials, he neglects to make a proper assessment of their impact at the level of the economy as a whole.

> Negative control, in this sense, seems a limited but clear manifestation of elements of working-class identity and opposition, if only at the level of the shop, the section, or the plant. (p.197)

Connor is certainly aware that the strikes and protests which took place prior to the onset of open crisis in 1989-90 usually occurred in *defence* of the normal or 'contractual' understanding between workers and the authorities (pp.220-25), but behind his theory of that 'contractuality' there lies little conception of an overall balance of power. In places he does argue that 'wage drift' eventually caused the authorities major problems, but ultimately he sees this phenomenon as no more than one of the standard "rules and operating procedures" which begat problematic results "almost automatically." (p.223).

Three Theoretical Positions

We now turn to three theses to which, in general, the above criticisms do not apply. Although the correspondence between a consideration of the working class and a general theory of the USSR is stressed to varying degrees in each case, we would argue that it exists in such a fashion as to allow each thesis to escape the more common 'empiricism,' at least in its more extreme forms. The idea of 'incorporation' (Lane) may be in irreconcilable contradiction with communist theoretical precepts, but it undoubtedly relates very strongly to a certain view, albeit a completely mistaken view, of the overall social formation. So do the theories of the 'social compact' (Pravda) and the 'historic compromise' (Zaslavsky), and these we have found to be of a limited instructive value.

The 'Incorporated Worker'

In his article on "Dissent and Consent under State Socialism" (1972) Lane states that the "entities" known as social classes were not major "actors" in what he terms the "state socialist" societies, and that these "societies" consequently appeared to be 'revolution-proof.' In later works he has developed his theory of one of these 'minor actors' and expounded his thesis that the Soviet industrial worker constituted a specific 'type': he or she was the 'incorporated' worker, as distinct from other 'types' which exist elsewhere. In his view, Soviet workers did not have an adequately homogeneous culture to qualify as 'traditional' proletarians. Nor were they respectful enough of their bosses to be counted as 'deferential.' Finally, they did not belong to the 'privatised' type either, since 'Marxism-Leninism' was the dominant ideology and workers were guaranteed jobs. (Lane and O'Dell 1978, pp.45-50). The Weberian nature of Lane's approach is self-evident.

Of interest in the present context is the way that Lane and O'Dell define the working class and understand workers' conflicts with the interests of the regime. We shall deal with these two matters in sequence. First, their approach to class is not Marxist, but sociological. For them, the Soviet working class included both manual workers and technicians and engineers; and 'non-manual workers' themselves formed a group which also included "employees of trade union and Party, officials in the Soviets, and professionals." Although this latter 'stratum' may have had a "specific cultural role," it was not 'disjunct' from the working class "in a Marxist sense," since the Soviet Union was a "politically unitary class society" which did not know any "class domination." (pp.4-6). Consequently, far from being an exploited class producing a surplus for appropriation by others, the working class was simply a set of occupational strata. It should further be mentioned that from this point of view, the concept of class is not at all fundamental: 'social inequality' appears as a matter not of class exploitation, nor even of any other class relation, but primarily one of 'stratification,' status, and differential 'occupational prestige.' (Lane 1971, 1976, chap. 7, and 1985a).[17]

Second, whilst they recognise that workers acted in ways which were problematic for the 'elites,' this is explained without reference to the *necessity* of struggle. Thus at first Lane and O'Dell perceive low productivity simply as a "cultural artefact" — a sort of leftover from the traditional peasant life-style — and as that alone. (1978, p.20). In this view absenteeism and drunkenness represent nothing more than "'deviant' attitudes," similarly derived and without "significant political implications." Since they do not conceive of social production relations as having been the foundation of Soviet society, it is not surprising that they view even "intense industrial conflict" — from strikes to the Novocherkassk uprising of 1962 — as having been "essentially economistic" and therefore devoid of antagonistic significance on the general social level. (p.48).

Although Lane changes his view slightly in his later works, the basic approach remains the same. Thus he accepts that lax work discipline is also conditioned by "the absence of structural unemployment, and by generally rising standards of living" (1985a, p.159); and further argues on a more general level that full employment strengthens 'labour's position *vis-à-vis* management.' (1987, p.3). But when he traces back the chain of cause and effect, though, he is constricted by his approach to find that what actually causes full employment in the first place is the ideology or 'ethic' of the regime, rather than material factors.[18] Rather than theorising full employment as a class relation determined by struggle, he understands it as a 'social policy' brought about by a 'legitimating ideology' and promoted by "three main interests: management, labour and Party." (p.231). Thus he continues to neglect the significance of a state of affairs where workers resist their rulers' need for them to work harder.

Such an approach to the nature and struggles of the Soviet working class leads directly to the concept of 'incorporation.'

> The authority structure is accepted. [Incorporated] workers participate in improving production, and they are closer to the administration both socially and politically than workers in capitalist society.... The trade union developed under the political authorities rather than against them. It is more an aid to management than a defence of strictly workers' interests. Its manifold social and welfare activites further the integration of the worker in the factory. (1985, pp.165-66)

Having thus identified "workers" with their State-recognised representation, Lane goes on to opine that "the structural features of Soviet society undoubtedly inhibit [class] opposition." This was so because "the threat of sanctions for anti-state activity has been effective in binding the worker to the system." As further support for this view — which is strikingly reminiscent of Friedrich and Brzezinski's a generation before — Lane quotes an American journalist's observation that Soviet workers spoke proudly of their own chief as 'a strong boss': indeed, workers "like[d] the feeling that someone above them [was] firmly in charge." (p.166).[19] It is also averred that the Soviet working class had "a general conception of serving the national interest."

Writing in 1985, Lane foresees that from the mid-1980s on there would be a "greater maturation" of the working class. (He does not explain what this means in a country supposedly without class domination). He then makes two predictions which have since been proven manifestly false. The first is that any major upheaval "can only come if there is association [of the working class] with other social groupings — say [*sic*] intellectuals or the scientific intelligentsia — and possibly if it is linked to a wider unifying theme like the question of national integrity." The second is that, since "the values of Soviet society [gave] the working class a leading role in its political organization," and "the ideology of state socialism [gave] the working class a legitimacy to press its claims," the authorities "[were] likely to respond to grievances and to compromise with the workers." (1985a, p.167). It is now, of course, common knowledge that working class standards of living have fallen more or less continuously since 1985, and that economic reform means mass unemployment.

It is clear from his book *Soviet Society Under Perestroika* (1992) that Lane has now updated his analysis in accordance with developments in the late 1980s. But the underlying theory remains the same. Thus he asserts that "labour productivity has *declined* because standards of punctuality, workmanship, and labour discipline *have been* poor" [emphasis added], and argues somewhat unconvincingly that a change in workers' attitudes to work resulted from "greater acquisitiveness and the rise of a consumer mentality." (p.161). Still neglecting to theorise the necessary struggle between classes, he keeps to the view that the manual working class was a "major support" for previous governments, and that it stopped being so only under pressure from economic reform. (This position is tenable only if one believes that the sole function of a government is to stay in office, and ignores its role as the administrator of capital accumulation.) Under the heading "The Rise of an Independent Workers' Movement," Lane then focuses exclusively on the (Russian-nationalist) United Workers' Front, and concentrates particularly on its demand for more workers' representation in the soviets. The term 'incorporation' no longer appears, but it would seem that Lane's basic conception is that whereas the workers used to be incorporated via politics, after a 'period of transition' they will eventually be incorporated via the market and the law. (p.184).[20]

The 'Social Compact'

Like Lane, Pravda too adopts a Weberian approach. In his article "Is There a Soviet Working Class?" (1982) he thus announces without explanation that "traditional Marxist class criteria seem unlikely to be useful in a society where the state owns the means of production,"[21] and proceeds to make use of the concept of the 'class group,' a sort of cross between Weber's notions of 'class' and 'status group.' A class group is defined as a 'multibonded' product of "converging dimensions of differentiation."[22] The social attributes necessary for membership of such a group relate to educational resources and 'prestige' as well as to work and the "material economy." (pp.2-3). But nonetheless, since Pravda focuses to a far greater degree than Lane on actual and potential areas of conflict, his work appears more useful in terms of the present study.

In the aforementioned article Pravda begins by looking at working class composition. He shows how, although there was no clear-cut divide between blue-collar and white-collar workers in terms of pay, among blue-collar workers as a group there were substantial differentials. Coalminers and skilled metalworkers could earn three times as much as factory or hospital cleaners, and the salaries of the most highly-skilled overlapped with those of middle-ranking engineers and managers. (pp.6-7). Moreover, in income and housing terms, the standard of living of skilled manual workers often outstripped that of the 'worker-technicians' who spent most of their time supervising automated machinery, and even that of the ITRs (*inzhenerno-tekhnicheskie rabotniki*, or semi-professional technical employees). (p.9). After further considering job complexity, education, and especially 'class identification,' Pravda discovers a 'working-class group' and a 'working-middle-class group,' both of which were distinct from the intelligentsia. By the criterion of self-identification the 'working class group' was comprised almost exclusively of blue-collar workers, whereas the other group (self-identifying either as 'employees' [*sluzhashchie*] or as 'middle class') included most of the ITRs, most white-collar workers, and those manual workers with a specialist secondary education. (pp.14-16).

Travelling 'forward' to the issue of contentment, behaviour and conflict, Pravda looks for differentiation by 'class group.' In terms of contentment, or lack of it, "on the pay or general material front," he finds little to distinguish the two groups; but in terms of national politics he discovers clear differences. Unskilled manual workers formed the least 'interested' and 'literate' group, whereas skilled workers, particularly those in the 'working-middle-class group,' seemed as "attentive to political events as their semi-professional middle-class counterparts," albeit less likely to understand what was going on. (pp.20-23).

Pravda finds that the indifference, caution and scepticism displayed by members of the 'working class group' at the national political level were not at all evident inside the enterprise. Indeed, at the workplace workers in both 'class groups' showed a high level of assertiveness. (See also Pravda 1981b, pp.58-59). But rather than reconsidering his category of 'class group' — which did not feature in his earlier work (1979a, 1979b) — Pravda prefers to state that this separation of the 'shopfloor' level of conflict from national politics made it unlikely that the working class would subject the *political* system to serious strain, since contentious issues were simply resolved 'informally.' For him it follows that it was the 'working-middle-class group,' or the 'new' (educated and skilled) working class which was the more "volatile." As a 'middle-class' group [*sic*], it had a "general vested interest in change," unlike the 'old' working class, which shared the 'upper-class' groups' taste for political and economic immobility. (1982, pp.22-24). The assumption on which such conclusions rest is clear: namely, if working class assertiveness does not consciously aim for reform, then it must be conservative. It is worth restating the opposite, communist view that faith in reformist politics acts against the only tendency in struggle which really challenges society 'at the roots': proletarian autonomy.

When Pravda begins with an analysis of the underlying relations between the top and bottom of society, however, his work appears from a Marxist viewpoint to be much more useful, even if at no point does he bend towards such a viewpoint himself. In his article on "East-West Interdependence and the Social Compact in Eastern Europe" (1981a) he states that

> People's relationship to the regime is conditioned by the authorities' satisfaction of what are largely economic welfare expectations. These expectations constitute what may be called a social compact between rulers and ruled, between those who run the workers' state [*sic*] and the workers themselves....(p.163)[23]

Although Pravda restricts his consideration here to Czechoslovakia, the GDR, Hungary and Poland, the idea is equally applicable to the analysis he has published of workers' activities in the USSR. (1979a). He shows how workers expected what they had learnt to expect: namely, in production, full employment, job security, slack labour discipline, and fairly 'egalitarian' wages regarded as welfare payments rather than related to performance; and in consumption, the availability of basic commodities, a slow improvement in the range of goods on sale, and stable prices. Moreover, whilst the "authoritarian and paternalistic state" demanded a high level of formal compliance, it required "minimal commitment of any real significance." (1981a, p.163; see also 1979b, pp.214-15).

Pravda presents a picture where the economic development necessary for producer and consumer growth was increasingly requiring a revision of the 'social compact.' He begins with production:

Three sets of problems affecting labor productivity are connected with the social compact production norms: absenteeism, full employment and job security, and the pace and quality of work. (p.166)

Pravda identifies both poor discipline (taking forms such as absenteeism, slack work and malingering) and worker-led mobility (moonlighting as well as upping and leaving one's job) as severe restraints on 'productivity.' He shows how, as attempts were made to circumvent such restraints, new problems such as burgeoning deficits and debts followed in their wake. In regard to consumption he cites rising consumer expectations and an aversion to the removal of subsidies as further problematic corollaries of the 'social compact.' (pp.170-74).

The basic problem facing the proponents of price rationalisation is the workers' tendency to conceive the relationship between prices and the standard of living in zero-sum terms.

And linking production to consumption, Pravda writes that talk of productivity-linked wage-rises to match price increases "arouses rather than allays workers' suspicions." (1979b, p.217).

Writing from a pro-reform point of view Pravda concludes that the development of more open and more complex economies in Eastern Europe will necessitate not only a replacement of the 'traditional' social compact with one where higher rewards are on offer for harder work and less security, but also the introduction of political reform. In his view,

in the final instance, the public's, and specifically the proletariat's, actual response to government measures depends on that regime's record and credibility. (1981a, p.178)

Whereas Lane implies that what he calls the "economistic" nature of industrial conflict distinguished it from class struggle proper, Pravda takes the opposite view that political participation — and, more specifically, a degree of independent workers' representation — is highly advisable precisely in order to control such conflict and divest it of its general objective antagonism in relation to the development of the economy. His insights into the 'social compact' — and into the need to change radically "the traditional social compact passivity of the population as citizens" (pp.178-80)[24] — clearly suggest an intensification of the elite's struggle against an 'obdurate' working class and a growth of political mediation as a safety-valve.

Pravda's analysis is very coherent. Having identified working class economic behaviour — he does not actually write 'struggle' — as a major problem for economic development — that is, for what was shown above to be capital accumulation — he considers ways to push back if not to vault the barrier it represents.[25] After describing (1979b, pp.233-34) how in the industrial sphere the Party was of negligible use in the articulation of workers' economic grievances and the mediation and resolution of conflicts, and before considering (pp.237-40) how workers' participation in management seems similarly unable to "provide a satisfactory solution to the problem of workers' dissent" he states starkly that

> in a more positive vein [*sic*], there is some evidence to show that more effective unions can help prevent workers' collective protests. (p.236)

As he explains elsewhere, the reason for this is that

> if they gain workers' confidence at the shopfloor level, unions can help divert conflicts into more controllable institutional channels. (1981a, p.180)

This is by no means a trivial point, but unfortunately Pravda does not go on to discuss the conflict between, on one hand, the efficacy of such diversion — by unions or by other means — and, on the other, the resilience, force and dynamic of workers' autonomous struggle.

To summarise, it should first be noted that at its most rigorous Pravda's view of the social compact is usefully centred upon an understanding of a relation of force between the exploiters and exploited, based on a fundamental division of interests. But its main weakness is that he fails to theorise the nature of economic growth, and still less its necessity, in terms of political-economic categories. Thus whilst in places he does recognise, from a reformist point of view, the 'awkwardness' of uninstitutionalised workers' resistance, he does not explicitly refer to the need for its institutionalised control as a need felt exclusively on one side of the class divide. Since economic growth has entered as an unexplained, untheorised necessity, it follows that the revision of the 'social compact' appears in terms which are similar: he does not discuss it explicitly as a development, or possible development, of the underlying class antagonism.[26]

The 'Historic Compromise'

Writing, like Pravda, towards the end of the Brezhnev period, Zaslavsky presents a theory of a 'historic compromise' between, on one side, the political regime, and on the other, the "populace." According to this view, the "existing distribution of power" is accepted, but only on three conditions: first, that prices stay low;

second, that employment is guaranteed; and third, that people remain "free to seek individual ways to improve their living standards." (1982, p.133).

In relation to Pravda's theory, Zaslavsky's theory appears more historical. Delving back further, Zaslavsky thus explains the Brezhnev period against the backdrop of the contradictions of Stalinism.

> When various groups of people pursue a similar course of action, spontaneous social movements are often formed. Political power at first attempts to suppress these outcomes but eventually ends up tolerating them. Even in the Stalin era, consent was only partially wrung from the population by the coercive apparatus: to a considerable extent it was voluntarily granted by members of some key social groups in exchange for actual or future benefits.

He continues:

> this holds even truer for the Brezhnev period as well and is, indeed, its distinctive feature. Soviet society is far from being a lump of clay that yields to any pressure from above; its internal policy does not merely depend on the whims of the party leadership. Brezhnev's period is characterized by a continuous dialectical interplay of state and society, which is not limited solely to governmental initiatives and the population's mechanical reaction but also incorporates mass popular actions that occasionally compel the state to yield. (p.135)

Thus he shows how the authorities were unable to enforce the 1940 ban on job-changing and eventually had to repeal it in 1956 (1979-80, p.47; 1982, p.135); and how the Kosygin reforms of 1965 were scuppered by semi-skilled workers among others. (1979-80, pp.48-51).

Evidently Zaslavsky ascribes great significance to the actual class struggle; and it is from a clearly classist perspective that he studies such phenomena as alcoholism (a double-edged "weapon" [1979-80, pp.53-54]), job-changing (pp.46-48), and migration (1982, pp.137-46). Of special interest is his analysis of the employment in closed cities of 'guestworkers' from the countryside (1982, especially pp.144-47). As regards the lack of work discipline he takes pains to point out that it

> clearly indicates a conflict between the party-state machine and large segments of the working class. It is important not to ignore or underestimate this conflict just because it is not accompanied by open and organized struggles. (p.160)

In his first prognosis, however, Zaslavsky fails to define actual antagonistic polarities. In an article originally drafted in 1978 he thus predicts that the "1960s type of economic reform will be resumed, since by the mid-1980s it will have become absolutely necessary" (1979-80, p.64), but does not really explain why the latter suggestion might be the case, or indeed what it actually means. Whilst arguing that the "equilibrium between workers' discontent and support may be seriously disrupted," he also takes the view that full employment will definitely continue, even under conditions of reform. Reform may come from 'above' or from 'below,' but working class living-standards will rise regardless. (pp.64-65). Thus reform no longer appears as a classist concept.

By 1982 — after the invasion of Afghanistan, the election of Reagan, and the acceleration of the US-Soviet arms race, albeit not towards the 'Cold War' bipolarity of the 1950s — Zaslavsky puts forward a view which is somewhat different. Like Pravda, he now argues that the 'compromise' only works as long as it can guarantee a steady improvement in workers' conditions, and that since such an amelioration can no longer be ensured, "the economic basis of organized consensus is shrinking." (1982, pp.155-56). Inefficiency is growing, the disproportion between heavy industry and the consumer sector is becoming increasingly dysfunctional, and the "semi-free" labour market gives both workers and enterprise managers scope to exert substantial pressure on the central planners. No longer is Zaslavsky convinced that living-standards will improve: he now argues that "workers themselves are the first to experience food and dwelling scarcity, [and] the first to be victimized by queues and black markets." (p.160). From the point of view of the system, work discipline and work incentives are becoming ever greater problems, and maintenance of the status quo — the Brezhnev compromise — no longer seems an option.

But whilst Zaslavsky now holds that a restructuring attack on working class living-standards, either through firmer centralisation or through 'technocratic reform,' is inevitable (pp.161-63), he fails completely to specify the extent to which he attributes causation to internal factors, such as the position and action of the working class, rather than to externalities such as diplomacy and security.[27]

In short, his concept of the 'historic compromise' seems to be a more social-democratic version of Pravda's of the 'social compact.' Initially endeavouring, perhaps, to adopt the viewpoint of the working class, he does not do so with a sufficiently profound view of the basic antagonism. At first he turns economic reform into a key category which will coincide with improvements for everyone. Then, having rejected this view, he paints a deterioration of working class living-standards as a sort of necessary result of the growing (general?) need to combat inefficiency. The unstated position seems to be that the workers' resistance, or indiscipline, has eventually turned out to their own disadvantage.

SUMMARY

In this brief chapter we have shown how a range of sovietological works have fallen short of relating a view of class struggle to a theory of the political economy.

Thus the theorists of 'totalitarianism' (Inkeles and Bauer, Friedrich and Brzezinski, Pipes) assume that the absence of 'independent' workers' organisations meant that the workers were unable to struggle as a class; and the 'revisionist' students of 'interest groups' either concentrate on divisions within the elite (Skilling and Griffiths, Hough) or else explain social tensions more broadly but on what is still a political basis (Cohen).

We have looked at a number of 'economic' analyses focused around concepts such as technological development, success indicators, and shortage. If the Birmingham school (Amann, Cooper, Davies) produce no political-economic explanation of the technological 'lag' they describe, nor has Nove tackled the question of the form of labour which underlies the category of the success indicator. Indeed, Nove has assumed *a priori* that Soviet society is reasonably accurately characterised in terms of universal conscription into civil and military service. Both the Birmingham school and Nove assume that growth was necessary without explaining why this was the case; and both eschew any theoretical concept of exploitation.

Roland, meanwhile, focusing on the inherent inefficiency of the indicator system, describes how workers took advantage of a state of affairs which was 'labour-power elastic.' But he does so only in terms of 'natural' factors such as the individual lack of 'moral motivation' and the end of the effectiveness of brutal methods once they were no longer a 'surprise.'

Interested above all in firm-level decision-making, Kornai does write, albeit confusedly, about the factors affecting wage-setting. But failing to offer a coherent theory to explain both the 'bargaining' power of the workers and the 'totalitarianism' of the enterprise, he neither deals consistently with the sale of labour-power nor points to any alternative form of its alienation. Like Roland, he too omits to discuss theoretically the conflict of interests between social groups.

Of those sovietologists who have written specifically about the Soviet working class, most have produced empirical studies of such matters as relative hardship, the mediation of disputes, or the rise of organisations during *perestroika*. Even Grancelli and Connor, who have produced studies with an undoubted historical basis, and have further focused upon widespread labour indiscipline and slack work, have omitted to relate their observations to a theoretical consideration of either the nature of the production relations or the subjective force of the working class.

Finally, we have considered three theses which, while not Marxist, nonetheless relate an understanding of the working class to a theory, or at least a view, of the system. These are those produced by Lane, Pravda, and Zaslavsky. Where Lane, however, repeating the Soviet propaganda that the ruling officials were not 'disjunct' from the working class, minimises the importance of lax discipline and holds that workers were incorporated into the system, both Pravda and Zaslavsky emphasise workers' opposition.

After first describing how the working class was divided between a 'middle class' group with an interest in change and and an 'old' group sharing the rulers' 'conservatism,' Pravda later explains that workers in general were involved in a 'social compact' according to which security was received in return for poor work. And he shows in particular how the need for economic development (itself left theoretically unexplained) caused workers' resistance to productivity to become an ever greater problem. From the point of view of the controllers of labour he suggests that more effective unions might help to divert workers' assertiveness and reduce its antagonistic effect.

On a slightly more historical basis Zaslavsky also studies the decline of what he calls the "historic compromise." If at first he suggests that reform will benefit the workers, he eventually reaches the view that it will involve a deterioration of their living-standards. But like Pravda he fails to define antagonistic polarities.

The relationship between the position of the working class and the nature of the political-economic system has not featured greatly in the work of sovietologists. Whereas the 'political' theorists either deny the existence of class struggle or else interpret conflict in general in terms of the interplay of Statist interest groups, the 'economic' theorists fail to explain either the form of exploitation or the basis of the need for growth. Indeed these latter two factors are not discussed with theoretical profundity even by those who write of a 'compact' or 'compromise' between the workers and the rulers. And since there is little theoretical consideration of the nature of antagonistic resistance to systemic imperatives, the basis of the need to revise relations with the workers remains to be properly explained.

Notes

1 For more general discussions of the history of sovietology, see Laqueur 1967 and Ticktin 1994b.
2 There are, of course, numerous works on Soviet politics which have dealt with one aspect of the 'polity' or other, or with several aspects in sequence. (See for example Schapiro 1967, M. McAuley 1977, G. Smith 1992, Ponton 1994). But only those which suggest a view of the nature of the society which lies behind the polity are of interest in the present context.
3 A similar point to that made in relation to studies of Soviet politics must also be made in relation to studies of Soviet economics. (See for example Schwarz 1951, Bergson 1964,

Gregory and Stuart 1981, Wilczynski 1982, Bergson and Levine 1983). Bergson's book on the economics of Soviet 'planning' (1964), for instance, is an empirically useful work on the functioning of the system of economic decision-making, but it does not offer a theory of the basis of the economy, let alone of class relations.

4   In his presidential address to the 85th annual meeting of the American Political Science Association (2 September 1989) Pye discusses the role of political science faced with what he describes as the "crisis of authoritarianism." In his view, what "with modernisation and the inevitable growth in the complexities of societies, the *only hope* for the long-run stability of *any* society [emphasis added] is learning how to manage the disorderliness of politics." (1990, p.16). Associated with the view that politics and the State are natural and eternal, and that no society could survive for very long without political management, there is the classic avoidance of the fact that the nature of any society is determined by its social production relations.

5   In a later work — but one based on substantially the same research material — Inkeles describes the USSR as a society with a "relatively open" class system, in which the differences between social class groups...[were] not defined by sharp discontinuities in income." (1968, p.106.) It is worth mentioning that he places the United States in the same category. See also Bauer, Inkeles, and Kluckhohn 1956, where it is held (p.188) that "the Soviet worker appears to take the factory and its special form of organisation for granted and as the natural way of doing things." From here it is but a short step to Schapiro's hard-right view that Bolshevik 'totalitarianism' "draws response from the fear of freedom, the envy, the anti-intellectualism, the chauvinism...of mass man...with his own mass morality, his crude egalitarian and levelling aspirations and his herd paranoia." (1971, p.276).

6   In an empirically rich work on the management of Soviet industry, another participant in the Harvard project avoids discussing class altogether. (Berliner, 1957). Other such studies include Granick 1961, Conyngham 1973 and 1982, and Berliner 1988.

7   This is also the view expounded in Conquest 1967.

8   A similar preoccupation is evident in Schapiro's work on The *Communist Party of the Soviet Union*, although admittedly he does accept that his aim is purely "to tell the story of a political party." (1960, p. ix). See also Armstrong 1961.

9   Marxist theory makes it clear, of course, that no society can ever be an essentially ideological system.

10   Cohen describes how all contributors to the US government journal *Problems of Communism* were subjected to prior vetting by the FBI. Although the editor managed to have the relevant ruling relaxed, it remained in force until 1977.

11   Nove has also described the Politburo as being the board of directors of the "USSR Ltd." (1980a, p.83), thereby echoing Meyer's earlier reference to the "USSR, Incorporated." (1961). The essential point which Meyer offers in opposition to the 'totalitarians' is that economic decisions, in both the USSR and the United States, are generally made by professional managerial executives. Rather than being part of a critique of Soviet production relations as capitalist, however, this view is founded instead upon a sort of economic version of the political functionalism of the 'interest groupers.' Thus there is simply a desire to describe the operation of a 'modern industrial' economic system, and no definition is given of the underlying social forms of production, consumption, and distribution. In this context it is not surprising that Nove has stated his agreement with Wiles's classic empiricist view that there is an "extremely obvious" connection between size (of a

'society') and alienation (of what, exactly, is not specified) (Wiles 1977, p.585, cited in Nove 1978, p.233); nor that he regards the free distribution of resources, along with other aspects of communism, such as the abolition of the "commanders and the commanded," as simply "cloud cuckoo-land." (1980a, p.78). A key empirical study associated with this kind of 'managerialist' empiricism is Granick's work *The Red Executive*, subtitled *The Organization Man in Russian Industry*. (1961). Granick's analysis is quoted approvingly in Galbraith's work on *The New Industrial State*, wherein questions of class are similarly avoided. (1972, pp.117-20).

12   Although in places Kornai does write of underlying categories, he does not really discuss the nature of Soviet production. Meanwhile Wiles, who like Kornai aims to produce a work on 'political economy' (1962), has written little more than an economics textbook based on numerous 'models' influenced by official Soviet ideology. Its distance from a political-economic theory — and *a fortiori* from a critique of political economy — is amply illustrated by the comments that "to say that 'really Stalin was a capitalist because he liked to accumulate capital' is just an idiotic play on words" (p.3); and that Stalin had to 'rely on the labour market' because "formal labour direction is indissolubly connected with the name of Trotsky." (p.132).

13   Kornai's confusion as to whether or not labour-power is sold is also evident in his statement that "wage costs are unrealistically low by comparison with what the labor is actually costing society." (1992, p.225).

14   The sociologist Parkin, meanwhile, assumes from the outset in a well-known comparative work that class itself is precisely a matter of 'stratification' and 'inequality'. Endeavouring to define the specificity of the Soviet context he writes that the "political values underlying the command system are part of a broader social philosophy in which the commitment to egalitarianism occupies an important place," and that "consequently, the powers available to leaders within this system have generally been used to combat tendencies towards inequality, not to encourage them." (1971, pp.182-83). These remarkable statements are predicate upon a lack of recognition of the reality of class in terms of production relations — and indeed simply of reality. In a work devoted specifically to the USSR, meanwhile, the sociologist Littlejohn begins by adopting a 'multifactoral' approach to class (1984, pp.28-41) and concludes that whilst class relations might 'possibly' exist in the "informal sector," such relations operate far more importantly "between state agencies and the *kolkhozy*." (p.267). In this context his main disagreement with the official Soviet ideology is his rejection of the view that there are two distinct social groups in the 'State sector': the 'class' of workers and the 'stratum' of *intelligenty*. Applying sociological methodology, he thus asserts that income statistics clearly show that "no category of agents seems to be capable of establishing privileged access to the means of production." (pp.263-64). Curiously, the well-known fact that this access was generally dependent on factors other than rouble income passes completely unrecognised.

15   Kahan sees the term 'class' — along with 'stratum' — as generally inapplicable to hierarchical societies, except "perhaps" to nineteenth-century Europe. (p.309). His view that "the only proletarians [in the USSR] are the working women" (p.305) should probably be read as an ironic reference to the term's literal meaning in Latin.

16   The artificial separation that Connor presents in such comments as that "*being* a class cannot determine how to *act* as a class" (1991, p.319) is famously avoided by Thompson in

his work on the working class in England (1963). The critical, revolutionary view can be summarised as the view that it is precisely class struggle that determines class.

17　Lane's sociological approach to class, and his consequent arrival at the concept of the incorporated worker, might be seen as parallel to the essentially functionalist approach to the Soviet economy employed by the Birmingham sovietologists.

18　Another sovietologist to study full employment is Granick, who perceives it (1987) as in many ways the determining characteristic of the Soviet economy. Concerning himself, however, exclusively with its consequences, he considers conflict only in passing, and then — in the same way as M. McAuley (1969) and others — only in terms of the official mediation of disputes.

19　The reference is to H. Smith 1976, p.305. Lane's extract is preceded in Smith's work by two lines of equally impressionistic character: "In their most admiring moments, Russians praise Stalin as the *krepki khozyain* [*sic*], the strong master. He held society together in his grip and they liked that feeling." Smith's work is one of many such journalistic accounts. Despite providing a wealth of not uninteresting empirical material, it is burdened with many such prejudiced simplisms, and is in our view inferior to Walker 1986 and even Binyon 1985, if not perhaps to Shipler 1983. All of these works remain overshadowed by the earlier *Journey Into Russia* (1964) by van der Post, an 'explorer' with a British 'special military' background.

20　The precise terms used are those of a 'reconciliation' of interests.

21　This statement suggests, of course, an ignorance of the fact that Marx's main theoretical concern was to criticise production relations, not legal relations.

22　An equally clearly Weberian approach, although nominally 'Marxist,' is adopted by Zukin (1978).

23　The concept of a 'social compact' had previously been used in Pravda 1979b.

24　In Marxist terms, one might suggest that the ruling ideology, unlike those of western liberal democracies, possessed minimal internal efficacy and existed mainly for reasons of foreign policy. The ubiquitous hammers and sickles and the large hoardings displaying slogans such as "Proletarians of the World Unite!" were of a less marked significance even than the symbolism which in Britain appears to be the nearest semiotic equivalent, namely the royalist and often Christian symbolism similarly displayed on coins and banknotes and at key judicial, executive, and legislative locations and occasions. Whereas the latter relates to real organisational aspects of the admitted hierarchy and privilege system of the specific British State, and at the same time (to a limited extent) reinforces national unity around the rulers' really-existing parliamentary-democratic regime ('constitutionality') — with major problems only where it confronts a rival in Northern Ireland — the 'socialist' ideology of the USSR could never hide the obvious fact that the Soviet system was not ruled by the workers. In other words, the official picture was self-evidently false. Indeed, since it was neither "the sigh of the oppressed creature" nor in any real sense the "universal basis of consolation and justification," it cannot even be likened to religion. (See Marx 1844, p.244). Slogans such as "Glory to Work," meanwhile, are best seen as a parallel to the "Work Liberates" slogans erected at the gates of concentration camps in Germany: in other words, as little more than an affirmation that might is right, and a threat of violence against those who would develop a language of class opposition towards a conceptualisation of the possibility of revolution. (This is something which Orwell describes brilliantly in

Nineteen Eighty-Four [1949], especially in his appendix on "The Principles of Newspeak." [pp.312-26]).

25　In comparison, Yanowitch's brief consideration that portions of the working class might resist the imposition of 'work reform' appears merely 'political' or 'sociological,' his main focus being upon political resistance and the resilience of the administration. Rather than theorise a deal, 'compact', or relation with the workforce of a general nature, he alludes instead to parts of a 'divided' working class which "have obviously found their niche in the network of privilege." (1985, p.163).

26　These criticisms apply equally well to the recent work by Cook entitled *The Soviet Social Contract and Why it Failed.* (1993). Although Cook inexplicably fails to refer to Pravda, she uses a concept of social 'contract' which, in this context at least, would seem identical to that of a social 'compact.' On an empirical level she brings the analysis up to the early 1990s, but she does little to aid the removal of the main theoretical weaknesses and perhaps even increases them. Thus in her initial definition of the "social contract thesis" she states that

> the contract thesis is based on the assumption that what the Soviet state delivered was precisely what its society most valued, that is, that party and people shared a conception of distributive and social justice that gave central place to material welfare and egalitarianism. (p.3)

In what follows, she does look more specifically at the thesis of a "contract" between the "regime" and "Slavic blue-collar" *workers* (p.4), but even so she often lapses into the somewhat less classist (albeit less nationalist) terminology of a "trade-off" between 'State and society.' And this she considers principally in terms of the government's policy of allowing a rise in living-standards in return for "political quiescence." (pp.80-81).

　　Whilst she shows in some empirical detail how under Brezhnev the central bureaucrats kept consumer prices down, employment relatively full, and 'social security' relatively secure, she avoids any substantial usage of a concept of actual *labour indiscipline*. Instead, she simply notes that the rise of working class unrest — mainly strikes — and eventually of independent workers' "activism" — that is, 'independent' trade unionism — coincided with the erosion of the social contract in a process which began around 1980 and came to fruition in 1987-90. (pp.75-81 and 150-79). As inadequate explanation, she gives little more than a *description* of the government's predicament, its policies and its skills, faced with the emergence of 'labour politics,' and against a background of what is once again simply assumed to be an objective social need for economic development.

27　In more recent analyses of both *perestroika* and the Yeltsin period, Zaslavsky has made minimal reference to the interests of the working class, concentrating above all on potential developments towards western-style democracy. (1987, 1993). The retrogression which such an approach represents in relation to his previous work has been amply shown by Rittersporn (1993).

5 The Class Struggle: A Critique of 'Marxist' Theories

In this chapter we consider the most important 'Marxist' theories[1] of the nature of the Soviet system from a single standpoint, namely focusing on how they approach the matter of the working class. In each case, we are interested in particular in how the overall view of the system relates to a theoretical understanding of working class struggle.

We divide the theories into three sets, according to whether they view the USSR as a 'degenerated workers' state', a 'capitalist' formation, or a 'mode of production *sui generis.*' The third group we subdivide further into early 'collectivist' theories, East European 'dissident' theories, later 'collectivist' theories, and a more recent 'mode of production' theory.[2]

THE 'DEGENERATED WORKERS' STATE'

The first position to be considered is the one formulated by Trotsky, the former War Commissar and rival to Stalin expelled from the Communist Party in 1927. In exile Trotsky arrived at a 'Bonapartist' explanation of the origins of Stalinism: in the present context, though, it is not that which interests us, but rather his ideas about the role of the working class within the society as a whole.

In *The Revolution Betrayed* (1936), subtitled *What is the Soviet Union and Where is it Going?*, Trotsky makes a number of statements about the working class which to the Marxist ear sound quite contradictory. At one point he scorns the announcement in *Pravda* that the Soviet worker "is not a wage slave and is not the seller of a commodity called labour power," and asserts that "the transfer of the factories to the State changed the situation of the worker only juridically." (p.228). Given his subsequent explanation that what characterises classes is "their position in the social system of economy, and primarily...their relation to the means of production," one would therefore be forgiven for thinking that what he sees as a purely juridical change in workers' conditions has left the working class as a class exploited by capitalism. But such is not his view, and only a few pages later, having argued that

> the nationalization of the land, the means of industrial production, transport and exchange, together with the monopoly of foreign trade, constitute the basis of the Soviet social structure (p.235),

he goes on to assert that these relations were sufficient to establish the "nature of the Soviet Union as a proletarian State." His confusion deepens when he then proceeds to describe how, if the means of production belonged to the State, "the State, so to speak, 'belongs' to the bureaucracy." (p.236). We are thus left with a State that was proletarian even if it was owned by a bureaucracy, and even if that bureaucracy was "in the full sense of the word the sole privileged and commanding stratum" in the society. (p.235). Accepting that the source of the bureaucracy's power and income was the State property under its command, Trotsky argues bizarrely (p.236) that it was precisely this aspect of its activity which preserved it as "a weapon of proletarian dictatorship."

If we concentrate on his view of the conditions endured by the working class, we see that he accepts that workers are obliged to sell their labour-power, and that property relations are such that the surplus product is extracted by a bureaucracy. But nonetheless, in his opinion, "the character of the economy as a whole depends on the character of the State power" (p.237), and the character of the latter is "proletarian" owing to the allegedly "proletarian" nature of the Bolshevik coup and the nationalisation measures introduced after 1917.[3] The only possible conclusion to draw from this is that workers' conditions are of minimal importance to the underlying nature of the system, which remains, at bottom, proletarian.[4] This is not to say, however, that Trotsky is not critical of those conditions, for in fact he makes no bones about criticising injustice, oppression, differential consumption, and so on, even if he had supported them when he himself was in the elite. Indeed, he even reaches the point (1939b, pp.30-31) of condemning the Soviet "workers' state" as "counter-revolutionary." But the only explanation he gives of the extent of workers' hardships is in relation to the "degeneration" of the Party he once helped lead — itself supposedly caused by scarcity (1936, pp.87-112) — and it cannot be said that he pays attention to forms of working class *resistance* — that is, struggle — at any level. Instead, he restricts himself to issuing calls to Soviet workers to defend the Soviet State (the 'Fortress of the Toilers'), and to deal with their problems by forming a new but traditional party, the legitimate heir of Lenin's, which would re-establish Leninist norms and clear out the 'parasites.' (1940, pp.281-84).

Trotsky's most important follower in the 'degenerated workers' state' camp has been E. Mandel, who also identifies Soviet conditions as 'transitional' between capitalism and socialism. (1974). Like Trotsky, Mandel bases this thesis (pp.8-9) upon the nationalised ownership of the means of production and the 'proletarian' nature of the Bolshevik seizure of power. As a consequence of his 'workers' statist' position Mandel creates an absolute theoretical division between, on one side, the interests of the bureaucratic elite, and on the other, the concrete relations of that elite with the working class. Thus he explains the massive growth rates of Stalinism with reference only to the "absence of the *rule* of the law of value" (1979, p.119) — which, for him, means the presence of some kind of planning

— and proceeds (pp.120-2) to assert that the "material privileges of the bureaucracy are essentially restricted to the sphere of consumption."[5] We are thus left without any consideration of accumulation in terms of production relations, as well as confused about in whose interests the accumulation actually took place, since it clearly did not take place in the interests of the workers. In other words, Mandel has no objective theory of the accumulation of the surplus product and its re-employment in production, without which the elite could not have administered any growth at all. The category of *control over the working class* — as a necessary feature of an economy which was founded upon accumulation but was not run by the workers — is completely absent. It follows, therefore, that Mandel has no theory either of workers' obstruction of this control.

When Mandel turns his attention to the crisis of the system, he can only be said to adopt a class perspective in the most superficial sense. Workers' organisation and struggle in the Gorbachev period thus appear simply as the result of poor living-standards, and their development is identified above all with activity within the political space opened up by *glasnost'*. (1989, pp.1-16, 68-84, and 167-81). Failing to analyse how the nature of the system was determined by the nature of class struggle, Mandel explicitly denies (p.8) that the malfunctioning of the system had anything to do with workers' 'laziness' or 'lack of drive.' For him, waste resulted exclusively from bureaucratic mismanagement. He is consequently able to write about the historical roots of the crisis (1991) without mentioning class struggle at all.

'CAPITALISM'

Having already considered the views of the main 'capitalist' theorists upon the nature of the Soviet system, we shall now consider their understanding of the Soviet working class. With allowance for the fact that contributions made by the council communists, Buick and Crump, Johnson-Forest, and the SPGB (all 'state capitalist'), as well as those by Gorter, Castoriadis, and Chattopadhyay ('capitalist') will be considered in Chapter 6, the order in which the remaining analyses will be considered is the same as in Chapter 2. We shall first take the 'state capitalist' theories produced by Wildt, Munis, Cliff, Bettelheim, Chavance and Sapir; and then the 'capitalist' theory argued by Bordiga.

'State Capitalist' Theories

Many conceptions of 'state capitalism' give hardly any theoretical consideration to the position of the working class, other than to record its exploitation and subjugation. Not surprisingly, these include the various conceptions based on views of the system which themselves lack substantial theoretical foundation.[6] They also include the view presented by Wildt, who holds that Soviet 'totalitarian state capitalism' made "all effective opposition" impossible (1979, p.54); or, in other words, that subjugation was absolute and the class struggle did not exist.

The Leninist Theories of Munis and Cliff

Even Munis, whose overall analysis of the political-economic conditions is focused around the category of the surplus product, proves unable to go beyond political rhetoric when writing about the working class. Thus for him,

> The extreme poles have for years been as follows: on the extreme right, the bureaucracy; on the extreme left, the proletariat. (1946, p.12)

His understanding of these 'poles' never becomes any more substantial than this, and a few pages later he avers that the proletariat's part in social distribution, which presumably includes the determination of its own income, is "precisely that of the slave." (p.15).

On a general level, Cliff too offers a theorisation seemingly capable of development, insofar as he draws a crucial connection between, on one hand, the subordination of consumption to accumulation, and on the other, the subordination of the workers to the means of production. (pp.34-38). As with Munis's work, there is no doubt that this is a more profound point than appears in Trotsky and Mandel's critique of 'parasites.' Furthermore, having identified the Soviet elite as a ruling *class* (pp.166-68), he does at least devote a chapter to the class *struggle*.

But it turns out to be the concluding chapter and to consist of a mere twelve pages. Whilst referring to a "relation of forces between the proletariat and the bureaucracy," Cliff fails to ask what for the Marxist is the crucial question: what form did the workers' struggle take? Instead, he looks at how the "more experienced and intelligent" workers were often able to travel upwards in the bureaucratic hierarchy; how the working class underwent a "dilution by raw elements"; and how these two factors combined to obstruct the rise of an independent — read: politically represented — workers' movement. (pp.255-56). No attempt is made to build on his brief earlier reference to sabotage as a weapon used against Stakhanovism. (p.22). Instead, we can read of "unlimited egoism," a bureaucracy that spreads lies without limits, and even "the absolute suppression of the masses." (pp.254, 257, and 258). Like Munis, he paints a picture somewhat similar to the one presented by the 'totalitarian' sovietologists; and the whole idea of a 'relation of forces,' a *struggle*, not being fleshed out, seems simply to vanish. What we are left with are merely comments on how improvements in the standard of living and culture would lead to increasing self-confidence and a growing impatience with the lack of bourgeois rights; whilst the absence of such improvements would sooner or later lead to "revolts of despair." (pp.259-60). Cliff summarises his position in the following terms: one day, a spontaneous explosion; for the time being, 'the volcano seems extinct.'(p.264).[7]

After the eruptions in the USSR and elsewhere in 1989, Cliff's ideas were applied to the changing state of affairs by Harman. In "The Storm Breaks" (1990) Harman suggests that the Soviet system entered crisis because it was unable to keep up with the worldwide shift towards 'multinational capitalism.' (pp.44-52). The crisis of the "old forms of rule" consequently brought about "enormous popular discontent," and that in turn created pressure for a transition to a new form of capitalist rule.

> Yet the transition itself involves disruption to the mechanisms which have kept the discontent in check in the past — the political and ideological apparatuses of the ruling class. The greater the level of accumulation and the levels of repression needed to sustain it, the greater the possibility of the mass of people taking advantage of this disruption to give expression to accumulated bitterness in a huge explosion of anger and action. (p.67)

Thus it cannot be said that Harman is unaware of there being a relationship between crisis and class struggle. But what exactly is that relationship? What caused the crisis in the first place? By asking these questions we can see that Harman is a long way away from hypostatising the antagonism between classes. In fact, when writing about the proletariat as the 'gravedigger' which undermined Soviet capitalism throughout its history, he refers only to its growth in size and the rise in its level of culture and education, and completely neglects even to mention its practice. (pp.41-43). Since he views things not from a class point of view but rather from a Leninist 'party' one — according to which the 'potential' of the working class is similar to steam to be 'directed'[8] — it is quite logical that faced with the crisis Harman ends up calling for support for political and even nationalist reforms. (pp.83-84).[9]

Bettelheim's Theory and Related Work

The author of the other best-known 'state capitalist' theory alongside Cliff's, namely Bettelheim, provides just as little analysis as Cliff does of the actual conditions of class struggle under 'state capitalism.' Thus most of his references to the working class are either statements concerning *negatives* — such as the non-subordination of the State to the labouring masses (1971, pp.58-59), or the absence of an adequate 'ideological revolutionisation' of the workers (1970, p.89); or else they take the form of rare asides concerning ideologically reinforced social immobility, other 'ideological relations,' or the power of managers to "invoke means of repression" and sack their employees. (pp.88-89). Although Bettelheim does not explicitly say that workers do not or cannot resist the conditions of exploitation, nor does he ever say that they can and do.[10] Hence the question of *how* they do is one that he does not even approach.

Chavance, meanwhile, whose work follows on from Bettelheim's, does not let this omission stand in his way. Unlike Bettelheim he understands fully that the "pressure from the base for wage-rises" is a phenomenon which is "inherent in the social contradictions of wage-labour." Although hardly a breakthrough in Marxist thought, this is in fact quite an advance in terms of the 'capitalist' theories of the USSR. Chavance is aware both of the gap between 'planned' wages and the wages actually received, and of the rise in consumption levels up to the 1970s. (1989, pp.24-26). In this connection, he then points to the poor quality of goods as being a sort of countervailing factor. (p.26). Underlying such phenomena Chavance identifies exclusively the absence or near-absence of unemployment, which he relates to the microeconomic shortage of labour. (pp.29-32).

Although Chavance does strive here to formulate a class-based critique of the overall Soviet political economy, the weakness of his account is quite straightforward: he omits to consider class struggle at the point of production. As a consequence, he neglects to consider the quality of goods precisely where it first appears: in the labour process. Apart from giving the observations noted above, he thus finds himself unable to analyse labour relations in such a way as to enhance the overall critique. The tension between workers and their conditions of exploitation — or between workers and the bureaucratic centre — appears simply as another characteristic of the Soviet system, alongside such phenomena as passive money, inconvertibility, and the shadow economy. It is considered only in terms of a structure-related 'conflict of interest,' not in terms of struggle; as something inherent but not fundamental.

Sapir also adopts Bettelheim's view of 'state capitalism,' but for his part has written more extensively on the workers. Having described the initial 'suppression' of unemployment as a means by which the authorities crushed labour turnover as a form of resistance, he proceeds to show how inside the factories there persisted a 'partial' or 'technical' unemployment as an intrinsic part of the 'shortage economy.' This unemployment within the workplace formed a contrasting backdrop to the well-known practice of end-of-period 'storming.' (1980, pp.163-65). In a subsequent work devoted specifically to "work and the workers" Sapir then considers mobility and storming in finer empirical detail. More importantly, he also pays notable attention to 'skiving' (*progul*), lateness, unofficial breaks, black work, and pilfering. (1984, pp.58-69). Having concentrated earlier upon how workers are constrained to act, he has thus progressed to a consideration of how they choose to act.

If this undoubtedly marks a development in his thought, though, it unfortunately remains an analytical and theoretical step of which Sapir himself seems completely unaware, and upon which he altogether fails to build. When we look for a theoretical conception of the overall relationship between class relations and the nature of the system we find that his work displays a consistency of the most 'objectivist' kind. In 1980 he does relate the strikes of 1962-63 and 1969-70 to the government's reform attempts (pp.179-85); but he nonetheless places a general emphasis primarily upon the problems caused by an economic institutionalisation of forms which are best suited to the period of intensive accumulation, and which from the rulers' viewpoint have become increasingly dysfunctional. (pp.162-71). With such an approach any dynamic of class relations will appear as merely epiphenomenal.

This becomes clearer when Sapir considers the world of Soviet work in greater detail. In describing rising labour turnover, alcoholism, and systematic breaches of labour discipline as products of "problems born from the crisis of regimentation [*encadrement*]" (p.96) he thus notably fails to consider how such behaviour on the part of the workers might have contributed to creating such a crisis in the first place. In this view, the "dysfunctions of the Soviet economy, whose consequences are felt especially in the area of work and its rhythms," are "inherent" in the existence of a high degree of competition for resources, both at enterprise level and between enterprises and ministries. (pp.72-73).[11] In the conclusion of his book, Sapir explains that these two "competing forms of economic logic" determine both the existence of full employment and the absence of a harmonious workplace rhythm. (pp.117-18). In the empirical consideration, then, he may refer occasionally to the class struggle; but in his overarching understanding of the Soviet political economy this struggle is not a basic factor. In considering the place of the workers he does refer to contradiction and to conflict, but the only "poles" which he defines in this connection are those of "integration" and "mediation." (p.101; see also 1989, p.32). Since these latter two terms properly relate to what happens *between* polarities, Sapir's formulation appears to be deprived of substantive meaning, but it nonetheless serves to demonstrate his lack of attention with regard to the consequences of the fundamental class relation. More recently he has expressed a view of the influence of the labour shortage upon workers' behaviour which is self-evidently mechanical, the prime connecting factor ostensibly being constituted by the "permissiveness" of the enterprises (that is, of the enterprise directors). (1992, especially pp.95-97).

Other 'Capitalist' Theory[12]

Bordiga shows a level of interest in the Soviet working class which is quite as low as Bettelheim's. Despite underlining throughout his work that Soviet workers are exploited by capital — in relation to which the State, like all States, occupies a subordinate position, the government being just one committee of the world capitalist class (1956-57, p.123)[13] — he shows little desire to look at the specific conditions workers endure and the forms of resistance which arise in opposition to those conditions. Thus in *Dialogue avec Staline* he writes of factory despotism and its Stakhanovist form, but confines his consideration of the workers' reaction to it to a mere half-sentence (1952, p.18) — which is sufficient space to mention 'storming,' but insufficient to give any sort of analysis or explanation. Even such a *reference*, though, is rare in the extreme.[14]

'MODE OF PRODUCTION *SUI GENERIS*'[15]

The final set of 'Marxist' positions to be looked at involve the theory that the USSR was neither a 'socialist' (workers') state nor a capitalist state, nor even a transitional or hybrid formation, but represented rather a new mode of production with its own contradictions and its own dynamic. First put forward in the late 1930s, this view has since been espoused and developed by a number of different theorists. First we consider the work of Rizzi, Burnham, and Shachtman; then the views of Djilas, Kuron and Modzelewski, 'Rakovski', and Feher, Heller, and Markus; then the 'collectivist' views of Carlo and Fantham and Machover; and finally a recent contribution by Clarke. Various other views are commented on in the notes.[16]

Early 'Collectivist' Theories

The 'bureaucratic collectivist' thesis originally arose in connection with the idea that capitalism was giving way on a world scale to a new social formation, and the arguments focused on developments in Hitler's Germany, Mussolini's Italy, and Roosevelt's United States, as well as on those occurring under Stalin in the USSR. In the Soviet context, Rizzi thus makes it quite clear that he sees the system as having resolved the contradictions which made capitalism 'unprogressive,' and he even leaves the question open (1939, pp.51-52) as to whether it might, in the long term, "improve the masses' conditions of life." Although he takes the view that the system was based on the exploitation of one class by another (p.63), however, he does not refer to any sort of struggle between the two classes, and ultimately his view of the powerlessness of the working class is as extreme as Friedrich and Brzezinski's.

> Members of the Russian working class are no longer proletarians, they are slaves, both economically speaking and in terms of behaviour. They kneel when 'the little father' passes and deify him....
>   ...The Russian worker, together with his union, has become part and parcel of the state...He is made to turn up, sheep-like, at political meetings; he is simply an unthinking element of a mass which is there to be manipulated by the bureaucracy. (p.81)

Two years after Rizzi's work appeared, Burnham published *The Managerial Revolution*, in which he argues that capitalism is being superseded by 'managerial society,' or rule by a class of managers who control production by means of the State. (1941, pp.69-71). Having identified 'Russia' as the country which has progressed furthest along this path (pp.151-52), he writes of a "triple problem" for managerial society (p.197): defeating the capitalists; "curbing the masses" so as to eliminate the threat of a classless society; and coping with internal competition, by which he means national competition among 'managerial states.' In his view, only the third can never be solved. The masses, for their part, have already been curbed, and

> their obscurely felt aspirations towards equalitarianism and a classless society were diverted into the new structure of class rule, and organized in terms of the ideologies and institutions of the new social order. (p.198)

It is sufficient to point out that this assertion, made almost a quarter of a century after the defeat of the workers' revolution, is not backed up with any evidence as to what Soviet workers were doing, what they were not doing, or even what kind of ideas they had, at the time when Burnham was actually writing the book. Nonetheless, Burnham refers repeatedly to the "masses" as having been "curbed."

The third main early 'collectivist' was Shachtman, author of *The Bureaucratic Revolution*. Unlike Rizzi and Burnham, Shachtman does not apply his view of the new collectivist mode of production either to national socialism in Germany or to the New Deal in the United States, and consequently does not make comparison a crucial part of his argument. (1940-61, pp.2 and 53-55). A second difference, more important in the present context, is that he denies the capacity of 'bureaucratic collectivism' — or its reform — to undermine the growth of what he sees as its basic contradiction: the conflict of interests between the exploiters and the exploited. But whilst recognising (p.16) that a "fundamental revolution" remains "inescapable," and underlining the inadequacy of reforms for shoring up the system (pp.18-19), Shachtman nonetheless gives remarkably little consideration to the actual conditions of struggle in the USSR at the time he was writing. Thus when looking at the post-Stalin period he identifies the fear of discontent as a major factor motivating the granting of concessions (pp.346-55), and even goes so far as to opine that after Stalin the successor regime could not "even think of maintaining itself without popular support" (p.346), but he fails altogether to relate such insights to any study of exactly *how* workers resisted 'bureaucratic collectivism' in practice. His view of the class relation consequently remains purely one-dimensional.

East European 'Dissident' Theories[17]

The 'mode of production *sui generis*' theory has also received support from various East European dissidents, beginning with the scholar who should perhaps be classed as the very first dissident of major importance, namely Djilas. A former Vice-President of Yugoslavia who left the League of Communists in 1954 after being stripped of his official posts, Djilas proceeded to develop the view that the Soviet-type systems were based on the rule of a class which was non-capitalist but still exploitative. The most useful passages of his seminal work *The New Class* (1957) are those where he writes of the "limit to exploitation," but unfortunately he fails to delve very deeply into the matter. Thus his account of how slave labour had to be scrapped because it was proving too costly for the regime (1957, pp.111-12) is all too brief. He further mentions concealed unemployment, but considers it only in terms of inefficiency, not as a class relation amounting to paying workers to do nothing. (pp.112-13). Third, he touches on how the system "leads inevitably to lack of interest on the part of the actual producers...to low quality of output [and to] a decline in real productivity," but the lens through which he examines the system is one marked 'Dogmatism in the Economy' (p.108), rather than 'Really-Existing Class Relations.' Ultimately, even as he recognises that the working class is "the class upon which production depends" (p.110), Djilas forgets the primacy of social production relations and eventually reaches the view (p.122) that "in the Communist system...economy has become concentrated politics; that is, politics play an almost decisive role in the economy."[18] By concentrating on politics and ideology, Djilas is consequently more denunciatory — especially of 'one-party rule' — than he is theoretically critical in a 'Marxist' sense.[19]

Kuron and Modzelewski's *Open Letter to the Party*, first published in Poland in 1965, represents an altogether more radical critique.[20] Being among the very few East European intellectuals even to *call* for a working class revolution,[21] these two theorists undoubtedly stand out from other 'dissidents' in terms of the amount of attention they pay to the position of the working class. Taking the view that the working class is exploited by a ruling class in the form of the central political bureaucracy, they argue that the form this exploitation takes is wage-labour. In other words, the only productive force which the ruling class does not already own is labour-power, which it is therefore forced to buy *en bloc* in return for wages. The goal of production is the accumulation of the surplus product on a correspondingly "national" scale. (1965, pp.25-27).

Kuron and Modzelewski proceed to relate the contradictions of the bureaucratic system, as manifested in economic crisis, to the class relations of production. Arguing that "production for the sake of production" means a tendency toward a disproportionate growth in Department One (means of production), they give the view that the logic of the system is to restrict the growth of consumption. Consumption *needs*, meanwhile, grow regardless, owing to "full employment,...the development of an industrial civilization, and...an improvement in the general level of social culture." (p.38). In the context of this contradiction, and unlike any of the 'Marxist' theorists considered so far, Kuron and Modzelewski describe workers' efforts to lower efficiency and product quality as amounting to a "massive social initiative."

> Like all social initiative, it is a conscious activity to realize the aims and interests of the people concerned....
>
> ...What we have here is...a contradiction between the class goal of the bureaucracy (production for production) and the interests of the basic groups who achieve the production (maximum consumption). In other words, it is a contradiction between the class goal of production and consumption, and it results from existing conditions, not from mismanagement. (p.44)

The problem, however, is that in their conception of the working class as subject they do not go far enough. When they come to discuss the nature of the 'social initiative' antagonistic to the bureaucracy they fail to draw a clear enough line between the obstructiveness of managers and technocrats on one hand, and that of the workers on the other. Moreover, they fail to spell out the fundamental point that sloppy work and upward pressure on wages are both forms of the same struggle: less work and more pay both mean a lower rate of exploitation. These confusions ultimately lead them to adopt the 'underconsumptionist' view (pp.38-39 and 44-45) that the low level of consumption actually inhibits the growth of production. In arguing that the scarcity of consumer goods in relation to nominal wage growth creates an 'inflation barrier' and the danger of falling real wages, and therefore constitutes a major barrier to growth (pp.39-40), they are neglecting two fundamental points: first, that the needs of the exploited are something imposed on the exploiters, to whom they are simply costs; and second, that the 'crisis' is something imposed back on the working class in the interests of exploitative society. Rather than seeing the 'crisis' as a class — that is, class struggle-determined — relation, Kuron and Modzelewski prefer to view it as a manifestation of a sort of 'decline' of production relations based upon production for the sake of production.

If Rakovski's[22] work is less radical than Kuron and Modzelewki's *Open Letter*, where the matter of class structure is concerned it is rather more scientific than Djilas's *New Class*. Like Djilas, though, Rakovski shows little interest in the working class as a 'really existing' subjective class force.

> The closer the two systems ['capitalist' and 'Soviet-type'] resemble each other at the level of the everyday life of the working class, the more difficult it is to avoid asking the question, why has the working class succeeded in having an organised influence on its conditions of life in only one of the two systems? Why is it only Western capitalism that has a workers' movement, whether reformist or revolutionary? There can be no doubt that this is the key question for every marxism.... (1978, p.14)

In fact, of course, this is the 'key question' only for those 'marxisms' which do not fully espouse the view that the history of class societies is the history of class struggles; and it reveals an assumption that the representation of the working class by the unions and the left is the same thing as the working class 'movement' itself. Consequently, even as Rakovski accepts that changes in the situation of the working class are difficult to interpret, he keeps to the view that workers' resistance in the Soviet-type countries is confined to the level of 'individual behaviour.' (p.38). And, like so many others, once he has mentioned such behaviour he fails to ask what the contradictory forces are which determine it.

All the same, Rakovksi does cautiously predict a growth in "the relative autonomy of the oppressed class," even if on the basis of a spread of intellectual non-conformism as well as on the basis of an objectively strengthened position of the workers' household. Since he links the latter factor to a growth in the strength of the individual worker's position in the labour market (p.103), it would be unfair to say that he neglects to consider class relations. Given that he further predicts that any future political crisis will also give greater scope to the workers, there is clearly a level at which Rakovski seems to describe fairly accurately the events which took place at the end of the 1980s. But theory should be more than description, and it is worth pointing out the theoretical weakness of his approach: namely, his drawing of a sharp distinction between, on one hand, developments centred around the objective strength of the working class — benefiting, according to Rakovski, from the ideological assistance supposedly offered it by the lower ranks of the intellectuals — and, on the other, the economic collapse of the system, which on the contrary he does not see as a possibility.

The final contribution to the dissident *oeuvre* requiring consideration is the work co-authored by Feher, Heller, and Markus.[23] (1983). Noting that the 'planning' process in Soviet-type economies is in fact a "multi-level bargaining process" among members of the 'apparatus' (Markus 1983, pp.49-50) — or, as it is later presented, a "very complicated process of semi-institutionalized competition...between the various horizontally and vertically articulated bureaucracies" (pp.77-79) — they advance the idea that the nationalised means of production are the property of the "apparatus" not as a 'collective' but rather as a 'corporation.' Thus the 'members of the apparatus,' whilst competitive among themselves, do not function as members of a capitalist-type ruling class wherein their own individual interests coincide in any important way with their interests as a collective; but rather as "trustees," as "representatives of the institutional interests of the apparatus as a corporate entity." (pp.60-69). In this view, since if every bureaucrat were promoted simultaneously, "there would be no advance at all" (p.61), bureaucratic interest is "non-additive." The interest or "goal" of the corporation, meanwhile, is defined as "the maximization of the material means under the direct control of the apparatus." (p.70). Given the tendency of the bureaucratic apparatus to expand and the absence of a non-bureaucratic mechanism which can bring individual bureaucratic interests into "correspondence" with the corporate interest, the result is structural 'economic irrationality.' (pp.63-66).

Although Feher, Heller, and Markus never clearly define what membership of the bureaucratic apparatus consists of, they accept that the material basis of "overall social domination" is the appropriation of a surplus. (p.126). But insofar as the interest of the individual bureaucrat is portrayed as operating most importantly in terms of the bureaucracy itself, it is hardly likely that this appropriation can be properly dealt with as a relation of production continuously imposed on the workers as a condition of their labour. And indeed the very recognition of the fundamental role of surplus appropriation is surrounded with numerous qualifications. Thus the authors reject any 'reduction' of the social structure to one of class dichotomy, and state that it is not determined by a single principal cause, "be it monopolization of social power, appropriation of social surplus or whatever." (p.129). Alternatively, the appropriation of the surplus, and the disposition over it, comprise "only the material foundation and economic component" of the apparatus's "monopolistic appropriation of all means of social organization and discourse."[24] The position appears best, if belabouredly, in their statement that the "antagonism between the corporate ruling group and the rest of society" is 'created, given substance, and perpetuated' by the "suppression of all group interest and of civil society." (p.131). The USSR is, then, a "political society" (Heller 1983, p.167; Feher 1983, pp.252-53); and since modernity, practicality and the presumed inevitability of scarcity supposedly necessitate the existence of either market or privilege (Markus 1983, p.92), the only realistic alternative to a Soviet-style "dictatorship over needs" would appear to be the introduction of a market. Economic rationality could then flourish, and the market's "spontaneous effects" could be 'counteracted' by self-management and political democracy. (Markus 1983, pp.91-95; Feher 1983 pp.284-86).

This raising of Soviet-type bureaucracy to almost archetypal status as the irrational *not-market* corresponds to a crucial lack of grasp of the underlying social function of the bureaucratic system — and indeed also of the market — in relation to the surplus. Such a weakness appears most starkly in the authors' avowal that

> the members of the apparatus are not constrained to act in a definite way by the position they occupy in the structure of social reproduction; they have to follow consciously the rules and objectives pre-set by the apparatus. (Markus 1983, p.116)

What is missed here is that it is precisely the position in terms of social reproduction which determines the fundamental role of any social agency. If the first part of this statement is simply nonsensical, however, the second is similarly obstructive of a clear analysis of the power relation between workers and exploiters. Thus the theory of the 'corporation' (p.117) slides all too easily into talk of the 'will of the sovereign' — defined, depending on the period, as that of the Bolshevik 'aristocrats,' the 'autocrat' Stalin, or the CPSU 'oligarchs.' (Heller 1983, pp.167-204). But the type of distinction between the political and the economic which is central to the methodology does not merely hinder the formulation of a critical understanding of the State: it also makes the possibility extremely remote of reaching a profound understanding of the struggle over the division of the social product.

Admittedly, the authors do note that workers resist the imposition of discipline and consequently maintain some sort of 'negative control' over their work. (Markus 1983, p.75). But little is made of this, and rather than being seen as a major problem for the rulers it is portrayed largely as a product of the irrationalities of the bureaucratic system. Indeed it is even presented as something which automatically backfires on the workers by leading to wage-cuts which workers are then led to compensate for by earning extra money working on the side. (p.75). As we shall see below in Chapter 7, though, this type of analysis is not simply superficial, it is factually wrong. And the assumption that wages in a given workplace are administratively pre-set and then simply handed over (p.72), at no time being the object of 'legitimate' bargaining (p.72, and Feher 1983, p.269),[25] only illustrates further the authors' lack of interest in how it actually comes about that workers receive such-and-such an amount of money in return for work of such-and-such a kind and quality. Questions, for example, of the significance of labour hoarding and the payment of bonuses are not even broached.

Nonetheless, this lack of a substantial consideration of the relations at the point of production does not prevent Feher, Heller, and Markus from stating that "the basic restrictions on the economic power of the apparatus emerge not in the sphere of production proper," but rather in the sphere of individual workers' choices as to what to consume, and to a certain extent, where to work. (Markus 1983, p.87).[26] But we note that even here the root of the resultant problems would seem to be the contradictions inherent in the totalising bureaucratic tendency — or 'will' — to 'internalise' such 'externalities,' rather than the effects of actual workers' struggle. (pp.51-52 and 87-88).

In the final analysis, the inadequate consideration of the relations between workers and exploiters corresponds well to the author's summary view that

> abstractly speaking, it is not in the interest of any government to keep its population artificially indigent....But whereas for the ruling classes in capitalism, abundance for the wage-earners [*sic*] is in itself indifferent...and can even be the source of profit [*not for the capitalist class as a whole*—NCF], it is not so with dictatorship over needs. An anti-capitalist enterprise, the latter was designed and planned as a negation of its opponent; as a result, the expansion of the individual or group need system [and] its variability...would mean the resurrection of precisely that individual on whose forced obedience, frugality and built-in servility alone the edifice of the anti-capitalist dictatorship can rest. (Feher 1983, p.261)

In the meantime,

> without a free social articulation of needs there can be no social rationality [and] this means that it is impossible for the regime to transcend the extensive period of economy and effect the transition to the intensive one. (p.263)

Thus it is held that the 'restrictions' which workers' choices in accordance with their needs actually do manage to force upon the 'corporation' — principally the ones they make as consumers — tend to push most of all towards the reintroduction of the market in what in effect would be the 'general interest' of the population. (p.269). The struggle involved in social reproduction — over the division of the product into wage goods on one side and the surplus on the other — is not held to be a factor of any major political-economic significance.

Later 'Collectivist' Theories

If the 'bureaucratic collectivist' theories of the Stalin period — especially those of Rizzi and Burnham — were in many ways rather simplistic, the newer version put forward in the 1970s was, despite its weaknesses, undoubtedly somewhat more nuanced. The reason for this is quite straightforward. Having a better vantage-point from which to view Soviet economic problems, not to mention access to eastern European theoretical works such as Kuron and Modzelewski's *Open Letter to the Party*, Carlo and Fantham and Machover were much more interested than their 'collectivist' forebears in discussing Soviet society's *contradictions*.

In his article on "The Socio-Economic Nature of the USSR," Carlo centres his attention on one contradiction in particular, namely that which exists between the forces and relations of production. This contradiction he finds expressed in three ways: the disproportion between the capital goods and consumer goods sectors; the impossibility of total coordination; and the low level of labour productivity. (1971, p.52).

Considering the first of these problems, Carlo argues that unlike in 'capitalism,' where "if machines for producing shoes are built, it will sooner or later be necessary to produce shoes," the growth in the Soviet primary sector[27] has "assumed pathological dimensions that threaten the very foundations of development." (p.53). Under 'capitalism' consumption levels have risen due to an increase in absolute wages, the appearance of a sizeable tertiary sector, and the expansion of credit; but under Soviet 'bureaucratic collectivism' they have stayed low, and as a result the system is in trouble. This trouble is so severe that ever since 1965 Soviet 'bureaucratic collectivism' has found itself gradually metamorphosing into capitalism. (pp.58 and 73). By arguing in this way, Carlo is repeating the mistake made by Kuron and Modzelewski, namely the assumption that consumer growth necessarily helps an exploitative system by providing a demand.[28] In fact, of course, producing shoes simply to sell to the workers is not *in itself* beneficial to any group of exploiters, since what the working class consumes is derived from the *necessary* part of the product, whereas the exploiters are only interested in the surplus. An increase in workers' consumption can only benefit the exploiters if it buys or enables a large enough growth in productivity.

When Carlo addresses the second problem, his terms continue to vary between the 'classist' and the 'non-classist.' In response to the question 'Why can't the system be planned?' he begins by stating that working class opposition has asserted itself in the plan-execution phase ever since the system came into existence, but follows this by considering *technical* problems of calculation and forecasting. He then suggests (pp.55-57) that the introduction of advanced techniques of computerised surveillance would bring its own problems, namely an increase in waste combined with the possibility of explosive opposition from managers, workers, and farmers. What has happened here is that the earlier mention of workers' opposition in connection with the prevention of (bureaucratic) planning, after being followed with a discussion of mere technical problems, has ended up being considered in purely hypothetical (and cross-class) terms of an 'Orwellian' future.[29]

The same lack of theoretical depth is evident when Carlo comes to consider the third aspect of the contradiction, namely labour productivity as a specific phenomenon. In stating that it is by means of low productivity levels that "the workers' rejection of the system expresses itself" (pp.62-64), he is going further than previous 'Marxists,' but even so he ultimately does little more than to affirm what is obvious: workers are disinclined to work well just so that bureaucrats can get better off. Meanwhile, even though he identifies the system's acceptance of a "moderate work rhythm" as being a concession to the working class that "is not exceptional but organic and normal," his political approach demands that he view the frustration of productivity as 'negative' as well as 'positive' in terms of the objective interests of the workers, since it lowers the chances of winning "the 'peaceful coexistence' race." (p.64).

If the strength of Carlo's work is that unlike the earlier 'collectivists' he brings into his understanding of the problems of the system a clear recognition of the importance of working class opposition, its weakness is that like Kuron and Modzelewski he fails to do so in a resolute enough manner. At best, his approach leads to an empiricism where issues of actual class antagonism appear but are not given a central place; at worst, he loses sight of exactly what is a problem for whom, for which class. Through confusion, he obscures exploitative society's basic contradiction, namely that which exists between the most important 'productive force,' the proletariat, and the most important 'relation of production,' the 'system' as a whole. Moreover, his implicit identification of the forces of production with the material means of production, combined with his explicit taking of sides in "the 'peaceful coexistence' race," shows an undeniable basic accommodation with the official ideology of the system he is endeavouring to criticise.[30]

In a later text concerning bureaucratic collectivism's crisis, Carlo similarly fails to draw adequately clear 'class lines.' Arguing that Soviet growth under the bureaucratic collectivist system had to remain 'essentially' extensive (1979, pp.6 and 9), he describes some of the problems faced by the bureaucracy in trying to develop efficiency. Thus he shows how military technology cannot be transferred into the civilian economy as in the bourgeois countries, owing to high costs and the structural innovation problem (pp.11-12), and how buying technology abroad is also no real solution, because sooner or later "the economy as a whole" will have to bear the costs. (p.8). (See also Carlo 1988-89, pp.32-33). Before reaching a far too superficial definition of crisis as a "difficulty in achieving the most important and central ends of the plan" (1979, p.26), he does explain his ideas in terms of class antagonism; but he fails to trace the development of this antagonism as an actual *rapport de force*, seeing it rather as a mere underlying fact. Hence he totally rejects the idea that 'Russian' workers are "opposed to an increase in the production of consumer goods since this would mean an increase in their working load," on the grounds that the black market and the 'consumer boycott' (constrained saving) show that worker-consumers "do not readily accept the system's delivery of consumer goods." (p.19) Here he is drastically missing the point, which is that the reason why the system is incapable of establishing a new deal of 'more goods for harder work' is that workers' resistance to work — and not just in consumer goods production — is too strong. If workers have no objection to 'more goods,' they are nonetheless not prepared to work harder to get them. Carlo's only counter-argument here, namely that the kolkhozniks work hard on their private plots, and that they are in no way "biologically different" from other workers (p.19), fails to hold, since the plots he mentions amount to privately-owned productive forces which are clearly unavailable to the majority of the proletariat. Carlo rightly stresses that higher-quality production is impossible without workers' collaboration, but rather than explaining the root cause of the problems which the bureaucracy faces in achieving such a deal, he simply blames them on the "system," which is "organically antagonistic." (p.24). Since he fails to identify the actual forms this antagonism takes, his view of it remains highly abstract.

Carlo's work ten years later on the "contradictions of *perestroika*" marks little theoretical advance, and may even be considered a move backwards. Failing to mention class antagonism (or resilience) even as one underlying cause of crisis among many, he focuses still more clearly upon the systemic bias against technological innovation as the prime determining factor. Consumer sector weaknesses and future unemployment and underdevelopment are understood solely on this basis. (1988-89, pp.32-33, 40-43).

A 'collectivist' view of the USSR has also been presented by Fantham and Machover, who state in a one-off pamphlet of 1979 that conditions prevailing in the 'second world,' together with those established or emerging in parts of the 'third world,' justify reference to a new mode of production running "parallel to capitalism." (1979, p.4). This 'state collectivist' mode of production they see as fulfilling a precise "historical role": namely, that of developing the productive forces and creating an industrial infrastructure wherever capitalism proves incapable of doing so owing to its global decline. (p.11). This is thus a repetition, with slight alterations, of the thesis first argued by Carlo.[31]

Fantham and Machover's originality lies in the extent to which they stress that Soviet conditions conform to a 'generally applicable model' of a mode of production bound to experience both 'progress' and eventual 'decline.' (Trotsky's view of necessary instability is emphatically rejected. [p.19].[32]) In relation to the working class the implications of such an alternative 'orthodox Marxist' approach would thus seem clear. Under the heading "The Historically Progressive Stages of the System," Fantham and Machover quote Kuron and Modzelewski on how from 1945 to 1960 "the achievements of Polish industrialisation...meant the realisation of a general social interest"; and they proceed to imply that class antagonism during that period was of little significance. In the next section, entitled "The Period of Crisis," they then point (pp.15-16) to the chronic problems experienced by the Soviet elite and the consequent ineffectiveness of 'planning' as shown by Ticktin.

The idea here would appear quite straightforward: namely, that in the 'progressive' phase of 'state collectivism' — that is, during extensive industrialisation — workers participate, but once that phase comes to an end they stop. Having earlier promised, though, that much of their discussion will revolve around the USSR (p.5), Fantham and Machover stop short of explicitly applying this thesis to that country. Instead, examples — as they see them — of 'participation' and 'working class identification with the system' are taken from elsewhere: and the USSR is used as the exclusive source of examples of antagonism, such as resistant labour rigidity and avoidance of hard work. (pp.17-18).[33]

All in all, what Fantham and Machover have to say about the Soviet working class is so confused that it does not lend itself to being summarised in coherent fashion. On the one hand, Soviet 'state collectivism' is seen as 'progressive' in relation to the capitalist conditions which pertained prior to 1917, and Kuron and Modzelewski are quoted as drawing a link between the mode of production's 'progressive' phase and genuine working class participation; on the other, Ticktin is referred to approvingly as demonstrating the low quality of work which has been there for as long as the system itself. Admittedly, after quoting the *Open Letter* Fantham and Machover do say that the contradictions may take very different forms and proceed at a very different pace outside Poland; but the gap between, on one hand, Kuron and Modzelewski's view as generalised here and, on the other, Ticktin's view as quoted, would seem logically unbridgeable. For the rest, one is presented with a series of points which are left theoretically unconnected. The working class suffers because consumption levels are 'comparatively' low — comparative to what? — but on the other hand employment is full, which means that dismissal is rare and productivity 'sticky upwards.' The only effective sanction against the working class is "repressive administrative control," but at the same time there is a "high degree of ideological control [which is] extended, even more strongly than in advanced capitalism, through the media, education and the family." Apparently in absolute contradiction with this last point, however, it is asserted in the very next sentence (p.18) that "state collectivism shares with all non-capitalist class systems a relative transparency of exploitation and oppression." Ultimately we are left with little more of substance than two basic points: first, low productivity conflicts with the bureaucrats' need to accumulate; second, there are no 'independent' trade unions.

Recent 'Mode of Production' Theory

The most recent contribution to merit consideration is that made by Clarke.[34] Although in 1990 he argues the 'Makhaevist' view[35] that

> the social base of state socialism [i.e. Soviet society] lies in the stratum of intellectual workers [such as] managers, administrators, scientists, technicians, engineers, social workers, and teachers (p.20),

by 1992 he has switched his allegiance to the view that Soviet society was based instead on the material relations of production. Attempting to analyse current economic contradictions in terms of production relations and class struggle, he outlines a view of the USSR which has a number of original aspects.

But unfortunately the theoretical underpinnings of his new view of the "Soviet mode of production" appear to be highly confused. Thus for him

> the Soviet system was based on a form of wage labour, but it was not based on social relations of capitalist production. (1992, p.3)

Clarke clearly believes (p.5) that the sale of workers' labour-power does not necessarily imply the existence of the category of abstract labour; but since he has not actually argued for this view it is sufficient merely to observe that this would necessitate a major — and definition-based — revision of Marx's categories which has yet to appear. Two further positions will serve to demonstrate Clarke's confusion even more sharply: first, his statement that the "basis of the Soviet enterprise was not capital, but the productive activity of the labour collective"; and second, his view that "the surplus was appropriated from the direct producers in kind." (p.7). Both are used to illustrate the non-capitalist nature of the system; but insofar as they apply equally well to the capitalism described by Marx, both fail.[36] In the absence of coherent definitions, Clarke's assertions that "capital did not exist in Russia" and that economic transactions were "essentially non-monetary" remain insupportable.

It is notable, however, that Clarke does not go as far as positing a non-capitalist mode of production based not only upon wage-labour but also upon the need to accumulate the material productive forces. Instead,

> the task of the enterprise administration was not to secure the expanded reproduction of capital, but the expanded reproduction of the labour collective. Any profits [*sic*] which remained to the enterprise, once it had met its obligations, were not appropriated as capital, but were generally spent on improving the working and social conditions of the labour collective. (p.7)

Certainly, production was not "subordinate" to the needs of the "collective" — indeed, the latter were "subordinated" to the production and appropriation of a surplus — but what in Clarke's view *determined* production was not any need of the system to expand the social product, but rather its "need to secure the expanded reproduction of the labour collective." (p.7) However much negotiation took place between enterprises and the centre, there was thus a clear correspondence between the 'task' of the enterprise managers and the needs of the system: the main aim of both sets of interests opposed to those of the workers was to expand the size of the working class.

Clarke proceeds to state in more 'classical' fashion that

> the development of the forces of production was constrained by the exploitative social relations of production, and it was this specific contradiction that underpinned the collapse of the administrative-command system. (p.8)

Two criticisms should be made of this view. First, the expansion of the working class which Clarke identifies as 'determinant' of production would seem very clearly to constitute one type of development of the forces of production. Thus while demographic factors are important it is hard to see which *production relations* might have constrained such development. Second, if Clarke is right, there would seem to be immense problems in identifying the "irrationality" of the system in the difficulty it faced in developing productive forces in general. For Clarke the system's nature and dynamic were determined by the need to expand the labour collective, not the other productive forces, whose growth would seem to have been peripheral or at most a by-product of higher employment figures. In what terms, then, can the failure to produce a peripheral effect appear "irrational," let alone critical? The answer could lie either with externalities or with some abstract 'law of historical progress' derived elsewhere than from a theory of Soviet reality — but once again Clarke does not follow the theory through this far.

A year later, in 1993, Clarke changes to a third view. Not only does he now refer to 'Soviet production' rather than to a Soviet 'mode of production' (1993a, p.7, n.1), he also moves away from his previous position on the need of the system to expand the 'labour collective.' The aim of production is now seen simply as the provision of surplus use-values to satisfy 'the Politburo and the military'; and the "specific form of exploitation" is associated with the effort of the centre to extort such a surplus by maintaining control over supplies. (p.15). In seeking to analyse the contradictions inherent in such a model, Clarke then describes how, since the managers are not subject to the law of value, their main problem is not that of controlling the labour process, but precisely that of acquiring the supplies over whose allocation the centre retains administrative control. As a consequence, in terms of the control of the production process the workers are allowed substantial leeway: their work might be subject to intensification, but how they work remains largely unsubject to external control. (p.16).

The question now arises of the form actually taken by the workers' control over the labour process, this control which is considered to contradict the interests of the rulers. Unfortunately, though, this is a question to which Clarke fails to give an adequate answer. Somewhat confusedly, he asserts that

> The fact that Soviet workers had a high degree of control over the way in which they produced [*i.e. over the labour process*—NCF] does not mean that they had power. Workers could try to escape from their oppression in individual ways, in the form of absenteeism, labour turnover, alcoholism and poor 'discipline' and 'motivation,' but they had little possibility of collective resistance. (p.17)

Soon he adds that

> the limits of workers' power were set by the norms and targets handed down from above." (p.19)

These two statements clearly contradict each other. Moreover, in analysing the class relations which correspond to the Soviet system, Clarke concentrates primarily on the limits imposed on workers' power, which he sees as enforced by means of piece-rates, stratification, union-administered benefits, and the enterprise-level labour surplus.[37] (pp.19-26). What he does not theorise is the actual assertion of this power in course of struggle. Indeed, where he does not deny that Soviet workers had any power, he clearly implies that they managed to acquire some power without struggling for it, as a sort of by-product of the nature of the system.

Despite his interest in the workers' struggles which have unfolded since 1989, Clarke seeks to explain the causes of the crisis of the system in terms which are remarkably non-classist. He begins by criticising the Soviet reformist view, associated with Gorbachev and others, that the administrative-command system had proven "well adapted to the economic priorities of heavy industrialisation in the 1930s," but by the 1980s had become increasingly irrational. (p.30). For Clarke,

> If the system was economically irrational from its inception, we cannot explain the *crisis* of the system by its economic irrationality alone. The system did not meet the needs of the Soviet people in the 1980s, but the system had not met the needs of the Soviet people in the 1930s, and it was never designed to meet their needs. The system was designed to meet the political needs of the nomenklatura... The crisis arose because the mechanisms which had kept a grotesquely repressive, exploitative and inefficient system going, despite its irrationality, for almost sixty years, had reached their limits. (pp.32-33)

The analysis here would seem to be largely rhetorical. It should be noticed, for example, that the term 'nomenklatura,' which might be applied to everyone from the Patriarch to a provincial newspaper editor, but not to the members of the Politburo, appears highly inappropriate. In addition, it is fairly obvious that Stalinist industrialisation did prove to be 'rational' in terms of the goal Stalin famously ascribed to it in 1931: namely, rapid enough economic development within 10 years to permit the avoidance of outright military destruction. (See McCauley 1981, pp.72-73).

Even if Clarke goes on to specify that by the 1960s it was the 'strategy' of extensive development which was beginning to 'reach its limits,'[38] he approaches only in passing the questions of what these limits were and how they came to be reached. The problem would simply be the continuing irrationality of the system, as manifested by the exhaustion of easily exploitable resources and by the "neglect of the reproduction of the technical, natural and human forces of production." (1993b, p.37). Low levels of workers' motivation are now brought in as one result among others of the low level of 'reproductive investment' in general. The sloppiness of this analysis is apparent once it is remembered that extensive growth is by definition precisely *not* dependent upon the reproduction of existing resources, but upon the mustering of new ones; and that the USSR can hardly be said to have exhausted the massive reserves of coal, oil, uranium, etc., which were so important to its economy. (See for example IMF et al. 1991).

Seeing high military spending as the main contingent factor threatening to turn stagnation into economic collapse, Clarke is ultimately led to stress that the 'timing' of the crisis was determined not by internal factors at all, but by "the relationship between the Soviet system and international capitalism." (1993b, pp.33-34). He then proceeds to discuss the effects of changes in the international terms of trade, especially the price of oil. In this view, the oil price rise provided an important breathing space after 1973, but the subsequent fall, together with the global debt mountain and rising grain prices, precipitated the onset of full-scale crisis in the late 1980s. What Clarke notably fails to discuss is the relationship between the underlying causes either of the crisis itself, or of its timing, to the specific relation of the workers to the labour process. And as if to underline this omission, he states clearly but without argument that the crisis was in fact not one of surplus production at all, but simply one of "surplus appropriation" and distribution. (p.47).

Clarke's desire to theorise the relation between the "development of class struggles over the social relations of production" and the "dynamics of the transformation of the Soviet mode of production" (1992, p.3) remains necessarily unarmed. He may have produced a useful analysis of the problems of privatisation (1992) and co-written informative accounts of the development of the 'workers' movement' since 1989 (Clarke and Fairbrother 1993b-f; Clarke, Fairbrother, and Borisov 1994), but since he has a theory neither of the class struggle in the previous period, nor of the accumulation of the productive forces, he cannot really relate class struggle to crisis in any profound, historical, or dynamic way. Above all, this would demand a preliminary recognition of the working class as a historical subject with 'radical chains,' and a quest to understand its self-assertion as the tendential negation of the existing order. (Marx 1844, pp.256-57). Whilst displaying a profound *interest* in the working class, Clarke appears very far from such an approach.

Given his non-recognition of class struggle prior to Gorbachev, it is hardly surprising that Clarke does not attempt to identify the nature of the force of the workers in terms of any sort of polarity or singularity. As a result, he gives far too much credence (1992, p.40) to the "management's identification of the enterprise with the labour collective," and eventually reaches the view that the most radical aspect of workers' struggle is its tendency to push for enterprise democratisation at meetings of worker-shareholders. (pp.40-41; see also Clarke

1993c, pp.240-41). Workers' actual practice at the 'point of production,' when they are actually working, is left out of the picture altogether. He undoubtedly does deserve credit for stating that it was the miners' strikes of 1989 and 1991 which brought the system down (1992, p.40), even if he excises this opinion from a later rewrite (1993c), but he imbues this statement with virtually no theoretical or historical force. Among the other weaknesses already mentioned, his democratism, limited theory of accumulation, and lack of critique of either the enterprise-form or the wage-form prevent him from achieving a profound grasp of the real antagonism involved.

SUMMARY

In considering what various 'Marxist' theories of the nature of the Soviet system have had to say upon the nature of the working class and its struggle, we have pointed to considerable weaknesses, and, in many cases, a remarkable level of superficiality. We shall now summarise the criticisms made.

We have shown how the understanding of Soviet political economy by the proponents of the 'workers' state' theory touches upon class conflict solely in terms of a static 'conflict of interests' in the abstractly differentiated sphere of distribution. It should therefore come as no surprise that there is no real consideration of the actual class struggle between the workers on one side, and the exploiters and their State on the other. Neither Trotsky nor E. Mandel have any real interest in any form of class struggle which might correspond to the overall political economy.

It is considerably more surprising that very much the same criticism can also be made of almost all the numerous 'capitalist' theorists who have also worked within 'Marxism,' from Cliff and Munis to Bettelheim and Bordiga. We have shown above how they too have done little more than to rhetoricise about the workers' total powerlessness. Harman, of course, can hardly ignore the struggles which have taken place since 1985, but aside from a few remarks about the growth of the exploited class since the 1920s, he paints a picture wherein the class struggle became 'actual' rather than just potential only under Gorbachev.

A welcome exception here is Chavance; but even as he describes the inherent tension between workers and the exploitative system, he fails to devote any attention to the *struggle* at the point of production. Sapir, meanwhile, pays greater attention to labour conflict — but he paints its forms as being unilaterally determined by capitalist competition, both between enterprise directors and ministries, and among the enterprise directors themselves. In this view, workers do struggle, but they do so only in mechanically determined ways which stem from causes but lead to no significant effects.

The first collectivist theorists, meanwhile, fail to study the issue of class struggle in much the same way as Cliff and Munis. Where Rizzi and Burnham refer directly to workers' powerlessness in so many words, Shachtman makes little effort to fit the concessions of the mid-1950s into his general theoretical critique.

Later *'sui generis'* work by 'dissidents' is somewhat more developed. Thus Djilas pays some attention to low-quality production, even if he sees it ultimately as a product of the overly 'dogmatic' orientation of the controllers of the economy. But the clear implication is that a less 'political' style of economic management would smooth over any problems of workers' lack of interest in economic efficiency. Viewing the role of the 'political' in just as extreme a fashion, Feher, Heller, and Markus later take the view that what problematic self-assertion there actually is on the part of the workers — seen largely as a matter of consumption choices — is oppositional to bureaucratic interests mainly because it pushes towards marketisation. For their part Bence and Kis, writing under the name 'Rakovski,' similarly omit to consider working class struggle in any more profound terms than those of individual behaviour and the 'objectively strengthened' position of the worker's household as a consumer.

Kuron and Modzelewski go much further, conceiving of the lowering of efficiency and product quality as a matter of a 'massive social initiative' rather than as an accumulation of individual reactions. But even as they scorn the idea that such a class relation depends on mismanagement, insisting instead on its roots in 'existing conditions,' they too display an over-determined interest in market demand and virtually end up arguing that higher workers' consumption would help the economy.

Subsequent 'collectivist' work by Carlo also has the merit of emphasising the importance of workers' opposition. Stating outright that low productivity is an expression of the workers' rejection of the system, he understands that the system must organically concede a 'moderate work rhythm.' But he fails to isolate the relation between the workers and the exploiters and home in on it with adequate rigour. As a result, when he comes to consider the crisis, he gives great weight to such factors as the petering out of extensive growth, and the structural innovation problem, rather than attempting to trace any material lines of determination from the class struggle.

Fantham and Machover's analysis, meanwhile, being very mixed-up, represents a step backward. They may emphasise low productivity, but their confusion over the essence of control (taking forms which are administrative, ideological and transparent) prevents them from formulating any coherent framework for understanding class struggle.

Writing about aspects of labour conflict since 1989, Clarke presents a theoretical analysis which is equally confused. Having moved on from his previous view focusing on the systemic need to expand the 'labour collective,' he admittedly points to the strength of the workers' position in relation to the labour process. But he fails to relate this to any dynamic consideration of the system's internal contradictions, and ultimately portrays class struggle as little more than a product of perestroika.

Of the many 'Marxists' who have presented theoretical views of the political-economic nature of the Soviet system, few have brought into their theorisation a consideration of working class struggle. And even those who have done so, such as Kuron, Modzelewski and Carlo, have failed to trace through the class polarities with consistent historical and theoretical resolution.

Notes

1   For an explanation of the significance of the inverted commas around the word 'Marxist,' see Chapter 1 above. Marxist work is considered in Chapter 6.

2   In the present context it is impossible to cover the full gamut of 'Marxist' works mentioning the USSR, many of which — for example, Marcuse's 'immanent critique' of the reigning Soviet ideology (1958) — have dealt only peremptorily, if at all, with actual Soviet production relations and the actual working class. We have therefore restricted consideration to the various critical theories of the material reality. Reasons for excluding 'Eurocommunist' and official Soviet and Chinese works are given in the Introduction.

3   It is earlier argued in the *Platform of the Left Opposition* (1927) that "the appropriation of surplus value by a workers' state is not, of course, exploitation." (p.13). This is in total contradiction with Marx's critique of political economy, which famously links surplus value, value, abstract labour, wage-labour, and capitalist exploitation. (1867, chaps. 1-6). But it is quite in keeping with the view Trotsky put forward when he was near the helm of the State, when he was keen to portray labour militarisation, one-man management and the generalisation of piece-rates as weapons wielded in the interests of the working class and socialism. (1920, chap.8).

4   Interestingly, this view is echoed by the Soviet 'dissident' Roy Medvedev, who in his largely empirical tome on Stalinism states his opinion — in agreement with "most Soviet historians" — that "Stalin's personal dictatorship did not completely abolish the dictatorship of the proletariat." In his view, "Stalin introduced many bureaucratic distortions into the system of the proletarian dictatorship, but he could not completely destroy the system. He received his mandate from the proletarian Leninist Party, after the victory of a socialist revolution. He did a poor job of carrying out the historical mission assigned to him, but he did carry it out to some extent, not only in the twenties,...but also in the thirties and forties — in the struggle against imperialism, for example...Unlimited personal power was a form,

the worst possible form, of the proletarian dictatorship; it was clearly *inconsistent with the nature of the regime* [emphasis added] and severely checked progress toward communism." (1971, pp.555-56.) In another equally empirical work, Medvedev views Stalinism in terms of "excesses," and asserts without elaboration that "many achievements of the October Revolution were not totally destroyed by Stalinism; pseudo-socialism has not managed to root out all elements of socialism from our social, economic, and political life." (1979, pp.196-97). Here too he gives no consideration to the conditions of the working class.

5   For the Trotskyist view of "the contradiction between the non-capitalist mode of production and the bourgeois norms of distribution," see E. Mandel 1968. For those who adopt a Marxist viewpoint it is clear that the contradiction that Trotskyists see between the relations of production and the relations of distribution simply cannot exist. As Marx puts it (1903, p.95), "The relations and modes of distribution...appear merely as the obverse of the relations of production....The structure of distribution is completely determined by the structure of production."

6   These are considered above in Chapter 2, note 1. In relation to the working class the Menshevik Iugov writes of low wages and poor labour conditions, but not of resistance and struggle. (1929, chap.15); and the same is true of Iurevskii writing a few years later. (1932). The social democrat Kautsky, meanwhile, who also for a time writes of Soviet 'state capitalism,' focuses mainly on political despotism and terror, rather than on the specific contradictions of class relations. (1919). The (communist) Workers' Group and Workers' Truth group, for their part, although they participated in the strikes of 1923 (Daniels 1960, p.210), are not known to have produced any theoretical work on the class struggle. And the anarchist Voline writes little about working class conditions of a theoretical nature other than to aver that the State's role as the only employer means that the worker is a "slave." (1947, pp.360-61). His consideration of class resistance under Stalinism is restricted to a brief reference to the sabotage and revenge attacks which occurred in response to Stakhanovism. (p.363).

7   Writing in 1971, Harman too restricts his consideration of class struggle to events that might happen in the future (p.66).

8   We would note here that Cliff clearly defends the use of force over the workers, albeit mediated through the 'workers' state.'

> In the transition period [between capitalism and 'socialism'] [labour discipline] will be the outcome of the unity [*sic*] of the two elements — consciousness and coercion....
> ...Whereas the workers will be both a disciplining and a disciplined factor, a subject and an object, the technicians will serve in reality only as a transmission belt, this time of the workers' state, even if they remain formally discipliners of the workers. (Cliff 1955, pp.128-29)

What appears to be an attempt at a dialectical conceptualisation is in fact simply a re-presentation of the familiar ideology of the modern representative State.

9   "Part of taking advantage of the political crisis of the transition is pushing to the limit the democratic demands of the radical democrats..." (p.83) "The majority workers, or at least the conscious socialists among them,...have to stand by the right of the national minority to form its own state if it wants to, regardless of the form of state the minority chooses to establish...The only way workers among the minority nationality will break from...[petty-bourgeois or petty bureaucratic] leadership is if they see a socialist workers'

movement among the majority nationality which is prepared to fight, in a more effective way than these leaders, against the reality of national oppression." (p.84).

10 Concerning earlier periods, though, he is confused rather than silent. Thus he refers to the 'blocking' of any organised action by the proletariat 'to transform the production relations,' but gives the main reason as being the adoption of incorrect ideological theses by officialdom. (1974, p.25). Meanwhile, when discussing the tightening of labour discipline in 1918-20 he still asserts that "this resort to coercion was only the secondary aspect of a situation whose principal aspect was the constitution of the proletariat as the dominant class." Workers who resisted were selfish and "strongly influenced by bourgeois and petty bourgeois ideas and practices." (pp.188-90). The same lens is also used to look at the struggles of the winter of 1920-21, including the uprising at Kronstadt. (pp.361-66). Bettelheim is less negative about the growth in workers' resistance to managerial authority in 1928, but blames the defeat of the 'mass movement' mainly on its lack or loss of support from within the Party. His failure to identify workers' struggle 'in itself' is shown by his very 'Maoist' attribution to General Secretary Stalin of an 'ambiguous' attitude, on the one hand genuinely calling for a continuation of 'mass criticism from below,' and for 'cultural revolution,' whilst on the other 'hesitating' to advocate a new form of 'really authoritative leadership.' (1977, 228-33).

11 A "high degree of competition" — or more accurately, generalised competition — is actually part of the basis of capitalism everywhere.

12 Meszaros's work does not fit easily into our system of classification by reason of his denial that the USSR was capitalist at the same time that he accepts that it was based on capital. (See our discussion of this view in Chapter 2, n.16). On one hand, he argues, the bureaucrats who personified capital in the USSR, unlike their capitalist counterparts, "could not exercise even a limited autonomy"; on the other, "labour could not be fragmented and atomized on the model of the capitalist labour process." Three reasons are given as to why the capitalist type of atomisation was impossible. First, "the immense enterprise of industrialization...as well as forced collectivization and forced industrialization" demanded "the highest degree of the socialization of production," which affected workers' consciousness. Second, the "ground of legitimation of 'building socialism' was the working class, and all talk about the 'proletarian dictatorship' and the 'leading role of the party' in it had to exclude quite explicitly the possibility of capitalist restoration and the subjection of labour to the alienating fetishism of the commodity." And "the third reason why the authoritarian discipline to which individual workers were subjected, no matter how severe, could not produce the result desired by the party leadership was that it could never be admitted that the recalcitrance of labour was a matter of *class antagonism*." (1995, p.668).

We would note that the second and third reasons are solely ideological, and essentially boil down to the view that the rulers were 'unable' either to strive openly for western-style atomisation or to admit that the workers were the enemy. The arguments are not based on an understanding of the political economy. If the rulers could lie about the overall position of the workers, what prevented them from benefiting from atomised private labour and lying about that too? And as for the first reason, labour's atomisation into 'private labour' could hardly be problematic for its alienated socialisation, when such atomisation is actually a necessary condition of precisely that alienated socialisation on which the existence of value — and hence of capital — depends. This is quite aside from the weakness of an argument which presents forced industrialisation as determining the supposed non-atomisation of labour only via its effects on workers' consciousness.

Meszaros goes on to state that

the workers, however, knew all too well that when they were violating the prescribed norms on a mass scale, *in front of one another*, and performing their role at a much lower level of productivity than they could, involved in all kinds of 'going slow', 'moonlighting', etc., they were not acting on behalf of a mysterious outside enemy but on their own behalf, *in solidarity with one another* which made their recalcitrant behaviour possible at all in an authoritarian system. (p.668) (emphasis added)

Although this is not linked in a straightforward fashion to the subsequent reference to the insufficiency — from the rulers' standpoint — of the fragmentation and alienation of labour, it is undoubtedly a statement about workers' struggle. Despite what appears to be a certain confusion with regard to the fulfilment of norms, it does say something about workers as a struggling collectivity. It is therefore unfortunate that it is not built upon. (For our own discussion of the subsumption of labour, productivity, and the power of the workers, see Chapter 7 below).

13   See also the discussion of Bordiga's work in Camatte 1974, pp.7-8.

14   Bordiga stresses above all that Soviet capitalism at the time he is writing is still in its 'developing' phase, and it is in this connection that the reason for his lack of interest in working class resistance becomes clear. For Bordiga it is not the onset or re-establishment of this phase which marks the victory — or even the process — of 'counterrevolution,' but on the contrary it is the establishment of its *permanence* and its labelling as (national) 'socialism' under Stalin. In the previous period, even if Lenin had seen the development of capitalism as a necessity — and denounced those who thought otherwise as 'childish' and 'petty-bourgeois' — he also saw it as temporary and did not call it 'socialism.' (See for example Lenin 1918b, especially pp.13-22). From Bordiga's point of view the key to the distinction between a developing transition and a counterrevolution is not the presence or absence of the categories of capitalism, nor yet the force of workers' actions against them, but "the dictatorship of the international communist party." (1957, p.482).

15   Whilst Bahro refers to Soviet society as 'industrial despotism' (1977, pp.83-119), his theory is so far removed from a class analysis as to exclude itself from consideration in the present context. "The concept of the working class no longer has any definable object in our social system, and, what is far more important, it has no object that can appear as a unity in practical action...Our society is no longer characterized by a 'horizontal' class division, but rather by a 'vertical' stratification, even if one which still has sharp transition points..." (pp.183-84).

16   Ticktin's theory, which denies the existence of a 'mode of production' in the USSR, is considered to be Marxist rather than 'Marxist,' and is considered in the following chapter.

17   On the grounds that they see Eastern Europe and the USSR as socialist, if not also for the fact that they use the terminology and methodology of Weberianism at least as much as they do those of 'Marxism,' Konrad and Szelenyi (1979) do not merit consideration in the main text. But by dint of their denial that those countries were 'workers' states,' and their use of at least some Marxian terms, they deserve parenthetical mention: for even while asserting that "the social structure of early socialism is organized in keeping with the principle of rational redistribution," and that "*in line with the rational principle on which its economy is based* [emphasis added], we regard this as a class structure, and indeed a dichotomous one" (p.145), they also recognise that "the interests of the workers are diametrically

opposed to those of the redistributors not only in respect to wages and other shop-floor issues, but also in matters of macroeconomic planning as well." (p.229). But since their focus is almost exclusively on the intellectuals, their analysis of working class interests is linked only tenuously to their theory of the nature of 'rational-redistributive society.' They thus argue that workers have an interest in technocratic reform insofar as it would create a link between productivity and wage-scales (p.230), but back this up somewhat unconvincingly with reference to the impetus it would supposedly give to consumer growth and the space it would make in the state budget for faster wage increases. Denying that labour-power is sold, they claim that it would be in workers' interests if it were, since removing the determination of the surplus product from "politics" would necessarily mean a rise in relative wages (p.226). Why this is so they do not say.

The Romanian theorist Campeanu is equally Weberian, and indeed owes a further debt to Parsonian structural functionalism. But despite expressing a preference at the beginning of his work *The Syncretic Society* (1980) for the tools of sociology over those of 'political economy' (p.4), he too employs a modicum of apparently 'Marxist' terminology. In presenting a theory of a *sui generis* (and anti-capitalist) "Stalinist mode of production" containing both 'capitalist' and 'pre-capitalist' elements, he thus proceeds to relate both kinds of element to the appropriation of labour-power. In this view, workers do sell their labour-power, but always to the State as a monopsonistic purchaser. (pp.25-26; see also Campeanu 1988, pp.119-22). Completely ignoring questions of labour mobility and of the influence of enterprise directors over wages and norms (see, for example, Kirsch 1972, chaps. 3 and 7; Filtzer 1986, chap.8; and Filtzer 1992b, chap.4), Campeanu then asserts in highly vague fashion that the price of labour-power, since it is fixed solely by the "subjective decisions of the regime," does not correspond to its value. (1980, p.17). The "power of value" has thus given way to the "value of power." (p.31). Consequently, even if the "articulation between production and consumption" is affected largely by "capitalist mechanisms" (namely, the wage relation), the "status" of labour-power in the economy — in terms of the allocation of work and the determination of the magnitude of the wage — remains affected by a political "regime" of "pre-capitalist complexion." (pp.52-53). In short, the sale of labour-power is real but its purchase is a sham. (p.81). Since Campeanu's rejection of the 'tools of political economy' has necessarily led throughout his work to a methodological separation of the critique of politics from the critique of economics, his attempt to bring them back together again must necessarily lead to such 'phenomenological' positions which to the materialist critic appear literally nonsensical. Since class struggle is a matter of political economy — and its critique — it has no place in Campeanu's work; but he clearly holds the view that workers in the USSR are completely powerless.

Third, mention must also be made of the Croatian scholar Horvat, who has described the Soviet-type countries as 'etatist.' While aiming to write a 'Marxist theory of political economy,' he too has adopted a Weberian optic in that his principal discussion of class has been focused upon 'stratification' and the fact that members of the 'masses' have less power than people higher up. (1982, pp.57-83). In discussing the alienation of labour, though — which he does not link to class — he states somewhat more profoundly that, just as in capitalism, the worker was both an object of bureaucratic political rule and an individual constrained to sell his labour-power. (pp.87-90). However, after then stating that unlike in the bourgeois world the source of reification under 'etatism' is "not the universalization of market relations but [rather] the universalization of bureaucratic relationships," he arrives at the view that "man is not reduced to a commodity but to the office he holds." (p.95). So what, then, does the sale of labour-power actually involve? Unfortunately none of these ideas is discussed in terms of the class relation, let alone in terms of class struggle.

18   Chen Erjin later presents a similar view, in the context of his portrayal of the Soviet system as a prime example of the 'revisionist mode of exploitation.' (1979, pp.72-87). His view of the worker under such a system as a "mere slave" (p.73), however, echoes the opinions of Rizzi and Burnham rather than those of the East European 'dissidents.' It should perhaps be added that his brief consideration of the USSR serves principally as a backdrop to what he has to say about China, and he does not study the former country in any depth. The Soviet emigrant Voslensky writes even more starkly, even if at greater length, of the fundamentally 'political' aims and basis of the ruling group. (1980, p.166). Arguing throughout his book that the "nomenklatura class" enjoys unlimited power, he suggests that the working class, although it produces surplus value, "has been plunged back into a system of extraeconomic forced labour as in the age of slavery or feudalism." (pp.146-75; see also pp.70-74). Hence there is no class struggle.

19   Of marginal interest is the fact that the publication of *The New Class* received backing from the CIA. (Blum 1986, p.128). Djilas has since renounced 'Marxism': see Djilas 1969. More recently, Djilas has described the Soviet crisis — somewhat expectedly — in terms which reduce it to a crisis of 'one-party rule.' (1988). In this view, everyone outside the CPSU has a need for democratic pluralism.

20   Although Kuron and Modzelewski deny that the USSR and the Eastern European countries were capitalist (1965, pp.26-28 and 35), they nonetheless theorise the existence in those countries of both wage-labour and capital accumulation; and even if they seem to portray a *society* that developed *sui generis* rather than just a *system*, they still avoid writing explicitly of a new mode of production. Their theory would thus appear to be rather confused. If they had written under different political conditions, however, and if they had written more on the world-historical context of their subject-matter, it is probable, we would argue, that they would have adopted a 'capitalist' theory. But since this point cannot be argued in the context of the present thesis, we have chosen instead to refrain from ascribing a theory to them which they themselves did not make explicit.

21   If from a communist viewpoint one has to remark upon a level of radicality in the *Open Letter* which was absent in the works of other dissident intellectuals — and which in light of the authors' anti-parliamentarism (p.75) and class-based internationalism (pp.65-72) might well be described as revolutionary — it should also be pointed out that when the period of sustained and open mass struggle began in Poland Kuron and Modzelewski changed camp completely. While Modzelewski was writing approvingly in the official press that "the only role to which Solidarity aspires is to be a recognized and respected social partner," Kuron put forward similarly nationalist ideas of a unity of interest between workers and rulers, and his role — alongside other leading figures in Solidarity — in encouraging workers to end their strikes made him an active and direct opponent of working class struggle. (See Simon 1982, pp. 31, 45, 52-53 and 85.) Whereas in 1965 Kuron had called for the arming of the working class (1965, p. 77), in 1981 he even opposed a strike demanding the release of workers who had publicised secret government plans for a repression (Simon 1982, p.38).

22   Marc Rakovski was the pseudonym of the two Hungarian writers Gyorgy Bence and Janos Kis.

23   Although in the 'Foreword' the authors claim collective responsibility for each of the book's three Parts, and note that each was the product of repeated discussion, they

nonetheless identify a main author in each case. Since the theoretical approach varies considerably, this is of more than bibliographical significance. Thus Heller, writing in Part 2 on questions of 'legitimation,' ideology, and consent, demonstrates little or no concern for underlying questions concerning the nature of the political economy, and for this reason her analysis is hardly very 'Marxist' at all — a weakness which for us is especially disappointing in view of the profundity and radicality of her earlier work on need. (1974). In Part 3, meanwhile, despite the fact that he ascribes a high level of significance to the categories of the rational and irrational, Feher undoubtedly shows a somewhat greater interest in the contradictions of the production relations, including those of the material relations between workers and rulers. It is, however, Markus, the author of Part 1, whose contribution is the least informed by Weberianism and the most by 'Marxism' — even if the former is still highly evident. Whilst in the main text we follow the authors' wishes by assuming joint authorship, in the references we take account of the variation by citing each author individually.

24 Such statements are hardly rare in 'social science,' the general rule being that the 'economic' is left undefined. Nonetheless, the view that society's material foundation is only one of its 'components' is virtually the defining characteristic of bourgeois empiricism. The absence of radicality is clear once it is understood that the idea of the economic being a 'facet' or 'component' of the social (Markus 1983, pp.105 and 131) — with the political being another and the cultural another — speaks more of the fragmentation of capitalist academia over the past two centuries than of the nature of social reproduction in an exploitative society.

25 The statement that "in conditions where employees have no right to autonomous professional or trade organizations, this indirect and spontaneous resistance *can have only* mild modifying effects" (Markus 1983, p.72, emphasis added) may perhaps be only borderline-absurd, but it surely calls for no great counter-argument when the authors omit to provide any argument in favour of it.

26 We would add that even the interest which these 'market socialists' show in workers' consumption choices remains superficial, insofar as they take the view, too simplistic for most bourgeois economists, that it is a "truism" that "people always want something more of everything." (Feher 1983, p.244).

27 'Primary sector' is used here to denote the production of means of production.

28 By making use in the Soviet context of a category remarkably similar to the capitalist category of 'demand,' it would seem that Carlo is leading his theory of the non-capitalist nature of the society onto very weak ground.

29 The reference to 'Orwellian' controls is Carlo's own.

30 This is also evident in Carlo's support for Mao's dictatorship in China, which prevents him from seriously envisaging what kind of society revolutionary workers might conceivably want instead of the USSR. In Carlo's view (p.58) "the Chinese model has proved that the bureaucratic road is not always inevitable."

31 "Bureaucratic collectivism can...arise naturally and develop only in underdeveloped countries." (Carlo 1971, p. 70). Or it can arise from the "degeneration" of a 'socialist revolution' (p.71). Carlo gives only one example of the latter, namely Russia, but even in that case he underlines relative economic backwardness as a factor. (pp.49-52). Leaving aside their mention of decline, then, a point which Fantham and Machover do not develop, we see that their disagreement with Carlo appears to be limited to specific examples such as China and Egypt. The former see these countries as respectively 'state collectivist' and 'state

capitalist'; the latter views them as respectively 'transitional to socialism' and 'bureaucratic collectivist.' (Fantham and Machover 1979, pp. 6 and 13-14; Carlo 1971, pp. 57-58 and 70-72).

32 For comparison, see Trotsky 1939a, pp.16-17.

33 The only exception is a one-sentence reference to working class organisations in Poland.

34 Omitting to theorise struggle, Roland has done little more than to state that full employment and the labour shortage, against a background of alienation, have led to poor discipline. (1989, p.146-69). Nor need Bayar's recent work on the 'party-controlled' (*partitique*) mode of production (1992) be considered, since no more is said about the actual class relation other than that it is exploitative and non-capitalist. (pp.222-24). Meanwhile Lefebvre, who presents an analysis of a mode of production which he prefers to term 'statist' (*étatique*) (1977), similarly omits to focus on the contradictions of class relations in the specific context of the USSR. It is undoubtedly the case that Burawoy has produced collaborative work which from a Marxist perspective is comparatively of much greater interest, insofar as he analyses in some detail the shopfloor effects (and non-effects) of post-1991 economic reform attempts in two specific Russian enterprises. (Burawoy and Hendley 1992, Burawoy and Krotov 1992). But our focus here is primarily on theoretical views of the political-economic nature of the economic system during the preceding, Soviet period, and in particular on the way such views have been related to overall conceptions of the conditions and activity of the working class as a class. And in this connection it is clear that Burawoy follows Konrad and Szelenyi (1979) in that even while he uses elements of Marxian terminology he adopts an approach which is primarily Weberian. Thus in terms of a view of the nature of the Soviet system, his theorisation has revolved principally around the construction of an 'ideal type' of 'state socialism' now ostensibly being replaced by one of 'merchant capitalism.' (See Burawoy and Krotov 1992, pp.18-21, and 1993, pp.52-54). He does, of course, utilise a concept of 'workers' control' of the labour process; but, as he and Krotov acknowledge (1992, p.19), this is largely derived from the work of Connor and Ticktin (see Chapters 4 above and 6 below, respectively), and explained in terms of the 'full employment constraint' theorised by Granick. (1987). Moreover, whilst it would be unfair to suggest that Burawoy omits to relate this concept to a consideration of workers' struggle, for in places he does indeed do precisely this (Burawoy and Krotov 1993, pp.60-64), the context in which he does so is solely that of the period of 'transition' since 1991, and that is not our concern here.

35 On Machajski see Avrich 1965 and Shatz 1967 and 1989; for a similar perspective see also Konrad and Szelenyi 1979.

36 This appropriation of the surplus *in naturalia* is cited in the same context by Feher, Heller, and Markus. (Markus 1983, p.31). If the argument is assumed to be non-circular — that is, not simply that the surplus is appropriated merely in kind because it takes a form which is not capital — the implication is surely that the category of capital can be understood outwith the context of social reproduction, investment, and accumulation — that is, *simply* as a form taken by each individual enterprise's 'surplus output,' alternative or 'extra' to its material form. This is hardly compatible with a profound grasp of the nature of capitalist political economy.

37 'Labour surplus' is Clarke's term for hoarded 'auxiliary' labour which was largely unskilled. (1993a, pp.21-22).

38 In fact, this is precisely the accepted Soviet reformist view of the late 1980s which Clarke supposedly rejects. See for example Gorbachev 1987, pp.20-21, and Aganbegian 1988, pp.100-09.

6 The Class Struggle: A Critique of Existing Marxist Theories

In this chapter we give critical consideration to the views of the Soviet working class which have been developed within Marxism. After commenting on the paucity of work produced by those adopting a communist approach, we analyse the positions of the Johnson-Forest tendency, Castoriadis, Ticktin, and Chattopadhyay. Our own theorisation is given in the chapter following.

THE NEED FOR A COMMUNIST THEORY

In the previous chapter we offered a critique of a number of 'Marxist' views of the Soviet working class, showing how they fail to grasp the polar nature of class antagonism and its centrality in the development of social contradictions. It follows that they offer very little that can be used to enrich a communist theory of the class struggle as it has undermined the conditions of exploitation in the USSR.

The first place to look for useful insights would now seem to be the texts of those who have consistently stressed proletarian autonomy and the subversion of wage-labour, such as the council communists, Situationists, and Autonomists. Working within the overall theoretical area described above as *communist*, these tendencies' most influential theorists have always kept in sight the importance of practical class antagonism. It would therefore be unfair to describe them as being unaware of the existence of class struggle in the USSR as a reality: for, in the abstract at least, given their general approach towards political economy, they quite clearly are not. On the other hand, though, the theoretical material they have actually published on the subject is very scanty, and it has to be said that they fail to consider the specific types of struggle engaged in by the Soviet working class with adequate theoretical rigour.

Various communist writers have, of course, published theoretical studies of the structure and functioning of Soviet capitalism, and we criticised their works above in Chapter 2 along with non-communist works on the same subject. But they remain very few, and it is notable that they do not include among their number any Situationists or Autonomists.[1] Moreover, the works which do exist have exclusively focused on the nature of the system rather than on the nature and vicissitudes of working class struggle. This gives rise to a certain incongruity; and council communists, usually anxious to stress workers' own experiences, have commented on the unfolding of working class struggle in the USSR in a fashion which is evidently wholly inadequate. Thus Gorter mentions the "urgent, clamouring demand of the Russian proletariat for independence," but only as an explanation of what lay behind the contribution made by the Workers' Opposition to the Bolsheviks' "trade union debate." (1921, p.4). At first glance, this would seem to be a very strange idea for a council communist to adopt; but when he later suggests (p.8) that revolutionary workers in Russia will eventually construct the equivalent of the council communist (and anti-trade unionist) General Workers' League of Germany (AAUD), Gorter makes it clear that his access to any hard information on the actual class struggle in Soviet Russia is minimal. He is simply not in a position to theorise about it.

Subsequent council communist analyses are similarly incomplete.[2] Thus Rühle, writing in the 1930s, may be able to describe the system put in place under Stalin (1931, 1939), but he omits to ask how the workers resisted its imperatives. Much the same is true of the councilists of the GIK. This is particularly striking given the thoroughness of their analysis of the events leading up to and immediately following 1917: for in that earlier context, rather than simply opposing workers' class struggle to Bolshevik Jacobinism and opportunism, they show how Bolshevik State policy not only interacted with the workers' movement but also grew out of the historical class relations, political structures, and global situation of the region. The method here is very reminiscent of Marx's descriptions (1850, 1852a) of the period around 1848 in France. Once they begin to consider the developments of the 1920s and 1930s, however, they fail to inform their critique with any such nuanced consideration of workers' struggle. As we have commented in Chapter 2, their reference to some kind of 'tendency' of proletarian struggle (GIK 1934, pp.24-25) is hopelessly muddled; and not surprisingly, they do not show why it was that the State was unable lastingly to 'master' it.

In theorising about the nature of Soviet capitalism, even Buick and Crump only touch on working class struggle — or potential for struggle — in two places. First, in referring to the massive expansion of the proletariat in the Soviet period, they write that

> as the working class grows in strength [i.e. in size], and as it becomes more educated, so the threat it poses to the rule of capital is potentially increased. (1986, pp.55-56)

Since they do not explain why 'education' should bring with it any potential threat to capital, they are doing little more than to make the observation that increasing numbers of people have an interest in revolution. This is not a statement about actual conflictuality. Later on, they describe the enormous turnover rate in 1956 as showing that the previous restrictions on labour mobility had caused a substantive build-up of "counterproductive social tensions." (p.76). There is undoubtedly a reference here to a relation of force, but they do not develop it as such, preferring to use it as evidence merely for the existence of wage-labour.

It is quite evident that the task of formulating a communist theory of working class struggle in the USSR has yet to be accomplished.

EXISTING MARXIST THEORIES

If above we have rejected 'Marxist' theories and called instead for a theorisation upon a communist basis, there remains another category of critiques yet to be considered: namely, those which, while not communist, should still be considered Marxist by dint of their clear prioritisation of the contradictions of the class relations of production. It is true that both Castoriadis and Ticktin have expressed strong support for democracy: the former advocates wage equality in a socialist 'transitional society' (1957, pp.125-27), while the latter not only suggests that the proletariat might come to power peacefully, but also states that in any case transition would involve large-scale nationalisation, secret ballots, and the gradual phasing out of the market, finance capital, and unemployment. (1990-92, pp.24-26). Neither Dunayevskaya nor James breaks completely with Bolshevism; and Ticktin remains heavily Trotsky-influenced (1992b) and sees nationalisation and the welfare State as constituting forms of the negation of capitalism, even as he understands that capitalism uses them and they are not socialist. (1983a, p.26). At the same time, however, Dunayevskaya and James, Castoriadis (in a certain period) and Ticktin have each managed to underline in no uncertain fashion the important disruptive role necessarily played by workers' power against the Soviet system. In many ways this realisation represents a major theoretical advance, and it has allowed them to make substantial contributions to Marxist critique. Chattopadhyay, for his part, may not exactly have homed in on the importance of struggle; but his avoidance of Leninist and social-democratic illusions has allowed him nonetheless to consider questions which directly concern the *rapport de force* between capital and the proletariat.[3] It is to the works of these critics that we shall now turn.

The Johnson-Forest Tendency's Theory

In Chapter 2 we showed how the Tendency's work on the functioning in the USSR of the categories of capitalist reproduction, within its limitations, represents a notable theoretical step forward. It is further the case that in her critique of the Soviet economy published in the 1940s Dunayevskaya becomes the first theorist to insist in the Soviet context on the importance of class struggle: not as an abstract goal, but in terms of a necessary actuality corresponding to the nature of the system. For this reason, her work is outstanding: in refusing to view the workers as mere objects, she once again breaks new ground.

In looking at the period of the first three five-year plans (1928-41) Dunayevskaya attempts to understand the class struggle by looking first at its specific pushes and pulls. It is from such a standpoint that she considers, for example, the law of 1932 by which workers' ration cards were transferred into the hands of the factory directors. Describing this decree as an attempt by the rulers to "turn wage slaves into outright slaves through legislative enactment," Dunayevskaya insists on the point that the statute

> failed to fulfill the desired end. Labor would not come to industry and when it did come, it left soon, after producing as little as possible. Since industry needed labor[,] the factory director 'forgot' to fire the worker for absence and slowups in production. (1946-47, p.316)

More generally,

> neither [the official] appeal [against competition among managers to hire labor,] nor the anti-labor legislation[,] nor the fact that the proletariat was deprived of the use of trade unions[,]which had become part of the administrative machinery of the state[,] accomplished the trick of straight-jacketing [*sic*] labor. (1942-43, p.54)

In short, as industry expanded apace, workers continued to take advantage of the increased demand for labour. Despite the desired aims of the ruling elite, it proved impossible to introduce 'slavery by decree.'

Dunayevskaya then describes how the agricultural crisis of 1933, and the consequent famine and unemployment, caused an increase in the influx of workers into the cities, which in turn allowed managers to discipline workers by means of the more 'natural' and 'bourgeois' method of the reserve army of labour. From 1935, this method was then replaced by Stakhanovism, another mainly 'natural' method based primarily on incentives for efficiency. Conceived of as a response to the ineffectiveness of the labour legislation of the foregoing period, this new policy was designed to avoid the failure which had beset the previous attempts to 'end depersonalisation' (or 'egalitarianism') by more despotic means. (1942-43, pp.53-54; see also p.316).[4] But these "natural" methods brought about natural results: the class struggle. The simmering revolt among the workers...only produced further chaos in production and a mass exodus of workers from the city.

In 1938, the State grew desperate.

> The 1932 law was revived and 'improved upon.' This still proved fruitless. In 1940 came the creation of the State Labor Reserves, and with it came the institution of "corrective labor": workers disobeying the laws were made to work six months with 25 per cent reduction in pay. (p.316)

But resistance continues even after this, as labour too shows "ingenuity." Where it cannot revolt openly, it either 'disappears,' or it slows up production, thereby preventing a rise in productivity. After the second world war, the rulers' demand for labour once again becomes very high relative to the available supply, and the rapidity of demobilisation makes a dead letter of "all" previous labour laws. The planners are forced to make an "unplanned declaration": an amnesty for all labour offences committed during the war. (p.316; see also Dunayevskaya 1958, p.246).

There are, of course, certain factual errors in this analysis. Unemployment did not rise in 1933: in fact, having risen throughout the middle and late 1920s, it starting falling at the turn of the decade and vanished altogether in 1931. (Davies 1986). Meanwhile, the working class response to Stakhanovism (Filtzer 1986, chap 7) did not involve a 'mass exodus' from the cities: such a strategy had last been employed during the civil war. (Nove 1982, pp.66-67). And the law against resigning from one's job without permission did not lose its force altogether until 1951, according to Brown and Helgeson (1966, p.16 and 1986, p.148, respectively), or until its repeal in 1956 according to M. McAuley (1969, p.47). But such inaccuracies are insufficient to undermine the overall strength of Dunayevskaya's work, which is twofold. First, there is her method: she constantly seeks to understand capitalist labour policy in terms of the power exercised by the workers in antagonism towards its implementation and efficiency. Second, on a more general level, she identifies a

> constant pull and tug between the needs of production for highly productive labor[,] which means 'free' labor, and the resort to legislative enactment to bring this about in hot-house fashion. (1946-47, p.316)

In relation to this second idea, it is important to realise that Dunayevskaya is not saying that excessive usage of 'despotic' means of discipline must in itself prove counter-productive, leading to the introduction of more 'natural' methods. On the contrary, she emphasises above all the resistance raised by the workers, and she explains the changes in labour policy precisely in reciprocal relationship to this resistance, rather than in fundamental terms of 'internal contradictions.' She stresses this point very clearly in her work of 1958, when she writes that

> [the] draconian anti-labor legislation [of 1940] records the terror of the ruling bureaucracy in the face of the revolt of the workers.
>
> The millions in forced labor camps are the true measure of the never-ending resistance of the Russian [*sic*] masses to the Russian rulers in the State, in the factory, and in the fields. Had the revolt not been so persistent, the terror would not have been so violent. (1958, p.237)

It is against such a background that Dunayevskaya explains the strike and uprising by slave labourers in Vorkuta in June 1953, whose significance she compares with that of the workers' movement in Soviet-occupied Germany the same year and those in Hungary and Poland three years later. (pp.249-57). For Dunayevskaya, the death-knell of Stalinism is sounded by nothing other than the actions of the workers.

Since, however, there were no revolutionary workers' councils in the USSR as there were in Hungary, these comparisons which Dunayevskaya makes at the beginning of her 'Marxist-Humanist' period are of little theoretical use. By conflating different manifestations of the workers' fight against Stalinism, she simply insists that such a fight existed and was important. Whereas in the 1940s she analyses the history of the Soviet system through the lens of the interplay between economic policy and working class self-assertion, when Stalinism comes to an end in the mid-1950s she falls back upon the mainly political and ideological concept of 'Russian totalitarianism,' pitted against the forces of 'freedom.' (p.248). As a result, she fails to focus on the specific characteristics of class struggle as acutely as she has done with reference to the previous period.[5]

The second main criticism to be made is that even in her work of the 1940s she fails to relate the specific characteristics of class struggle to the specific characteristics not just of labour policy, but of the Soviet political economy as a whole. This is not to belittle her achievement in insisting on the necessary and permanent nature of the workers' struggle against the imperatives of the system; it is simply to note that such considerations do not illuminate to any significant degree her work on the functioning of the political-economic categories of capitalism in the specific Soviet context. (1946-47, p.314, for example). As a result, her theoretical grasp of the effects of workers' class struggle remains on a general level, concerning little more than its adverse influence on the growth of productivity.

It is now necessary to consider the work of her longstanding co-theorist James,[6] who in 1950 penned what was presented as the Tendency's most important document, namely *State Capitalism and World Revolution*. Perceiving that

> the whole tendency of the Stalinist theory is to build up theoretical barriers between the Russian [*sic*] economy and the economy of the rest of the world [,]

James declares early on in this work that he intends to help break down such a separation by explaining Soviet development in the context of capitalist development globally. (p.39). In addition, he states very clearly that the key to understanding the nature of the Soviet system must be based principally upon a 'concrete analysis of labour' both inside the USSR and without. He thus sets himself theoretical tasks whose solution would undoubtedly represent a major advance.

Unfortunately, though, in seeking to explain the development of the USSR

> by the development of world capitalism and specifically, capitalist production in its most advanced stage, in the United States (p.39)

James does not quite achieve his goal. Whilst his work on American Fordism, the workers' reaction to it in the sphere of production, and the bourgeoisie's forced creation of the welfare State (1950, pp.39-44) is undoubtedly pathbreaking and highly important,[7] it is not matched by any correspondingly profound analysis of the labour process and the development of class relations in the USSR. He gives instead an account which is both rudimentary and very schematic. According to this, the "Russian Revolution in 1917 [first] substitutes for the authority of the capitalist in the factory the workers' control of production"; next, after the 'blip' of labour militarisation on the railways is rectified by Lenin in the 'trade union debate,'[8] "mass activity" begins to be alienated and production "bureaucratised" in the years 1924-28. At the end of the 1920s abstract mass labour then comes into its own when government policy demands the creation of "lots" of it in the race to "catch up with capitalism."[9] The introduction of Stakhanovism in 1935 constitutes "the counter-revolution of state-capital"; and Molotov's speech in 1939 about increasing production *per capita* rather than just gross output marks a further change in the "mode of labor." (pp.44-47).

> We can say that 1937 [*when elaboration began of the third five-year plan*—NCF] closes one period. It is the period of "catching up with and outdistancing capitalism" which means mass production and relatively simple planning. But competition on

a world scale and the approaching Second World War is the severest type of capitalist competition for world mastery. This opens up the new period of per capita production as against mere "catching up." Planning must now include productivity of labour. (pp.47-48)

This analysis may seem impressive but in fact it is offered without any strong empirical basis. Its main inadequacy is not simply, however, James's apparent ignorance that productivity growth was always an aim of every plan; nor even his omission to consider the actual progress of productivity, which fell during the first five-year plan period (1928-32) and seems to have risen during the second and third. (1933-41). (See Nove 1982, chaps. 8-9). It is this: unlike in his consideration of American Fordism, James makes no reference in his consideration of Soviet Stalinism to any reaction by the workers against the moves of their exploiters. His comparison of Soviet Stalinism both to conditions under Ford before unionisation (1950, p.40) and to what conditions would be like if Ford was totally successful (p.48), therefore, rather than being based on an analysis of workers' struggle, is based largely upon the assertion that the worker in the USSR is "reduced to an appendage to a machine and a mere cog in the accumulation of capital." (p.48).

From ascribing less weight than Dunayevskaya does to the force of Soviet workers in production, James later jumps to ascribing more, thereby becoming able to consider Soviet conditions in a much more stimulating way. But it is nonetheless evident that the theoretical consideration of the USSR in *Facing Reality*, published under the joint signatures of James, Lee, and Chaulieu (Castoriadis)[10] in 1958, is influenced most of all by earlier work by Castoriadis rather than by any of the Johnson-Forest tendency. (pp.29-34 and 51-54). Moreover, whereas Castoriadis, notwithstanding certain weaknesses criticised below, later builds upon the ideas about the USSR which are expressed in this book, James himself produces no subsequent work on the subject of any substantial theoretical depth.[11] For these reasons we leave over dealing with this text until the following section.

Castoriadis's Theory

After first writing that in the USSR "the proletariat is completely reduced to mere raw material in the production process" (1949a, p.85), and before returning to an even more 'totalitarian' view of Soviet "slave capitalism" (1977, p.8), Castoriadis similarly succeeds for a time in focusing with some acuity on the real struggle of workers against the Soviet system. Once he has decided in May 1949 that "the class struggle [in the USSR] exists" (1949a, pp.139-40), the importance he attributes to its effects grows steadily over the following several years.

Recognising that working class 'counter-influence' on production is a result of class struggle Castoriadis forages further into ground first opened up by Dunayevskaya in the mid-1940s. He points to two forms of struggle in particular, both of which are "tied, more or less indirectly, to the distribution of the surplus product." The first is theft — of tools, products, semi-finished goods, raw materials, and machine parts — which "assumes massive proportions" and provides a relatively large proportion of the working class with a means to make up for their "terribly inadequate wages." The second is what Castoriadis terms an "active indifference" toward the results of production, manifested on a qualitative level as sloppy work and on a quantitative level as a slow production rate. (pp.139-40).

Whilst in 1949 Castoriadis does not exactly criticise such struggles, he has yet to view their impact on the system as being particularly great. For him they may be "subjectively sound class reactions," but their "point of view" is nonetheless "objectively retrograde." Still a Leninist, he takes the view that

> in the long run, if the class struggle of the Soviet proletariat is not afforded a different way out, these reactions can only bring with them this class's political and social degradation and decomposition. (p.140)

Ultimately he understands their "point of view" as being one of desperation, similar to that ostensibly possessed in a previous epoch by 'machine-smashers.' The ideological nature of this opinion, according to which real forms of struggle lead to degradation (Castoriadis does not actually write 'lumpenisation') — unless, that is, a different outcome is "built" upon "revolutionary struggle" — is self-evident. What Castoriadis fails to recognise here is that struggle is always a struggle of power against power: any form it takes can be recuperated, incorporated, or defeated, but so long as it retains a force antagonistic to exploitation it cannot be 'retrograde.' It is only possible to hold otherwise if one has a concept of 'progress' as some kind of class-neutral term outside of the basic antagonism. (See Perlman 1983).

Castoriadis's assessment of Soviet workers' struggle soon changes, and after the death of Stalin he commits himself much more (1953) to the view that working class opposition carries considerable power: not only as manifested in the strike movements in Czechoslovakia and the GDR, but also in the USSR itself, as permanent pressure on the needs of exploitation. Analysing and explaining the changes in the USSR in the spring and summer of 1953, he points in particular to the amnesty granted in March to many of the inmates of the camp system, and to the major price-cuts announced on 1 April. In his view such concessions cannot fully be explained by the conflict between dictatorial centralism and the need for internal bureaucratic stability: whether they are "apparent" or "real," a "second factor" is at work:

> This is the need to attenuate the fundamental social contradiction of this system of rule, the workers' opposition to the regime.

He continues:

> Russia's [*sic*] low productivity results from the workers' nonallegiance to a system of production that cheats them as well as from a miserable standard of living combined with terror. The resulting permanent economic crisis becomes much more serious as the technical and economic level of the country rises. Canals can be dug with concentration camp prisoners controlled by the whip as long as some of their skin is left on. But modern industry requires that the worker maintain at least partial allegiance to his job, and this allegiance cannot be obtained by terror pure and simple; to obtain it, he must be given some interest in the economic results of production...We must think that Russian *workers' opposition has become sufficiently strong to initiate some specific concessions*. (p.248) (emphasis added) (See also Castoriadis 1954, pp.278-80)

In *The Proletarian Revolution Against the Bureaucracy* (1956) he goes still further, becoming the first person to argue that it is working class resistance that is the "ultimate cause of the failure of the 'Plan'." (p.65).[12] In this text Castoriadis no longer focuses simply on concessions, but on *crisis*. Workers refuse to work hard and to participate in work organisation, they work sloppily or even stay away from work altogether, and the 'plan' simply collapses. (pp.68-69). For the exploiters it is impossible to establish a set of aims and then see them realised.

Using quotes from the Soviet leaders at the Twentieth Congress of the CPSU (also 1956), Castoriadis shows how

> neither production bonuses nor Stakhanovism, neither the GPU nor prison camps, provide the Russian factory director with the means to discipline workers and to *impose* on them a set of norms and pay rates. He is obliged to *come to terms* with them. (p.72)

Thus although the eradication of wage levelling has been an official aim of the 'plan' (and of reform) ever since Stalin came to power, it has always proved impossible, because workers are simply too strong to allow it. As a result, the workers' struggle against wage differentials goes "as far, if not further," than it does in factories in France or the United States. (pp.70-72). Summarising the Marxist view, he then states very simply that the Soviet dictatorship

> cannot now and never will in the future be able to prevent the workers from struggling against exploitation with means that the exploited always have at their disposal: the refusal to cooperate in production, which can be manifested in an infinite number of ways. (p.76)[13]

This view is then restated in the text published jointly with James and Lee in 1958, and similar references are made to Khrushchev's complaints at the same congress about wage-levelling and the receipt of inordinately high wages by certain categories of workers. The First Secretary is shown to be blatantly aware that the system's achievement of its aims is constantly being problematised and disrupted by pressure from the workers in production. (1958, pp.31-33).[14]

Castoriadis writes that the working class enters into revolt not just

> against the low standard of living as such, in the absolute — a notion that indeed hardly makes any sense...[but rather] against the *stagnation* of its living standards...(p.75)

One can criticise the imprecision of this formulation,[15] but it is more important to point out that Castoriadis is unable to take the next step: namely, that of explaining *how* various forms of struggle are part of the same autonomous movement, and *how* they tend to undermine the production of surplus-value and hence the bureaucratic system. Instead, falling back on his libertarian political approach, he arrives at the confused theory that the basic 'dynamic' contradiction in Soviet society — and capitalist society generally — is that which operates between 'exclusion' and 'participation.' Whilst this is not, of course, a Marxist view, paradoxically the terms in which Castoriadis conceives of this contradiction approach those of the traditional 'Marxism' he rejects. Thus rather than taking a proletarian 'point of view' (the struggle being about everything that can be got hold of, now), he takes the view that the basic contradiction lies in the fact that capitalism needs both to solicit participation and to forbid initiative, simultaneously. (1960-61, p.282). Insofar as these are needs felt only on one side of the class divide, the polarity so sharply visible in his writings of the mid-1950s becomes much hazier.[16]

Thus Castoriadis is never able to use his insights to help produce a theory that might explain fully the relationship between workers' struggle and the breakdown of the system; nor the reason why the first industrialised economic system to break down was highly bureaucratic, rather than bourgeois and based on the market. In 1977 he still mentions the "permanent implicit struggle of workers

		POSITION ON THE NATURE OF THE SYSTEM		
		WORKERS' STATE	CAPITALISM	*SUI GENERIS* FORMATION
	NONE	Trotsky, Mandel	SPGB, Wildt, Munis, Cliff, Harman, Bettelheim, Bordiga, Gorter, Rühle, GIK, Buick/Crump	Rizzi Burnham
TREATMENT OF CLASS CONFLICT IN RELATION TO THE NATURE OF THE SYSTEM	HIGHLY CONFUSED	-	-	Fantham/Machover Clarke
	TANGENTIAL	-	Chattopadhyay Chavance Sapir	Shachtman/Djilas Feher/Heller/Markus Rakovski Carlo Kuron/Modzelewski
	ESSENTIAL		Dunayevskaya/James Castoriadis *[Present Theory — see Chap.7]*	Ticktin

Figure 6.1 Theories of the USSR: The Consideration of Class Conflict

against the system in production," and points to 'Russia' as being of all the industrialised countries the "prime candidate for social revolution." (1977, pp.13-15; see also 1981a, p.8). And he even makes a reference to the "permanent crisis of production" which results from workers' resistance. (1977, p.9). But he simply makes this assertion and fails to develop any materialist critique much further than that. He is consequently able in the very same text to describe the Soviet 'social regime' as being a "slave capitalism" or "bondage capitalism" whose totalitarian oppressiveness *and control* outdoes even those of the Nazis. (p.7). Betwixt these two assertions, he suggests that the supposed inability of the working class to influence events "openly" leaves the way open for full-scale "bureaucratic irrationality." (p.8). This highly undeveloped usage of such terms as 'resistance' and 'control' (which one might conceive to be inversely related to each other), 'openness' or the absence of it (from whose viewpoint?), and 'irrationality' (by what criteria?) only demonstrates how the critical materialism of his earlier works is no longer present.

Ticktin's Theory

The third body of work to be considered is that developed by Ticktin since the early 1970s. If he is clearly not the first theorist to emphasise the connection between the nature of Soviet exploitation and the role of the workers in the production process — this having been done before him by Dunayevskaya, James, and Castoriadis, and to a lesser extent by Kuron and Modzelewski and Carlo — he undoubtedly does so in a much more thoroughgoing way than is evident in previous efforts. (See Figure 6.1). A second aspect of his work is that even despite his denial that the Soviet system is capitalist, he binds his analysis of it very closely to an understanding of capitalism's historical development and the contradictions of that development. (See, for example, 1994a, pp.92-93; or 1987a, pp.20-24).[17] In the present work, of course, it is the former aspect which concerns us most; but in view of the interrelation and 'interpenetration' of the two aspects, it is necessary to consider first the more general theoretical context which he has constructed.

The Idea of Capitalist Decline

Taking Ticktin's work as a whole, we see that behind his theory of the nature of the USSR there is one idea which is more basic than all the others: namely, that capitalism is in decline. Closely associated with this idea — so closely, in fact, that it often appears as a restatement (1994a, pp.80-83) — there is the idea that the present epoch, considered historically and globally, is one of transition to socialism.

> We live in a world where the old order is dying, where capitalism is in decline, and the world is in a transition to a new mode of production that has not yet been born. In this epoch three sets of laws are operating: the laws of capitalism itself, the laws of a declining capitalism, and the laws of transition. This book [*about the USSR—NCF*] has really been concerned with the last. The fundamental law of the transition period is that of the growing conflict between incipient and often distorted forms of planning and the market. (1991c, p.185)

It is no surprise that in epochs of transition

> there can come into existence...unstable combinations of forms deriving from capitalism, and attempts to overcome it. They are not simply bits of one formation and bits of another but new forms altogether which are like unstable chemical compounds which may decay into their component parts but are not themselves the component parts and may have few properties in common [with them]. (1976, p.28)

Rather than being, say, a development of — or simply a successor to — the geographically specific 'Asiatic mode of production' (1978, pp.39-42), the Soviet social formation is just such a "compound." On one hand, as a symptom of decline, it represents a (temporary) "victory of capitalism in preventing a move to socialism." (1991c, p.186; see also 1987a, p.23). On the other, as a monstrous symptom of the transitional epoch defined by that decline, it contains forms neither of planning nor of the market. Neither capitalist nor socialist, it is not transitional and it is not even hybrid. It is instead 'non-historical,' a non-mode of production with no 'essence' and no 'mature form.' (1991c, p.14; see also 1978, p.61).

In order to be able to discuss the issue of capitalist decline it is first necessary to realise that it is not straightforward. In fact, four separate statements can be associated with it. These are as follows: 1) capitalism is declining at the present time; 2) capitalism must eventually enter a decline, because of its very nature; 3) capitalism is bound eventually to disappear; and 4) communism cannot be prevented forever and is historically inevitable. (See Figure 6.2). In the present context, of course, it is 1 and 2 which are the most relevant; but in criticising Ticktin's arguments we have found it necessary to draw important distinctions both between 2 and 3 and between 3 and 4. By arguing in support of 2, Ticktin evidently feels he is strengthening the case not only for 3 but also for 4, so it is worth pointing out at the outset that the criticisms which follow are directed solely at the arguments in favour of 1 and 2. The historical certainty of an

1. CAPITALISM IS DECLINING

2. CAPITALISM MUST DECLINE

⇓

3. CAPITALISM MUST DISAPPEAR

⇑

4. COMMUNISM IS INEVITABLE

(Note that neither link is reversible in direction)

Figure 6.2 Capitalist Decline: Four Concepts and Two Necessary Links

irreversible victory of communism (statement 4) is not in question; and indeed its recognition is considered to be intrinsic to the entire communist theoretical approach. (See Chapter 1 above, where it is accepted that the overall movement of history paves the way for future communism. [Marx 1852b, p.64, and 1932, pp.90-91]. See also A. Cohen 1990.) It is not capitalism's disappearance which is in dispute, but rather its putative decline.

'Current Decline' First to be considered is the idea that capitalism is declining now, since this is the idea which crucially underpins Ticktin's entire explanation of why a non-capitalist social formation could exist in the USSR for so long. In defence of this thesis he cites the development of one capitalist form in particular: namely, finance capital. More particularly, he focuses on its increasing tendency to abstract itself from long-term productive investment in industry; and in so doing he has undoubtedly produced useful and important work on the subject, which among other things has pointed up very clearly the uselessness of Lenin's. But nevertheless, the argument leading from the contradictions of finance capital to the decline of capitalism remains highly faulted. (1986a, pp.1-4). In this view, capitalism declines because of the tendency of money-capital (M) to strive towards (but never reach) autonomisation from production. This striving contradicts the basis of capitalism, namely the production and realisation of new value. (1983a, 1986a, 1994a). And since the tendency must necessarily grow, the society itself is eventually bound to decline. As a result, in the absence

of the subjective condition of a conscious revolutionary movement, there is thus a growing likelihood of the rise of (bastard) 'forms of the negation of capitalism,' and an increasing occurrence of historical 'accidents.' (1983a, 1991c chap.10; see also 1987a, pp.23-24).

But if the contradiction which Ticktin identifies indisputably exists, and in terms of the expansion of global money markets is indeed intensifying (Davis and Davidson 1991, pp.89-95) — and for the time being seems bound to intensify further — this does not in itself provide adequate proof of decline.[18] The matter of whether or not capitalist society is declining raises an obvious epistemological question: how would we know? If increasingly irrational financial conditions are a cause of decline, then what are its symptoms? First, then, there is the view that the actual performance of capitalist production is falling further and further behind its potentialities. (Ticktin 1994a, p.69). In this connection we shall simply point out that any objective verification of this highly subjective assertion would depend among other things on a profound study of the history of capitalist science, which Ticktin fails notably even to call for.[19] In the second place, he argues for the existence of decline, as indeed he should, on concrete empirical grounds. He mentions, for example, the rise of unemployment and the run-down of British manufacturing industry in the interests of the City (1986a, pp.12-15), the enormous expansion of the non-value producing military industrial complex in the United States (1991c, p.185), and the more general rise of irrationalism, drug use, and the mafia. (1994, p.75).[20] He further cites the growth of what he terms 'needs-based' sectors such as 'education,' health, and public housing, even if they are currently being reduced. (1983a, pp.40-41; 1987a, pp. 21-23 and 27; 1994a, p.83; see also 1991c, chap. 10). He also points to forms such as nationalisation and central economic administration, which he describes as inherently non-capitalist, even if highly useful to capitalism; and as non-socialist too, even if such "intermediate forms" are supposedly socialism's necessary prerequisites. (1987a, p.21-24). More recently he has added to the list, citing increasing racism as evidence of the "progressive removal" of commodity fetishism; State intervention and the "nationalisation of money" as evidence for the decline of value; the "break-up of the production unity of the workers" as evidence for the decline of abstract labour; and the limited usefulness of the rulers' traditional tool of unemployment as evidence for a decline in the labour market. (1994a, p.83).

The logic of this argument would clearly imply that at some time in the past capitalism existed in a relatively pure, mature, healthy state. In short, if capitalism's vigour is declining then it must once have been at a maximum. In this golden age of capitalism, two conditions would have been apparent. First, labour would have approximated much more closely than it does today to the capitalist ideal of abstraction and interchangeability; and second, unemployment would have functioned smoothly across the entire labour market. (Any search for a period when capital dominated labour using forms which were exclusively non-racist would clearly be quite fruitless). Whereas the first condition, then, was obviously not the case prior to the organisational developments associated with Sloan, Taylor, and Ford,[21] the second was clearly no longer the case during the implementation of the policies associated with Hitler, Roosevelt, the second world war, and Keynes. In seeking to specify a period when both conditions were satisfied, then, we thus arrive at around the year 1930 — hardly the best of times to pick as capitalism's peak moment of health.

In the final analysis, though, Ticktin's theory of current decline must stand or fall according to an appraisal of the present. It then appears that decline's most important empirical indicators can be grouped under two main headings: first, the granting of concessions in the area of social expenditure and the control of institutions, at least in the 'first world'; and second, the growth in several areas of the general economic role of the State, in terms of both unproductive consumption and administrative control. These two factors are held to be highly contradictory to the nature of the system, and form the nub of the argument.

Let us take first the issue of structural concessions. The question we should pose straightaway is this: what does government spending on working class health, for example, actually involve if not a socialised form of the wage? We recognise, of course, that a substantial proportion of 'health spending' actually goes to rich physicians, managers, large shareholders of companies selling drugs, computers, and equipment, and so on, in a process which can rightly be termed the distribution of surplus value from exploiter to exploiter. But exploiters gain money from selling food too, and as with food, the main function of health treatment provided to the working class is to *reproduce labour-power*.[22] And since the value (not including surplus value) of *any* commodity is its average cost of production, there is no reason why this should not apply to the labour-power commodity (which by definition contains no surplus value, but produces it); and notably does not provide a counter-argument to the definition of the wage as the cost (or price) of the reproduction of the worker. (Dalla Costa 1971). It should thus be evident that the introduction of 'public' health provision, social security benefits, and subsidised housing, which together constitute the main parts of the *social wage*, amounts above all to a wage-rise, or at least to a change in the form of payment. In short, structural concessions are made in the course of class struggle: and from capital's point of view this becomes a struggle to offset them — along, of course, with any other forms of wage-rise — against an increase in productivity: that is, against the production of relative surplus value. (See Marx 1867, chaps. 12-15). They can hardly be described as inherently non-capitalist in any sensible way, since they do not demand a revision of what is most fundamental in the basic capitalist category of the wage. Any "measure of power" supposedly conceded to the working class in the form of the right to vote, meanwhile (Ticktin 1994a, p.75), would seem to be wholly illusory and at any rate of no political-economic importance.[23]

Nor is the military economy necessarily *critically* problematic for capitalism. It is true that at least in the short term State military expenditure is consumptive of surplus value. But the part of it paid to the sector's workers still takes the form of a wage; and it is surely bizarre Marxism to argue that the wage-form of the price of labour-power is real or illusory according to the character of the commodity produced. In return for the expenditure as a whole, the rulers receive arms which can hardly be defined as a burden. Those which are actually 'consumed' are used to rule, divide, and kill proletarians (always), as well as to bolster particular capitals against their competitors (almost always); while even those which are stockpiled indefinitely tend to spin off competitive technologies such as nuclear power or satellite communications. Neither of these uses is exactly unprofitable, and so it is only superficially meaningful to classify them as *simply* 'unproductive consumption.' Both uses ultimately assist in the social reproduction of capital. The final part of the arms economy involves weapons which prove to be totally useless, thereby amounting only to a drain on surplus value. But even if the often politically-determined expense were to become too high, the world's rulers would surely find it much easier to economise in this area — witness the signing of treaties on conventional forces in Europe (CFE) and strategic arms reduction (START) in 1990 and 1991 — rather than reducing their expenditure on more straightforward (and cheaper) forms of luxury consumption such as, say, first-class air travel or privileged access to healthcare.

There remains the issue of State administrative control, and in fact it is this that forms the basis of Ticktin's principal argument. In short, the growth of various forms of State intervention is understood to express a tendency towards the organisation, concentration, and centralisation of capital which necessarily undermines it. But this too is faulty. Thus it is not at all clear why increasing capitalist organisation should perilously undermine capitalist competition — or why the bourgeoisie's use of the State should backfire. Competition has never been totally free, so why should even the future rule of One World Government necessarily involve its elimination? Restriction, even severe, is not abolition, or even, necessarily, de-generalisation. For that matter, centralisation does not even imply restriction, insofar as competition can become 'internalised' and simply given manageable forms in which to operate. A move to centralised policy-making at a global level might well enable capitalism to cope more efficiently with its problems; and in fact it might be undertaken for precisely this reason, since the modern State is nothing but the form in which the capitalist ruling class asserts its common interests. (Marx and Engels 1846, p.78).[24] It is a weapon wielded by the ruling class in advance of those interests, and there is no fundamental contradiction between the State form and the value form. Policy/politics is essentially an arm of economic rule.

Ticktin's inadequately critical view of the State form, which is perhaps the clearest weakness of his theory of decline, leads him to ignore some of Marx's most important observations. A critic agreeing with Marx's critique of the capitalist State form as the "illusory 'general' interest" (1846, p.46), for example, could hardly assert, as Ticktin does, that "the introduction of annual parliaments with the right of everyone to vote would make any capitalism unviable." (1994a, p.75). And instead of arguing that arms production is "geared for public use, rather than private or corporate consumption" (Ticktin 1987a, p.21), they would surely view the very word 'public' as an ideological term which expresses very neatly precisely that illusory representation to which Marx refers.

We would further argue that it is only possible to view the advance of the State as being in inherent contradiction with the nature of capitalism if one holds that among the main features of a future 'socialist society' would be, first, the continued existence of money and commodities; and second, the 'hindrance' by the State of the accumulation of capital in 'private hands.' (See, for example, Trotsky 1936, pp.55-56). That Ticktin shares Trotsky's view is evident in his position on the "gradual" elimination of finance capital in a context where nationalised firms operate for a time within a market.[25] (1990-92, p.24). From this standpoint it is quite reasonable to see any expansion of the role of the State in contemporary capitalism as serving to increase the possibility of a move to 'socialism' in the future. Apparently, then, the 'laws' of a declining or late capitalism progressively weaken all the main capitalist forms except the State form, which they only serve to strengthen. This form comes to function in an increasingly 'non-capitalist' manner, and seems positively to reach out for the 'anti-capitalist' role which supposedly lies in store for it in 'early socialism.' The problem with such a view is that by reclassifying the State as some sort of 'contradictory' form it involves a rejection of the necessity of destroying all capitalist forms by revolutionary means. It is a social-democratic view founded on a grave misunderstanding of the polarisation of class subjects.

It would hardly be unfair to draw a connection between Ticktin's work and the more 'orthodox' *a priori* identification of 'normal' or 'mature' capitalism not with the capitalism of 1930 but with the 'classical' capitalism which lasted from Marx's time until the first world war. For most intents and purposes, then, the changing conditions of present-day capitalism — or indeed capitalism since the mythical 'October 1917'[26] — might just as well be termed 'post-classical.' On this assumption, virtually all 'non-classical' forms (nationalisation, pension funds, even universal suffrage) appear to be non-capitalist, or at least symptomatic of a capitalism which is somehow warped in relation to the supposed 'ideal form' of generalised *laissez faire*. Capitalism is assumed to have flourished most in the period which followed the Industrial Revolution, only to have become bogged down in a mire of problems prior to the twentieth-century rise of mass production, mass consumption, and 'mixed economy.' The social-democratic view that nationalisation and political democracy will also be features of a future 'socialist revolution' (Ticktin 1990-92, p.24) can subsequently serve as an indicator that the analysis is on the right lines. For those locked into such a view, it is then but a short step to explaining away the extraordinary development which capitalist production has undergone since 1945 in terms of an epochal "strategy of delay" on the part of the bourgeoisie. (Ticktin 1994a, p.88). But in the face of this development — in aeronautics, chemicals, electronics, and plastics; in entirely new industries such as genetic engineering, information technology, and the nuclear and space sectors; and involving enormous changes in consumption and the ideology of consumption — such a non-historical conceptualisation is signally unconvincing. Indeed it fails to lend itself to any substantial use other than the Trotskyist struggle to declare a 'rotten' capitalism moribund after nationalising the monopolies.

'Necessary Decline'   Quite apart from the view that capitalism is in decline now, the second aspect of Ticktin's theory of decline is the view that capitalism *must* decline, owing to its very nature. Regardless of whether or not this has already started to happen, it is understood to be a matter of historical certainty. This aspect of the theory, then, concerns the objective reasons which will bring about capitalism's final demise at some point in the future. But in this area too the theory invites criticism. Indeed, the problem is more than simply the 'essentialist' assumption that capitalism's decline, just like its 'maturity,' is implied by its nature, as if it were a biological organism[27] or physical entity. In criticising 'declinism,' Tillium has recently argued as follows. If capitalism disappears then there are two possibilities: either it is destroyed by proletarian revolution and replaced with communism; or else it is replaced with "some new kind of despotic and exploitative society with a non-value basis yet to be defined." (1994, p.13). In the first case, the strengthening of revolutionary forces prior to their victory would obviously have corresponded to a weakening of capitalist forces prior to their defeat. In other words, the capitalist system would have experienced the exacerbation of severe problems in the run-up to its overthrow. These problems, or weaknesses, can be considered from two points of view. From a proletarian point of view, since the build-up of the revolutionary movement would be experienced as primarily subjective and assertive in nature, it would surely make little sense to conceptualise the underlying tendency in terms of external factors defined by the objective decline of the opposition. On the contrary, the historical tendency of the

period would appear principally as a communist advance, and there would be no reason to understand capitalism's disappearance in terms of its decline. Only from capital's point of view might such an understanding appear reasonable. But even then, the possibility of a forestalling of communist revolution by forces organised around an embryonic non-capitalist form of exploitation is sufficient to show that even severe problems for capital do not *necessarily* make revolution more likely. In practice, of course, such a possibility may well remain remote, and capitalism's weaknesses may indeed make a revolution more likely — but this does not follow necessarily from the nature of capitalist society.

Mention of the second case is, of course, highly subversive of received opinion: but in considering it we might first picture a future which brings the most 'monstrous' forms imaginable, so 'monstrous' — rule by a single neurocomputer, perhaps, or technetronic slavery, or both — that they prove incompatible with the continued existence of a society based on value. We would argue that it is only possible to discount the possibility of such a future if one occupies the ground of dogma. As Tillium has suggested, there is no way that it can be shown that such forms might not in fact herald, on a world level, the creation of an exploitative society of a wholly new kind, a 'higher form' of exploitation wherein the control over labour is more effective than it is under capitalism. If this, then, is what the future brings, capitalism would surely not have 'declined,' like some modern version of ancient Rome. On the contrary, it would have succeeded.[28] (Tillium 1994, pp.13-14). To speak of monstrous 'accidents' or barbarism — in effect, of 'the end of history' — is no effective counterargument. From a classist perspective, this only has to be a very faint possibility for Ticktin's arguments for 'necessary decline' to be shown not to hold.

The sole remaining possibility is that the new system's control over labour would be intrinsically *weaker* than capitalism's. In that case, since capitalism would have failed itself, we should be quite justified in speaking of an objective capitalist decline. But to show that the decline of capitalism is a possibility is not at all the same thing as showing that it is a historical certainty. And besides, it is clearly impossible to judge now the ease or otherwise of undermining or overthrowing a future system which at the moment does not even exist. One could, of course, conceivably argue that the USSR was just such a system, but even if one managed to show that its control over labour were of qualitatively unparalleled inefficiency, this would not yet be sufficient to show that it was non-capitalist in nature. And finally, even if it were such a system, in the present context this would not be a sufficient basis on which to argue for an actual capitalist decline, for one should further have to show that there operated a global tendency towards the rise of formations of a Soviet type.

These, then, are some of the weaknesses in the basis from which Ticktin argues, first, for capitalist decline; then, for the increasing likelihood of the rise of bastard formations; and finally — given a Leninist view of the Bolshevik coup as a 'major blow' against world capital, and a Trotskyist view of 'Stalinist counterrevolution' — for the possibility that the political economy of the world's largest country, although crucially supportive of capitalism, might itself be non-capitalist in nature. Given this basis, and in particular the characterisation as non-capitalist or potentially non-capitalist of various forms which are really capitalist, Ticktin's explanation of the global context of Soviet non-capitalism must be adjudged to be seriously inadequate.[29]

Soviet Political Economy and the Class Struggle

If when studying western countries Ticktin seeks principally to identify the 'laws of decline and transition' whose existence he has first derived on the basis of a philosophical concept of capitalism as quasi-organism, when studying the USSR he adopts an approach which is altogether very different. Since he does not see the USSR as a 'historical' society — as one which, in orthodox terms, was 'necessary' — he is completely disburdened of any Engels-type concepts of the growth, maturity, and decline of such societies.[30] As a result, he is able to focus very tenaciously upon the contradictions of the production relations: and in particular, upon the form of the surplus product, the relations between classes (or between workers and the 'elite'), and — underlying everything even if in a capitalist context (that is, in the context of what he himself recognises as capitalism) he pays them little real attention[31] — the contradictions of the *labour process*. The pioneering force of his analysis lies to no small degree in his insistence on the linkage of these three areas.

The Form of the Product and Control Over Labour   Influenced by works by Baran and Sweezy (1966), and by Baran alone (1957), as well as by Marx's *Capital*, Ticktin adopts as his main initial concept that of the *surplus product*. This is defined as that portion of the social product in excess of the part used to meet the "immediate needs of those engaged in productive work." (1991c, p.10). In case the concept of productive work, which usually denotes work productive of surplus value, might prove confusing, he hastens to define it as work productive of the surplus product itself; and it becomes clear in the course of his critique of the USSR that in fact he makes no distinction between 'productive workers' and the working class as a whole. (Again, this is not a view he would express about capitalism. But it is, of course, the view of Dalla Costa [1971] and Negri [1979, pp.63-65, 182-84].) In the Soviet context, then, the surplus product is the part of the product in excess of what becomes the income of the workers: it includes the privileged consumption of the ruling elite, the allocation of State resources to the armed forces and the KGB, and the accumulation of stocks and means of production. If the nature of capitalism flows from the fact that the workers (or, for Ticktin, the 'productive' workers) produce a surplus product in the form of surplus value, the nature of the USSR must correspondingly be explained in terms of the form of the surplus product there.

Before analysing the form of the surplus product, it is necessary, of course, to discuss the form taken by the control over its extraction, and this means looking at production, at labour. In Marx's words, quoted by Ticktin (1978, p.38),

> the specific economic form, in which unpaid surplus labour is pumped out of direct producers, determines the relationship of rulers and ruled, as it grows directly out of production itself and, in turn, reacts upon it as a determining element. (1894, p.927)[32]

But one must start with a general framework. At the outset, then, Ticktin holds two ideas to be self-evident. The first is that Soviet workers are exploited: in other words they produce by alienating their labour. Obvious to all reasonable observers, this scarcely requires lengthy derivation. Soviet society is clearly exploitative. As a result, there can be no real planning, since that could only occur in the absence of antagonistic interests setting social group against social group: that is, in socialism. Since in the USSR there is an antagonism between groups or classes — that is, struggle — the rulers find it impossible to gather all the information they need and are therefore unable successfully to realise their formulated objectives. (1973a; see also 1978, pp.44-48). The well-known empirical evidence Ticktin refers to in the course of his analysis provides, as we shall see, overwhelming support for this basic thesis.

His second tenet is quite another matter. This is that the "all-important" form of the product is use-value. (1991c, p.11). In other words, Soviet society is not founded on the production of exchange-value, and is therefore non-capitalist in nature. Regardless of the weaknesses of the 'capitalist' positions argued previously, however — two of which at least Ticktin has criticised in convincing fashion (on Bettelheim, see Ticktin 1976; on Cliff, see the remarks in Ticktin 1973a, p.20, n.1) — we would suggest that this can scarcely be justified as a preliminary assumption. If he is certainly correct in holding that the concept of surplus product is more basic than that of surplus value, since the latter is a form of the former, we would argue that he is not so entitled to grant an unopposed place to the concept of use-value. Admittedly, he has presented arguments against the idea that the USSR knows the existence of exchange-value (1973a, pp.36-38, 1976, pp.23-25, and 1991c, pp.133-34),[33] rather than just leaving the assumption undefended. But the problem is that he has accepted as the best opposing argument Bettelheim's view which is based upon formal rouble transfers between enterprises. (Ticktin 1976). (See the discussion of Bettelheim's work in Chapter 2 above, where we refer to Ticktin's critique). The nettle which he has not grasped successfully is the larger issue of inter-enterprise competition and of competitive relations among the elite in general. On one hand, he holds that the members of the elite "are eternally atomized in a more competitive environment than under capitalism" (1991c, p.37), and that bargaining within the economic administration "has always been the nature of the system." (p.169). On the other, in relation to the price-system he has written that "the point is that there is no competition whatsoever." (1976, p.25). These statements are not, of course, contradictory: what Ticktin is arguing is that competition is not mediated by the setting of prices. But he has yet to trace the form of competition properly through to its economic base.[34] This weakness is most glaring when he writes that "within production itself, without competition, profit is nothing other than a technical phenomenon." (1973a). The problem here is that he has not first shown the absence of competition in order subsequently to explain that rouble profit does not play the role of a competitive mechanism: on the contrary, it is clear from the context that he is really arguing the converse, namely that competition is not a fundamental economic relation of production because rouble profit is not its mechanism. This is not a logically tenable argument.

When Ticktin considers the internal nature of the USSR, he is thus no longer weighed down with the matter of the necessary decline of capitalist categories. Paradoxically, this means that once he assumes that control over labour does not take the characteristically capitalist form of commodity fetishism (on which, see Perlman 1968), he is able with impressive theoretical rigour to unpack aspects of the fundamental form which it actually does take. (See especially 1991c, chap. 7). Identifying in particular a specific form of the atomisation of the worker, he proceeds to show how it is highly contradictory. On one hand, it involves a 'total' bureaucratic dependence, negatively definable as the absence of economic independence at any level; on the other, it involves a politically enforced "individualisation."[35] The Soviet form of the atomisation of the worker can then be defined as the process by which these two poles interact; and it is the enforcement of this atomisation which has determined the entire nature of the "Soviet regime" since the late 1920s.

Soviet atomisation as a form of control is further contradictory in that it has no firm roots in the socialisation of labour: for Ticktin it is not enforced by internal economic means such as the domination of a universal equivalent. As a result, it obstructs and indeed prevents the rulers from attaining effective control over the labour process. Insofar as the worker is constrained, in this model, to work where, when, and for how much the authorities dictate, he is certainly controlled. But insofar as he "relates to his own work process rather than to other workers" (1991c, p.12; see also 1978, p.45), rather than to the "factory" or "society as a whole" (1991c, p.120), he retains a partial control over the process of his own work on an individual level. (See especially Ticktin 1976, pp.41-43). In exercising direct control over the division of labour through means which are essentially administrative (and originally terroristic), the Soviet ruling group finds it impossible to exert full control over the actual labour process on the shopfloor, and is led to undermine the conditions of its rule by conceding a limited degree of 'negative control' to the workers.[36] From its point of view, atomisation is productive in that it forces the workers to work; it is counter-productive in that not being economic (that is, firmly rooted in the socialisation of labour) it inadequately dominates how they work. From the workers' point of view, on the other hand, this individualised and partial control over the pace and quality of work reduces the onerousness of their employment; but it remains the most that can be conquered so long as the system of bureaucratic dependence remains in existence. And what is more, it results in the production of shoddy or rarely available consumer goods which do not match up to their requirements.

This highly contradictory form of control over labour defines the "relations within production in general" (1973b, p.15); and relying on Marx's *Grundrisse* (1939, pp.94-98) Ticktin explains how these relations necessarily imply a corresponding form of distribution of both workers and means of production within the production process. In other words, they imply a structure of production wherein "because the elite does not control the means of production, its control over appropriation is imperfect." (1973b, p.15). The result is chronic inefficiency throughout the economy, which manifests itself as *waste*. Defining this phenomenon theoretically as "the use or lack of use of the surplus product in a manner that fails to lead to a product" (1991c, p.11),[37] Ticktin deserves credit as the first critic to explain it in terms which are fundamentally class-based and political-economic.

Waste takes several forms. (Ticktin 1973a, pp.27-32). First, there is the low quality of production. This can take the form of the production, in both Departments, of goods which wear out or break down very quickly, leading to the rise of a gigantic repair sector. More workers are employed in mending machines, for example, than in manufacturing them. It can also take the form of the output of goods which are simply unsuitable for the purpose for which they are made. (See for example Nove 1980b, pp.98-99). Second, there is the slow coming on stream of new technology, a problem which has been shown by many observers to be an endemic and increasing problem for Soviet policy-makers. Aspects of this include slow diffusion and innovation, slow integration of technological imports, and to some extent problems further up the technological cycle too. No measure introduced by a Soviet government was ever able to circumvent fully the well-known obstacle of 'success indicators,' which always disfavoured the option of undergoing the re-tooling, teething problems, and other shake-ups attendant upon the introduction of new equipment and processes. (See Berliner 1976, Hanson 1981, chaps. 3-4, Amann and Cooper 1982 and 1986, and Gomulka 1986; see also Nove 1980b, pp.166-72 and Aganbegian 1988, p.144-46). The third form of waste is the high level of under-employment, which is also usually accepted as being a major feature of the Soviet economy. (See for example Lane 1987, pp.136-40 and Granick 1987). And fourth, there is that which could be called "the underutilisation of capacity, existing or potential." Under this heading can be counted the stockpiling of unused parts; the stoppages due to bottlenecks and to breakdowns in supply either of raw materials or of machinery; and the slow pace of plant construction. In short, the 'system' of incentives for efficient production and accumulation is itself utterly inefficient. Vast quantities of resources, including labour-power, stand idle, are poorly utilised, or otherwise go to waste. Soviet use-value is defective use-value.

The next point is that the overall context is one where the economy must necessarily grow. For those who see the USSR as capitalist, of course, this does not cause any great theoretical problem. Since value growth is part of the definition of capital in the first place, capitalism without accumulation would be like fire without burning. But once the capitalist nature of the economy is denied, the empirically evident systemic need for growth comes to demand a full consideration of its own, and Ticktin must therefore offer an explanation as a crucial part of his overall theory. Thus he writes:

> The dynamic in the society is provided by the movement of the process of socialized production. The more socialized the nature of labor and so production (i.e., the more integrated the division of labor), the more difficult it is for the worker to be atomized around his labor process and the more difficult is it for the elite to obtain compliance with their commands. Democracy becomes an ever-present necessity. The elite are driven by their position as organizers of the economy to expand it, in order to buttress their own control. This is done both by assuaging the demands of the workers for more consumer goods, more jobs, more creative jobs (i.e., social mobility), etc., and by their own needs to maintain control. (1991c, pp.121-22)

It should be noted here that Ticktin is not presenting the demands of the workers as a cause of the increasing socialisation of labour. On the contrary, not only has he earlier described the socialisation of labour as a method of control over the workers (p.121), but he also takes the increase of this socialisation effectively as a given in the context of "modern industry." (p.125). Nor are the workers' demands being presented as the underlying reason for the need for growth, since that place is allotted to the increasing socialisation of labour, and the greater leverage acquired by the workers operates as some kind of mediating term. (See especially p.117). Unfortunately, though, since the increasing socialisation of labour would also seem to be predicate upon growth as a prior assumption — or at least upon some kind of economic development — the analysis is somewhat incoherent.

A few pages later, he writes that

> the elite are themselves based on the necessity of growth precisely to avoid the disintegrating nature of the society. Growth is the only means whereby some consumer goods can be produced, some mobility ensured, and stagnation avoided. (p.123)

Leaving aside the avoidance of stagnation, which is a synonym for growth rather than an explanation, and ignoring the assurance of mobility, reference to which is similarly redundant, we note that growth is held to be necessary not simply for the production of consumer goods in greater quantities, but for the production of any consumer goods at all. Indeed, a lack of consumer goods is built into the system since they are "the end-product of a process of production that never reaches its logical end." (p.123). This, then, is the crucial point. On a more general level, in the production of producer goods as well as in the consumer goods sector, the ruling elite is constrained to perform the "juggling act" of effectively employing each period's surplus to patch up the endemic inefficiencies of the production system. Ticktin describes how

> the defective nature of the Soviet product is both a cause and a result of the system of production in the USSR. It results in the formation of an enormous spare-parts sector and a hypertrophied construction sector developed to supply parts that have failed in one form or another or to complete construction projects that seem never to reach their natural conclusion. Additionally, more raw materials are required both to supply the expanding industry as well as to supply the defective goods that unnecessarily guzzle inputs. The vicious circle is developed further with the need to have an ever-expanding producer goods industry, as the defective producer goods absorb ever more resources, most particularly in the spare parts and construction industries. As a result, the consumer goods sector is starved of those resources. The worker receives a below-subsistence wage and has even less reason to work to capacity, and every reason to permit the over-absorption of raw materials and to produce shoddy goods. The bureaucratic apparatus is then expanded to control all these features, which is in turn a further drain on resources.... All of these qualities

of the Soviet product lead, therefore, to two immediate consequences: a massive waste of resources and an immense shortage of goods. (p.137)[38]

By means of the concept of inefficiency he has now explained many of the main characteristics of the Soviet economy.[39]

If we might have expected to read, though, that the need for growth exacerbates the problem of inefficiency, the suggestion is actually the other way around:

> In the final analysis, then, the elite are based on growth because of the inefficiency of the regime. Its instability and constant destruction of use values requires ever more use values. If the product were not contradictory in having use values that are only partially useful, then the elite could have a much lower growth rate. (p.125)

The argument runs like this. The increasing socialisation of labour gives the workers more leverage, but this is only a subsidiary factor in the systemic need for growth. A stronger factor is the endemic inefficiency of the entire Soviet production system, which leads not simply to the need for growth, but to growth which is inefficient. Spare parts and construction sectors mushroom. As a necessary consequence — and this is pivotal to the entire analysis — inefficiency itself grows.

The question which Ticktin has now arrived at concerns the kind of growth which is actually achieved, and the meaning of inefficient growth in terms of the social product. (chap.8). In other words, we are now in a position to deal directly with the nature of the surplus product. If the country were seen as capitalist, of course, one would look to explain both growth and inefficiency in terms of both the fundamental class relation and the opposition between use-value and exchange-value. In that context, use-value is personified by the proletariat and exchange-value by the controllers of capital. Exchange-value dominates, and its necessary growth, in generalised form, provides us with a definition of the essence of the capitalist system, of capital itself. But since Ticktin assumes that in the USSR use-value does not interact or even co-exist with any contradictory opposite of any kind, the problem, while remaining one of theorising the class relation, is on quite another plane. It can only be one of theorising a division within the category of use-value itself.

Inefficiency implies, of course, a certain degree of efficiency, and so he starts by conceptualising actual utility, or "real use-value." The remaining aspect of the product — that is, of the defective use-value produced — concerns things or aspects of things which are not as they should be, not as they conceivably could be if production were more efficient or carried out according to a different system. Involving as it does the expenditure of real labour-power and the investment of real resources, this part cannot rightly be characterised as illusory or fictitious. Since it does exist as a material possibility, Ticktin thus defines it as "potential" and "imagined or intended" use-value. (pp.12 and 134). In rapid succession, he describes inherent contradictions between the product's "imagined nature" and its "actual nature," its "bureaucratic or organized nature" and its "real form," and its "apparent" form and its "real" form. (p.134). (It must be noted here that the Aristotelian terminology adds little in the way of clarity.) Having pointed to a contradiction in the case of machine tools between "ostensible function" and "actual operation" he then uses mathematical terminology to identify the underlying contradiction as being the contradiction between the "imaginary" product and the "real" product. This, then, is the contradiction to which

> all categories are subject, in the same way that the contradiction between use value and exchange value governs capitalism. (p.136)

But the categorial analysis does not stop here, for this contradiction itself arises only "on the basis of a prior contradiction": namely, the contradiction between, on one hand, an administered form of the product, and on the other, use-value. (p.136). The bureaucratic administration of use-value is necessarily contradictory in a most fundamental sense since

> there is no way that a center of any kind can have either the knowledge of the nature of use values or the means of implementation of decisions over use values that corresponds to real situations. The direct producer must have a degree of autonomy to produce a good that conforms to needs. He must also have an incentive to do so. Direct instruction does not provide such an incentive, unless accompanied by a democratic process of decision-making. Put differently, behind the administered form of the product lies a form of control over labour. (pp.136-37)

There is, of course, a hint here of the Trotskyist position that the key to the 'transitional period' is provided by 'nationalisation under workers' control' — what other meaning might be attributed to the penultimate sentence of this extract? (see also p.39) — but we would argue that it is of much more importance to underline the strength of Ticktin's theoretical approach. Above all, this lies in his uncompromising insistence that all of the Soviet system's problems "go back to labour" (p.116): in other words, to the specifically Soviet form of control over labour. In relation to the work of Dunayevskaya and Castoriadis (and *a fortiori* Sapir), it is apparent that Ticktin's theory of the resulting political-economic contradictions, and in particular those relating to the wasteful form of the product, marks a substantial theoretical advance. Admittedly, there is a failure to explain the economic significance of the 'intended' or 'imaginary' form of the product at the level of bureaucratic competition and the related field of the distribution of the surplus. (In Chapter 3 we ourselves have given considerable weight in this same context to the concepts of bureaucratic exchange-value and bureaucratised money.) But at the same time it must be noted that the concept of "potential use-value" is much more concretely rooted in the real conditions of production than it is in the work of Baran, where it denotes merely the productive potential which currently goes to waste in market capitalism but which would be put to good use in a future socialist society. (1957, pp.132-134 and 142-55).

Since Ticktin's foundation of his critique of the nature of the Soviet product upon an understanding of the contradictory production relations is not in dispute, the question becomes one of assessing the extent to which the corresponding antagonism between exploiters and exploited remains evident once the analysis reaches the categories which define the contradictions of the product and surplus product. Taking up the explicit analogy which he himself makes with the division under capitalism between use-value (human need) and exchange-value, we arrive at the following question: in whose interest does the imaginary product, the apparent or intended form of the product, exist? If this question sounds inadequately materialist, it can be rephrased as follows: in whose interest is potential use-value actually produced — or, rather, wasted? The answer is fairly simple. In terms of the Soviet economic system, the production and wastage of potential use-value is not in the interest of any particular social group. It is not only not in the interests of the workers, it is also thoroughly dysfunctional to the system of their exploitation. No-one needs it. It is a by-product of a class relation where the rulers can neither unproblematically make concessions nor successfully impose discipline and viable productivity bargains. Faulty use-value is not even a way of ensuring that workers' consumption — that is, the wage — is partly fictitious in magnitude or character, since illusion is not an issue. In this sense, poor-quality goods are not a sop to the poor. Nor are they a disciplinary instrument, since it is in the rulers' interests to maximise the extraction of the relative surplus, which means spending no more of the workers' labour-time on producing labour-reproductive goods than they have to according to the state of the underlying relationship of force. They do not then, serve the interests of the exploiters. Nor, evidently, can faulty use-value be in the interests of the exploited, since it needlessly expands the amount of time they have to work and be at the workplace. There is thus not even any substantial struggle over the issue, since all social groups are opposed to its existence. In short, we have a third term, a non-class term, a term which although derived from the class relation is somehow squeezed out of it to take on a highly significant role of its own.

It might be argued, of course, that even in countries which are generally recognised as capitalist the class-based contradictory nature of the product allows the growth of types of waste which are injurious to all classes. Regardless of whether this point should be conceded in terms of empirical reality — and stated this simply it is certainly disputable — it should surely be conceded as a hypothetical possibility. But be that as it may, the description of Soviet waste as a social relation which actually defines the nature of the social product is quite another matter. The issue is not merely a problem which the system experiences, but rather it is the system's fundamental political economy, the very nature of Soviet society. While one form of the social product, namely potential use-value, is not personified by any class or group, and is in no-one's interests, the opposing form, namely actual use-value, is personified by all classes or groups, and is in everyone's interests. In other words, unlike in capitalism the exploiters in the USSR do not 'personify' a specific form of the social product. What they personify at this level is surplus actual use-value. When the analysis is put like this, the appropriation of the surplus product seems to be a matter of little more than parasitism. And indeed it is but a short step to identifying the "fundamental law" of the regime as being one of a conflict between the "law of organization" and the "law of self-interest" of each individual unit. (1973a, pp.35-36; 1991c, p.118-19). Whatever Ticktin's intentions are, by this time the theory has become far removed from the class contradictions of the real control over labour, and to present the former law as a description of the movement of a contradiction between central control and the specific interests of the elite, and the latter law as describing the development of a contradiction between the atomised worker and socialised labour, would appear to be little more than a cosmetic exercise. (1991c, p.118). In short, the fact that Ticktin's theory of the contradictory form of the Soviet product is not as 'classist' as Marx's theory of the contradictory form of the commodity under capitalism can no longer be avoided.

The Issue of Class   In fact it is evident from Ticktin's writings on the meaning of class (1978, 1987a, 1991c, pp.86-88) that this last assertion is not one that he would dispute. In his view, the ruling elite of the USSR does not constitute a class, and nor does the working class in that country, except in a "non-scientific" sense. (1987a, p.20).[40] This is principally because there is a total lack of "forms of collectivity" (p.18), whereas the existence of classes is predicate not only upon a communal environment, but also upon the possibility of combination and the existence of class consciousness. A class relation is "more than the simple existence of a relationship in production": it has to be both collective and dynamic. (pp.11-12).

Regarding the Soviet ruling elite, one must of course agree that under Stalin there was immense instability and mobility across the entire privileged part of society — not to mention the other part, nor the promotion of workers into that privileged part — and that *prima facie* this is a fair basis on which to argue that that group did not constitute a class. But nonetheless, by the time of the Brezhnev period — the 'time of stagnation' (*zastoinye vremena*) — the accession to membership of the privileged section (elite plus the higher intelligentsia) took on a much more hereditary character, even as social mobility continued. As far as many graduates were concerned, there was thus an increasingly evident bottleneck or glass ceiling to social promotion. (Ticktin 1991c, p.62). Hence even if one were to concede that under Stalin the rulers did not form a class, a strong case could be made that eventually there came a time around the 1960s when they did. By this time the system for generational transmission of ruling group membership attained a degree of relative stability. Ticktin's reference to the necessary individualism and brutal competition within the elite is of little relevance in this context, especially when it is recalled that the bourgeois class is also necessarily internally competitive at one level. (1978, p.43; 1987a, p17). Moreover, whilst he argues that the elite is bereft of collectivity, he in fact also argues that it is precisely the *absence* of individualised private access to the means of control over the surplus product which demonstrates that the Soviet ruling group takes a non-class form. (1987a, p.17). If control is partial, rather than non-existent, then he should not have it both ways by asserting that it is neither collective nor individual. And since the crucial question relates to the control which really is exercised over the extraction of the surplus product, rather than that which is not, nor is it very convincing to rely on the point that this control *is* chronically partial. (1973b, p.16; 1987a, p.18, 1991c, p.61).

Moreover, if there is to be any meaning in the term 'political economy' at all, political competition must also be understood as economic competition: that is, in this context, as competition among those who exercise a degree of control, however limited, over the surplus product. For this reason, any explanation of control over the extraction of the surplus product with reference simply to the security service, the State, and administration is bound to be inadequate. We would further argue that in assessing 'collectivity,' one should look at the stability or instability of composition rather than the forms of control based on 'direct dependence,' or the mediation or even brutality of rivalry within the elite. It would seem, then, that since the 1960s the strongest remaining argument against classifying the rulers as a class is simply this: that part or much of the elite often finds it difficult to prevent the downward mobility of its offspring into less privileged places in the intelligentsia. (Ticktin 1973b, pp.15-18; 1991c, pp.60-61; see also Hosking 1985, pp.381-82). But one might equally well describe this state of affairs in terms of the tendency of numerous sons and daughters of the ruling class to fall down into intermediate strata, or, more vaguely, into the middle class.[41]

It is further possible to argue that the question of stability of composition should be tackled primarily in terms of the relationship of the ruling section as a whole to the extraction of the surplus product, regardless of membership turnover or rapid expansion or even Stalinist terror. A group, of course, is greater than the sum of its members. Agreeing that there has to be more than a simple relationship to production, one might hold that the ruling group forms a class only on condition that it exercises sufficient power to ensure its own self-reproduction. Under the internal reign of terror associated with Stalinism, then — from which the security service itself was not immune — there was never any great threat to the important *functional positions* within the ruling group. Perhaps even more importantly, the institutional means of reproduction of ruling group membership, such as educational institutes and officer training, were never put in danger either of abolition or of a removal of this kind of function. The growth of party, union and army bursaries in higher technical institutes after 1928, for example, may have involved a major shake-up, but in no way did it change the function of advanced formal education in preparing students for positions of hierarchic control. (Hosking 1985, pp.174-77). If this is of notable significance, as we would argue that it is, then the exploitative ruling group which had centred around the Bolshevik elite since 1917 first took on the characteristics of a ruling class as early as the early-mid 1920s, once the economic and military aspects of alienated order became relatively less unpredictable. This was, of course, the position of the Workers' Truth group at the time. (1922).

But regardless of the position that is taken, the issue of whether or not to call the rulers a class is actually secondary, and Ticktin is mistaken in giving it such importance. The main point is that a ruling group existed that benefited from the exploitation of the workers: that is, from the extraction of an alienated surplus product, even if control over it was only partial. As he himself has shown, the political economy of the country can only be fully understood in terms of the nature of the control over this extraction, and this necessarily means theorising the opposition between, on one side, the exploitative system and the group or groups who control it and benefit from it, and on the other, the workers. Thus it is no accident that Marx did not write at length about the exact meaning to be ascribed to the term 'class' with reference to such groups taken individually. Instead, in a passage cited by Ticktin (1987, p.12), Marx and Engels write that

> the separate individuals form a class only insofar as they have to carry on a common battle against another class; otherwise they are on hostile terms with each other as competitors. (1846, p.68)

The context here is the formation of the bourgeoisie, but what is crucial is the use of the term 'class' to explain the necessity of struggle. In other words, since the concept of class struggle is prior to that of class, the question of class must be tackled by first looking at how the social groups stand opposed to one another. We show below how Ticktin's main argument that the ruling elite is not a class — namely, the limited extent of its control over the labour process (1991c, p.61) — leads to considerable confusion on this issue.

There is, though, a difference between the question of whether or not the rulers are a class, and the corresponding question concerning the workers. On the side of the rulers, clearly there can be numerous different kinds of control over the extraction of the surplus product, over its distribution, and over alienated labour, and hence different kinds of controlling group even within market capitalism. (Hitler, for example, used means of control other than the reserve army of labour). But whatever its form of control, an exploiting group is necessarily deprived of the chance of achieving a final victory, since owing to its nature it can only have as the essential aim of its struggle the maintenance of the exploitative system. Prior to the categories of form of control and of role within the control system, and therefore of more fundamental importance in understanding the contradictions of the system, there is thus the category of the workers' alienation of their labour. For their part, the working class produces everything, but at the same time it is totally dispossessed of the means of production. By achieving victory in its struggle, then, it negates the entire exploitative political-economic system. In other words, if it does struggle as a class then that struggle is potentially universal, potentially communist, and posits the permanent abolition of all classes. (Marx 1844, p.256). The 'essence' of this struggle is thus necessarily of a higher order, since in comparison with the 'essence' of the struggle of the ruling group it calls more into question. It follows that the matter of whether or not the working class is a real class is more important than that of the precise term to be allotted to the ruling group. By denying that there has been a process of working class self-formation, Ticktin is in fact denying the necessary material reality of working class struggle in the USSR.

His argument is as follows: given that the control over the working class takes the form of a special kind of atomisation, and that corresponding to this the workers have a limited and individualised form of control over the labour process, then consequently the working class does not have the requisite degree of (subjective) collectivity to be called a class. (See especially Ticktin 1987a, pp.16-18; and also 1991c, pp. 86-87). Unfortunately, though, whilst he formally praises Thompson (1963) — if not his followers — for using a dynamic concept, the imprecision of Ticktin's thought on the subject is evident when he writes that

> the problem with just seeing the formation of the class as a process is that it ignores the nature of the process and so its political economy. All too easily then class is transformed into a woolly concept, which is ultimately entirely

subjective since consciousness and conscious struggle play the only role left to play. (1987a, p.12)

This may well be a useful critique of the Thompson school, but Ticktin's confusion of the subjective with the conscious constitutes a major weakness in his understanding of the working class.

If a process or force is subjective then that does not mean that it is necessarily conscious. On the contrary, it means that people are acting in their interests. And it is not in dispute that members of the working class are acting in their interests in a fashion which is antagonistic towards the interests of the ruling group. Their actions are necessarily subjective. What Ticktin is suggesting, then, is that workers in the USSR act in their individual interests rather than in their class interest, and hence do not form a class subject, a class in struggle which has an effect on the forms of political economy. He does, of course, recognise that it is the opposition between the workers and the ruling group which helps to determine the nature of the political economy in the first place: he is simply arguing that there is no *dynamic* at all by which the two social groups, as opposed to the political authorities and the individual worker, enter into actual conflict with each other. But if this were true, one would hardly expect the agglomeration of individual behaviour-patterns to have any great political-economic effect over a period of time, or at least not on the general conditions of the main social groups as social groups. If there is such a thing as a working class interest, then it is reasonable to expect working class people to act in that interest, even if the extent to which they do so is then open to question. On a theoretical level, it is hard to see how the opposition could fail to take an antagonistic form unless it were purely 'structural' and synchronic, or in other words purely static. And if this were the case, then the system itself could hardly be based as it is upon the necessity of growth. No specific form of growth actually achieved would negate the fact that if the group of labourers stands in opposition to another group, and at the same time there is growth, then the relationship between the groups must be dynamic. But it is precisely this dynamic, or antagonism, between groups with a specific shared relationship to production which defines the class struggle. This is the first main point.

The second point involves the empirical evidence for collectivity, and is best illustrated with reference to sloppy work. (See for example Berliner 1957, pp.136-48, Nove 1980b, pp.194, 259, and 357, and Lane 1987, pp.102-09). Let us take, then, the oft-quoted practice of 'storming,' by which workers work relatively very quickly towards the end of each plan period, with highly detrimental effects on the quality of work. (See for example Nove 1980b, pp.227-28). In the context of interconnected modern industry, it would surely be stretching the concept of non-collectivity too far to suggest that the general speed-up and fall in work quality were together simply the result of a summation of individual choices within the parameters of the bonus system. When it is realised that a refusal to co-operate with the speed-up by even just a few workers would affect the rate of speed-up by most of the other workers, and hence the nominal fulfilment of the plan, it becomes apparent that there must be some sort of collective approach if the word 'collective' is to retain any meaning at all. The general level of work quality must similarly vary within collectively determined limits. Not only must there not be a state of affairs where some workers are too conscientious, thus slowing down the overall speed-up, but similarly nor can there be a minority of workers who are so unconscientious as to allow an excess of breakdowns in production. Overall, this collective approach not only affects the form of the product, but also, as a factor in the state of relations between workers and management and between management and the bureaucratic centre, it leads to the payment of larger bonuses than would otherwise be conceded. Meanwhile the corresponding slowdown of production early in the next plan period must also in some way be read as evidence of a collective operation. (And indeed the time gained during breakdowns must enhance the collectivity of the workplace atmosphere.) The worker's relation to his work is clearly not, as Ticktin has it (1978, p.52), purely an individual one.

Ticktin would be right, of course, if he meant simply that the workers in the USSR do not yet form a consciously revolutionary class, a fully collective class-for-itself, since this could evidently only exist at the point at which the exploitative system was overthrown. Equally importantly, it could only exist on a world scale.[42] But the fact that he means more than this is clear from his arguing that the working class as a class has already come into being (albeit not "fully") in the advanced countries under bourgeois rule. (1987a, p.13).[43] He has not written at length in support of this view, and his view of some sort of correspondence in this context with supposedly 'transitional' forms such as nationalisation and State-sector employment, not to mention 'capitalist decline,' has remained largely implicit. (pp.14-16). If one assumes though, that the critique of both the USSR and market capitalism should be based upon an understanding of the opposition between workers and rulers, Ticktin's theory should surely lead to the conclusion that since the Soviet rulers have considerably less control over the labour process than the bourgeoisie, and are therefore not a class, then the workers in the USSR must have more control over the labour process than their counterparts in market capitalism, and therefore are a class. On the question of whether or not the workers constitute a class, it is certainly quite reasonable to look at the actual character of the control that they manage to exert; but it would still seem that if the limited political-economic *extent* of the rulers' control is cited as a sufficient condition for the non-class nature of their group (Ticktin 1991c, p.61), then to concentrate in the workers' case upon the *form* of control involves a clear case of moving the analytical goalposts.

It is instructive nonetheless to consider why it is that Ticktin holds that the workers in market capitalism do constitute a class. In this regard he has made it clear that his underlying empirical argument concerns the significance of the 'western' model of the trade union. Despite being highly critical of its evolution, then, and although he accepts that it is a 'ruling class' form which has to be replaced,[44] he still presents the trade union form as being a 'form of proletarian organisation.' (1987a, pp.10-11). But any preliminary impression that this is compatible with a communist opposition to trade unionism can hardly be sustained once it is realised that the only real evidence that he cites for the existence of a degree of workers' control over the labour process in the 'West,' and indeed for its fundamentally collective form, is the existence of union membership and union negotiation. (p.17).[45] Correspondingly, the main empirical evidence that he alludes to for the absence of working class collectivity in the USSR is precisely the absence of 'genuine' trade unions. (p.16). Thus at some level he evidently holds the view that working class collectivity outside of a revolutionary period must necessarily take a union-type form. But one only has to introduce a critique of trade unionism as *false* consciousness and *false* collectivity, as a means of capitalist control over the workers, to see that such an understanding of collectivity is not at all based on the 'objectivity of the subjective' — that is, not on that of the working class subjective — but rather on forms of institutionalisation represented by union-mediated negotiation, productivity deals, and formal 'social contracts.'[46] The fundamental mistake here, derived from his theory of decline and transition, is the failure to recognise that if the concept of working class collectivity is used to define the class nature of the working class rather than, say, a shared culture, then it is quite meaningless unless it is understood as denoting a form of class assertion. Formal deals, mediation, and institutionalisation are not the crucial issue, and nor is representation. Since Ticktin's concept of currently existing class subjectivity is dependent upon its current mediation by western-type social democracy and trade unionism, and since his view of its potentially revolutionary significance outside of these forms is primarily constructed in terms of its future politicisation in a hypothetical struggle for a Statist transition (1993, p.131), his denial of its existence in the USSR is not at all compelling. What is missing from the entire analysis, both political and economic, of both the USSR and the 'West,' is a concept of class autonomy.

The great paradox of Ticktin's work is that despite this omission he does, like Thompson, have a concept of workers' power — and, in effect, of working class power — as a force which is independent of politically institutionalised 'consciousness.' (1991c, pp.149-51). Unlike most of the 'collectivist' and 'state capitalist' theorists Ticktin is thus in profound disagreement with the view of the 'totalitarian' sovietologists (and others) that workers in the USSR are mere slaves or quasi-slaves. The third main point to be made, then, is that without a concept of class antagonism, and therefore of class autonomy and class subjectivity, such a disagreement is of little meaning. In short, what is missed is that regardless of the existence or non-existence of western-style unions, or of any form which is similar, no measure of power can be conceded to the dispossessed group without a struggle.

The Issue of Workers' Power   It is now necessary to deal with Ticktin's theoretical discussion of the issue of workers' power. This he looks at from two viewpoints in particular: firstly, in terms of the labour indiscipline which corresponds to the Soviet elite's lack of effective control over the labour process; and secondly, in terms of the gradual increase in workers' power which has corresponded to the elite's increasing problems in achieving viable growth.

The first consideration concerns the underlying facts of the Soviet economy. Here Ticktin has pointed to five specific factors which give the worker (and the use of the singular person here should be well noted) a certain degree of "latitude." (1976, pp.35-38). These are as follows: the nature of mechanisation, which has involved low tolerance levels and frequent breakdowns; the growth of a large repair sector, mechanised even worse than the industry it services; the lack of rhythm in production brought about by breakdowns in equipment and supply; the underemployment contingent upon the inefficiency of technological introduction; and, fifth, the regime's allowing of "slack norms and slack discipline" for "historical, political and technical reasons." (p.38). As a result of all these factors, enterprise managers find themselves dependent upon the "goodwill" of the workers in ensuring nominal fulfilment of planned targets, and must therefore permit a "lower rate of work and poorer performance to make up for the special calls required." Indeed, a "necessary wage" is allowed to be established by 'spontaneous pressure' (inverted commas in the original), at a level above which there is "no point in going." The rate at which the workers work is similarly determined "from below." On one hand, then, managers concede to the workers so as to safeguard their own positions in relation to the bureaucratic centre (pp.35-36); and on the other, there is slack production discipline because "the working class will tolerate nothing else." (1973a, p.41).

The task now surely arises of drawing a distinction between the causes of poor discipline which lie in the workers' objective environment, and those which are brought about subjectively and assertively by the workers themselves. Since workers act within and upon their environment, and indeed are part of that environment, it is evident that the causes interact: but to use this as a reason to avoid making a distinction would only be to beg the question, for "latitude" clearly implies a scope of action. But unfortunately Ticktin's analysis of the latter set of causes has remained insufficiently thought out. Thus towards the close of his earliest major text on Soviet political economy, he writes with little real theoretical attention that

> what the working class maintains [in terms of slack production discipline in the USSR] it does almost in the same way as trade unions do in the West: through non-co-operation or direct action: strikes. (1973a, p.41)

It should be clear from the above references to his later writings on class that this is not a view which he cares to retain, let alone develop. Indeed in his recent full-length work he categorically rejects it, writing that the (partial) control which the workers exert over the work process

> is not the same control as in mass production in the West, where workers can resist through unions or collective sabotage. (1991c, p.85)

But by doing so he merely presents a highly abstract and simplistic contrast with the 'West,' constructed above all upon his unshakeable view that the USSR is not a capitalist country and the working class is not a real class as it is elsewhere.

Regarding the subjective aspect of the static side of the control exerted by the workers the analysis is highly insubstantial. Admittedly he has mentioned that some workers take advantage of full employment to change their jobs, but even this observation is parenthetical and at any rate it can hardly be developed given his continued insistence that such voluntary job-hopping does not imply the existence of any kind of labour market. (1991c, pp.83-84). The statement that "where labour is increasingly scarce, it becomes more powerful" is thus left without a proper explanation. (1990, p.98). Furthermore, since he depicts the wage not as a real wage but simply as some kind of ration, Ticktin deals only very confusedly with the wage as an object of struggle. On one hand, writing in the middle of the Brezhnev era, he depicts the worker's possession of roubles as a secondary and politically-economically almost negligible factor in his or her access to food, clothing, and other goods (1976, p.34), such that "a bonus of an extra five or ten roubles a month for most workers is meaningless." (1973a, p.37). On the other hand, he later cites precisely the rise of wages under Brezhnev as evidence that the workers did very well during the 'years of stagnation.' (1990, p.98). Nor does he deal with the refusal of work any more clearly, and indeed does not even reach the preliminary point of recognising that this refusal might actually be *positive*, to whatever degree, from the point of view of the workers. We are thus left without a useful discussion not only of the forms of working class self-assertion, but also of its aims.

At the same time, though, in turning to the second consideration, namely that of the dynamic aspects, we must recognise that his work on the position of the workers does have the great merit of being founded upon a theory of the development of the contradictions of the production relations over time. Indeed, it is this theory of the dynamic of Soviet accumulation, and of the endemic contradictions and weaknesses in the nature of that dynamic, which has come to underlie and inform his entire analysis. Other theorists, such as Carlo and Sapir, have also produced works with a strong 'historical' orientation, but Ticktin's work stands out from these not simply by dint of its rigorous foundation upon Marxist categories such as surplus product and accumulation, but also — and this is crucial — in terms of the central place given in the discussion of accumulation to the changing position of labour.

He has thus been able to cut completely through a widely held view of the problems of Soviet accumulation, namely that which explains the underlying difficulty as being the need to shed forms which once were sufficient to allow 'extensive' growth but which have increasingly become a burden now that what is needed is 'intensive' growth. (See for example Carlo 1979, pp.6 and 9, Sapir 1980, pp.162-71, and Clarke 1993b, p.37; Nove 1982, pp.378-89; and also Gorbachev 1985c and 1987a, pp.20-21, and Aganbegian 1988, pp.100-09). Ticktin rightly holds that this view minimises or even ignores the total difference in nature between labour-power and other resources. In other words, it is little more than a theory of diminishing returns which, by eschewing the concept of surplus product, fails to vouchsafe exactly "what it is that is supposed to be diminishing." As he points out, there has been a shift from agriculture to industry since at least 1930, and machinery per worker rose enormously even in the early Stalin period. And there is no evidence that there was a greater objective shortage of energy resources in the 1980s than there was before. Since the USSR "has always worked on the basis of ignoring the consequences of exhaustion of men, materials, land, and equipment," the theory of extensive and intensive growth can hardly explain why it has reached "a new stage of absolute exhaustion." (Ticktin 1983b, pp.113-16; 1990, pp.98-99).

The first factor which he points to in formulating an alternative explanation is the erosion of the available sources of new labour. Most women were already working by 1940 (one might add, outside the home as well as within it); the use of labour from the satellite countries after 1945 was of limited importance;[47] and, most importantly of all, the inflow of labour from the countryside to the towns began to dry up under Brezhnev and came almost to a halt by the mid-1980s. (1990, p.98; 1991c, p.138). Up to a point the elite was able to use this inflow to skew the economy towards the construction of new plant, thereby circumventing the inherent systemic problems in introducing new technology; but eventually the reduction in the supply of new labour could only mean that fewer new factories could be built and thus less technology introduced. The necessary result, correctly predicted by Ticktin from 1973, was chronic economic stagnation and crisis. There should be no doubt that the basic thesis of the *Critique* journal has been proven true.

The second factor he gives concerns the more general context of 'modern industry.' Thus

> the weaknesses inherent in the nature of the system have now attained their developed forms, which were only embryonic in the earlier phase. The more industrialised and intensively developed industry becomes, the more important become questions of reliability, suitable technique, punctual delivery and overall high quality....

But these too are best explained in terms of labour. As Ticktin puts it,

> ...when the task is simply carrying bricks from one point to another a policeman can ensure its successful completion. But no policeman can ensure that the wall of bricks is built straight, or that complex, specialised, and interconnected industrial operations are carried out as they should be. (1983a, pp.114-15)

Where labour is more specific, and production more integrated (1991c, p.142), the usefulness of the former, purely administrative means of controlling labour must necessarily decline.

Working from such an understanding of Soviet economic development Ticktin introduces two related concepts at a more abstract theoretical level. These are the absolute surplus product and the relative surplus product. Before discussing their application, though, it is necessary to make two preliminary points. First, it is worth recalling that for Marx the concept of surplus product denotes a general category of which surplus value is the specific capitalist form. (1894, chap.51). In other words, if it exists in societies not based on value then it must take forms which are quite different in nature from the form of surplus value. Second, the distinction he makes in the context of capitalism is that which differentiates absolute from relative surplus *value*. (1867, pp.283-667). What he does not do is to distinguish between absolute and relative forms of the more general category of the surplus product. Indeed, the fact that surplus value is a form of the surplus product does not in automatic fashion imply that absolute and relative surplus value must be the forms taken under capitalism of the more general categories of the absolute and relative surplus *product*. To posit the existence of such general forms is to make a theoretical step of sizeable proportions. Even if he omits to make it clear, then, Ticktin's introduction of these concepts in 1978 is wholly original.[48]

Second, since the concepts are derived by analogy with their 'value equivalents' under capitalism, it makes sense to recall what these capitalist forms actually are. Absolute surplus value, then, is the aspect of the rate of surplus value which relates to an increase in the working day. (Marx 1867, pp.283-426). The rate of surplus value itself, also known as the rate of exploitation, is defined as the result of dividing the mass of surplus value by the size of the wage, assuming both quantities to be expressed in terms of average socially necessary labour-time. As long as surplus value can be expanded only by increasing the working day, and capital has simply taken over a previous mode of labour, the subsumption of labour under capital is said to be purely formal. (p.1021). Only when formal subsumption begins to be "differentiated within itself" by means of an expansion of the scale of production — and this involves a second kind of increase of absolute surplus value, namely an expansion of the workforce — is the foundation constituted of what Marx calls the "specifically capitalist mode of production." (p.1022). The immediate process of production can then be transformed on a specifically capitalist basis, and

> a complete (and constantly repeated) revolution takes place in the mode of production, in the productivity of the workers and in the relations between workers and capitalists. (p.1035)

This is known as the real subsumption of labour by capital, and is founded upon the reduction of necessary labour-time: that is, of the value of labour-power. Capital no longer simply subordinates the labour process, it continuously transforms it. Or, as Marx and Engels put it earlier in the *Manifesto*, it constantly revolutionises production. (1848, p.36). There is now a production of relative surplus value, which means that the quantity of surplus value produced per hour increases even if the number of hours worked stays constant. (Marx 1867, pp.429-639 and pp.1034-38). Indeed, since "the production of relative surplus value completely revolutionizes the technical processes of labour." (p.645), the length of the working day can even fall. But given that characteristics of absolute surplus value extraction can and do continue into the period of relative surplus value extraction, the concepts of formal and real subsumption are the more fundamental.

It would now seem that if one is arguing that the mode of production in the USSR is capitalist, as we have done in Chapter 3 above, then the application of these concepts to the Soviet economy is more a matter of 'how?' than 'whether.' (See Chapter 7 for an explanation of the specific functioning of the categories.) If, however, one holds, as Ticktin does, that it was non-capitalist, and then proceeds to create more general concepts of relative and absolute surplus *product*, then theoretical problems arise as to what exactly the distinction between these forms is supposed to mean. On one hand, of course, the definitions appear straightforward: the absolute surplus product is raised "through the extension of labor time or the reduction of the standard of life"; and the relative surplus product appears as a result of the raising of productivity through the application of the new machinery and technology acquired as part of the existing surplus. (Ticktin 1991c, p.145). It is quite simple to understand that

> the workers resisted the introduction of forms of extraction of the relative surplus, as a method of reducing the extraction of the absolute surplus. They worked poorly or took action to contain the effects of the introduction of new technology. The result was overmanning, technology that was outdated even when introduced, high costs of installation, and little savings from the introduction of the new machinery. On the other hand, had the new machinery not been installed, nothing would have been produced. The growth in the absolute surplus then masked the failure to raise the relative surplus by itself or even in itself for considerable periods of time.

As long as costs of inefficiency could be contained through the employment of more labour to construct new factories, "the question of costs was secondary." (pp.145-46). But the method and conditions of extraction of the absolute surplus product led to the extraction of a relative surplus product which was not only systemically inefficient, but also quite incapable of itself becoming the basis of the system.

On the other hand, the clarity of the theoretical foundation vanishes once the supporting definition of the system as value-based is removed. First of all, there is a small problem with the concept of the absolute surplus product. It is quite clear, one could argue, what it would mean in the context of ancient Egypt, where production was relatively uncomplex — two pyramids being twice as many as one pyramid — but in the context of the USSR, given the complex plethora of industries and products and the weft of interconnected paths of distribution, it is not so clear at all. Since the concept involves the theorisation of the size of the overall surplus product in objective terms, one should surely have in mind some substance or other which is embodied in all products. Otherwise, the concept becomes impossible to pin down in a complex economy where all the sectors are growing at different rates and indeed the production of some goods is declining. But the one substance which fulfils this role is labour-time. Superficially, of course, it would appear reasonable to assume that an expansion of the overall product predicate upon an expansion of the labour-force must be 'absolute' as opposed to 'relative'; but theoretically that would mean that one is theorising in terms of a rise in the number of labour-hours expended. Given especially a context where the rates of work exhibit a notable variance, that could only mean relying upon a concept of average labour-time, or an hour of labour-time in the abstract. But by this time one has already arrived at the expansion of value as the essence of growth.

The problem is greatly exacerbated when the discussion moves to the concept of the relative surplus product, for in this connection one should surely posit from the outset some kind of overall social indicator founded upon the average working-day and some kind of line that can be drawn within it between necessary and surplus labour-time. And that, of course, regardless of how the line moves, implies abstract labour and surplus value. The only way around this problem, it would seem to us, would be to keep the analysis at the level of the individual enterprise — or, better still, the individual workshop — for only at this level might it be considered reasonable to conceptualise a change in the number of hours worked as against a change in output per worker-hour in the absence of a concept of value. This could then be tied up with the concepts of atomisation and the absence of planning. But this way out is in fact illusory, since, given that the resources consumed by workers at each workplace are produced at countless other workplaces across the country, it is quite absurd to conceive of the category of necessary labour-time as limited in operation to the level of the workshop. Moreover, at some workplaces, no necessary use-values are produced at all: how many Kalashnikov assault rifles or Zil steering-wheels per day can be counted as one worker's necessary production? And how many soles made for inferior-quality shoes by a worker in a footwear plant can be counted as part of the social surplus? One might conceivably wish to argue that the system of surplus production was *completely* fragmented and unintegrated, but this could hardly be married to an application of specific concepts of the absolute and relative surplus product (and indeed the rate of exploitation) at a macroeconomic level. It is not surprising that Ticktin gives no full definitions.

The most one could reasonably argue would seem to be that more and more surplus labour has been employed in producing a social product which in a large number of specific workplaces is inadequate to ensure the fulfilment of a large number of the specific growth requirements of the ruling group; and that when the inflow of new workers dried up the problem grew critical. In other words, it was easier for the system to have new plant constructed than to raise productivity; and by this means the rulers met most of their growth requirements for a certain period of time.[49] But whilst it is not denied that Ticktin's explanation of this economic movement in terms of labour relations is an important theoretical achievement, it would appear that the concepts of relative and absolute surplus product are only sustainable at a macro level if the theory of the Soviet system as non-capitalist is discarded. And at that point they reduce to the concepts of relative and absolute surplus value.

It is now necessary to consider the aspects of the theory which link the relationship between labour and growth to the specific issue of workers' power. Once more we are looking for a differentiation betweeen objective and subjective aspects, but this time on a historical or dynamic level. Objectively, then, there is the clearly expressed view that as the rate of increase in the labour supply has declined, and labour has become more scarce, "the control over surplus labour, and hence over the worker, has been reduced." More specifically, the possibilities for directing labour were lessened as the workforce grew more attached to specific skills and locations. (1983b, p.113-14; 1986b, pp.126-27). The shortage of labour increased the need to concede to labour. Wages had to rise, and under Brezhnev they rose considerably. Workers' control over the labour process, albeit negative, was reinforced. A second factor cited as strengthening the workers' hand is the large size of Soviet enterprises. (1991c, p.87).

The subjective side is dealt with in relation to three stages. In the first, during the early 1930s, the workers wrested a large degree of control over the labour process. (See Filtzer 1986). After that, they were controlled "through forms of force" (Ticktin 1991c, p.85), and the "rate of exploitation" rose. (1978, p.58). Then under Khrushchev and Brezhnev they increased their control once more. (1991c, p.85; see also Arnot 1981 and 1988, and Filtzer 1992b). Over time, then, "workers have acted in a more collective way to establish their norms." (1991c, p.87). Blue-collar wages in industry rose considerably, and workers' consumption demands have become more pressing. (pp.87 and 149). In addition, "the nature of performance in the labor process has deteriorated," and the propensity to strike increased dramatically at the end of the 1980s. (p.144). As a result of the workers' increasing strength, the rulers have been forced to make concessions. Ever more urgently, they need to control the workers through the market, which necessarily implies the use of unemployment.

But despite the undoubtedly impressive classist nature of the analysis, the theory retains the overall weakness that the strength of the workers is depicted as both actual (witness the above examples of its effects) and "potential." (1991c, p.87). The key idea here is that the increased power of the workforce was consequent upon the "increasing socialisation of labour," (p.146) which implies a kind of philosophical position that it started out as a potentiality which became ever more intense until it had to become actual. Workers' subjective self-assertion, then, appears as a necessary product of the integration of the division of labour in an advanced modern economy. As a result, the 'objective' and 'subjective' aspects of workers' power may certainly be considered as closely related, but only insofar as class conflict appears as simply an aspect, albeit the most significant aspect, of some kind of mystical movement of the socialisation of labour. It is as if workers' power were separable from workers' struggle.

Under Brezhnev the power of the workers increased, and helped bring about a rise in wages; but since the late 1980s it has served most of all to scare the rulers away from imposing mass unemployment, and has prevented the extraction of the relative surplus from becoming the basis of the economy. (In Ticktin's terms, the elite cannot establish capitalism.) The question thus arises as to whether or not the power of the workers is still increasing. If it is, then why is the workers' position not being objectively enhanced in terms of real wages and conditions? And if it is decreasing, then why is the system not entering a phase of better health? Once such questions are posed, the fundamentally dichotomous nature of the exploitative society becomes far less apparent, and it is evident that the category of the increasing power of the workers is not conceived of in the rigorous sense of class autonomy, expressed outside of and opposed to the development of the Soviet economy. To assert that "the whole dynamic of the system is toward its own demise" would make sense so long as it is taken to mean that the system is increasingly inefficient; but the same cannot be said once Ticktin adds the words "and overthrow by the workers," since that is virtually to equate the dynamic of the system with the dynamic of the workers' struggle. (1991c, p.87).

The weakness is in fact especially evident when he comes to consider the tendency of the workers' struggle towards the overthrow of the system. Thus he writes that once

> the social nature of production forces its way through society the power of the workers will not be unmediated and hence there would not be even the temporary existence of a working class movement: there would be the simultaneous establishment of workers' control with the elimination of the elite. (1987a, p.19)

One's first impression might be that this amounts to an understanding that the autonomy of workers' struggle is totally antagonistic to political mediation, but in fact that is very far from being the case. Indeed, Ticktin has asserted quite openly that "the workers cannot blindly develop their own theory, in the absence of intellectuals" (that is, according to context, non-worker intellectuals) (1991b, p.11), and that if their struggle is to come to full fruition they first need a party. (1993, p.131). He has also argued that whereas

> some elite members are entirely useless and others are merely policemen, ...its [the elite's] predominant membership would remain in position, stripped of rank, privilege and power, in a socialist society. (1976, p.43)

On a political-economic level he has even stated in so many words that if the working class comes to power in the USSR the market would actually be restored. (1979, p.13).[50] Presumably the territory could then play its proper part in a global reformist transition wherein market relations were abolished gradually in the 'classically' conceived fashion. Such 'orthodox Marxist' positions, we would suggest, leave traces in the overall theory of the USSR and ultimately ensure that his consideration of the antagonistic nature of class relations remains necessarily incomplete.

Chattopadhyay's Theory

The question of the form of surplus (absolute or relative) is also considered by Chattopadhyay. (1994). There is, however, one major difference in approach: since Chattopadhyay sees the USSR as capitalist, he does not need to theorise the existence of forms of a non-value nature, and is thus able to make use of familiar concepts relating to the political economy of capital accumulation. Remarkably, he is the first exponent of a 'capitalist' theory to deal with what is surely a key question: was the capitalist subsumption of labour in the USSR formal or real?[51]

Chattopadhyay's underlying view is that

> the accumulation of capital in the USSR through time has been an amalgam of the elements of original accumulation of capital, formal subsumption of labour under capital, and *certain phases* of the real subsumption of labour as envisaged by Marx.... (p.61) (emphasis original)[52]

More specifically, since the old pre-capitalist methods of production have already been transformed, subsumption is more than simply formal. At the same time, however, Soviet capital accumulation is not based on what is usually associated with the real form of subsumption: that is, the continuous technological revolutionisation of production. Rather it is based on the quantitative extension of production on a given technical basis. Reference is made to the 'one-shot' technological 'infusions' represented by the deployment of advanced imports (p.70), but the general position is that technical 'revolutionisation' lies essentially in the past and is absent as a property of the form of capital accumulation. The key point is that real subsumption takes place in the context of a *"once-for-all and not continuing* transformation of the method of production." (p.35; see also pp.64-72).

What, then, was the basis of the specific form of real subsumption? After noting the rapidity of the 'original expropriation' organised during the period of 'superindustrialisation,' Chattopadhyay gives the view that without continuous revolutionisation the tempo of accumulation could only be maintained

> by means of the prolongation of the total (social) working time, intensity of labor used [,] including enforcement of discipline, and bringing into the fold of productive

labor those who were still outside of it: mainly women, in other words, increasing the totality of absolute surplus value.

In particular he cites the move to continuous, three-shift operation in the factories, as well as methods of labour intensification involving 'socialist competition,' shock work, Stakhanovism, the raising of norms, and the introduction of piece wages. (pp.64-65). And although he accepts that a rise in productivity did take place, he asserts that this was mainly

> due to the concentration of capital with corresponding changes in the "social combination of labor," to the "upward revision of the existing technological and labor norms" including "improved labor discipline" [,] and, more importantly, a change in the composition of output through shift of labor from agriculture to industry. (p.66)[53]

It would also seem that the absence of a "qualitative" change in the technical composition of capital (pp.64-66) was compensated for by the availability of "abundant natural resources" as well as the existence of a large "reserve of labour." This latter point is especially stressed:

> if the exploitation of the already employed laborers cannot be increased by raising the rate either of absolute or of relative surplus value, the capitalist class requires the enrollment of supplementary labor power to make the (material) elements work as capital. (p.65)

To summarise: the form of real subsumption was based on organisational changes which involved the intensification of labour but not the raising of the technological composition of capital; and on the expansion of the labour force. In consequence there was a "more or less symmetric increase in fixed capital and natural resources along with the employment of more labour." (p.66).

Before criticising this view we need to recall what the concepts of formal subsumption and real subsumption actually refer to. Formal subsumption, then, is the form of subsumption associated with the extraction of absolute surplus value alone: that is, with the lengthening of the working day, and in particular of the portion of the working day in which the workers produce the surplus product. From the point of view of capital accumulation the employment of more workers represents a step forward, within this mode of subsumption, since it not only allows economies of scale but also provides a spur to the technological transformation of the production process which transforms the basis of subsumption. Subsumption thus becomes real when the old techniques are replaced with the new, and major increases in surplus value come from increasing the portion of surplus labour-time within a total labour-time (per worker) which may be constant or even falling.

Let us look first at the part of the basis of Chattopadhyay's theorised form of real subsumption which relates to the quantitative expansion of production. How is it that such expansion can cause subsumption to be real without involving a technological advance? The root of the argument would seem to be that if peasants formerly working outside of a capitalist environment, using pre-capitalist, traditional techniques, are made to engage in wage-labour in an environment where the techniques are more modern, then the subsumption of their labour must be real insofar as the labour process is one which has been thoroughly transformed by capital. There is undoubtedly a case to be argued here. On the other hand, however, since the object of discussion is precisely the relationship between necessary and surplus labour-time, considered not statically but dynamically – statically, the terms absolute and relative surplus value are without meaning — the type of real subsumption theorised by Chattopadhyay is not simply inefficient: it barely manages to qualify as real in the first place. *Ceteris paribus*, the lack of technological change is simply compensated for by an increase of the mass of surplus value, by means of what is effectively 'original accumulation.' The principal difference in relation to such accumulation in England is that in the USSR the deracinated peasants are forced straight into industry. But unless the analysis is taken forward, with reference to a profound consideration of the development of class opposition within industrial production, the issue of real subsumption fails to connect with the question of relative surplus value.

The second factor is the intensification of labour. In this context the main weakness of Chattopadhyay's theory is the absence of any definition. It is one thing to refer to shock work, Stakhanovism, and increased discipline; it is quite another to assume that they were successful. Filtzer argues that in important respects they were not (1986); and as we have seen, Ticktin uses the lack of efficient control over the workers at the point of production as an important component of his critique of the entire political economy. Marx devotes a chapter of the first volume of *Capital* to questions of productivity and labour intensity where he differentiates between the two categories in order to study changes in capitalist production. (1867, pp.655-67). Chattopadhyay, however, asserts abstractly that an increase in labour productivity, in the absence of a change in the techniques and technologies of production, *can* still result from an increase in the intensity of use of both labour and equipment. (p.38). Later, apparently more concretely, he refers to official Soviet figures to show that "with a consistently much higher rate of growth of constant capital compared to living labour there was no corresponding growth in the productivity of social labour." (p.77). But he does not explain how the ratio between constant capital and variable capital could grow even only slightly faster than the productivity of labour (in this general sense), when the former appears to be an index of the latter; or, to put the point differently, when the additional constant capital must itself be produced. From the point of view of capital, it might be possible to investigate this type of problem with reference to inflation; from the point of view of the working class one would certainly have to theorise a distinction between productivity and labour intensity in a precise fashion; but in neither case does Chattopadhyay oblige.

Our third criticism concerns both areas simultaneously: the issue of productivity as well as the growth of industry relative to agriculture. Indeed we would argue that they are very closely related. Let us consider the core issue concerning the rate of surplus value: the ratio between the number of hours spent producing the surplus and the number spent producing goods consumed by the workers. Is it not apparent that moving workers from agriculture into industry reduces the number of labour hours spent producing food, and therefore, assuming the workers drafted into industry do not spend their entire day producing goods for workers, actually increases the overall rate of surplus value? Of course workers' food consumption could fall, in which case the increase would be absolute rather than relative, but if we assume that it does not fall, does this not imply that some sort of technological change must take place in agriculture itself? These are issues which we shall tackle at length in Chapter 7, but for the time being we simply note that Chattopadhyay's writing off as "inconspicuous" a 70% increase in officially aggregated agricultural output between 1960 and 1985 is surely inadequate; as is his omission to reconsider the question of productivity growth even once he has mentioned that according to official figures the agricultural share of total employment fell from over 50% to 20% between 1940 and 1980. (p.96). Brief references to food imports and declining agricultural growth rates are surely insufficient in this regard. (pp.95-96).

Fourth, the development of other sectors too, such as space technology, would seem to constitute further evidence that productivity growth occurred on a significant scale, most definitely not unassociated with change of a qualitative and technological nature. In view of Chattopadhyay's paltry consideration of the issues raised, we feel justified in posing the following crude question: could the rulers really have been able to send men into orbit and rockets to Venus by herding former peasants into the industry of the 1920s? Admittedly he does accept, if only in a footnote, that technological change did occur, and clarifies his position by arguing that "*continuous* technological changes" were "rather limited outside of [the] military and aerospace sectors" and mentioning that "the rate of growth of productivity was at a fairly high level only for a very limited period, namely, during 1951-60 when its annual rate reached five percent."(p.81, n.7). But whatever his view may be of what constitutes limitedness and what is high or low, these points are surely sufficient demonstration of the major inadequacies inherent in his particular theory of the specific Soviet form of real subsumption: that is, as based not on continuous technological revolutionisation but rather on extensive and 'symmetric' growth.

The questions he raises — formal or real subsumption, the specific form of real subsumption, productivity, labour intensification, technological change — are of the highest importance. And we welcome the fact that they are raised by the exponent of what is by no means the weakest 'capitalist' theory of the mode of production. But to our mind the very raising of them demonstrates the need for a placing of focus on the fundamental opposition of class interests and its development over time, with reference above all to the expenditure of labour-power and the specific dynamic relationship between the working class and capital. In this sense, Chattopadhyay's work is stimulating. In regard to meeting this need, however, he does little more than to describe "people's needs as a residual." (pp.93-94; see also p.133). He points, for example, to falling life expectancy and deteriorating conditions of health. In regard to consumption, he briefly mentions its falling share of total investment, and then, immediately following, the declining rate of its growth. (pp.93-94). In regard to production, he cites low-quality work as a sort of mediation through which "over-accumulation" puts a brake on "the accumulation process itself"; and alludes to competition for labour in connection with the labour shortage whilst omitting to discuss its effect on wages. (p.136). But if questions of surplus value and subsumption are to be dealt with properly then surely the movement of the wage deserves much more profound consideration than this. There is nothing mistaken in quoting Gerschenkron to the effect that the "investment interest of the government" is "constantly opposed to the consumption interest of the population" (p.93), but as soon as the mode of production is understood to be capitalist in nature this is no revelation. The issue arising is this: what forms has the opposition taken?[54]

SUMMARY

The first point to be made in summary is that the number of substantive Marxist contributions to an understanding of the relationship between the history and nature of Soviet political economy and the history and nature of working class struggle is very small. One might have expected communist theorists especially to have shown a great interest, but in fact they have paid it minimal attention.

On the other hand, the same cannot fairly be said of Dunayevskaya and James (until the later 1950s), Castoriadis (ditto), or Ticktin (since the mid-1970s). Material is evident in the works of all four, and especially those of Ticktin, which stands well apart from the non-classist or inadequately classist material considered in Chapter 5.

Credit for being the first to insist that the nature of the Soviet system necessarily implies the reality of class struggle must go to Dunayevskaya in the 1940s. In considering the Stalin period and its immediate aftermath, she breaks new ground in her attempt to define Soviet labour policy in terms of the vicissitudes of the class struggle. It is thus unfortunate that she fails to link the analysis to her work on the specific functioning of the political-economic categories of Soviet capitalism. Her one-time collaborator James, meanwhile, produces work which is somewhat less theoretically refined before eventually reaching agreement with Castoriadis. From the 1960s onwards neither Dunayevskaya nor James produces work of similar interest.

During the 1950s Castoriadis also stresses the importance of workers' opposition to the Soviet capitalist system, in his case with special reference to the Khrushchev period. Thus in a landmark text of 1956 he becomes the first person to identify working class resistance as the ultimate cause of the failure of the 'Plan.' But he fails to theorise the underlying nature of this resistance. In the 1960s he rejects Marxism and adopts the view that the essential contradiction of the Soviet system (and capitalism in general) is that which opposes its bureaucratic nature to its need to solicit initiative from below. Eventually he reaches what is virtually a 'totalitarian' theory of Soviet 'slave capitalism.'

A further significant contribution to the theory of the relationship between class conflict and the nature of the Soviet system has been that produced by Ticktin since the 1970s. We would argue that the advances he has made on previous work are quite outstanding. His central achievement has been to identify an underlying contradiction between the ruling elite's limited control over the surplus product and the workers' limited control over the labour process. Despite denying that the USSR knew either history or real classes, he has developed an understanding of this contradiction in a resolutely historical and classist fashion.

Since, unlike the others considered in this chapter, he holds the position that the USSR is non-capitalist in nature, he is then faced with theoretical problems concerning the system's need for growth and the nature of the growth achieved. These, though, he has dealt with in meticulous fashion. In particular, he has developed a theory of a defective form of social product, determined by the specific forms taken by the elite's control over labour and the workers' partial control over the labour process. Actual use-value stands in opposition to potential use-value and waste. With these concepts he has undoubtedly explained the various well-known characteristics of the Soviet economy with a materialist profundity which has not been evident in the works of previous theorists.

Certain problems remain, though, in his insistence that the system is riven by the contradictions of an administered form of use-value rather than an administered form of exchange-value. In particular he has proposed the existence of forms he describes as the absolute surplus product and the relative surplus product which he has insufficiently distinguished from forms based on value. This has meant that in the final analysis his view that the USSR was non-capitalist does not stand up. And in denying that the working class is a real class he has made the focus on class struggle blunter than would otherwise be the case. He has thus developed what is essentially a theory of class antagonism (or at least a theory of the movement of class opposition) in the absence of a concept of class autonomy. In addition, his theoretical achievements remain rather obscured by an 'orthodox Marxist' theory of transition, based on a somewhat mystical view of the necessary movement of the socialisation of labour.

For his part, Chattopadhyay has produced work which is weaker than Ticktin's in the sense that he gives little or no consideration to the overall significance of forms of opposition in the workplace. But in the context of a theory which has the merit of holding the mode of production to be 'capitalist but not State capitalist,' he raises questions which nonetheless do point up the need for such consideration. Thus the inadequacies of his discussion of the specific and 'limited' form of capital's real subsumption of labour flow partly from the absence of an adequate grasp of the underlying conditions of class struggle; but in doing so they demonstrate *malgré soi* that in order to investigate the form of subsumption the radical critic must prioritise an understanding of precisely those conditions.

We would conclude that although a certain amount of work has been done on the importance to Soviet political economy of the dynamic opposition between classes, there remains to be constructed an adequate theoretical account of that importance with specific reference to working class subjectivity and autonomy. This, then, is the issue to be dealt with in Chapter 7.

Notes

1   The Situationists make no references to the class struggle in the USSR apart from superficial comments as to future prospects. In addition, in early years they seem to have been signally over-positive about the intelligentsia. Making what by any standards is a facile parallel, Vaneigem in 1962 thus places the role of the "Eastern bloc's" intelligentsia in the same category as "the workers' struggles presently beginning in England [*presumably, wildcat strikes*—NCF]," of both of which "much can be expected." (1962, p.93). It would certainly be inaccurate to see the early writings of this highly voluntarist thinker as containing the most precise elements of the Situationist critique, but nonetheless in 1969 even the more historical-materialist Khayati could write, without argument, that "the courageous isolated protests voiced in Moscow after 21 August [*in 1968: the day of the*

invasion of Czechoslovakia—NCF] herald the revolution that will not fail to break out soon in Russia itself." (1969, p.264).

Nor have the Autonomists ever studied this area. For his part, Negri simply writes a few years after the Polish events of 1980-81 that in the 'socialist societies' the processes of real subsumption (of labour by capital) "have not yet been fully developed," and that "there still exists a margin within which class struggle of a traditional kind can take place." In this regard, the Polish case is held to be "typical." More generally, the 'socialist societies' seem to be tending "towards the predominance of military structures in the supervision of exploitation." (1986, pp.179-80). Those knowledgeable in the field, however, would hardly see Poland, with its mass union, prevalent Catholicism, and army coup, as having been typical even at that time.

At the end of 1989 Negri produces some comments about the events then taking place in 'the East,' but in terms which are arguably actually opposed to those of an Autonomist critique. Proposing that the 'question' in the Soviet-type countries is that of "understanding what might be the rules for the democratic management of economic entrepreneurship," he goes on to assert that "in the East, within the revolution, people are experiencing a new form of democracy: the democracy of work, a communist democracy." (Let us note in passing that the meaning hardly changes if the term 'entrepreneurship' is translated instead as 'enterprise'). By this time the rebels against the Soviet order in whom Negri is most interested are "the students, scientists, workers linked to advanced technologies, intellectuals, and in short, all those who deal with abstract and intellectual work," whom he sees as representing a new kind of producer: "a social producer, manager of his own means of production and capable of supplying both work and intellectual planning, both innovative activity and a cooperative socialization." (1990, pp.171-72). Such a view makes Vaneigem's praise for the intelligentsia of the late Khrushchev period seem comparatively moderate. Not a specialist in Soviet affairs, Negri appears to be completely unaware of the contempt the Soviet intelligentsia in general harbours for the proletariat (and peasantry) (on which, see for example Ticktin 1973a, pp.39-40, 1973b, and 1991a, chap. 5); not to say theoretically completely unconcerned with their material place in society and the historical forms of proletarian struggle. His view represents Gramsciism taken to an extreme, where the concept of 'organic intellectuals' (see Gramsci 1929-35, pp.5-23) is replaced by 'intellectual workers' as virtually a distinct productive class. It is hardly distinguishable from the position taken by Bahro. (1977).

2   For a recent, mainly empirical councilist 'dossier' on class struggle in the Yeltsin period, see Echanges et Mouvement 1993-95. This material does, however, contain a brief but very useful theoretical summary of the division within the post-Soviet Russian ruling class (p.50), to which we shall refer in the final chapter.

3   In some ways the SPGB can be bracketed together with Chattopadhyay (see Chapter 1, Note 17 above), but this does not appear to be one of them. Thus after commenting on the absence in the USSR of political democracy, they simply assert without further evidence that the Soviet rulers have "hoodwinked" their subjects into believing that rule by secret police, concentration camp, and executioner" is the "best of all possible worlds." (1946, p.101).

4   For a much fuller discussion of the intricacies of the attempts to introduce more labour competititon, both before and by means of Stakhanovism, see Filtzer 1986, pp.91-115.

5   Dunayevskaya's later work is of much less critical interest. In her introduction to the 1963 edition of *Marxism and Freedom*, she writes as follows:

After the Russian admission, in 1943, that the law of value operates in Russia, there was no further point to continue the detailed analysis of their State Plans. My analysis of the Five

Year Plans, therefore, stopped with World War 2, and thereafter focused on the Russian assault on Marx's *Capital* and his *Economic-Philosophic Manuscripts*. (1963, p.20) This statement clearly illustrates the weakness of 'Marxist-Humanism.' See also Dunayevskaya's later, largely journalistic declaration that the coming to power of Andropov in 1982 "reveals the state of the degeneracy of state-capitalism as a whole"; and the support she lent to Solidarnosc in Poland. (1982).

6   It should be remembered, of course, that James's book of 1950, like Dunayevskaya's early articles of 1942-43 and 1946-47, formulated the ideas of the Johnson-Forest tendency, not just those of one individual. Indeed the former text, which was presented as the summation and culmination of the tendency's theoretical work, did not originally bear James's signature. (See Dunayevskaya 1958-72, p.3; and Cleaver 1979, p.46). Since we now know, though, that James was the author, we have chosen to present the material in such a way as to point up the various strengths and weaknesses of the Tendency's critique in relation to those of the two authors' later works, which were notably rather discordant. (James, Lee, and Chaulieu 1958; Dunayevskaya 1958).

7   As Cleaver has rightly pointed out (1979, pp.45-48 and 54), this work anticipates Autonomist work of a decade later.

8   This is not quite an accurate representation of Lenin's position, for in fact he defended labour militarisation whenever he perceived it to be necessary in the interests of the regime. Thus at one time he drafted a decree imposing "martial law for labour militarisation" in a belt stretching 30-50 versts (20-33 miles) either side of the railway lines. (Nove 1982, p.73). Arguably one factor in the 'trade union debate' which came to a head in 1921 was a power struggle between the head of the government and the War Commissar.

9   The inverted commas in this sentence are James's.

10 Although, according to Dunayevskaya (1958-72, p.3), Chaulieu (Castoriadis) denied having written or signed this work, nonetheless in the second half of the 1950s James's group did enter into a rapprochement both with Castoriadis's group Socialisme ou Barbarie and with European council communists such as Brendel and Maasen. (Johnson et al. 1956). Whatever precise role Castoriadis played in its production, it is readily apparent that he exercised a substantial influence on its content; and one only has to read the texts he wrote in 1954 and 1956 (q.v) to realise that in relation to the critique of the USSR it was his influence which was overriding. In other words, by 1958 James had adopted Castoriadis's position on the class struggle in the USSR rather than the less considered position of the Johnson-Forest tendency. (See also note 14 below).

11 By 1963 one of James's main interests is to defend the role of Leninism. In highly tendentious fashion, he thus endeavours to separate Leninism from the "theory and practice of the vanguard party," which he denies was ever its "central doctrine" or even a 'special' one. (1963, p.327). Such an apparently bizarre position marks perhaps an even greater theoretical abdication than Dunayevskaya's formulation of 'Marxist-Humanism.'

12 He also mentions bureaucratic 'cliquism' and the technical problems of hierarchical supervision, but understands them to be less important and less basic.

13 This translation has been slightly tidied up.

14 Although the elaboration of the fundamental position on the class struggle in the USSR should be ascribed mainly to Castoriadis, the depiction of the USSR in this collective text is somewhat more rhetorical than it is in Castoriadis's writings as sole author. Thus it is argued that, since the workers know their work better than anyone else does, even at gunpoint they retain a certain say in the setting of norms. As long as capitalism lasts,

"modern industry cannot be run in any other way." (pp.31-33). These comments apply to the entire capitalist world, but unfortunately in the limited space allotted to conditions in the USSR several uncritical and blanket comparisons are made with shopfloor relations in the United States which detract from the critique of the former. It is stated, for example, that "workers in Russia have created shop floor organizations which control production and discipline management in much the same way [*sic*] as American workers." Unrigorous comparisons like this clearly fail to provide convincing support for the assertion that the 'Russian working class' is "the most powerful in the world except for the American." Since it does not follow either that it is the former which is "far more dangerous to the ruling class," this is explained instead with reference to the alleged occurrence in 'Russia' in the last fifty years of "three great revolutions," in each of which "the workers took the lead." (p.34). According to context the 'third revolution' apparently denotes de-Stalinisation, whereas the first two presumably occurred in 1905 and 1917. Such a formulation is, of course, largely dogmatic. Given the rather more considered analysis of the USSR published by Castoriadis alone, as well as the more considered analysis in this collective text of conditions in the United States (pp.20-29) — which follows on from earlier work by Johnson-Forest and James in particular — this can almost certainly be ascribed to James or Lee rather than to Castoriadis. The assertion that "long before Khrushchev spoke of de-Stalinization, the workers in the plants had de-Stalinized themselves," (p.34) is undoubtedly interesting, but it is unfortunately made without any substantial consideration being given to the forms taken by either 'workplace de-Stalinisation' or indeed Stalinism itself. In short, it would appear that in support of Castoriadis's (profound) work on the USSR, James is offering comparisons with his own (also profound) work on the United States which themselves, being crude, remain weak.

15 The idea that working class people have a low standard of living "as such" does indeed involve a confusion of the relative with the absolute. But at the same time it must also be recognised that their 'standard of living' — let us disregard the inadequacy of this term — is not only always low relative to that of the exploiters; it is also low relative to need. If this latter sense were what was intended, to call it "low as such" would be quite correct, even without the recognition that need is closely related to struggle. In the *Road to Wigan Pier* Orwell rightly rejects the curious 'view' of the middle class snob that "It isn't the same for them as it would be for us." (1937, pp.16-17).

16 See the distinction drawn between Castoriadis's approach and that of Autonomist Marxism in the first section of Chapter 1 above. See also the criticisms of Castoriadis in Aufheben 1994, pp.25-27.

17 "There is indeed one world but that world is governed by the law of decline not the law of value, by the decadence of value not by its apogee. That necessarily implies that in different times and different places value exists in different degrees, or not at all." (Ticktin 1987, p.24). But what exactly are the 'degrees' that value can exist in?

18 In addition, while Ticktin is right to begin a discussion of finance capital with Britain, developments in that country merit no special weight in any argument that the problems of finance capital have led to a decline of capitalism globally. Britain, and indeed the United States, are quite evidently in 'decline' in a number of ways (see Ticktin 1994a, p.73); but, more importantly, a theory of the decline of the global capitalist system should explain what is happening in countries which are rising. The tendency of financial outflows from Japan, for example, to take the form of direct investments as well as investment in shares and bonds, which apparently contradicts Ticktin's argument, should not be written off in a

single sentence. (1986a, p.10). In South Africa the 'fracturing of abstract labour' has indeed come to hamper capitalist efficiency (Ticktin 1991d); but in Japan the effect is quite the opposite, and there the 'dual labour market' has proven to be very good indeed for business. (Crump 1989). (For a pro-capitalist 'geopolitical' description of Japanese economic growth, see Kennedy 1988, pp.537-40 and 591-608).

A second point, which we shall simply note, is that theorists of decline should be able to show convincingly that what appears to be an ongoing technological revolution is in fact something else. The communist theorist Tillium has recently argued the opposite view. (1994). Our theorisation of forms of money makes it fairly easy to suggest that capital could overcome the problematisation of the relationship between money-capital and the forces of production by imposing a technological revolutionisation of the form of money. Such a proposition has not been supported at length, but nor is it easy to disprove. The capitalist development posited would not abolish the underlying contradiction; and since it would involve the introduction of *new forms of control* over the forces of production and, as part of that, a restructuring of the class relation, it would evidently be subject to resistance. Moreover, the contradiction might once again become severely problematic at some time in the future: that is, once this particular technological revolutionisation had become a 'given' and capital had undergone a period of development on the basis of its institutionalisation. Perhaps that would even necessarily be the case. But what we do not accept is that the rulers' problems must steadily intensify, preventing capitalism from entering a new period of its domination.

19 For the moment we are making general criticisms of Ticktin's idea of decline in order to probe weaknesses in the overall basis of his 'exceptionalism.' The question of potential and actual surplus, first theorised by Baran (1957), is a complex one, and we shall deal with it in greater depth below in a specifically Soviet context.

20 A more astute critic would surely see irrationalism as directly implied by commodity fetishism; drug abuse, whether legal or illegal, as an advanced form of social control which expresses such fetishism — as do fashion, television, cinema, and numerous kinds of home, personal, and indeed 'collective' consumerist entertainment; and the mafia as expressing in a number of ways the very essence of capitalist society (the ideology of honour in business, the subordination of politicians and public officials to the cause of profitability, and so on).

21 On the role of the Taylorist 'scientific management of work' in the dissociation of the labour process from workers' craft skills, and hence in the increasing abstractification of labour, see Braverman 1974, chaps. 4-5. No subsequent re-skilling or creation of 'quality circles' and so on should detract from the force of Braverman's analysis of capitalism's second industrial revolution.

22 Some 'health' treatment, of course, is neutral or actually harmful in its effect. One issue raised is the interaction between, on one side, forms of self-justification concerning the distribution of revenue among the ruling class, and on the other, the relationship of this class with the working class, in terms of both the imposition of control — including false consciousness — and the making of concessions. An understanding of such an interaction — in a geographical rather than a sectoral context — is demonstrated in Tillium 1997.

23 As Marx realised, political democracy is connected principally with the expansion of the power of the bourgeoisie against previously dominant property interests. (1843b, pp.232-33). In the present century there has also become apparent a strong — and we would argue unbreakable — relationship between enfranchisement and the bourgeoisie's use of

its mass media, and hence with the capitalist struggle against the class self-assertion of the proletariat.

24   On this definition, the State is more than the legal State, and includes various hidden parts.

25   Ticktin's critical stance towards 'market socialism,' founded on his insistence upon an absolute incompatibility between planning and the market (1979, 1990-92, 1991c, pp.175-80), wears somewhat thin once it is realised that the 'socialist' government he envisages would in no way refuse to print money.

26   "Only in this [present] epoch, and this is the nature of the epoch, could a real alternative to exploitative society be contemplated. It is real because a real revolution conducted in the name of this alternative has taken place." (Ticktin 1978, p.53). No substantiation is offered for any of the several distinct assertions within these lines.

27   It is possible, of course, especially in view of Engels's work (1877-78, 1896-1925) to interpret some of Marx's work as being based solely upon a philosophical and 'natural-scientific' view of the interplay of 'objective laws.' (See, for example, Marx's postface to the second edition of Volume 1 of *Capital* in 1873). It is, after all, an undisputed fact that Marx wanted to dedicate Volume 2 of *Capital* to Darwin, author of the work *On the Origin of Species Through Natural Selection, or the Preservation of Favoured Races in the Struggle for Life* (1866) — even if, as McLellan has shown (1973, pp.423-24), Engels's speech at Marx's graveside in which he equated the views of Marx and Darwin is highly misleading. Given, though, Marx's rejection of philosophy (1844, pp.249-50), his insistence on the unity of theory and practice (see, for example, Marx 1845), and his insistence in the *Manifesto* on the centrality of class struggle (Marx and Engels 1848), it would seem much more useful to be wary of any 'objectivist' self-commentaries written under the later influence of contemporary capitalist science, and to reject them accordingly. (See McLellan 1973, and Levine 1975 pp.423-24). As Debord puts it,

> what closely links Marx's theory with scientific thought is the rational understanding of the forces which really operate in society. But Marx's theory is fundamentally beyond scientific thought, and it preserves scientific thought only by superseding it: what is in question is an understanding of struggle, and not of law. (1967, para.81)

Discussion of this matter cannot be developed further in the present context.

28   It should be recalled that, just as the disappearance of capitalism is not a sufficient condition for the inauguration of communism, the 'success' of a capitalism which gives way to a more efficient form of exploitation does not undermine the historical certainty of this inauguration.

29   This is not to suggest that it was necessarily impossible in this century for a large country to have had a non-capitalist political economy, even one which underwent rapid development; but simply to criticise Ticktin's explanation of the context in which it was possible.

30   As we shall see, though, whilst Ticktin has no concept of the USSR's maturity, he does have a concept of its decline. (1990, 1991b). In his own terms this would appear to be highly problematic.

31   With reference to the forms of control associated with capitalist decline, he writes that "the attempt to control workers on the shopfloor using the labour process cannot be dignified with the term strategy. Rather it is a particular tactic adopted within the overall social democratic or Keynesian strategy." (1994a). This statement appears remarkable given that capital is self-expanding value and surplus value is produced by labour. Thus the increased consumption associated with Keynesianism is dependent of course upon changes in production.

32   This is the translation quoted by Ticktin. Our reference is to the Penguin edition, in which the translation is slightly different.

33   More precisely, Ticktin's view is that exchange-value was known exclusively in the black market (1991c, p.133), but in the absence of value (M-C-M´) and hence of the law of value. He recognises that since 1989 the rouble has also become important in bargaining between legal enterprises, but sees this as essentially a matter of mediated barter (C-M-C´). It follows, in his terms, that Russian money, by which he means the rouble, is still not real money, or 'money as money.' (1993, pp.125-26; see also Ticktin 1992a).

34   Ticktin is by no means an orthodox Trotskyist, but his view on the relationship between Soviet politics and economics reveals a glimmer of the Trotskyist position on the 'political' nature of 'Stalinist' exploitation. (See Trotsky 1936, pp.248-49). "The individual has a political relation to his workplace in two senses: firstly in terms of control and secondly in terms of the necessity to work." (Ticktin 1978, p.53). After writing that "the economic relation can only exist through the political relation, so that the economic relation is expressed through a political form," he then adds that this political form supposedly 'limits' the nature of the economic relation. (p.55). Later he writes that

> in the West [*i.e. capitalism*—NCF] the atomisation is economic, fundamentally caused by commoditisation of labour power, whereas in the East [*i.e the USSR and countries with similar regimes*—NCF] it is fundamentally political, though based on a political economy of a kind conducive to this political atomisation. (1987a, p.16)

What he does not recognise properly is that in any exploitative society a political relation is at the same time an economic relation. More simply, it distributes resources which are socially determined as scarce: in fact, it necessarily concerns the organisation of the scarcity which is denoted by the word 'economy' in the first place. There is a clear correlation here with an aspect of his work we have criticised above: namely, his downplaying of the continuity of the essentially economic role of the State in capitalism.

A further relic of Trotskyism is evident in his insistence that the USSR was always unstable. It is impossible not to notice the high degree of esteem shown for the former War Commissar (and advocate of labour militarisation [1920, chap.8]) in the following sentences:

> Trotsky, who still regarded the USSR as a workers' state, was nonetheless moved to remark in 1937 that the USSR under Stalin was politically worse than Germany under Hitler. *In other words* [emphasis added], the absence of a market and the strong internal controls reflect extreme instability, not stability. (Ticktin 1991c, p.9)

If the Soviet social formation had really been that unstable it would hardly have survived the second world war. Even if it were not defeated, as Trotsky thought it would be due to its instability (1936, p.227), it certainly would not have won so completely. Attempting to rescue the idea of 'permanent instability' Ticktin is forced to explain it in the much vaguer terms of 'unviability,' and to accept that Trotsky "appears to have been wrong in his time frame." (1991c, p.61). On both counts the special pleading is self-evident.

The somewhat fanciful notion is also noted that it was the course of events in the USSR during the late 1920s — rather than, say, the defeat of the international revolutionary movement by 1921, or the second world war, or the post-war boom — which determined the whole nature of the world-historical epoch in which we now live. (p.185). Connected to this there is the strong but somewhat confused view that the ability or inability of the rulers to impose the market and therefore mass unemployment is related very closely indeed to the overall conditions in the outside world of (market) capitalism. Thus in 1987 Ticktin describes as "inevitable" the prospect that the Soviet rulers will conclude a deal with their counterparts in the US and open up their territory to the world market. (1987b, p.196). As well as fulfilling the needs of the Soviet elite, this would also enable the American rulers to "shore up" their own position. In 1991 he goes so far as to assert that an opening up of the USSR to the world market is a necessity for global (market) capitalism too, and would actually enable the latter to escape its "crisis." The trouble now, though, is that the USSR cannot get to the market because that would mean confronting the workers head-on. (1991b, pp.15-19). If for the sake of argument one accepts these two assertions, one might then ask why the big banks would be unable to offer large enough loans to key multinationals to enable them to make sizeable concessions to workers in the USSR at the same time as conquering the country for the world market. These loans could surely then be paid back out of the increased profits which would accrue once the rest of market capitalism had pulled out of its "crisis." Alternatively, one might ponder awhile the obvious implication that the workers' limited control over the labour process in the USSR is the most important factor in the current history of the world. Since the area has only around 5% of the world's population, and a similar percentage of world output — and considering that even the importance of oil in the world economy is bound to decline — the analysis would appear to be a severe case of the purest academicism. (Gross output figures for 1988 in US $ trillion [constant 1988 prices] were as follows: US, 4.8; Japan 2.9; Germany [East plus West] 1.4, USSR, 1.0; World, 18.7. By 1990 the Soviet economy was smaller than the French and about the same size as the Italian. See United Nations 1993, pp.232-39.)

35   The choice of terms here appears inappropriate, since etymologically the term 'individual' (that which is indivisible) is virtually identical in meaning to the term 'atom' (that which cannot be cut). A second point is that, as Ticktin recognises, atomisation is not at all a social relation unique to the USSR. Through television and other means it plays a crucial role in Japan and the countries of the advanced West too. The importance of the analysis lies in the critique of its specifically Soviet form.

36   In using the term 'negative control' Ticktin doubtless does not mean to evoke any cybernetic connotations.

37   For Ticktin, Soviet waste is not directly comparable with the 'unproductive' sector under capitalism. Indeed it is all the more problematic for the Soviet rulers given that within the Soviet system it is use-value which is "all-important." (1991c, pp.11-12). But in fact this insistence on the non-capitalist nature of the USSR adds little extra weight to the argument that its inherent wastefulness was an especially chronic problem. Capitalism does indeed depend upon the production of new exchange-value, but at the same time all commodities — in this context, all new production — must necessarily have a use-value as well as an exchange-value. Exchange-value certainly dominates; use-value even falls, as Debord has rightly pointed out (1967, para. 47): but this does not make it impossible to imagine a local form of capitalist system in which the production of use-values is so highly inefficient as to hinder the production of exchange-value and therefore the general interest of capital. If all machine-tools suddenly began to wear out twice as quickly, the production of exchange-value would obviously be drastically reduced — and not just because of market competition. Subject to a more rapid turnover but without any quickening of production, fixed capital would become much more expensive, per period, in value terms.

38   It should be noted that the category of the producer sector is not equivalent to that of heavy industry, which includes, for example, car production. Nor is it the same as the defence

sector, not even in the broadest possible sense. For an example of the type of traditional view which Ticktin has successfully and deftly undermined, see Voslensky 1980, p.141.

39   Where Ticktin identifies Soviet society's central economic feature as being wastefulness, and then proceeds to analyse the categorial interactions which make it so, Füredi, who does not employ a comparably precise critical method, holds rather that the most distinctive feature is the overall "lack of any dynamic of development." (1986, p.79). Omitting to develop analytical categories in any profound fashion, he succeeds mainly in demonstrating that it is possible to adopt various aspects of Ticktin's critique while remaining an avid defender of political Leninism. It is also worth mentioning that Füredi's empirical knowledge of the field is not very great, and he thus makes such inexcusable errors as to assert that it was only in the 1960s that the law of value was first officially portrayed as "an essential component of the transition to communism." (p.113). (See in rebuttal the well-known textbooks by Leontiev et al., 1943, and Stalin 1952).

40   Füredi has adopted an identical position. (1986, pp.179-83).

41   Our context here is that of the control over labour. Whilst daughters and sons of high-up State administrators during, say, the Brezhnev period, tended not to take up posts as senior as those of their fathers, and often had less control over labour, they usually managed, of course, to live very comfortable lives. And the privileges they enjoyed did not exactly exclude career prospects. In Walker's words,

> the striking feature of the privileged children of the Soviet leadership...is their reluctance to follow in their parents' footsteps and seek to climb the ranks of party power. Even those who go into public life, or into the party hierarchy of the *Nomenklatura*, do not choose the kind of career pattern which leads to the central committee or the Politburo. The jobs they choose are those which allow them to continue to live in comfort, with access to Western luxuries and, if possible, a life abroad. (1986, pp.198-99)

42   Ticktin, however, writes of individual countries 'going socialist.' (1990-92, p.19). In the editorial preamble of the *Critique* journal, meanwhile, there may be a rejection of the "concept of socialism in one country" but there is also a denial of "the possibility that a country could be both socialist and undemocratic." (See for example Critique 1994). The clear implication here is that if a country is not an undemocratic country then it might be ... a socialist country. He has also written that "socialists have to fight for socialism on a national basis, even if they are internationalist, simply because the State is national." (1990-92). Not only is this logically false, since socialism (that is, communism) is not founded on the basis of the State; it is also incorrect in content since the State-form is global.

43   This is a summary of Ticktin's position, which is actually self-contradictory. Thus in a single article he asserts first, that the working class "came into being over time, threatened the society and has since constituted a permanent feature of a society which is no longer a classical capitalism"; and then that "classes exist in potential or essence all the time but...only when the immediate circumstances are propitious can we say that the class has come fully into being." (1987a, pp.13-14). The problem is that by concentrating on class formation in the context of 'laws of transition' supposedly now in operation he has removed the focus from the class struggle.

44   In the description of the trade union as a 'ruling class' form of proletarian organisation, the inverted commas are in the original.

45   Ticktin's actual words are:

> [In the USSR] the individual reacts spontaneously and individually with disastrous results for the product. In the West, the worker is part of a union, which negotiates

control over the production line. The individual can be controlled through the reserve army of labour or through the wage system, neither of which are relevant in the USSR. (1987a, p.17)

But in fact many kinds of 'workers' control' over the work process, such as hoodwinking time-and-labour specialists, are not negotiated by unions at all. Moreover, Ticktin is forgetting that the majority of workers in the 'West' are not unionised.

46   It is also based upon a serious underestimation of the general level of socially-enforced atomisation in countries more capitalistically advanced than the USSR.

47   He does not mention war reparations, but clearly the same argument would apply.

48   Previous critics have failed to notice this, or at least to comment upon it. (See for example E. Mandel 1979 and Molyneux 1987). These concepts are criticised here for the first time.

49   On the depletion of available new sources of absolute surplus value, see also Arnot 1988, pp.59-64.

50   In a different context, part of the basis on which Trotsky criticised the Soviet industrialisation drive at the turn of the 1930s was precisely the "adventurism" of the rejection of market mechanisms. (1936, pp.66-73).

51   Negri has referred very briefly in an Eastern European context to the incomplete development of capitalist real subsumption (see Note 1 above), but the issue can be said to be discussed for the first time by Chattopadhyay.

52   Although this is a summary of Chattopadhyay's position, the details of which we are about to discuss, we cite it here as representative of his mode of presentation. The position summarised is not unreasonable, but the reference to Marx in this context most certainly is. As presented here (see also pp.35-36), the idea that only 'certain phases' of real subsumption were evident in the USSR clearly implies that Marx conceived of at least three 'phases' of real subsumption. We do not accept that the analysis elaborated in *Capital* and other works supports this belief; nor that the figures concerning Soviet economic growth point to "a clear case of capital accumulation on the basis of an inadequately changing technology or largely on the given technical basis as Marx had envisaged." (p.72; see also pp.66 and 77). Chattopadhyay's commitment to presenting his work as ultra-orthodox leads to confusion; which in view of the importance of the questions in which he is interested, as well as his non-reformist grasp of Marxism, is especially unfortunate.

53   The references here are to Nove 1982, pp.233-35.

54   In his very last footnote Chattopadhyay writes that

the alienation and apathy of the Soviet workers in regard to the regime did not, however, mean their simple passivity in the face of the regime. Workers' opposition to the regime manifested itself to a non-negligible effect throughout the Soviet rule in different forms.

And he goes on to quote a poet quoted by two dissidents to the effect that what the regime calls bourgeois sabotage is in fact proletaran sabotage. As evidence of workers' "continuing opposition" to the "regime" he also mentions the high prison and labour-camp population and the Novocherkassk uprising of 1962. (p.163, n.25). But these are references of a parenthetical and even journalistic character, and there is no consideration of workers' opposition in terms of its political-economic significance.

7 The Class Struggle: An Autonomist Marxist Theory

In this final chapter we develop an understanding of the struggle of the working class in opposition to the needs of Soviet capital. The overall structure is similar to that of Chapter 3. After giving expanded Autonomist Marxist definitions of the underlying categories of the class struggle under capitalism in general, we proceed to develop an Autonomist understanding of the significance of that struggle in the USSR.

DEFINING THE CLASS STRUGGLE UNDER CAPITALISM

The class relation in capitalist society can best be defined as the conflict between, on one side, those who do not possess any control over the means of production, but who, being the producers, are the sole source of new value; and on the other side, those who do possess such control by dint of controlling capital. It is fundamentally a relation of production.

It would certainly be quite feasible to begin a theorisation of this relation on the basis of subjective proletarian experience. But since that experience necessarily involves struggle, a second route to a theoretical understanding involves looking first at the pole of capital (as discussed in Chapter 3 above) in order to grasp what it is that proletarian subjectivity *opposes*. It will then be possible to start to understand theoretically why and how it does so, and to proceed to look at the pole of the working class on the basis of this understanding. And it is this second route which will now be taken. Given that working class struggle must to some degree obstruct the *control* of capital — that is, capital's control over itself, its well-being — there is a need to understand that control in terms of its temporal field of operation, the capitalist production cycle.

Surplus-Value Versus the Wage

The Capital Circuit

The circuit of capital involves two processes which for analytical purposes can be considered separately. The first is *investment*, or the injection of capital into production; the second is *sale*, or its realisation once production has occurred.

In all capitalist production projects capital is invested partly in labour resources and partly in means of production. In other words, capital divides into two portions. (See the upper half of Figure 7.1). On one hand, there is the capital invested in plant and materials, which Marx defines as 'constant' capital or c; on the other, there is the capital invested in labour-power, which modern mystified jargon knows as 'human capital' but which Marx denotes as 'variable capital' or v. In the case of the first portion, it becomes clear during the course of production that it is simply transferred from the plant and raw materials to the product. Its exchange-value is therefore passed from one use-value to another. (Marx 1867, pp.310-16). (If this were not the case, one would have either a 'magic machine' or else a black hole into which no controller of capital would wish to invest.) The second portion, meanwhile, has the unique property of being able to generate new value in the course of the 'consumption' of what it has bought: that is, labour-power. This is because the upkeep of workers, unlike the purchase and upkeep of plant, gives them the strength to produce additional value in excess of the value of their own maintenance. (pp.316-19).

It follows that the employment of wage-labour cannot be defined simply in terms of circulation, nor indeed in terms of the mere consumption of a material commodity by its purchaser. The crucial point is that the human beings who receive v (wages), being deprived of any control over the means of production, alienated from them, and exploited by capital, are forced to produce a surplus which takes a value form (s). This surplus is the lifeblood of capital expansion and therefore of capital. As Marx puts it,

> the production of surplus-value — which includes the preservation of the value originally advanced — appears therefore as the determining purpose, the driving force and the final result of the capitalist process of production, as the means through which the original value is transformed into capital. (Marx 1933, p.976)

Control over capital is thus necessarily the control, direct or indirect, over the extraction of *surplus value*.[1]

The next step in the analysis is to look at the category of surplus value in relation to the end result of capitalist production, and thus in terms of the composition of the product sold. (Marx 1867, pp.329-32). As depicted in the lower half of Figure 7.1, this product is divided into three portions, one of which is subdivided further. First, there is the reproduction of constant capital (c). Second, there is the part of the product consumed by proletarians — namely, that which is reproductive of labour-power — which is defined here as the quantity of products upon which the wage (v) is spent (wage goods). The third part of the

INVESTMENT *Productive* *Consumption* <small>WITHIN PRODUCTION</small>	Constant Capital	Variable Capital	
SALE *Realisation* <small>OUTSIDE OF</small> <small>PRODUCTION</small>	Reproduction of Constant Capital	Wage Goods (incl. Social Wage)	Exploiters' Consumption + Accumulation Fund

Figure 7.1 Capitalist Production: The Two Moments of the Cycle of Capital

product, the surplus value (s), is itself split into two portions. The first of these, constituted by the resources consumed by the exploiters, is most easily described as 'revenue.' These resources play no further part in the capital circuit, which in fact they leave. The second is constituted by the resources which the exploiters use in expanding production, and forms the accumulation fund. These resources remain capital. Indeed they are necessary to capital's very nature, since the point is that they are subsequently reinvested with a view to the production of even more surplus value. (pp.738-61).

Since capital's essence is determined by its accumulation, it is thus the *accumulation* of surplus-value, rather than the personal consumer tastes or privileged consumption of capitalist investors — or indeed any mythical origins in Protestant 'asceticism' — which provides the motive for capital circulation. In Marx's well-known words: "Accumulate, accumulate! That is Moses and the prophets!" (p.742). For some exploiters it may be the opulence of their consumption which determines their feelings of well-being at any given moment, or indeed the size of the gap between their own living-standards and those of the proletariat; but it is accumulation which permits the growth of capital and nourishes the health of the capitalist system which they control.[2] More specifically, the accumulation of surplus value provides the essential motive for each of the two 'moments' of the capital cycle: that is, both for the investment in forces of production (means of production and labour-power), or M-C; and for the realisation of the value of the product through its sale, or C-M´.

The Labour-Power Circuit

An understanding of the essence of investment and sale — that is, of the two sides of the relationship between C and M — does not in itself, though, even once the categories are grasped as parts of a single whole, provide a fully adequate basis for an understanding of capitalism's class contradictions. (See Lebowitz 1992, pp.35-59). This is because, as Marx stresses in the Grundrisse, the theorisation of each of these categories involves a consideration of capital principally through the lens of circulation, even if it is true that the relations of circulation are understood to be a constituent and indeed essential part of the overall relations of production. Thus he explains (in a style frequently characteristic of the 'Notebooks') that

> if we examine the entire turnover of capital, then four moments appear, or, each of the two great moments of the production process appears again as a duality: we can take either circulation or production as the point of departure here. This much has now been said, that circulation is itself a moment of production, since capital becomes capital only through circulation; production is a moment of circulation only in so far as the latter is itself regarded as the totality of the production process. The moments are: (I) The real production process and its duration. (II) Transformation of the product into money. Duration of this operation. (III) Transformation of the money in the proper proportions into raw material, means of labour and labour, in short, into the elements of productive capital. (IV) The exchange of a part of the capital for living labour capacity can be regarded as a particular moment, and must be so regarded, since the labour market is ruled by other laws than the product market etc. (1939, pp.520-21)[3]

If investment and sale describe moments III and II respectively, we have yet to consider capitalism's class contradictions in *direct* relation to production: in other words, in such a way that circulation is understood through the lens of production, and capital through the lens of labour, rather than the other way around. We therefore need to look more closely at Marx's 'moments' I and IV.

In parallel to the two moments of the circuit of capital described above, we see that there are also two moments of the 'circuit of labour-power.' The first is its *exertion*, or employment in material production; the second is its *regeneration*, or reproduction outside of material production.

In a consideration of the actual 'production process' in which the exertion of labour-power takes place, it must first be recognised that the process has 'unity.' Insofar as production is organised according to the end of the extraction of surplus value, it is value which "enters as subject." (Marx 1939, p.311). Labour is labour for capital; and capital "appears as a force of expansion, as production and reproduction, and always as command." Production is not partly capitalist and

EXERTION *Consumption* *by Capital* WORKERS' EXPERIENCE WITHIN PRODUCTION	Necessary Labour-Time	Surplus Labour-Time
REGENERATION *Reproduction* WORKERS' EXPERIENCE OUTSIDE PRODUCTION	Consumption of Wage Goods (incl. Social Wage Goods) (Dependent on Housework + Childcare)	

Figure 7.2 Capitalist Production: The Two Moments of the Cycle of Labour-Power

partly something else. In that they produce surplus value, workers are working in the way that capital requires them to work. In fact, the quantification of surplus value — more generally, its comparative quantitative assessment (see Chapter 3 above) — is only possible insofar as capital commands production as a whole. (Negri 1979, pp.75-76). "The process of the production of capital does not appear as the process of production of capital, but as the process of production in general." (Marx 1939, p.303).

It will readily be seen, though, that class antagonism has not been negated. Although use-value and exchange-value are brought together within the capitalist production process, another 'determination of labour' is to be found "inasmuch as it is separated [from capital] and exploited." (Negri 1979, p.70). This is comprised of the categories of *necessary labour* and *surplus labour*, as shown in the upper half of Figure 7.2. In Negri's words:

> a relation is established which contains a *specific measure*: the measure of labor necessary to the reproduction of the force of labor acquired by the capitalist and submitted to the general relation of capital. (p.70)

And this 'specific measure' can only be that of *necessary labour-time*, defined as the socially-averaged portion of the working day which workers spend in production of the resources that they and their dependants consume. If the part of the social product consumed by proletarians takes X labour-hours to produce, capitalist exploitation can then be defined on the basis of the fact that the physical and mental capacities which are refreshed or 'reproduced' in the course of its consumption are themselves exploited for $X + \Delta X$ hours.

Despite occurring within a process of production dominated by capital, and despite defining the *value* of labour-power, necessary labour is therefore the labour that produces products which satisfy the *needs* of socialised workers. From the point of view of the workers these needs, and labour's capacity to fulfil them, cannot be seen as a mere 'residue or appendage' of capitalist development. Here, therefore, there is a radical clash between points of view and between interests. As Negri has shown, at the very heart of the restoration of the workers' productive capacity which the fulfilment of these needs permits, there is thus

> a dynamic relation, an attempt by the working class to reaffirm the indispensable consistency and the necessity of its own composition, constant counterpart of that capitalist force which tries to under-value the workers and their necessary labor. (1979, pp.70-71)

And the form of this relation is the opposition between necessary labour and surplus labour, between production which meets the needs of the workers and production of surplus value.

It is precisely in asserting their needs, in expanding them and fighting for them — indeed, in just defending them — that workers act antagonistically with regard to the production of surplus value. Moreover,

> in the struggle between the two classes — which necessarily arises with the development of the working class — the measurement of the distance between them, which, precisely, is expressed by wages itself as a proportion, becomes decisively important. (Marx 1939, p.597)

Or, as Negri puts it succinctly, the 'relation between surplus labour and necessary labour' is itself 'the relation between the two classes.' (1979, p.97). The value of necessary labour "is *the result of the class struggle*, when it fails to become the dictatorship of the proletariat." (p.133).

Whilst being productive of goods which fulfil needs, necessary labour is, though, just like surplus labour, 'consumptive' of the workers' capacity to produce. In short, it tires workers out. Hence labour is only one moment of the 'labour-power cycle' which includes not only the exertion of labour-power, but also its *regeneration*, its reproduction.[4] Since the value of any commodity is precisely the cost of its production (in terms of average socially-necessary labour-time), and since under capitalism labour-power itself takes the form of a commodity, it follows that what distinguishes the expenditure of labour-power under capitalism — that is, wage-labour — is expressible as the capacity to produce value *in excess of the cost of its own production*. (See Marx 1867, pp.274-77, and 1939, pp.263). The applicability of the term 'production' to the labour-power commodity thus follows directly from Marx's theory of value. Such production, or reproduction, constitutes the second moment of the cycle, and it is this that we must now examine. (See the lower half of Figure 7.2).

From a proletarian viewpoint it should be clear that under the heading of the reproduction of the worker we must place his entire life outside of material production. In other words, it involves his consumption not only of goods bought in the shops, but also of the resources used up in building and repairing his accommodation, in looking after his health, in teaching him facts, 'facts,' and attitudes at school and college, in producing his car if he has one, and indeed in cooking his meals and cleaning his house.[5] (Dalla Costa 1971). Also included in the worker's reproduction are his leisure activities. Moreover, reproductive consumption evidently includes not only the consumption of goods which increase the worker's physical, intellectual, and emotional strength, such as food, lodging, healthcare, educational resources, and various types of games; but also the consumption of goods for psychological reasons which are actually detrimental to health or intellect, such as cigarettes and propaganda. It includes the engaging in activities which in themselves are free, such as sex and face-to-face conversation; in those which are not quite free, such as walking; and indeed in those which mainly involve giving money away in exchange for illusions, such as most types of betting. It is rapidly apparent that the reproduction of the worker is a relation replete with its own internal divisions and contradictions.[6]

It is, however, the class contradiction implicit in the nature of capitalism which determines the contradiction which is most fundamental in the social relation defined as the reproduction of labour-power. Indeed in this area the underlying class contradiction appears perhaps even more starkly than it does in the form of the contradiction between necessary and surplus labour-time. It is as follows. From the point of view of the workers the salient characteristic of their reproduction is *enjoyment*. In other words, it is the fulfilment of needs whose importance must necessarily be determined subjectively.[7] (Lebowitz 1992, pp.125-33). But from the point of view of social capital the salient characteristic of the workers' reproduction is its *cost*.

Certainly, for the workers, enjoyment is not wholly reducible to the consumption of goods which have come to the end of their circulation on the value cycle, or even to the consumption of goods *tout court*. But since virtually all activities outside the workplace are mediated through resources which take a commodity form, we are quite justified in stating that the level of assertion of workers' needs is manifested in the size of the wage. For the controllers of capital, meanwhile, the wage bill appears as a necessary evil in relation to the surplus value extracted from the workers. Once the worker's income or wage is understood as the ticket to the permitted enjoyment of resources, the antagonism between needs and surplus value becomes extremely clear in all its profundity.

Once the term 'wage' is defined according to this antagonism, though — that is, in relation to the labour-power cycle and the underlying political economy of capitalism — then it must denote more than just the pay-packet received from the employer. Thus many of the resources which go to reproduce the worker are in fact paid for by State authorities, either centrally or locally. For example, in a number of countries workers are allowed access to various limited types of healthcare regardless of how much they have contributed individually to insurance schemes. And children are given some kind of schooling, and thereby prepared for entry into wage-labour, even if their parents have been unemployed for many years. There are all sorts of resources which working class people are permitted to consume in the course of their reproduction which they do not pay for out of their salaries according to the quantity they consume: these often include certain inferior kinds of healthcare, accommodation, schooling, library services, refuse collection, recreational facilities, and sometimes entertainment and contraceptives. As long as these resources are consumed as part of their reproduction, from the workers' point of view they go to meeting their needs; from capital's point of view, on the other hand, they are a cost which goes to building up the workers' capacity, or their children's future capacity,[8] to carry out surplus labour and thereby produce surplus value. The lack of congruence between the two viewpoints is determined by the fundamental conflict of class interests, and can only reinforce the theoretical position that the wage includes the 'social' wage as well as the individual wage.

Taxes are evidently raised from everyone, or almost everyone, to pay for these resources, but this should not be allowed to obscure the fact that no accounting system designed and administered by State bureaucrats can alter the nature of the underlying relationship. These resources are produced by the workers, and they are consumed by the workers in a contradictory way that both fulfils needs and regenerates their capacity to be exploited. In other words, the consumption of such resources is a part of the necessary-labour-to-wage-goods cycle which defines the circulation of labour-power. It cannot but be included within the "small-scale circulation" which Marx defines as that part of the capital circulation process involving the payment of wages and their recoupment in return for wage goods. (1939, pp.673-68).

The 'unity' of the capitalist production process, according to which necessary labour is permitted to be expended solely on the basis that surplus labour is also expended, therefore corresponds to a fundamental contradiction in the lives of the workers. This contradiction sets production, the conditions of which are completely alienated from them, opposite labour-power reproduction, the conditions of which are not. Capitalist exploitation thus carries antagonism to a very profound level.

Control Over Capital and Labour-Power

Given the capitalist necessity of controlling the extraction and accumulation of surplus value, it follows that a degree of capitalist control must be exercised not only over the circuit of capital, but also over both moments of the circuit of labour-power.

Control over the circulation of capital (M-C-M´) in general — that is, not simply the 'small-scale circulation' of necessary labour and wage goods — was defined in Chapter 3 as the specifically capitalist function of money. At this overall level, money's function can be described as the movement of capital in and out of production. It is money which permits and mediates control over this movement on a 'generalised' foundation. On the 'investment side' money is thus the means for assessing the potential profitability of decisions concerning the creation, expansion, or continuation of specific productive enterprises; and at the same time it is the generally accepted means of implementing such decisions. On the 'sale side,' it is the means by which commodities are circulated from one controller to another until eventually they reach the 'end-user' or consumer; and it is also the generally accepted means of assessing the actual profitability of the original investment decisions.

Considered at this level, capitalist control is not immune from class contradictions. However, given that the class contradictions of such control have yet to be considered in the context of the bureaucratic form of money which operated in the USSR, and given that bureaucratic money has been identified as the key distinguishing characteristic of Soviet capitalism, little more can be added until that form is considered in specific context below. In short, since the analysis given in Chapter 3 involves a contribution to the overall critique of capitalist money, it would be methodologically wrong to theorise the general class contradictions of money without considering the operation of class contradictions in the USSR.

Control over the moments of the labour-power cycle, for its part, can be broken down into control over production and control over the reproduction of labour-power.

Capitalist control over production involves, of course, control over a certain kind of investment, namely investment in labour-power. It can also be viewed as the investment of labour-power which has already been bought. But since labour-power is a special kind of productive force (and commodity), being a human ability rather than a property of things or a type of thing, capital's control over it involves specific aspects which lead us closer to the essence of the capitalist class relation. First, people dispossessed of the means of production must be controlled in such a way that they are made to alienate their labour-power. In other words, they must be made to make themselves available for exploitation, for work in return for a wage. This is not especially difficult, once they have been uprooted from subsistence production, and as long as the armed defence of the means of production is functioning properly. Second, capital must have some degree of control over where workers work: namely, over their mobility. This too is related to the function of money. Third, workers must be made to work in a manner conducive to capital's needs. In other words, they must be controlled once they are actually at work. This does not necessarily mean that they have to obey all orders handed down to them, immediately and without question, according to both letter and spirit; but it does require the imposition of limits on their freedom to behave as they would wish, especially when this freedom might be used collectively and consciously. And fourth, they must be made to engage in surplus labour. In other words, they must be made to work long enough to produce surplus value.

The second area of capitalist control to concern the working class in direct fashion is the control over workers' reproduction. From capital's point of view this appears as a special kind of control over sale: namely, the control over the sale of wage goods to the working class. In short, it corresponds to a degree of control over working class consumption. This need not, of course, take the form of a precisely differentiated control over exactly what the workers consume. But it must be such as to allow the reproduction of adequate numbers of workers, and of workers who are sufficiently fit, trained, and otherwise prepared for capital's purpose of the production of a surplus. Controllers must also ensure that resources are directed to this end first and foremost.

One aspect of this control is straightforward and simple, involving the enforcement of the rule by which workers can only take things from shops in return for money: that is, for wages. Clearly this specific form of the law of private property — or 'privilege,' from the Latin *privus*, private, and *lex*, *legis*, a law — requires the availability of force. Another aspect concerns the administration of the social wage in all its forms. A bureaucrat in an environmental ministry, for example, insofar as he sets standards for 'acceptable' levels of pollution, exercises control over working class reproduction; and so does a health official charged with deciding on the limited delivery of medical services. The same can also be said about a doctor with the power to make decisions affecting a patient's physical well-being — or, more to the point from capital's point of view, decisions which affect a patient's ability to work and the length of time for which he will remain able to work; a 'policymaker' in the area of official 'education,' who organises access to such-and-such resources on condition that a worker's child is exposed to such-and-such capitalist indoctrination; and indeed any official, in health, 'education,' housing, social work, or elsewhere, who exercises significant influence in determining the restricted and 'acceptable' distribution of resources among the working class.[9] In effect, control over the distribution of the social wage is control over the 'sale' of social wage goods, and force is available in this area too to prevent unsanctioned access. Taken as a whole, capitalist control over the means of labour-power reproduction, whether delivered in return for money taken from the individual pay-packet or as part of a 'social' budget, is simply the control over the amount and type of resources that working class people are allowed to consume.

In both areas of control over labour-power, capital thus exerts a degree of power over the working class: on one hand, by controlling labour, or the 'consumption' of labour-power; on the other, by setting wages, both individual and social, thereby controlling the regeneration or 'production' of labour-power. Insofar as capital controls labour-power for a single end, namely capital expansion, we must again notice the 'unity' of the relation.

But although the basis of wage-labour is capital's drive to accumulate, the contradiction between surplus value and human need is ineradicably present at each moment of the labour-power circuit. On one side, capital's drive to accumulate is 'personified' by its controllers. (Marx 1867, pp.739-40). On the other, human need, a social category opposed to capital, is itself 'personified' in a generalised way by those who, dispossessed absolutely of the means of production, stand opposed to the imperatives of capitalist control. It is this opposition which takes the form of class struggle. Working class people not only resist capitalist control of production; but at the same time, by exerting pressure for wages, both individual and social, to be higher than capital would otherwise set them, they also resist capitalist control over the reproduction of labour-power.

Workers' Power Versus Capitalist Growth

In Chapter 3 we described how money and the commodity, once capitalism became dominant, took on specifically capitalist forms which are best understood in terms of the generalisation of exchange and the establishment of a growth drive as the basis of production. It is now necessary to return to these latter two categories in order to anchor the points made so far.

Regarding the activity which produces capital, namely the specifically capitalist form of labour, we introduced two terms in particular. The first was 'wage-labour,' used to denote the expenditure of labour-power which is alienated by being sold: or, in other words, the 'consumption' of labour-power bought and sold for a wage. The second was 'abstract labour,' introduced as a way of focusing upon the same form of labour from another angle: namely, with reference to socialisation not by means of the power of the associated producers, but rather by means of the generalised exchange of products. It will be noticed that in both cases the consideration concerns *exchange*: that is, first, of the ability to labour, hence 'wage-labour'; and second, of the products of labour, hence 'abstract labour.' In terms of the nature of capitalism, value-producing labour was not discussed in specific relation to the category of capitalist *growth*.

If neither money nor the commodity necessarily contradicts either exchange or growth, it should be clear that wage-labour is different. Since, of course, the controllers of capital only employ labour with the intention of making an overall profit, we know that it too is based on growth. But it is in the nature of the wage relation that it necessarily introduces a tension into the actual achievement of growth. This is because successful growth, defined as the reinvestment of surplus value, is necessarily conditioned by the size of surplus produced. That size, in turn, stands in opposition to the size of the wage; and the size of the wage is determined by class struggle.[10] Consequently, whereas the proletarian class struggle does not, outside of a revolutionary crisis, affect the predominance of the category of exchange, it does tend to pull down the rate of capitalist growth. The existence of such a tendency is indeed intrinsic to the entire capitalist mode of production.

Dynamic Capitalist Control Versus Working Class Struggle

But of course in capitalism growth does occur. To consider the dynamic of the class relation — between control and resistance, between capital and need — it is now necessary to introduce further concepts. Particular attention must be paid to capital's ability to accumulate and develop the productive forces without either totalising or losing its control over labour. What must be discussed is not simply the relationship between wages and surplus value, but rather the movement of that relationship in the context of capitalist growth.

This is best grasped initially as the movement of the relationship between necessary labour and surplus labour. (Marx 1867, chaps. 12-17). If the working day is represented by the line from A to C,

$$A\text{———————}B\text{———}C$$

where AB represents necessary labour-time and BC surplus labour-time, the issue is thus what happens to AB and BC over time.

Capital has three ways of changing this relationship. The first is simply to make the workers work at the same pace, for the same wages, but for *more hours*. All of the extra time worked will then be surplus labour. This can be represented graphically by a lengthening of the line BC as point C moves to the right and points A and B remain fixed. The second is to raise *productivity*, leaving the length of the production cycle, the amount of wages, and the length of the working day fixed. Through introducing changes in equipment and technology, the controllers of capital thereby raise the rate of surplus-value, or s/v. From a working class point of view this ratio is known as the rate of exploitation. Point B moves to the left; and, since other things are assumed to be equal, A and C stay put. Particularly important to this method are changes in the wage goods sector, since any decrease in necessary labour there will lower the value of labour-power, and hence the proportion of necessary labour, throughout the economy. The third way is to increase the throughput of items produced and consumed: in other words, to raise the overall rate of 'turnover.' For the workers this appears as an increase in the pace of work. In theoretical terms this can be distinguished from a change either in the number of hours worked or in the material means of production. It is as if capital somehow forces more time into less. Since the daily wage is assumed to remain fixed, this too can be seen as shifting point B to the left; but is said to represent an increase not in labour productivity but rather in labour *intensity*.[11]

According to the definitions given in Chapter 6, the first method relies on the production of absolute surplus value, while the second and third rely on the production of relative surplus value. It will also be noticed that the first method is of limited effectiveness when used alone as a basis for accumulation, since it does not make a necessity of the 'revolutionisation' of the means of production in the interests of capital. Thus although, for example, the limitation of the working day was bitterly opposed by British industrial capitalists throughout the first half of the 19th century — and undoubtedly marked a victory for working class struggle — its generalisation actually assisted in the institutionalisation of the capitalist drive for 'intensive' development based on the extraction of relative surplus value.[12] Marx describes this institutionalisation, identical to the move to the real subsumption of labour, as marking the 'adequate realisation' of capitalism's inherent tendency to produce "as much surplus value as possible." (Marx 1933, p.1037).

For their part, the second and third methods are often employed concurrently, as mechanisation and computerisation, for example, tend to imply. Nonetheless, it is instructive to distinguish between them for critical purposes.

Productivity

A rise in productivity amounts to a reduction in the proportion of the working day worked as necessary labour. (Marx 1867, pp.429-38). If no workers are laid off this involves, ceteris *paribus*, an increase both in the number of physical units produced and in the quantity produced per man-hour. (See Kay 1976 and 1979a, pp.72-78). Moreover, since on the given assumptions there is a rise in surplus labour-time, there must also be an increase in the rate of surplus value. In relation to such a straightforward example of the extraction of relative surplus value, it is clear that the workers' struggle for higher wages constitutes a counteractive force.

A further important point to be made in regard to productivity is that since wages and labour intensity are held fixed, one enterprise on its own is unlikely to experience a growth in productivity of substantial proportions (unless it successfully monopolises the use of an advance in technology). This is because on these assumptions a sizeable reduction in necessary labour-time can only result from a reduction of the labour-time content of wage goods in general.

But it is precisely by lowering the overall value of labour-power — that is, the number of hours of labour spent on producing wage goods — that productivity growth creates a certain leeway in which wages can rise at the same time as the rate of surplus value. A hypothetical example will illustrate the point. Thus let us assume that the initial rate of surplus value is 60% and the length of the working day is fixed at 8 hours. A growth of productivity by 67% will then cause a reduction in necessary labour-time from 5 hours to 3 hours. In itself, this represents a growth in the rate of surplus value from 3/5 to 5/3: that is, from 60% to 167%. If the workers are now able to force a wage-rise of, say, 33%, the time spent on necessary labour will increase from 3 hours to 4 hours. The rate of surplus value will thus fall back to 4/4, or 100%, but it will still be higher than the 60% at which it stood originally. Overall, necessary labour-time will also have fallen, namely from 5 hours to 4 hours. But the rate of its fall will be lower than the growth in its productivity: or in other words, lower than the growth in the quantity of goods which a single hour of it can produce. Hence the quantity of goods consumed by the workers will rise, even if the value of the wage has fallen. And, to take one last but highly significant index, the ratio between the quantity of goods consumed and the total time worked, or the 'value of labour,' will also have risen.

By raising the rate of exploitation in opposition to the workers' struggle, productivity growth thus creates the potential for capital to make concessions to that struggle even as the rate of surplus value rises.

Labour Intensity

The third method, that of labour intensification, involves an increase in the pace of work. (Kay 1975, pp.157-67, 1976, and 1979a, pp.74-78). This can be said to involve the expenditure of more labour by the same number of workers in a given time period. There is, of course, a theoretical problem with the ascription of meaning to the term 'more labour' in this context, given that value is defined upon the basis of labour-time. But nonetheless it would seem logical to suggest that given identical enterprises, more value will be produced in one subject to speed-up than in one where the pace of work remains constant. *Ceteris paribus*, this too brings an increase in the quantity of output, but in this case one which is based on an acceleration of turnover. As before, wages are assumed to be constant in a given period, but the number of 'projects' or production cycles which occur in that period is increased; and it is this which leads to a rise in the rate of surplus value.[13]

For his part, Marx considers the category of labour intensification only briefly, and in the relevant pages of *Capital* he does not discuss it in detail at the level of the overall social product. (1867, pp.533-43 and 660-62, and 1894, pp.339-42). From the point of view of capital, of course, this omission would seem quite reasonable, since an overall intensification of labour everywhere to the same degree would simply establish a new base-line from which further attempts at intensification would then be launched by industry and area according to the relation of class forces. In many ways the change would appear as indistinguishable from an increase in output brought about by an increase in the length of the working day. (See Marx 1894, p.340). Apparently, then, the change might sensibly be filed together with the extraction of absolute surplus value.

Indeed this would not seem wholly meaningless even from the point of view of the working class. Thus in discussing labour intensification Kay writes with some justification that a worker subject to rapid speed-up can produce a quantity of output in eight hours "as though" he has worked for 16. (1976, p.75; Marx 1867, p.534). It can hardly be disputed that working hard for a short time is in some ways subjectively comparable to working in a more relaxed fashion for longer. On the other hand, it is equally clear that between the intensification of labour and the extension of the working day there are also quite substantial dissimilarities, not least in terms of limits. The basis of these dissimilarities surely requires a theoretical explanation.

On further consideration it becomes apparent that this reference to the 'subjective' comparability of the two methods — a comparability which is by no means unrealistic — is not at all tangential either. In fact it allows us to take the analysis forward. Both in the period of absolute surplus value extraction and in the period of relative surplus value extraction the workers resist the hard work involved in submitting to capital's control over their labour. But whereas in the former the struggle is against a lengthening of the working day and in favour of its reduction, in the latter the workers resist capital's tendency to impose more work by struggling to do less work *per given time*. The opposition of classes thus points up both the comparability and the distinction.

A point must therefore be made which Marx did not make explicit in *Capital*:[14] namely that an increase in the pace of work is limited by the level of workers' resistance to work. And since the fight to do what is subjectively determined to be less work is in necessary *antagonism* with capital's striving to increase labour intensity, it is just as intrinsic a part of the workers' side of the class struggle as is the fight to raise wages.

A growth in labour intensity can also be compared in its effects with a growth in productivity. On one hand, then, it is different, since in itself it

> does not affect the mass of use-values produced nor their value — it merely reduces the time of production. If labour is intensified threefold, for example, exactly the same amount of labour produces exactly the same amount of commodities embodying exactly the same amount of value; only the period of production is reduced to one-third. (Kay 1976, p.60)

On the other hand, it is similar. Thus, given that in this example capital can now extract surplus value from three production cycles in the time it used to take to extract it from one, it would seem quite straightforward that it can now 'afford' to concede higher wages (per period) in much the same way as it can after raising productivity.

Once again it is useful to look at a hypothetical example. As before, let us take the initial rate of surplus value to be 60% and the length of the working day to be 8 hours. A growth in labour intensity of 56% will thus determine conditions which are "as if" the workers are working for 12.5 hours. The analysis can now proceed in two different ways. The first relies on the assumption that the figures apply to a single enterprise. Since intensification will then be of minimal effect on socially necessary labour-time averaged out at the level of the whole economy, it would seem reasonable to retain as a value-stick the productiveness of an hour of labour-time prior to the change. In these terms the working day may have effectively increased, but necessary labour-time stands as if unchanged at 5 hours. The rate of surplus value has thus gone up to 150%. An enterprise wage-rise of 25%, corresponding to an increase in necessary labour-time to 6.25 hours, will then cause it to fall back, but only to 100%, at which level it will still be 40% higher than it was at the outset. Although this rate is the same as the one achieved in the example of productivity growth, the quantity of goods the workers consume will now have fallen relative to the 12.5 hours they are thought of as working.

In the second part of the analysis we assume that the intensification of labour occurs throughout the economy. At this level, it is apparent that we must now use as our value-stick an hour of labour-time after the change has occurred. And this means that the final figures for necessary and surplus labour need to be adjusted accordingly. Since the working day has not really risen to 12.5 hours but is still 8 hours, it would now appear to be split between 4 hours of necessary labour and 4 hours of surplus labour, which would be a similar result to the one reached in connection with a rise in productivity.

Labour intensification is not, however, such a simple matter, as is clear from the fact that we must now reconsider our implicit assumption that the length of a production cycle is a single working day. In the consideration of labour intensification in a single enterprise such a simplification was acceptable, since the reproduction both of the means of production and of the workers was assumed to be dependent upon the consumption of goods produced elsewhere in the economy in enterprises which were not themselves subject to speed-up. But it would actually be self-contradictory to retain this assumption in any consideration of speed-up at the level of the whole economy. The idea that workers work "as if" for more hours than they really do will still retain its usefulness as a reminder of the real subjective sense in which labour intensification necessarily leads to a fall in the 'value of labour.' Indeed a change throughout the economy is only possible as the summation — in fact, the integration — of numerous changes within specific enterprises. But in terms of the value of labour-power it cannot be retained.

The analysis must now centre upon the increased pace of *turnover*; or, from capital's point of view, the difference between the rate of surplus value per project and the rate per unit time. This has been studied in profound fashion by Kay. (1976, 1979a). In particular he focuses on the distinction between 'absolute turnover,' or the overall turnover of capital both constant and variable; and 'relative turnover,' or the turnover of variable capital relative to that of constant capital. From a resolutely classist point of view he thus shows that one of the main aspects of the increase in absolute turnover is the increasing "colonisation of time by capital." Under this heading he counts not only capital's striving to control the production process with ever finer precision; but also the phenomenon of "accelerated depreciation": the "foreshortening of the life of products, whether due to physical reasons or the dictates of fashion," and the general fall in the quality and durability of goods made available to the working class. (1979a, p.78-85; see also Kay 1975, pp.165-67 and Packard 1961). Kay notes in particular the great significance of the car; and how, in relation to this highly important wage good, "superficial changes and accelerated depreciation have been developed into a fine art." (1975, p.166).

If the wage per project stays constant as the rate of absolute turnover increases, then evidently both the wage and the rate of surplus value will rise per unit time. Once again, the rise in the latter will allow scope for a rise in the former. Moreover, the growth of the working class 'market,' as long as it is kept within limits, can actually be used as a support for growth in intensity and productivity: and this in fact was the basis of Fordism and indeed Keynesianism. As was shown in advanced western countries after 1968, however, the antagonism over the wage is by no means negated.[15] (Kay 1975, pp.167-83; see also Armstrong, Glyn, and Harrison 1984, p.260). There is no special reason why the wage per project should remain constant, and the struggle over its determination does not lose its basis in irreconcilable class antagonism.

In the case of relative turnover, Kay stresses that "everything hinges on the distinction between capital *advanced* and capital *employed*." The main benefit which capital draws from this distinction is the ability to reinvest repeatedly what is effectively the same variable capital during the lifetime of a single investment in (fixed) means of production.[16] (1976, pp.63-66). In the terms of our example, then, capital can now be considered to fit into a single day an additional 56% of the 'working day' originally identified with a single production project. This does not mean that an office worker who has to punch more keystrokes per hour, for example, thereby acquires a need for proportionately more food. But the fact that this is a boon for capital is precisely the point. What it means is that the initial variable capital will circulate 1.56 times per day rather than only a single time per day. (It is not relevant here that no individual enterprise will actually achieve such a rapid turnover, since the period of consideration could just as well be six months or a year.) Meanwhile the constant capital will only be consumed once. *Ceteris paribus*, this will raise the annual rate of surplus value.

There are various implications. For capital the key relationship is now that which exists between the rate of relative turnover and the rise in the 'organic composition of production' itself defined as the ratio of constant capital to variable capital advanced. As growing productivity and intensity cause this ratio to rise (Marx 1867, pp.772-74), increasing relative turnover determines a relative fall in the amount of constant capital embodied in each commodity relative to the variable capital employed during its production. This ratio has been termed the 'organic composition of the commodity.' Kay has also shown how within production a main result of increasing relative turnover is a fall in current employment, or the number of workers employed at a moment in time, relative to long-term employment, or the number of worker-hours employed during the lifespan of the fixed capital with which they work.[17] And on an overall level, we see that even as workers are faced with ever greater quantities of objectified labour at the workplace, the commodities circulating in the sphere of reproduction now contain increasing relative quantities of labour.[18] (1976, pp.62-69).

Kay does not discuss working class resistance at length, but he certainly recognises that the capitalist development of turnover involves the development of the opposition of class interests. And, as Negri has stressed with reference to

EXTRACTION OF SURPLUS VALUE	*Capitalist Strategy*	*Tendency of Working Class Struggle*
ABSOLUTE	Longer Hours	Shorter Hours
RELATIVE	Higher Productivity	Higher Wages
	Greater Labour Intensity	Higher Wages, Less Work

Figure 7.3 Class Struggle: Some Concepts

capital's 'real subsumption of society,' it must always be the movement of this opposition which provides the background to the critique. (1979, pp.112-18). Thus the labour intensification involved in absolute turnover is resisted by means of the fight for slacker work; whereas relative turnover, which in terms of the relationship between v and s effectively brings together the categories of labour intensification and productivity growth, is subject in addition to pressure from the struggle for higher wages. Even the effects of any unemployment caused by increasing relative turnover can be resisted by the struggle to defend the social wage.

To conclude: two points are clear. First, as a struggle which is antagonistically both rigid and autonomous, working class struggle does not undergo a fundamental change in its nature under conditions of advanced capitalist development. As capital extends its colonisation of time throughout society[19] — that is, in both production and reproduction — the struggle of the workers for less work and more wages necessarily continues to undermine that domination. (See Figure 7.3). Indeed, more than this, the 'density of contact' between the contending forces increases.

Second, whereas the workers' struggle for *higher wages*, although oppositional to capital, can gain limited concessions within contexts both of growing productivity and of labour intensification, the struggle for *less work* cannot gain concessions on the basis of any similar 'deal.' In other words, the imposition of more work and faster turnover does create space for raising real wages, but does not in itself create space for concessions to the struggle for less work. Since it is closely bound up with the increasing capitalist domination of time, it does, of course, involve the advance of the capitalist side of the struggle; but since it is based upon the falling 'value of labour,' it meets resistance which, however mild or intense in effect, is intrinsically less recuperable.

THE CLASS STRUGGLE UNDER SOVIET CAPITALISM

Given that the mode of production in the USSR was capitalist (see Chapter 3), it follows that there must have been a struggle between the working class and the interests of capital. The remaining task is thus to consider some of the forms which that struggle took, in the specific context of the bureaucratic capitalist relations in that country. A detailed historical study would, of course, involve the consideration of all the various developments in government policy, economic management, and workers' resistance, over the entire Soviet period: that is, during two periods of wartime, two subsequent periods of limited liberalisation (NEP and de-Stalinisation), and during what compared with the rapidity of collectivisation and the industrial 'Great Leap Forward' have been relatively protracted periods of stagnation and crisis. These topics cannot be covered exhaustively in the present context. Within a structure roughly similar to that of the previous section, however, we now look at the struggle between capital and the working class in the USSR, identifying the areas in which it occurred and underlining the broad forms of its political-economic significance.

Surplus Value Versus the Wage

In order to understand the relationship between surplus value and the wage in the USSR it is necessary to identify the circuits of capital and labour-power in the specific Soviet context. In other words, there is a need to point to the class contradiction in investment, sale, wage-labour, and the regeneration of labour-power. After briefly doing this, we shall then look at the control over these circuits in specific relation to bureaucratic money and the Soviet forms of control over labour.

The Capital Circuit

The 'investment moment' of the Soviet capital circuit involves the ploughing of bureaucratic/blat money into production projects. Thus a capitalist interest, whether an individual bureaucrat or a bureaucratic body, is said to 'invest' bureaucratic clout. In the case of an enterprise director who exercises direct control over an enterprise, this will be done directly, in terms of specific directives concerning the use of the means of production under his control. In the case of an official in an industrial ministry, Gosplan, or a CPSU committee or secretariat, who holds control within a complex bureaucratic web, it will be done indirectly through that web itself.

In Chapter 3 it was argued on the basis of the primacy of the categories of exchange and growth that this bureaucratic clout functions as capital. It follows immediately from this, given the basing of the category of capital on that of value, that this capital is divided between investment in means of production and investment in labour-power. And given simply the fact of capitalist exploitation, it also follows that workers produce surplus value in excess of their own consumption and that of their dependants.

Certainly, in view of the largely nominal or passive role of the rouble in the producer goods sector, it is an even more striking fact in the USSR than it is in western countries that one cannot numerically quantify the ratio between surplus value and the wage. But this does not do any damage to a theory of the foundation of the categories of value and surplus value upon the category of an abstract form of labour. At this level the class antagonism in the USSR is straightforwardly that of capitalism as described above.

The moment of the capital circuit constituted by sale — the receipt or 'realisation' of bureaucratic/*blat* money in return for a product — is thus riven by class division. Part of the social product goes to the reproduction of the constant capital embodied within it; part is consumed by proletarians and goes to reproduce labour-power; and part goes to provide both for the consumption of the exploiters and for the accumulation fund. The emphasis given to accumulation in Soviet economic policy has already been noted. Of course ultimately it will be bureaucratic considerations which determine whether or not a project has been completed successfully, and if so, then to what degree. But these are precisely among the functions of capitalist money. And in the USSR as everywhere else where capitalist conditions of production prevail, the accumulation of surplus value is necessarily opposed by the struggle of the proletariat for its own expanded reproduction.

The Labour-Power Circuit

In the production process it is abundantly clear that production as a whole is carried out not in the interests of the workers but rather in the interests of those who exploit the workers. Those with the power to determine the construction or expansion of enterprises, their product range, and what is to happen to their output, are evidently not those who work in them. The people who manage enterprises, run Gosplan, occupy executive office in the ministries, or sit on the Politburo, do not themselves produce.

Meanwhile the workers do, of course, consume a portion of the total social product. Given the generalised exchange in which mediation by bureaucracy and *blat* plays a very large part, there is no need to revise the concepts of socially-averaged necessary labour-time and its counterpart, surplus labour-time. One portion of the working day goes to produce wage goods; the other to produce surplus value. Theoretically a ratio must be involved even if empirically its numerical value cannot be discovered. And this ratio must be the result of class struggle.

Nor does the second moment of the labour-power circuit, namely labour-power regeneration or reproduction, call for any revision of the overall theory. The worker is given a ticket to the permitted enjoyment of resources; and to the exploiters this ticket is a cost. Part of the ticket takes the form of roubles in the pay-packet, and another part takes the form of rights to use 'social' resources. The fact that in the USSR the line between these two parts of the ticket is often very blurred is not without importance; but it should not be allowed to detract from the fact that the ticket as a whole corresponds both to the level of fulfilment of the workers' needs and to the size of the labour *costs* incurred by the controllers of capital.

Control over Capital and Labour-Power

Control over the Capital Circuit   Since control over the investment cycle is the main function of capitalist money — indeed its defining function — the statement that throughout this part of its cycle money is principally bureaucratic is identical in meaning to the statement that control over the Soviet investment cycle takes on specific bureaucratic characteristics. And once the moment of investment (as distinguished from sale) is understood as the taking of implementable decisions concerning the instigation or enlargement of production projects, its control by bureaucratic means appears as a familiar feature of the Soviet economic system.

In Soviet enterprises the funds for 'capital investment' (*kapital´nye vlozheniia*) — that is, the investment of capital in the material means of production — are formally drawn from two main sources. These are the State budget, the implementation of which is the responsibility of the industrial ministries; and the enterprise's own funds, especially those labelled 'retained profits' and 'amortisation.' (See Nove 1980b, p.246). Whereas in the first case the enterprises receive the go-ahead for production projects directly from the ministerial authorities, in the case of investment monies drawn from within the enterprises the usual reality is that they are simply allowed to keep funds earmarked for investment purposes in the central 'plan.' (See Lane 1985a, pp.21-22). This does not, however, mean that the enterprise managers are powerless in matters of investment and are simply pawns of the ministries and 'planning authorities.' Rather, it means that the power that they do have is to a great extent exercised by *blat* and by bureaucratic means in the course of the processes of 'plan' formulation and revision. (See above, Chapter 3).

Control over investment is, of course, control over capital and over the means of production in the form of capital. It is not itself shared out between exploiters and workers. *Within* the exploiting sections of the population, however, the bureaucratic reward system does reinforce a major division between enterprise managers and what for the sake of simplicity can be termed the central bureaucratic elite in industrial ministries, Gosplan, and the central organs of Party and government. It is not especially important whether or not these two social groups are referred to as separate classes or as two parts of the same class. What is important is the highly apparent fact that some controllers of investment (enterprise managers) are more directly confronted by the workers than others (the central elite). This division within the ruling class thus relates in quite a clear fashion to the overall class opposition between the workers and capital.[20]

How it does so has been discussed in detail by Filtzer, even if he himself denies the capitalist nature of the mode of production and remains theoretically restricted by 'Ticktinist' exceptionalism. (1986, pp.257-61). With empirical reference to both the pre-war Stalin period and the Khrushchev period he has shown that it was in the nature of the Soviet system for enterprise managers to make concessions to workers in opposition to the objectives and interests of the central elite. (1986 and 1992b; on the Brezhnev period, see Arnot 1988; on the Gorbachev period see Filtzer 1991 and 1992a). In particular he has shown how from the 1930s onwards, not being subject to the disciplinary weapon of unemployment, the workers appropriated

> considerable control over the individual labour process, most notably their work speed, how they organized their work, and the quality of the products they produced or the operations they performed.

Managers, meanwhile, who were

> under their own pressures to meet production targets under near chaotic conditions [*the context is that of the 1928-41 period*—NCF], had little choice but to accommodate. Managerial concessions to workers were of two types. First were those to do with

violations of labour discipline. This was a simple function of supply and demand: workers were scarce and managers could not afford to fire workers who committed grave violations of labour discipline regulations. As the regime imposed more stringent penalties for absenteeism, lateness, alcoholism, and insubordination, managers found themselves having to take a more active role in insulating workers from these sanctions. The second type of concessions was more complex and had a more direct bearing on the relations of production within the Soviet enterprise, as managers increasingly had to accept the workers' partial control over the work process. Managers needed not only to hold on to their workforces, but to achieve some basic degree of co-operation in order to minimize the disruptions to production endemic in the Stalinist system. They therefore came to tolerate workers' substantial control over how they used their work time, did little to combat the persistence of irrational and inefficient forms of work organization, accepted relatively high levels of defective or poor quality output, and took steps to protect workers' earnings by keeping output norms low and inflating their wages. (1986, p.256)

One does not have to accept the utility of the term 'control' to describe the workers' struggle against the system's need for their engagement in hard work to recognise that what Filtzer is describing is precisely the negative effect of workers' power on the efficiency of that system.[21]

The salient points at the moment are that the disposition of forces was such that concessions had to be made to the workers; and that these concessions were made at enterprise level. Workers' power thus directly affected capitalist control over the investment moment. And this was especially evident in relation to the division between enterprise managers and the central bureaucratic elite.

Output plans, then — that is, targets for successfully realised investment — were lax, at least once they were fully 'revised.' More specifically, they were lax compared to what they would have been if the central bureaucrats had been able to achieve greater prevalence vis-à-vis both the enterprise managers and the workers. From the individual manager's point of view, this was in fact a prime aim, given that he did not want to be penalised for not reaching prescribed targets. To this end resources were concealed and productive capacity was underestimated in negotiations with ministerial and planning bureaucrats.[22] (See for example Berliner 1957, pp.160-81, and Nove 1980b, pp.102-11). But from the workers' point of view lax plans could only mean the obtaining of concessions over production targets and norms, as Filtzer has shown with reference to both the 1930s and the 1950s. (1986, pp.148-49, 222-29 and 229-32; 1992b, pp.111-17). Moreover, in the sphere of distribution (mediated by bureaucratic money) there was chronic inefficiency in terms of both the delivery of supplies and the quality and suitability of goods. (Rutland 1985, pp.120-21, 128-32, and 135-37; see also Bergson 1964, pp.293-97 and Nove 1980b, p.357). This too involved concessions to workers' capitalistically dysfunctional low malleability. In short, the imposition of capitalist control was inefficient to such a degree that enterprise managers ended up acting in opposition to the overall needs of capital and in 'collusion' with those of the workers.

The question now arises of the extent to which the capitalist control over the capital circuit was held down by workers' class struggle, and the extent to which it was held down owing to inefficiencies inherent in the bureaucratic form of money. In other words, to what extent would it have been in the bureaucratic interest of an enterprise manager to push for relatively low plan targets regardless of the power of the workers in his enterprise? Was he not necessarily interested simply in the easiest route to the overall nominal fulfilment upon which his own bonus depended? In the final analysis, could he actually care about the actual physical quantity and quality of what was produced?

In answer to these questions it must be noted that the entire theorisation given so far implies that as a controller of capital the enterprise manager was essentially interested in the expansion of the capital under his control. The productive forces — that is, both the material means of production and labour-power — appear accordingly as a means for the accumulated reproduction of money, which in this context means the reproduction of bureaucratic clout. It is in these terms alone that the controller of capital is interested in production, and it should not be a surprise that the physical characteristics of output appear merely as a subsidiary consideration. At the same time, though, this does not mean that production is unimportant, since the entire capital circuit is essentially a matter of the control over labour which is productive of a particular form of surplus, namely surplus value. (See Marx 1867, pp.742-43). Hence the actual imposition of this control — that is, the control over the operation of the means of production — is crucial.

Two points will make it clear that the interests of Soviet enterprise managers did indeed depend upon the maintenance and expansion of their control over labour. First, once norms and targets had been established, at however low a level, it was indisputably in the interests of the enterprise managers to see that they were met. The reason why they wanted targets to be kept down was precisely so that they could be fulfilled — and indeed over-fulfilled — by the labour of the exploited. In such a context it cannot be said that the opposition of managerial interests to those of the workers was reduced in intensity simply by dint of the making of concessions. Second, it is known that whereas enterprise managers usually wished to keep targets down, they simultaneously struggled to raise the level of inputs: that is, of investment. (Nove 1980b, pp.103-11, Dyker 1983, pp.35-38, and Rutland 1985, pp.132-35).[23] There is thus a contradiction between this interest of the individual manager and the interests of capital as a whole. From the point of view of capital as a whole it is evidently preferable not simply to maximise output but also, while maximising overall investment to this end, to *minimise* the level of investment *per output*: in other words, to maximise the overall ratio of surplus value to investment, known as the profit rate. Enterprise managers, on the other hand, aimed to *maximise* investment per output. But the socialisation of production makes it quite apparent that between the interests of managers and those of overall social capital there is also an identity. Material inputs do not appear out of thin air: they must first be produced. As we have seen, the rate of investment is first of all dependent upon the extraction of adequate quantities of surplus value.[24] And this surplus value is extracted precisely in enterprises.

For Soviet bureaucrats and managers the interplay of the collectivity of interest with the conflict of interest is simply a specific example of the existence of the interests of social capital in an environment of generalised competition.[25] In the simplest of terms: controllers of capital fought among themselves in bureaucratic fashion for the distribution of surplus value and control over the productive forces. And the amount of control available overall was a function of the class struggle against the working class. In a discussion of the problems involved in controlling Soviet capital the question of the distribution of emphasis between the power of the working class and the 'inherent' inefficiency of the bureaucratic form of money is really a non-question, since the concept of the efficiency or inefficiency of that form — or indeed of the market form — is only meaningful with reference to the historical development of the class relation.

Control over the Labour-Power Circuit   The control over the circuit of labour-power has already entered the discussion of the control over the circuit of capital. In this section we describe some of the apparent characteristics of Soviet control over the labour-power circuit in specific relation to the control over labour-power's exertion and reproduction.

In the section above on the control over labour in capitalism in general, this control was described as having four main aspects, and in the Soviet context it is convenient to mention each in turn.

First, then, workers must be available for exploitation. Above all, this means that they must be deprived of access to the 'reserves' which would otherwise allow them the means to live outside of the capitalist mode of production. In Russia there were already several millions of proletarians at the time of the first world war, but the really rapid expansion of their numbers occurred during the programme of rural collectivisation and accelerated urban industrialisation imposed under Stalin. Enormous quantities of workers were made available for capitalist exploitation with unprecedented speed. (See Davies 1980a and

1980b). Soviet figures thus describe how between 1928 and 1932 the number of official proletarians more than doubled, rising from 11 million to 24 million, and how in the same period the number of 'collectivised' rural *households* rose from a mere 400 000 to 15 million. (*Narodnoe Khoziaistvo* 1958, p.494 and 1917-77, p.461). Since *kolkhozniki*, despite being allowed to keep a portion of their own produce, were ultimately proletarians involved in relations of their own specific kind, we can rightly speak of a four-year period in which the proletariat trebled or even quadrupled in size. What is more, the process did not simply involve a massive use of armed force: by means of famine it also led to millions of deaths among the dispossessed. (See for example Dalrymple 1964 and Conquest 1986). The analogy of the accomplishments of this primitive capitalist accumulation with the effects of a policy of war is unavoidable.

Second, it was stated that capital must have a degree of control over workers' mobility. In the USSR the way that this control was exercised was similarly subject to its own specific development. In short, it involved a differing mixture of 'labour conscription' and rouble-based and other incentives in the various different periods.

After capital went on the offensive in production in 1918 (Brinton 1970, S. Smith 1983, Jones 1984), the main means of ensuring that the workers who did not leave the cities worked where they were meant to work were despotic. Labour militarisation was imposed under the political leader of the armed forces, Trotsky; and Sovnarkom issued a decree on 'universal labour service' at the beginning of 1920. (Carr 1952, pp.213-18, and Brinton 1970, p.59). Under NEP the form of control then changed to that of the rouble. Although industrial management within the factories was by no means 'liberalised,' the workers who returned to wage-labour in the cities came voluntarily. Once around 1928 the working class had regained the numbers it had in 1913 (*Narodnoe Khoziaistvo* 1917-77, p.461), there came the Stalinist upheaval. Under Stalin there was considerable use of slave labour, which evidently involved the forced movement of labour, but this tended to be confined to certain extractive industries and the construction of large-scale infrastructure. (Hosking 1985, pp.197-99). In the 1930s the principal factor motivating labour mobility in most of the urban economy remained the role of rouble wages and material incentives. (Filtzer 1986, pp.135-44, Helgeson 1986, pp.146-47). Voluntary labour turnover was really only brought to an end upon the imposition of draconian labour rules in 1940-41. (Filtzer 1986, pp.233-53 and Grancelli, 1988 p.45-46). In response to the German invasion entire industries were then moved East to the Urals, and whole ethnic populations—including Chechens, Crimean Tatars, and Kalmyks — were forcibly resettled. The forced movement of labour continued in massive quantities between 1943 and 1946, and many who had worked in the German camps under the SS were transported to work in Soviet camps under the NKVD.

(Solzhenitsyn 1973, pp.81-86). In the mid-1950s not only was the use of slave labour wound down, but in the rest of the economy the ban on voluntary turnover was removed. From then on, such capitalist control as there was over the movement of labour was mainly effected through the rouble — hence, for example, the higher wages in the far North and parts of Siberia (Fakiolas 1962, p.32 and Brown 1966, pp.42-44) — and through other employment-linked incentives in areas such as housing. (Grancelli 1988, pp.144-50). Organised forms of control, such as graduate placement schemes, Komsomol appeals, and the famous system of *propiski* (residence permits), were comparatively much more limited in scope. (Helgeson 1986, p.147; Oxenstierna 1990, pp.101-19).

Third, capital must have a degree of control over the actual process of work. It is rather simple to demonstrate that it did. Thus not only were workers assigned particular tasks, but they were subject to various punitive measures for violations of discipline. These included the issuing of warnings, the temporary transfer to lower-paid work, the ignoring of their wishes as to the allocation of time off for holidays, and, importantly, dismissal. (See for example Andrle 1976, pp.71-72). That workers could complain to legal authorities and sometimes won (Brown 1966, p.209, M. McAuley 1969, pp.204-48, Andrle 1976, p.72) — or that sometimes they could break rules and avoid dismissal (see Filtzer 1986, p.256, quoted above) — should not detract from the point, which is not that managers had complete control, but simply that they did have some control.

Fourth, workers must work long enough to carry out surplus labour and thus produce surplus value. The easiest way to illustrate the scale on which this took place is to point to the official capital investment rate and the size of the military sector. Whereas the rate of capital investment, measured in roubles, was a feature of every plan, the size of the 'defence' sector, as is well known, was substantial. It is thus evident, given that the basis of the economy was generalised exchange, that workers in general worked for more hours than were necessary to produce for their own consumption. High rates of absenteeism (Arnot 1988, pp.75-76, Connor 1991, pp.171-74) did not remove the basic fact that enterprise management necessarily had a degree of control over the amount of time for which the worker worked.

In regard to the reproduction of labour-power, clearly the resources which workers in the USSR consumed were passed to them on the basis that they had permission to receive them. Either this permission took the form of individually possessed roubles, or else it took the form of various 'social' rights. From capital's point of view, these resources added up to the cost of the workers' reproduction.

In the first instance, the setting of piece-rates, norms, and bonuses, and therefore of wages, was clearly in hands which were not those of the workers. The role of official trade unions and 'production conferences' (Bienstock, Schwarz and Yugow 1944, p.40-46, Andrle 1976, pp. 69-71, Kahan and Ruble 1979, and Ruble 1981) should not be allowed to obscure the fact that in order to understand the nature of the workers' influence on wage-rates it is first necessary to recognise that they themselves did not control them (that is, set them). Nor did they control prices, which were also set by the controllers of the economy. Many goods, of course, such as milk, butter, children's clothing, and housing were formally subsidised (A. McAuley 1979, pp.288-89, and Cook 1993, pp.43-44 and 85-87), but this only reinforces the point that the function of the roubles in a worker's pay-packet was simply to serve as part of her overall reproduction-ticket.[26]

The second part of the wage includes all the resources consumed by the working class which were not given solely in return for workers' roubles per unit consumed. In the above section on capitalism in general these were described as including limited provision for education, health, and various other social services. In the Soviet context it is apparent, however, that the distinction between the individual wage and the social wage was not as clear-cut as might be presumed. At one end of the spectrum of the 'social' wage there were thus the familiar cases of schooling and medical care, the availability of which to proletarians did not generally depend on employment. (Chapman 1963b, pp.129-38). In the middle there were 'social insurance' benefits, the payment of which was sometimes reduced for those employees considered to have a poor work record. (A. McAuley 1979, pp.284). And at the end of the spectrum closest to the individual wage, there were numerous types of benefit which, whilst not freely available to anyone with enough roubles to pay for them, were nonetheless distributed to individuals whose rights were assigned according to their specific position as wage-labourers. (A. McAuley 1979, pp.260-301; see also Grancelli 1988, pp.63-64). The prime example here was, of course, housing. Other resources, paid for directly out of the enterprise's 'social fund,' included holiday accommodation and the provision of crêches. Many of these resources were distributed by enterprise trade union bureaucrats. (Brown 1966, pp.128-35, Ruble 1981, pp.87-89).[27] At the same time there was often considerable variation in the distribution of such 'social services' even within a single large enterprise, and Grancelli has pointed out that "those who find themselves at the 'back of the line' are usually unskilled auxiliary workers." Together with variation according to plan fulfilment, this differentiation can only point up the similarity of this type of 'social' provision to that which was mediated by roubles in the pay-packet. (Grancelli 1988, pp.144-45).

Since the social wage took such a plethora of forms, it is clear that the capitalist control over its setting was distributed among various types of bureaucrat, not only in the health, educational, and industrial ministries, but also in enterprise management and the trade unions.

Workers' Power Versus Capitalist Growth

Given that the interests of the workers lay in their assertion of their own needs in opposition to those of the production and accumulation of surplus value, it is now necessary to identify the main forms of assertion of those needs in resistance to the forms of control described above.

To start at the beginning, it is necessary to note that the massive expansion of the proletariat during the Stalinist 'great leap forward,' considered by itself, stands out as one area in which capital managed to achieve full success. Once resistance to land seizures by the capitalist State was crushed with military force, the scope for living entirely outside of the capitalist system was effectively eradicated.[28] The main consideration must therefore be of forms of proletarian resistance which took place *within* the framework of capitalist domination.

The first of these was worker-led labour mobility, sometimes referred to as voluntary or unplanned labour turnover. As Brown has shown, workers tended to leave their jobs in a way that was dysfunctional for the economic system. The main reasons for such voluntary mobility included poor wages, inadequate accommodation, poor working conditions and work-related benefits, and sometimes the simple desire to return to the worker's parents' home town. (Fakiolas 1962, p.23, Brown 1966, pp.32-39; see also Kahan 1962, p.19, and Grancelli 1988, p.205). The principal dysfunctional effects included the loss to capital of potential work time when workers were between jobs, lower initial productivity once they moved to their new jobs, and the necessary costs of retraining. (Brown 1966, p.34; Romanenkova 1991, p.174). From capital's point of view the provision of enterprise-linked housing and State housing loans tended to a certain extent to ameliorate the problem, but it remained an ever-present reality. (Fakiolas 1962, pp.25-26). Indeed the need to attract and keep hold of workers, especially skilled workers, caused enterprise managers both to raise basic wages (Berliner 1957, pp.170-78,[29] Nove 1980b, pp.207-12, Filtzer 1986, pp.212-22) and to introduce incentives based on the length of continuous employment in one place. (Helgeson 1986, p.150). Worker-led mobility thus led directly to the making of concessions.

At the same time, it was clearly not the case that capital needed to fix labour and to restrict turnover altogether. Rather, there was an inconsistency between the turnover it required and the turnover it faced. (See Standing 1991, p.241). As Fakiolas has shown, this led to the rise of special problems in the 'developing' areas of the far North and Siberia. In this case, what was particularly problematic was the behaviour of "migrant but trained" workers, mainly of urban origin, who were aware of the "relative comforts and facilities in the older urban centres." (1962, p.34). Their migration back and forth *en masse* was not the kind of mobility which capital needed, which on the contrary was a large one-way movement leading to lasting settlement.[30] More generally, Helgeson has shown how the demographic reality of migration, far from being the result of an effective policy of discouraging independent 'job-hopping' while simultaneously using official channels to encourage labour to migrate to developing regions, was rather an effect of "millions moving where they pleased." (1986, pp.146-49; see also Zaslavsky 1982, pp.137-46). From the capitalist point of view, of course, the poor housing and inadequate medical services in the developing areas were not the essential problem: it was the workers' rejection of them that was.[31]

The second main form of resistance was low-quality production. This very well known feature of the Soviet economy has been discussed by Berliner (1957, pp.136-48), Bergson (1964, pp.295-97), Nove (1980b, pp.194, 259, and 357), Hewett (1988, pp.78-86), and others. In sovietological terms this is essentially a problem of the absence of a market and the inadequate role of consumer preferences as an incentive. It is thus effectively assumed that a properly functioning market capitalism would express the 'general interest' of the population and would therefore increase the quality of output. More concretely, the problem is considered to be an effect of excessive administration. In the terms of a fundamental critique, though, the inefficiency of Soviet capitalism's administrative system is only meaningful in terms of the inadequacy of *capital's control over labour*. Thus it stands as the great merit of the *Critique* school to have discussed poor quality in relation to the basic opposition in production. (Ticktin 1973a, 1976, and 1991c; Filtzer 1986, 1992b, Arnot 1988). Even if Ticktin denies the capitalist nature of the production relations, he undoubtedly demonstrates a profound understanding of the methodology of the critique of political economy when he insists that all of the Soviet rulers' problems "go back to labour." (1991c, p.116). Indeed, what else can they go back to? In the terms of a critique of Soviet capitalism, the low-quality production constantly bemoaned by Soviet authorities and sovietologists alike cannot be anything other than a crucial index of the underlying class relation. In short, it is describable as the result of the exertion of labour-power in such a way that production is of a lower quality than the capitalist rulers would have wanted. Essentially this meant that the rates of surplus value production per project and of project turnover per unit time were lower than they would have been had workers worked in greater accordance with the needs of capital: that is, had they resisted the imposition of those needs less.

The clearest evidence for the fact that the rulers were forced to make a 'structural' — that is, lasting — accommodation with the workers' imposition of low-quality production was the large size of the repair sector. Ticktin has described how this became one of the main features of the system, up to the point where more people were employed repairing broken-down or inadequate machinery than actually making it. (1973a, pp.25-28). Given the exertion of labour-power on what in the case of, say, machine-tools or tractors was effectively a drawn-out process of production, the organic composition of production was lower than it would have been otherwise.[32] Thus the investment of capital in the highly labour-intensive industrial repair sector could only work against capital's need to raise the rate of relative turnover too.

The third form of resistance was absenteeism. Although it was in the interests of managers to under-estimate the number of days lost, there can be little doubt that in the USSR 'voluntary absence' from work was widespread. (Standing 1991, pp.247-48). One estimate places the rate of "under-utilisation of workers" for this reason at more than 10%. (Seeger 1981, p.83). A survey quoted by Connor found that only 10% of workers in factories and offices were still at work during the last hour of the working day. (1991, p.173). The causes of absenteeism have variously been listed as drunkenness, the need to queue, and the excessive role of "non-wage benefits" — that is, the enterprise social wage — in the income of the worker; but the main point here can only be that the opposition between the needs of the workers and the needs of capital accumulation appears in an extremely pure fashion in this particular form of resistance. It is, of course, quite possible to be an alcoholic and still turn up on time each day for work, just as workers and their dependants are quite capable of organising queueing collectives where the person actually doing the queueing is not simultaneously supposed to be at the workplace. A profound understanding of absenteeism must begin with the grasping of the fact that by staying away from work workers *chose* to reduce the amount of time for which their labour-power was exploited. They chose to do other things than work for their employer. And the fact that absenteeism, along with drunkenness at the workplace, was one of the commonest reasons for dismissal (Godson 1981, p.117), clearly demonstrates that this choice necessarily involved the rejection of disciplinary constraints. Its prevalence was one of the measures of the independence of working class struggle.

The forms of working class struggle can be summarised in terms of resistance to the specific areas of capitalist control. The first area of such control, the *making available* of workers for capitalist exploitation, or the expansion of the capitalist mode of production, was noted above to have been one of full success, at least when considered on its own. But the same cannot rightly be said of the other areas. The second area, that of *workers' mobility*, was at one time controlled partly by military means, but from the 1950s onwards principally by means of rouble and benefit incentives. As part of their resistance, workers took advantage of the high demand for labour-power to push up wages. Overall, they struggled to impose mobility according to their own needs rather than those of capital. The third form of control was the capitalist control of the *production process*. Being in general the remit of enterprise managers, this was imposed by means of familiar rules concerning the allocation of work and bonuses. Workers, however, took great advantage of the capitalist 'planning' system by forcing concessions at enterprise level concerning wages, norms, and, importantly, the quality of production. In effect, they forced enterprise managers to use their own positions vis-à-vis the central bureaucrats to ensure that accommodation was made to the exercise of workers' power on the shop-floor. Finally, the fourth area, that of the *working day*, was of course controlled by capital; but absenteeism, together with the chronic rate of equipment breakdown resulting from the poor quality of inputs — that is, of the labour which produced those inputs — ensured that workers managed to work for less time than the rulers would have preferred them to.

By resisting capitalist control, and thereby tending to increase the wage as a portion of the social product and to lower the rate of capital accumulation, the workers' struggle necessarily tended to reduce the overall rate of capitalist growth.

Dynamic Capitalist Control Versus Working Class Struggle

But despite the problem of workers' resistance, Soviet capitalism evidently did experience growth. Indeed, as the figures given in Table 7.1 show, growth rates were enormous for much of the Soviet period. What must now be considered is the political-economic form of this growth, and its significance for the working class in terms of labour-time, wages, productivity, and labour intensity. As described above, these are the crucial aspects of the historical class struggle between the working class and capital.

Relative Surplus Value Extraction

The first question to be asked is whether or not the USSR knew the extraction of relative surplus value.[33] Although many of the consumer goods on sale to the working class — cars, television sets, refrigerators, vacuum cleaners, and so on — only became available to proletarians in, say, Britain, once capitalism in that country had entered the period of relative surplus value extraction, in the USSR there were nonetheless a few factors which might conceivably indicate that the same was not true there. Thus it might be recalled that by the time of *glasnost´* in the late 1980s members of the ruling class such as Gorbachev and Aganbegian were referring to the need to take the economy into a period of 'intensive growth' and out of a period where growth was primarily 'extensive.' (Gorbachev 1987, pp.20-21, and Aganbegian 1988, pp.100-09). It would surely be wrong to ignore such serious pronunciations as meaningless. The suggestion might also be made

Table 7.1 Soviet Growth, 1913-90

	1913	1928	1932	1940	1950	1960	1970	1980	1989	1990
Coal[a]/Mt	29	36	64	166	261	510	624	716	740	703
Steel/Mt	4	4	6	18	27	65	116	148	161	154
Electrical Energy/GWh	2	5	14	49	91	292	741	1294	1722	1726
Haulage[b]/Mtkm	126	120	218	494	713	1886	3829	6481	8173	7931
Cars/1000	-	-	-	5	65	139	344	1327	1217	1259
Television Sets/1000	-	-	-	-	37 (1952)	1726	6682	7528	9938	10540
Refrigerators/10^6	-	-	-	4	1	530	4140	5925	6465[c]	6499[c]
Housing Construction/10^6m^2		4 (av.1918-28)	11 (av.1929-41)		40	83	106	105	129	118
Urban Workers and Sovkhozniks/10^6	12.9	11.4	24.2	33.9	40.4	62.0	90.2	112.5	115.4	112.9
Kolkhozniks[d]/10^6	-	0.8	22.5[e]	29.0	27.6	22.3	16.2	13.5	11.9	11.9

Source: Narodnoe Khoziaistvo 1958, pp.242, 299, and 494-95; 1962, pp.202-03 and 501; 1965, p.435; 1917-77, pp.201, 206, 208, 389, 460-61, and 495; 1922-82, p.196, 217, and 402; 1990, pp.6, 100, 397-98, 407, 422-23, 451 and 582; and *Sel'skoe Khoziaistvo* 1971, p.446.

Notes: [a]Coal quality not considered. [b]By all means of transport. [c]Includes freezers. [d]Includes fishing 'collectives.' [e]Figure not published. Estimate based on assumption of 1.5 working kolkhozniks per household, as in 1940. (Ratio calculated from figures in *Nar. Khoz.* 1956, p.128, and *Sel'. Khoz*, 1971, p.446).

that capital did not establish the degree of control over the labour process which would allow it to achieve the 'complete revolutionisation of the technical processes of labour' which Marx saw as essential to the move to relative surplus value extraction. (1867, p.645). Thirdly, it is well known that the slowdown in growth in the 1980s did coincide with the fall to a very low pace of the migration of workers into the towns from the countryside.

On further consideration, though, these factors can hardly be made to stand up in defence of the idea that the country remained enmired in the extraction of absolute surplus value. There can be no doubt that the growth of production was huge.[34] If this were to have occurred simply as a result of absolute surplus value extraction, there would have had to have been a considerable rise in the number of hours worked. But the reality is that neither the facts on the length of the working day, nor those on the quantitative expansion of the proletariat, support such a thesis. The eight-hour day introduced in 1917 (under often severe pressure from workers: see S. Smith 1983, pp.65-68[35]) was reduced to seven hours in 1927,[36] and although it was raised back to eight hours in 1940, it was shortened to seven hours once again in 1956-62. (Brown 1966, pp.270 and 304-05, and Conquest 1967, pp.118-22).[37] Moreover, as the data in Table 7.1 demonstrates, the growth of output in principal sectors between, say 1940 and 1970, was much more rapid than the growth of the proletarian population. Thus whereas the population of urban workers plus *sovkhozniki* grew by 166% — a figure which becomes only 69% if we include *kolkhozniki* — the output of coal, steel, and electrical energy and the figure for total haulage by all means of transport (in tonne-kilometres) grew by 276%, 544%, 1412%, and 675% respectively. The typical working week, meanwhile, contained six eight-hour days in 1940 and five seven-hour days in 1970[38] — a fall of 27%. Taken together, these facts can only mean that Soviet capital did indeed successfully enter the period of relative surplus value extraction. The decline and eventual end of growth cannot therefore be explained solely by the fact that the number of hours worked stopped increasing.[39]

And so the analysis must now focus more specifically upon the growth which relative surplus value extraction actually permitted. In particular we must differentiate in broad terms between productivity growth and labour intensification.

Productivity

On an overall level, a growth in productivity must necessarily depend on a reduction of the amount of labour-time expended on the production of wage goods. The prime example of this in the development of capitalism in any country is, of course, the capitalist revolutionisation of agriculture. This is so for various

Table 7.2 Soviet Agricultural Development, 1913-90

	1913[a]	1928[a]	1940[a]	1950	1960	1970	1980	1989	1990
Sown Area/10⁶ ha	118	113	151	146	203	207	217	210	208
Rural Population/10⁶	131	[b]	131	109 (1951)	108 (1961)	106	98	98	98
Grain Yield/kg.ha⁻¹	690 (ave. 1909-13)	760 (ave. 1924-28)	860	740 (ave. 1946-55)	1020 (ave. 1956-65)	1420 (ave. 1966-75)	1490 (ave. 1976-85)		1730 (ave. 1986-90)

Source: Narodnoe Khoziaistvo 1958, p.491; 1961, p.311; 1967, p.7; 1970, p.27; 1975, p.312; 1922-82, pp.9 and 244; 1989, pp. 420 and 434; 1990, pp.67 and 470-71.

Notes: [a]Post-1945 borders. [b]No reliable figure available (see Lorimer 1946, pp.133-37); official American figure for pre-1939 borders is 123.3 million. (Chapman 1963a, p.271).

reasons. Thus if peasants who previously spent much of their working time in subsistence production are not only to be turned into surplus value producers but also to be made productive of surplus value in increasing amounts, clearly the time that *must* be spent in the countryside producing food for each proletarian must be reduced. (See Marx 1894, p.773). The capitalist development of agriculture, and the associated expropriation and proletarianisation of the vast majority of the peasantry, involves a process of agrarian mechanisation and industrialisation of epochal significance. Without this, there simply cannot be a successful movement into the period of relative surplus value extraction.[40]

In the USSR as in Tudor England, there was a capitalist 'enclosure' of agriculture.[41] Unlike in England, however, in the USSR the development occurred under the aegis of industrial capital, and led very rapidly to the sector's industrially-mediated technical development. There has, as is well known, been some controversy among sovietologists over the precise contribution made by agriculture to industrial capital accumulation during the period of the first Five-Year Plan; but in the present context this matter is not especially significant. (See Millar 1970 and 1974, Nove 1971, and Ellman 1975 and 1989, pp.106-10). What there can be no doubt about is that in these years the size of the industrial proletariat greatly increased owing to the intake of dispossessed peasants. More important are the developments which took place over a longer period.

In the long term, one of the most important indicators is the urbanisation of the Soviet population. Thus as a percentage of the whole, the rural population fell from 82% in 1913 and 84% in 1922 to 67% in 1940 and 34% in 1990. Although it contained the same number of people, 131 million, in 1940 as it did in 1913, it fell back to 108 million in 1960 and has been around 98 million since 1980. Meanwhile the sown area grew from 118 million ha in 1913 to 150 million ha in 1940 to 208 million ha in 1990. (See Table 7.2). Given these figures it is not surprising that under Stalin agriculture underwent considerable mechanisation: a process which was generally accomplished by the time of Khrushchev. One set of figures will illustrate this particularly clearly. In 1932, the use of tractors accounted for 19% of tillage, 20% of sowing, and 10% of harvesting; in 1940, the figures were 62%, 56%, and 46% respectively; and in 1956 they were 98%, 97% and 89%. (*Narodnoe Khoziaistvo* 1958, p.491). The figures for agricultural growth in subsequent decades show that productivity continued to grow under Brezhnev too. In 1990 the rural population was lower than it was in 1960, but the grain yield per hectare had increased substantially even if the sown area had increased only marginally. In general this was due to chemicalisation. (Zh. Medvedev 1987, pp.312-13.). Leaving aside any consideration of the specific problems of Soviet agriculture (see for example Dovring 1980 and Zh. Medvedev 1987, pp.334-60), we see that in this vital wage goods sector, considered in the long term, there was a clear indication that products cheapened

Table 7.3 Per Capita Consumption of Food, Clothing, and Housing, 1913-88

	1913	1928	1932	1945	1950	1958	1968	1978	1988
Meat[a]/kg	29	32	17	15	27	38	48	57	66
Milk[b]/kg	154	17	113	108	145	224	285	321	356
Fabric[c]/m^2	13.4	13.4	12.7	7.5	17.8	26.0	29.5	33.7	38.1
Housing Space (Urban)[d]/m^2	6.3	5.8	4.9	3.9 (1944)	5.0	8.2[e]	10.8[e]	12.9[e]	15.3[e]

Source: meat and milk for 1928-58, and urban housing space for 1928-50, from Chapman (1963a, pp.238-39), who takes figures for meat and milk from official American figures (see p.274); fabric for 1928-58 estimated from per capita output/m (Chapman), converted to consumption/m^2 by multiplication by ratio for 1913 (for 1928 and 1932) and by ratio for 1960 (for 1945, 1950, and 1958). (*Narodnoe Khoziaistvo* 1968, pp.286 and 596); all figures for 1913 and 1968-88, and urban housing space for 1958, from *Nar.Khoz.* (1958, pp.272-73 and 461; 1968, pp.7, 286, 580, and 595-96; 1917-77, pp.7 and 511; 1978, pp.7, 397, and 412-13; 1988, pp.117-18, and 165).

Notes: [a]Includes poultry and lard. [b]Includes dairy products, converted back to kg of milk. [c]Includes fabric made from cotton, wool, linen, silk, and synthetics. [d]Per head of urban population. [e]Official Soviet figures from *Nar.Khoz.* clearly calculated on different basis from those of Chapman, who gives a figure for 1958 of 5.5m^2.

in terms of average socially-necessary labour-time. In value terms, such a development necessarily tended to bring about an overall cheapening of labour-power throughout the economy.[42]

If productivity growth is to be understood in terms of the class relation, then logically the next matter for consideration is the movement of workers' wages. As was explained above, the wage is defined by the quantity of resources consumed by the working class in the course of its reproduction, not simply by dividing the number of roubles in the pay-packet by the price level of goods in the shops.[43] In order to concentrate on the underlying opposition, it is thus best to focus directly on the movement of living-standards.

There can be no doubt that in the long term real wages did rise. (See for example, Chapman 1963b, pp.165-88, H. Smith 1976, pp.74-107, A. McAuley 1979, pp.23-27, Walker 1986, pp.76-78, and Connor 1991, pp.117-18). This is evident in the growth of consumption in four fields in particular: food, clothing, housing, and consumer durables. Thus Chapman has noted how the consumption of meat and milk, for example, fell between 1928 and 1950, but more than made up the gap by 1958. (1963a, pp.238-39). In subsequent decades it continued to rise.[44] Thus the figure for per capita meat consumption in 1988 compared with 1958 had risen by 74% and the corresponding figure for milk by 59%. Similarly, between 1958 and 1988 the consumption of fabric of all kinds rose by 54%. Over the same period, urban per capita housing space, which Chapman gives as lower in 1958 than in 1928 — and indeed lower than the official figure calculable from *Narodnoe Khoziaistvo* for 1913 — officially rose by 87%.[45] (See Table 7.3). A rise in consumption of 'consumer durables' (*potrebitel'nye tovary dlinnogo pol'zovaniia*) is also evident. Thus whereas prior to the second world war the only such good with a widespread distribution was the timepiece, by 1965 there were 24 television receivers, 21 washing-machines, and 11 refrigerators for every 100 families. By 1990 the figures had risen to 107, 75, and 92. (See Table 7.4).

Thus the development of Soviet capitalism, especially after the second world war, allowed productivity growth to coincide with wage growth. In short, there was a 'deal' with the working class of the sort discussed above with reference to capitalist development in general. The length of the working day fell, and wages rose, as productivity and quantities produced increased. Clearly at some point growth came to an end, whether that was in the late 1970s, as Ellman argues (1982), or whether it was as late as 1990. (*Narodnoe Khoziaistvo* 1991, p.7). Given that wages continued to rise as growth declined, the 'deal,' endangered for some time, was eventually called off under Gorbachev. (See for example Cook 1993).

Since, however, the whole basis of the relationship was that productivity and wages would increase simultaneously, this is by no means an explanation of why it was that growth actually came to a halt. Nor can Cook's pointing to the rise of

Table 7.4 Distribution of Consumer Durables Per 100 Families, 1965-90

	1965	1970	1975	1980	1985	1990
Time-pieces	319	411	455	518	530	574
Television Sets	24	51	74	85	97	107
Radios	59	72	79	85	96	96
Refrigerators	11	32	61	86[a]	91[a]	92[a]
Washing Machines	21	52	65	70	70	75
Sewing Machines	52	56	61	65	65	61
Vacuum Cleaners	7	12	18	29	39	48
Cameras	24	27	27	31	34	33
Cars	[b]	2	[b]	10	15	19

Source: *Narodnoe Khoziaistvo* 1968, p.596; 1978, p.413; and 1990, p.142.
Notes: [a]Includes freezers. [b]Figures not available.

'independent' activism in the late 1980s provide an answer. (1993, pp.150-79).
It is not enough to recognise that wages were too high to allow the continuation
of capitalist growth, because it is always true that the level of wages (per project)
contradicts the level of productivity, whatever the level of growth. In the abstract,
given that material living-standards in the USSR were considerably lower than
they were in the advanced West (Connor 1991, pp.125-32), as was productivity,
one might suppose that the dynamic deal could have lasted a lot longer than it did.
The present context is not, of course, a comparative one, but the contrast makes
it clear that in order to proceed it is necessary to look beyond the aspect of the
capitalist growth dynamic defined simply by productivity and wages. It is
now necessary to consider the class relationship in terms of capital's need to
intensify labour.

Labour Intensity

From a working class point of view, labour intensification necessarily takes place
at an enterprise level, involving the doing of what appears to be more work in the
same amount of time. Since this often occurs simultaneously with an increase in
productivity, it is instructive to differentiate clearly between the two processes.
Whereas a rise in productivity, then, involves a change in the means of

production, a rise in intensity involves the acceleration of the production project, of the speed of project 'turnaround.'

The first point to be noted about labour intensity is that it does not lend itself to empirical quantitative analysis and is best discussed qualitatively. In relation to the rate of absolute turnover, then, the qualitative dynamic to be considered is that of the intensification of work, its speeding up, along with the general speed-up of circulation. This has effects both in the sphere of production itself and in the sphere of reproductive consumption. The dynamic of relative turnover, meanwhile, is the acceleration of the rate of investment in labour-power relative to the rate of investment in fixed capital,[46] which causes a divergence between the organic composition of the commodity and the organic composition of production. These areas will now be considered in turn.

Regarding absolute turnover, it is apparent from the above discussion of the control over labour that the level of labour intensity in the USSR, considered statically, was low. Stories such as those of factory workers covering screws with glue and banging them in with hammers are well known, but the point here is that in the producer goods sector such sloppy work necessarily led throughout the economy to two main effects. The first was the chronic rate of equipment breakdown, and the consequent high level of 'unintended stoppages' in production, including because of material shortages. The second was the necessity of a large amount of repair work wherever the equipment was used. The combined effect was not, as might perhaps be superficially inferred, to increase the rate of turnover at the expense of quality; rather it was to reduce the rate of turnover relative to what it would have been if workers had worked more 'conscientiously.'

The next area to look at is that of the ramifications of the turnover rate in the sphere of labour-power reproduction. Although labour intensification does not create space for a 'deal' in the same way as a growth in productivity, an increase in turnover, as mentioned above, does create the conditions for the rise of a 'consumerism' involving accelerated depreciation and what can broadly be termed 'fashion.' The merest glance at social conditions during the bulk of the Soviet period is enough to demonstrate that this this was not as prevalent there to the same extent as it was and is in the advanced West. For most of the USSR's existence, the culture of the 'throwaway society' did not achieve a substantial penetration into its territory. This was particularly clear in relation to the car. Although ownership per family did rise from the very low rate of 1 in 50 in 1970, it had yet to reach a figure of 1 in 5 even by 1990. (Table 7.4). Cars were expensive and hard to acquire and there was not the same 'rate of consumption' as in the West. (See H. Smith 1976, pp.77-78).

We thus arrive at the position that capitalism in the USSR experienced qualitatively greater problems in institutionalising labour intensification and the acceleration of turnover than it has done in the capitalistically more advanced

West, at least since the 1950s and 1960s. Owing to the workers' persistence in offering labour of poor quality, the degree of capitalist control over the labour process remained weak in any dynamic sense. And this was also evident in the fact that the rate of turnover of 'consumerist' consumption was also relatively low. In short, the workers' resistance to hard work acted as an important magnet slowing down the capitalist 'colonisation' of time, both inside and outside of production. Not only did this resistance indicate the level of oppositional 'rigidity' in working class composition; but insofar as it signified a low level of co-operation with the imperatives of capitalist growth even despite rising wages it also indicated a substantial 'autonomy.'

Perhaps the clearest indication that Soviet capital also felt the problem in the sphere of relative turnover was the size of the industrial repair sector. As has already been noted, the investment of capital into the repair of machinery is in effect the continuation of investment into machine production. Moreover, repair work is evidently highly 'labour-intensive.' In Marxist terminology, then, the ploughing of resources into industrial repair work involves the investment of capital into labour-power in Department One. Thus the famous prioritisation of Soviet heavy industry — more precisely, producer goods — did not involve an automatic and unopposed rise in the organic composition of production. On the contrary, the size of the repair sector was a significant factor which actually tended to reduce this composition in that Department. At the same time, though, since repair work — in machine industry at least — should rightly be classified under the heading of production of the means of production, it necessarily had an *upward* effect on the organic composition of each commodity. Both of these effects worked to hinder the acceleration of relative turnover.

The conclusion to be drawn is this. As became clear after the second world war, the degree of control which Soviet capital exerted over the workers was quite sufficient to allow an increase in productivity and the creation of leeway for the granting of wage-rises. Soviet capitalism did, in other words, enter the period of relative surplus value extraction, as is also evidenced by technological advances particularly in agriculture. Its development, however, was severely hampered by the fact that the workers were strong enough nonetheless to offer significant resistance to the intensification of labour and therefore to the acceleration of turnover. If it would be unreasonable to hope to provide a reliable quantitative estimate of the degree of intensification that *was* achieved, it would perhaps be less so to state that it is quite possible that there may actually have been a *deintensification*. As Department One grew and the socialisation of labour advanced, the effect of the resistance to hard work may actually have provided a spur to the stepping-up of resistance. It seems to us, however, that the question as to whether there was such a deintensification cannot be verified at the present stage of research. But what we can be sure about is that there eventually came a time when the 'productivity deal' came to depend on a level of labour intensification which Soviet capital was simply unable to deliver within the framework of the existing economic system. That system can therefore be seen to have been based on an inefficient form of the real subsumption of labour.

The Problem of Labour from the Viewpoint of Soviet Capital

If it is indeed the case that labour intensification was the prime need of a Soviet ruling class beset by economic stagnation caused by the inefficient form of labour's real subsumption, then of course this is something of which their principal advisers would be expected to be well aware. Moreover, one would expect the problem to have been widely talked about *prior* to the onset of a full crisis. Since economic crisis marks a strategy of a large-scale and severe assault on working class living-standards — through means such as mass unemployment, formal wage-cuts, inflation, or indeed war (see Cleaver 1979, pp.87-89) — it does not in itself mark the establishment or renewal of a dynamic. In effect, it is simply a rapid redistribution of wealth away from the working class. This evidently brings its own policy problems and topics for research, but what is more important in the present context is the longer-term problem of the *restoration of a viable dynamic of capitalist growth.* If the above theorisation is correct, then there should certainly have been an indication of its correctness in the research reports of the rulers' clearest advisers prior to the appearance in the 1990s of shorter-term questions of crisis and crisis management.

We would argue that a recognition of the need for labour intensification was indeed a crucial feature of the most important capitalist analyses made in the USSR during the Gorbachev period. In fact, this is clear even from Gorbachev's own speeches. In his 'accession' speech to the Central Committee plenum in March 1985, for example, he refers to the need for an 'acceleration' (*uskorenie*) of economic development. This term, which for a time became a buzz phrase in public debate,[47] was particularly closely associated with the official thesis that what was required was the introduction of a greater role for 'intensive growth.' (See for example Gorbachev 1985b, pp.129-30, 1985c, pp.252-57, and 1986, pp.27-68). Although it was soon dropped — in favour of the *glasnost'* and *perestroika* heralded by the world's media from 1986 to 1990, not to mention *demokratizatsiia* — the original concept of acceleration is much more revealing on a political-economic level. A month before he became CPSU General Secretary, Gorbachev revealed the substantiality of the thinking which underlay the concept when he stated that alongside the necessity of rapid technical development there was the "no less important" task of the efficient use of means which already existed. In short,

> we should not put faith in the machines of the future, nor use their absence as a screen behind which to hide poor work. To adopt a waiting position is to lose time — and time is everything. (1985a, p.121)

Given his understanding of the linkage of the two economic 'tasks' —technological change and 'better,' more intensive work— Gorbachev's later announcement at the CPSU's 27th Congress in February 1986 that it was necessary to make the workers 'interested' in their work, 'morally' as well as materially (*zainteresovat´ ikh moral´no i material´no*), should not be dismissed as mere speechifying. (1986, p.30). Although the idea of acceleration was sometimes used to support the somewhat fanciful notion of the achievability of a literal quickening of the growth rate (see Aganbegian 1988, p.9), it also denoted, more profoundly, the breaking of the worker's general attitude in the workplace.

Among the two most important academic theorists inspiring government economic policy at this time were the economist Aganbegian and the sociologist Zaslavskaia; and it will be instructive to look at their contributions in turn, and more specifically at their views on the workers.

In a text devoted to the issue of the "transition to intensive development," Aganbegian presents the underlying problem facing the Soviet economic administration as being "the negative tendencies in the dynamic of efficiency," and poses the rhetorical question of how to overcome these tendencies in order to achieve a "qualitative leap forward." (1988, pp.104-05). The solution he explains, is two-sided. First of all (*prezhde vsego*), there is the need for a mobilisation of the

> organisational, economic, and social reserves and potential through the better use of existing resources and the existing technical basis of production; the strengthening of discipline and order; the raising of qualifications and responsibility; and the raising of people's interest in their work [*usilenie zainteresovannosti*], etc.

Second, there is the issue of scientific-technical progress. (p.106). *Uskorenie*, in this view, depends on the 'organic combination' of the two factors. (pp.106-07). Such an analysis is not, of course, wholly 'classist,' but it should be noted that he does not hesitate to place the task of making workers 'interested' in their work at least at the same level of importance as the technological development of production.[48]

Zaslavskaia, who is perhaps best known in the West as the author of the seminal 'Novosibirsk Report' of 1983,[49] goes much further in a 'theoretical' direction; and from the present point of view she can be seen as a more acute analyst. Reporting to a conference hosted jointly by the Central Committee of the CPSU, the USSR Academy of Sciences, and Gosplan, she introduces into official Soviet discourse for the first time an idea which clearly indicates an attempt to cut through the ideological deadwood in order to address the ruling class's problems in a pragmatic fashion. This is the idea that the development of production relations is 'lagging behind' the development of the productive forces. (1983, pp.88-89). Thus she argues that whereas over several decades the "size and value of the means of production" have grown many times over, as has the technical level of production, the *form* which growth has taken has been contradictory. On one hand, she states,

> the level of productive labor has greatly increased, but on the other, the scale of damage inflicted upon society through careless labor, violations of labor and technology discipline, irresponsible attitudes to technology, etc., [has] also risen. (1983, pp.91-92)

This, then, put succinctly, is the principal problem. Having recognised that "man is often the weakest link in the technological chain" (p.92), she notes that there has been a gradual "increase in the technological demands made on the labor behaviour of the workers." The whole point of her analysis is that since the workers have been strong enough not to accede to these demands, or not to accede to them to an adequate degree, the problem of their attitude to their work has necessarily grown worse. The main 'production relation' which needs to be changed is precisely that of the workers' behaviour.

In considering the road to a solution, she calls for research into the right kind of incentive schemes. Removing all possibility of doubt about what she is saying, she writes that

> it is in the interests of socialist society, while regulating the key aspects of the socioeconomic activity of the workers, to leave them a sufficiently wide margin of freedom of individual behaviour. Hence the necessity for directing behaviour itself, i.e. the subjective relationship of the workers to their socioeconomic activity. Administrative methods of management are powerless here. The management of behaviour can only be accomplished in an oblique fashion, with the help of incentives which would take into account the economic and social demands of the workers and would channel their interests in a direction which would be of benefit to our society. (pp.95-96)

Later she makes the further clarificatory point that

> any serious reorganization of economic management must be accompanied by a certain redistribution of rights and responsibilities among various groups of

workers. Thereby, the expansion of every group's rights is, as a rule, combined with an increase of responsibilities; and a decrease of responsibilities goes hand in hand with a reduction of rights. (p.99)

She thus focuses extremely sharply on workers' resistance to the needs of 'society': that is, of Soviet capital.

This preoccupation is also apparent in texts she produces after Gorbachev has come to power. In calling for an enhancement of the "creative activity of the masses," she writes that under today's conditions,

a sober, skilled, and reliable worker produces tens and hundreds of times more products [than he did in the 1930s]. An irresponsible or inebriated worker, on the other hand, who produces defective products in enormous quantities, who breaks valuable machinery, who puts an industrial livestock complex out of action, or who causes trains to crash into one another, causes scores and hundreds of times more damage even than the Herostratuses of the past. (1986a, p.4)

In this context, it is hardly surprising that in another text of the same year she describes the 'resolution' of a broad 'complex' of problems as being a powerful means by which the "human factor" (*chelovecheskii faktor*) can be successfully "intensified." (1986b, p.73; see also Loginov 1989, pp.102-11).

Such analyses as this, produced at the time that they were, can only corroborate the view that the development of Soviet capitalism came increasingly to depend upon the intensification of labour.

THE CLASS STRUGGLE IN THE USSR: ITS SPECIFICITY

It is now necessary to describe the specificity of the class struggle in the USSR, the related overall form of development of Soviet capitalism, and the critical position arrived at.

Soviet Capitalist Development and Workers' Power

As became apparent in the discussion of the development of the opposition between working class autonomy and capitalist growth, the specificity of Soviet economic development lay in the one-sidedness of the extraction of relative surplus value. Thus whilst the two aspects of successful growth under western Fordism and Keynesianism — productivity and intensification — were closely intertwined and indeed interdependent, in the USSR there was a division between them which eventually proved critical.

The theoretical conclusion, then, cannot be that relative surplus value extraction is necessarily two-staged, and that the Soviet administrative-command system was functional only in the first stage. Such a theory would have little explanatory value in regard to why such a periodisation has not been especially evident elsewhere. (Consider, for example, the importance in the West of the car industry, both in terms of the production process itself — it was the birthplace of the conveyor-belt — and in terms of the 'planned obsolesence' of its products. [See Kay 1975, pp.166-68]). On the contrary, the causes of the problems faced by capitalist development in the USSR must necessarily lie in the specific history of the underlying antagonism: the class struggle. And working class struggle in the USSR can only properly be understood in relation to its opposition to the efficiency of capitalist growth.

In these terms, two factors in particular stand out. The first is the importance on the capitalist side of the Russian (or Soviet) *State bureaucracy*. Crucial in the organisation of industry since the time of Tsar Peter I (1682-1725) (see for example Crisp 1972, Milward and Saul 1977, pp.334-35, and Kochan and Abraham 1983, pp.114-15), this was the natural weapon for capital to employ not only in 1917-18, faced with enormous unrepayable debts (Carr 1952, p.143) as well as the *force majeure* of working class struggle against the bourgeoisie; but also at the end of the 1920s, when the new urban ruling class tied itself to a policy of extremely rapid urbanisation and industrialisation. More specifically, what Stalinism amounted to was the massive employment of quasi-military means by the ruling class in struggle: in political-economic terms, the control by *responsible officials* of capital investment both in means of production and in labour-power. The role of such officials, or administrators, became the defining characteristic of Soviet economic management even after concessions had to be made to workers' mobility in the 1950s. This was not 'despotism' in the sense of full central control, any more than it was real 'planning.' Rather, it was a local form of capitalist command and competition based on the functioning as money-capital of a bureaucratic, restrictedly-fluid form of the general equivalent And this latter form was to a great extent based on the prioritisation of rapid investment and productivity growth.

The second factor is the form of *working class power*, which according to the present analysis subverted the capitalist strategy of extreme prioritisation of 'gross output' by seemingly conceding to it. As workers used mobility to force managerial concessions on wages, especially in the Brezhnev period, the intensification of labour appeared to be a non-issue as long as the 'ratchet effect' was functioning properly. Put simply, the workers had wage drift, the rulers had the fulfilment of plans formulated 'from the achieved level' (*ot dostignutogo*). Under these conditions *poor-quality labour*, as a political-economic reality, operated against the increase of turnover, both absolute and relative, and what is more it actually reinforced the prevalence of full employment. This in turn allowed the workers to make more use of mobility, and so on. At the same time, by holding back intensification, poor-quality labour prevented even the offering of a new 'deal' based on the rapidity of consumer turnover: that is, on 'consumerism.'

The one-sided nature of the strategy of Soviet capital, closely bound up in practice with the organisation of the ruling class upon the basis of the bureaucratic form of capitalist money, led it to be brought into 'stagnation' by workers' power: not in a way that was subject to political mediation and representation, but in terms of resistance to capital's drive to develop the political-economic means of its control. The lack of representedness of this form of class struggle corresponded very closely to what was identified above as the irrecuperability of the struggle against hard work. The 'productivity deal' which existed, then, was literally that — a deal on productivity — which, given the resistance of the workers and the prevalence of concessions to workers by local managers, involved minimal class co-operation on labour intensification.

Operating at the same time as the deal over productivity, predicate upon an increase in the socialisation of labour even if technological development tended to be skewed towards newly-constructed plants, the high level of refusal of hard work tended inevitably to bring down the rate of profit. What was worse, from the point of view of capital, was the fact that the controllers of capital — those who possessed significant bureaucratic clout — had to a great extent to rely upon productivity growth as an *alternative* for intensification. Indeed this can be seen as providing the material basis for the Stalinist ideology of the 'primacy of the productive forces': that is, of the material means of production. It is therefore highly revealing that when Zaslavskaia issued her resonant call for the ruling class to face facts, fund a programme of truly functional social scientific research, and attempt to remould working class composition according to the interests of 'society,' this was precisely the ideological target on which this proponent of the 'human factor' concentrated her fire.

The Form of the Crisis

If the economic crisis in the region were caused by the strength of a revolutionary movement — that is, if the existence of exploitation itself were endangered — there and in the rest of the world, the central question would clearly be the 'epochal' one of 'capitalism or communism?' Since, however, the crisis is the result of the vanishing efficiency of an inefficient form of capital's real subsumption of labour, caused by the workers' resistance to labour intensification over a period of several decades, the circumstances are very different.

Seen from the point of view of the working class, the crisis is a continuing defeat. Contrary to the received opinion, there is thus a level at which both Gorbachev and Yeltsin have had remarkable economic success: each of them has overseen a large fall in living-standards for most of the working class. Conditions have been deteriorating for at least a decade and could deteriorate further, all the way to famine. There have already been reports of slave labour (see Ticktin 1992a, pp.253-54) — although by no means on a Stalinist or Hitlerist scale — and the export of slaves to cities such as Berlin and Vienna. (See for example Franchetti and Conradi 1996 and A. D. Smith 1996). Vodka prices are kept low as a matter of government policy (Meek 1996a and 1996b) — in early 1996 in Moscow a bottle cost the same as two loaves of bread (Scott 1996a) — and between 1987 and 1993 male life expectancy fell at the rate of one year per year: that is, from 65 to 59. (Mihill 1995). Another factor here has been the assault on health provision: government spending on this sector, as a proportion of GNP, was cut by half in 1992. (Gluschenko 1993). But since for some years the economy has been contracting on a large scale, it is clear that even this success in attacking the working class has been unable to provide capital with a solution to its central strategic question: the establishment of a secure basis for new growth.

Seen from the point of view of the controllers of capital, the crisis has taken the form of a crisis of the pre-existing bureaucratic form of money. It was this crisis, then, which was the main cause of the end of the Soviet political system. As the rate of surplus value fell, there was a growing opposition between capital in the form of means of production, C, and capital in the form of bureaucratic clout, M. By the beginning of the 1990s many of those with a great deal of bureaucratic clout on paper — in the CPSU Central Committee, say, the CMEA, or the Politburo, not to mention the Party's General Secretaryship — found that it did not give them anywhere near as much control as it should have done over the use of the means of production to provide a surplus. Bureaucratic money, in other words, was found to have been subject to great *inflation*. Many bureaucrats raced to 'cash in' their holdings: into hard currency (including gold), influential positions in organised crime, deeds to buildings, or control over the supply of raw materials.

The unevenness of monetary inflation in its bureaucratic form meant that a chronic restrictedness of bureaucratic monetary fluidity was always likely to be a feature of the crisis. For those who understood this, the convertibilisation of the rouble into hard currency, which most western commentators had not expected to see for decades, if at all, came as no surprise. Fluidity was encouraged where it was easiest to grow, since elsewhere it was blocked. Foreign policy considerations were no impediment whatsoever, and too much revenue was being spent on nuclear stockpiles anyway. The mafia economy, always concerned more with distribution than production, and which had been growing for several years, came into its own.[50] Such convertibilisation, however, has encouraged fluidity only within a very small part of the economy. The exchange rate has rocketed and the Russian stockmarket is one of the the riskiest in the world. From the point of view of Russian capital as a whole there remains the problem of *internal* convertibilisation, the profitable convertibilisation of 'money in general' for means of production, and of means of production for money. And this itself is only a manifestation of the underlying problem, which lies *between* the two moments of exchange, in the sphere of production. This is the problem of the productivisation of capital, the creation of surplus value.

In the absence of a solution to the problem in production, monetary problems have exacerbated a fault-line within the ruling class. This division has been described by the editors of the *Echanges* journal, using revolutionary material from Russia itself. On one side, there are the State bureaucrats, ex-CPSU nomenklatura, and mafia; on the other, there are the industrial officials in control of productive plant, to which they seek or have already acquired legal possession. Members of the first group are "linked to commercial capital" and have "monetarism" as their typical ideology; members of the second are linked to "industrial capital" and have "mercantilism" as theirs, meaning that they see the "commodity as a source of wealth but not wealth itself." "Commercial capital" seeks the rapid accumulation of monetary wealth but is in no hurry to "integrate itself into the productive process"; whereas industrial capital is highly concerned with the preservation of the means of production even if at the same time it wishes to buy it at cheaply as possible. (1993-95, p.50).

The underlying political-economic state of affairs becomes even clearer when it is understood as the crisis of the form of money. On one side, then, there is control over capital in its monetary form, by State officials and mafia bosses, who control both roubles and traditional-style bureaucratic/*blat* money. The non-stabilisation of the general equivalent in a particular form has meant that assassination is a constant possibility — as something to avoid experiencing and to consider commissioning — in the top circles of both finance and the government. (Scott 1996c). Bodyguard loyalty is of the highest importance. On the other side, not unaffected by this atmosphere, but embodying capital in another form, there is direct control over the means of production. Each form of capital needs the other, but they stand opposed. The crystallisation may not be total,[51] but its degree is a measure of the depth of the crisis.

Capital's Need for Growth

The conditions of achievement of a new dynamic are easiest to understand once Soviet capitalist development is understood in the context of world capitalist development. The 'advanced western' form of real subsumption, then, based on both productivity growth and labour intensification, and bringing 'consumerism' as one of its effects, is not at all a 'stage' which the whole of the former USSR must enter if capitalist production is to advance. Capitalist development has never been this simple; rather, in some areas it has taken the form of so-called 'underdevelopment,' where both real wages and productivity are much lower than they are in the most advanced areas. In these areas there has been little evidence of a real subsumption based on the 'advanced' model. It is certainly possible to argue that they have to some extent entered the period of relative surplus value extraction, since productivity has certainly risen to *some* degree, but at the same time the level of technology is relatively low and the form of subsumption is less advanced even at this level. The second major difference with both the capitalistically most advanced countries and the USSR is the existence of very high levels of unemployment. It is in these areas that the unemployment caused by global capitalist advance is concentrated.

The capitalist form of growth in the USSR was to some extent intermediate between the so-called 'first' and 'third' worlds. Now that its usefulness has come to an end, one possibility for capital in the region would be to introduce a mixture of the two other forms. One can thus envisage the creation of islands of technologically advanced industry, in areas such as the Baltic coast and perhaps St. Petersburg. Wages would not be high, and presumably much of production would be export-related; but the internal market would not be negligible. Turnover would to some extent be accelerated and labour intensified. Perhaps this could also occur in the oil and gas industries. Elsewhere, whole regions would be run down in a massive devalorisation of constant capital. There would, of course, be a degree of cherry-picking: the mining of gold and diamonds would continue. But there would also be hyper-unemployment, or — a variation on the theme — a reduction in population which is arguably already underway. Profitability would depend upon the payment of very low wages, and perhaps also on the lengthening of the working day: that is, on absolute surplus value. Life expectancy would continue to fall. This could also involve the migration of cheap labour either abroad or to the technologically more advanced areas. In some areas of this vast region of the world, most of the remaining employment would probably be in farming — under conditions which could be extremely brutal. In others, the two forms of development would occur simultaneously.

This, however, is merely a hypothesis and we do not see a way out for capital at all in the short term. We are certainly very doubtful that production is about to pick up, as is currently being suggested. We are much more sure that in the face of sustained direct assaults on the majority of the working class, attempts to increase the intensity of labour for a minority, and the official building-up of the spectacle of consumerism with extremely limited provision of the goods, major struggles lie ahead.

SUMMARY

In formulating a theoretical understanding of working class struggle in the USSR we have emphasised throughout its relationship to the fundamental categories of capitalist political economy.

For this reason we start by discussing the issue of capitalist control, with detailed reference to the circuit of capital (investment and sale) and to the circuit of labour-power (exertion and regeneration). A Marxist understanding is presented of the necessary opposition between working class autonomy and capitalist growth.

The growth which does occur is then considered in terms of the dynamic class relation: that is, the class struggle. Distinguishing between absolute surplus value extraction and relative surplus value extraction, we show how under relative surplus value extraction — more precisely, capital's real subsumption of labour — the struggle takes two forms. First, there is a struggle over the wage. In this area, productivity growth creates space for the capitalist concession of higher 'real wages,' but only on condition that the value of necessary labour-time falls. Second, there is a struggle over labour intensity. In this connection the concepts are introduced of absolute turnover, relative turnover, the organic composition of production, and the organic composition of the commodity, the latter two being taken from Kay. Here, it is argued, the intensification of labour does not create space for any concessions to the struggle for *less work* in the same way that a growth in productivity does for concessions to the struggle for *higher wages*.

Moving the focus of consideration to capitalism in the USSR, we begin by demonstrating the class opposition implicit within each moment of the twin circuits of capital and labour-power. Soviet specificities include the role of bureaucratic/*blat* money in investment, and the related division within the ruling class between the central bureaucratic elite and the enterprise managers. It is noted, first, how it was at enterprise level that concessions were made to the workers over both work quality and norms; and second, how the position of the enterprise manager, whilst it involved a contradiction between his own interests and the interests of capital as a whole, did not remove the fact of a fundamentally shared capitalist interest in the extraction of surplus value.

With reference to capitalist control over the labour-power circuit, we consider four aspects in particular: proletarianisation, mobility, control over the labour process, and control over the time worked. Proletarianisation, or the making available of workers for capitalist exploitation, is held to be the only area of unqualified capitalist success: the others are noted in turn to have been forms of control which met permanent resistance. Looking then at the reproduction of labour-power, we draw attention to the role in the USSR of the social wage, and more specifically the enterprise social wage.

The discussion then focuses on the opposition between workers' power and capitalist growth. Three forms of working class struggle are noted: namely, worker-led labour mobility, low-quality production, and absenteeism. These are shown to have involved resistance to the three specific areas of capitalist control over labour-power already mentioned.

The nature of Soviet capitalist growth is then considered in more detail in the context of the dynamic class relation.

It is argued on the basis of Soviet economic statistics that Soviet capital did achieve some success in extracting relative surplus value. More specifically, it is shown that productivity growth coincided with a general rise in real wages throughout the post-war period. But it is noted that nonetheless the levels of both productivity and wages did not reach western levels.

The discussion then necessarily moves to the area of labour intensification. We proceed to show that in various ways the acceleration of turnover was restricted by the force of workers' struggle, and in particular by the prevalence of low-quality work. In regard to the rate of absolute turnover, the high level of work stoppages, along with the size of the repair sector, are described as major retarding factors. And the fact that the absolute turnover rate was indeed low is backed up with reference to the weak level of penetration of 'consumerism' on Soviet territory, especially in terms of car ownership.

The size of the industrial repair sector is then argued to have retarded the rate of relative turnover too, increasing the ratio between investment in Department One and investment in Department Two whilst tending to reduce the ratio between the organic composition of production and the organic composition of the commodity.

The conclusion is reached that Soviet growth and the Soviet economic system were based upon an inefficient form of the real subsumption of labour. This is backed up with brief reference to some of the strategic writings which appeared in the USSR in the mid-to-late 1980s. Attention is drawn to such concepts as those of 'acceleration' (*uskorenie*), the need to increase workers' 'interest' (*zainteresovannost*) in their work, and the importance of the 'human factor.' (*chelovecheskii faktor*).

The specificity of capitalist development in the USSR is described from both sides of the class divide. On the side of capital, investment was largely in the hands of responsible officials and was geared towards the prioritisation of investment and productivity growth. On the side of the proletariat, concessions were certainly made to the capitalist need for increased gross output, but only at the expense of the absence of any real co-operation on labour intensification. As wages rose, the rulers seem to have responded by using output growth as a sort of alternative for intensification. The scale of concession in this area of capitalist control brought economic stagnation — and an ever-increasing strategic need for the rulers to force up labour intensity by whatever radical means are necessary.

Lastly, we describe the form of the current crisis. Above all this is a crisis of a specific form of capitalist development associated with specific forms of class struggle. For the working class it has meant a major fall in living-standards which could yet deteriorate further. For capital, it was heralded by the large-scale inflation of bureaucratic money and the eventual collapse of its fluidity and coherence. No viable form of money capital has so far been established, and indeed there is a major division within the ruling class between, on one side, the controllers of abstract capital or money (government officials and mafia bosses); and on the other, the controllers of concrete capital or means of production (industrial officials and directors). These groups need each other but stand opposed.

Both Gorbachev and Yeltsin have been successful insofar as they have overseen a fall in wages, both individual and social. But this in itself is no way out of the crisis. In the absence of a new form of development, the convertibilisation of the rouble for hard currency has necessarily had a very restricted effect. What capital requires more is the establishment of a new form of money internally, as a moment of productive capital, and this demands first and foremost a revision of the organisation of labour. It is suggested that the form of development most likely to be viable would involve a division in the economy: on one side, there would be a technologically advanced sector based on some degree of labour intensification; on the other, a sector based on very low wages and a longer working day, associated with what might reasonably be called hyper-unemployment. But even as capital is still limbering up for this sort of development — and it may continue to do so for several years — working class people will increasingly face the alternative of struggle of an increasingly radical and organised kind or else a further deterioration in living-standards.

Notes

1   On the production of surplus value as the essence of the capitalist valorisation process, see especially Marx 1933, pp.989-91 and 1939, pp.321-26 and 373-447.

2   This is not to deny that accumulation also permits the growth of the exploiters' privileged consumption. As Tillium has shown, privileged consumption cannot reasonably be described as 'accidental' to the underlying nature of capitalism. (1994, p.17). The point in the present context, though, is that since value is founded upon competition — as the means by which it regulates production — the controllers of capital are compelled to reinvest surplus value so as to ensure its continued production. (See Marx 1867, p.789). Since it is in the nature of the system that if a capitalist interest does not seek to expand the production under its control, then it will be taken advantage of by its more rapacious rivals, it is clear that the exploiters as a whole could only introduce 'zero growth,' and thus consume the entire surplus, if they were to abolish generalised competition. But at that time the form of exploitation would no longer be capitalism.

3   In the *Grundrisse* Marx states explicitly that "Moment IV belongs in the section on wages" (1939 p.421), and disagreement has since arisen as to whether or not his plans to write a book on wage-labour (as part of a six-volume work) were or were not fully realised in Part 6 of Volume 1 of *Capital*. See for example, arguing that they were fully realised, Rosdolsky 1968, chap.2, especially pp.56-62, agreed with by E. Mandel 1976, p.29; and, arguing that they were not fully realised, Rubel 1973, pp.220-21, Lebowitz 1992, pp.12-34, and Shortall 1994, pp.185-97. Negri, meanwhile, although ascribing fundamental importance in his consideration of Marx to the theory of wage-labour and the working class as subject, holds the distinctive view that "Marx didn't write a separate book on the wage because his whole work constantly returns to this theme." (1979, p.134).

Although the development and contradictions of Marx's publication plans are not of central importance in the present context, a few comments on Marx's view of the determination of wage-levels will be in order. Thus in the *Grundrisse* he writes that the supposition that wages are at a minimum level is necessary in order to establish the "laws of profit," insofar as "they are not determined by the rise and fall of wages or by the influence of landed property." He then goes on to state that

> however the standard of necessary labour may differ at various epochs and in various countries, or how much, in consequence of the demand and supply of labour, its amount and ratio may change, at any given epoch the standard is to be considered and acted upon as a fixed one by capital. To consider those changes themselves belongs altogether to the chapter treating of wage labour. (1939, p.817)

This can be compared with what is said in Volume 1 of *Capital*, where it is held that

> the value of labour-power is determined by the value of the means of subsistence habitually required by the average worker. The quantity of the means of subsistence required is given at any particular epoch in any particular society, and can therefore be treated as a constant magnitude. What changes is the value of this quantity. (1867, p.655)

In this area the main theoretical advance — first made explicit in unpublished form in the *Grundrisse* (see 1939, p.282), omitted in the *Contribution* of 1859, but stressed throughout *Capital* — lies in the focusing on the category of *labour-power* rather than simply on that of *labour*. And indeed it is this which forms the basis of Marx's 'abstract social labour' theory of *value* and *surplus value*. Unfortunately, though, he does not reach the stage of theorising changes in the value of labour-power which are determined by changes in the quantity of goods consumed by the workers. This has allowed the fact that this determination can occur to become obscured. But in fact such determination is quite straightforward, given that the value of labour-power is equivalent to the value of the workers' consumption, and therefore to the quantity of 'average socially necessary' labour-time which is expended in producing the goods consumed. In short: if the quantity of goods consumed changes, then, other things being equal, so do the quantity of necessary labour and the value of labour-power, *as a matter of definition*. The corresponding partition of the social product among classes is evidently a matter of class struggle.

As Kay puts it,

> the short answer to the question — what process determines the level of socially necessary consumption and the value of labour-power? — is the class struggle. A more complete answer situates the class struggle within the general development of production, the value of commodities, the pattern of output and the type of techniques employed. But the fact remains that the value of labour-power is not determined by economic forces defined in the narrow sense: there are no market laws to be discovered that stipulate the level of necessary consumption; no strict correlation between wages and the technical conditions of production.... [The] class struggle, the relentless opposition of the working class to capital, is not an extraneous assumption plucked from nowhere to patch a hole in an economic theory; the class struggle is nothing but the concrete expression of the law of value; or, to put it the other way round, the law of value is the general theoretical statement of the class struggle. (1979a, p.90)

Marx's critique of political economy as given in Capital should thus be seen as a critique of capital's nature and internal laws, wherein the issue of class struggle has been provisionally — but only provisionally — 'closed.' (See especially Shortall 1994; and also Cleaver 1979 and Lebowitz 1992).

4   The moment of the circulation of labour-power defined by its reproduction is also a moment of the circulation of capital. This area will be recognised as that in which Autonomist Marxism has made its principal theoretical contribution. In preparing the following analysis we have found Negri 1979 especially useful; and also Dalla Costa 1971, Cleaver 1979, and Lebowitz 1992.

5   An indispensable part in the reproduction of employed labour-power is played by housework, most of which is done by women. By helping to reproduce such labour-power, which takes a commodity form, this work is evidently productive of value. Equally clearly, it is atomised to a qualitatively much greater degree than work outside the home for a capitalist employer. It is instructive, however, to consider the fact that the housewife's own reproduction involves not only her own work in the home, but also her consumption of commodities which are themselves produced by employed wage-labourers. Thus the reproduction of her own labour-power, which constitutes the basis upon which she is able to carry out work which is productive of her partner's labour-power, and of her children's in the future, is itself a moment in the *cycle* of value and therefore of capital. Given the socialised essence of value, Dalla Costa is therefore right to insist that housework is productive of surplus value. (1971, pp.32-33).

It is additionally necessary to recognise that female houseworkers are usually economically exploited by male working-class partners. Perhaps the easiest way to show this is with reference to the fact that women considered to be of an 'employable age' usually engage in work for an outside employer as well as doing the bulk of the housework in the family home. Even when they do not have an outside job they normally work longer hours than their partners who do. But this exploitation, although atomised in its own specific way, also serves to keep wages *in general* at a lower level than would otherwise be the case. It is therefore a part of the overall relationship between wage-labour and capital.

6   This is a point which Negri misses quite badly. In order to reinforce a view of a proletarian sphere of 'self-valorisation' which is wholly antagonistic, he thus asserts that "small-scale circulation seems to reject the functions of money, even though money can function within it in terms of simple commodity circulation." (1979, p.138). The implication is that the function of money defined by M-C-M´ is *successfully* rejected. But even if wage rigidity and workers' struggles do indeed antagonise the M-C-M´ function, this is still a remarkable over-stating of the case. The fact that the (socialised) worker produces surplus-value only *after* he has been sufficiently 'reproduced' to do so, and not while he is being 'reproduced,' is not of overriding importance in a society based on generalised exchangeability and growth. That Negri has bent the stick too far is evident when he proceeds to state that "money exchanged between proletarians is use-value" (p.138), thus forgetting that the use-value of all money is precisely — and exclusively — its exchangeability: namely, the fact that it has exchange-value. In reality, the reproduction of workers is permitted precisely on the basis that they will continue to produce surplus value. (Marx 1939, p.421). Their needs and struggles do conflict with this basis, but this does not mean that the basis ceases to be a basis! As a result, a multitude of contradictions is introduced into workers' reproduction 'off the job.' In this respect Dalla Costa's theorisation, in which she emphasises the oppression of working class women (1971), is in advance of Negri's. (See also Kay 1979a, pp.84-89).

7   It might be argued that needs are principally objective. Certainly the existence of objective needs for food and shelter is indisputable. But humans need food and shelter so that they can stay alive as subjective beings who feel, think, and choose, not merely as beings in the objective chemical-mechanical sense.

8   "The owner of labour-power is mortal. If then his appearance in the market is to be continuous, and the continuous transformation of money into capital assumes this, the seller of labour-power must perpetuate himself 'in the way that every living individual perpetuates himself, by procreation.' The labour-power withdrawn from the market by wear and tear, and by death, must be continually replaced by, at the very least, an equal amount of fresh labour-power. Hence the sum of means of subsistence necessary for the production of labour-power must include the means necessary for the worker's replacements, i.e. his children...." (Marx 1867, p.275).

9   In the 'social wage sector' as in other sectors, the case of managers is straightforward: since they control wage-labourers, and therefore variable capital, they are clearly exploiters. On the other hand, of course, in any organisation which is not directly repressive the position of non-managerial white-collar staff is usually proletarian. We are not suggesting for a moment that all town hall clerks or nurses, for example, are controllers of capital, any more than that could rightly be said about a grocer's or newsagent's delivery boy. It should be clear that the bigger the decision concerning resource distribution, the higher up the ladder it is made. Moreover, senior controllers of capital — again, in organisations which are not directly repressive — tend not to allow underlings to have substantial control over resources unless they also appear convincingly at ease in a managerial, that is, anti-proletarian, role. This is a good example of capitalist class consciousness.

10 See note 3 above.

11 For a useful theoretical discussion of labour productivity and labour intensity, and their development under modern market capitalism, see Kay 1975, pp.157-67, 1976, pp.59-62, and 1979a, pp.72-78.

12 At that time in Britain this institutionalisation was manifested especially in the spread of piece-rates. See Marx 1867, pp.411-16, 694-700 and Hobsbawm 1968, pp.123-24.

13 In an important text, Kay has argued that

> the maintenance of the rate of profit with rising real wages in the post-War period — at least until the late Sixties — which has been analysed almost exclusively in terms of rising productivity, is probably due, in considerable part at least, to the intensification of labour. [And] if Marxism is to be used as a means of analysing working class experience as a basis for revolutionary political action, this matter is much more than a footnote to the theory of the rate of profit. (1976, p.62)

14 It is not held that what follows marks an important methodological advance in relation to Marx. Rather it is seen as *implicit* in the relevant section of *Capital*. Thus he ends the consideration of labour intensification by stating that

> If the intensity of labour were to increase simultaneously and equally in every branch of industry, then the new and higher degree of intensity would become the normal social degree of intensity, and would therefore cease to count as an extensive magnitude. But even so, the intensity of labour would still be different in different countries, and would modify the application of the law of value to the working days of different nations. The more intensive working day of one nation would be represented by a greater sum of money than the less intensive day of another nation. (1867, pp.661-62)

It might be suggested, certainly, that he is simply denying the relevance of a concept of intensification at the level of overall social capital. But in this context we would mention the footnote which he appends to the end of this section. In this brief note he comments that

> the most infallible means of reducing this difference [in terms of quantity of output] between the product of the English and of the Continental working hour would be a law shortening the length of the working day in Continental factories." (p.662, n.4)

It is possible, no doubt, to debate the amount of irony that should be read into the phrase "most infallible," but in our view it is more important to recall the importance at that time of the *struggle* over the length of the working day. He has already made it clear that this issue was one of workers' struggle "on both sides of the Atlantic"; and indeed he has referred explicitly to the demand of the International for the introduction of an eight-hour day across the capitalist world. (pp.411-16). It cannot rightly be held that Marx was unaware of any linkage between the intensity of labour and the class struggle, when he links it — albeit without elaboration — to what he saw as the pivotal issue for the internationalisation and advance of working class struggle at the time. The reality was that in the second half of the 19th century the main issue in the class struggle concerned the fight to limit the extraction of absolute surplus value. We would suggest that the struggle over intensification itself, which is a form of increase of relative surplus value, was one of the areas which Marx would have dealt with at greater length in the book on wage-labour.

15 The relationship between the end of Keynesianism and, on one side, the workers' successful struggles for higher wages and the impact of the radical social movements of 1968-72 and,

on the other, the rising organic composition of production and the related return of mass unemployment in the advanced western countries, cannot be gone into here.

16   The material means of production include both the instruments of production and raw materials. Under capitalism, this division takes the form of the division between fixed capital and circulating capital. In relation to turnover Kay thus discusses the ratio between, on one side, the total of the fixed capital present all the time and the circulating capital used up in each project, and on the other, the variable capital advanced. (1975, pp.134-36). The assumption in the present context is that all constant capital is fixed. This simplifies but does not undermine the demonstration of the relevance of turnover to the class relation.

17   The 'absolute' rate of turnover of fixed capital is of course another issue.

18   This shorthand expression refers to the rise in the ratio between, on one side, the value of the living labour-time worked during the commodity's production, and, on the other, that of the labour-time embodied in that portion of the means of production the value of which has been transferred to the commodity.

19   In our opinion Kay's Autonomist Marxist views on the falling "organic composition of the commodity" and capital's increasing "colonisation of time" strongly suggest a need for a cross-fertilisation with Debord's Situationist critique of the capitalist spectacle as the "technical realization of the exile of human powers into a beyond" and of "spectacular time." (1967, para. 20 and chap.6). There is a very real need to base a critique of modern false consciousness upon a critique of capitalist political economy, and it is possible that Kay's demonstration that commodities undergo an increasing level of 'human input' could point the way towards a theoretical explanation of the development of advanced false consciousness as a political-economic necessity in advanced capitalism. This project, however, which has yet to be embarked upon by those engaged in revolutionary theoretical critique, clearly lies beyond the terms of reference of the present thesis.

20   We would argue that since capitalism is a mode of production which is global, the controllers of capital and those who have access to such control constitute a capitalist ruling class on a world level. The bourgeoisie is thus one section of that class, and the Soviet bureaucratic elite, including both central bureaucrats and enterprise managers, is another. It is hardly convincing to call the director of an enterprise employing, say, a hundred workers under a regime of 'one-man management' anything other than a member of the ruling class, even if he is not a member of the smaller and more central ruling elite within that class. (As a rule, nor will the owner of a firm of similar size in Britain be a member of the central ruling circles in that country). It is, however, convenient to refer to the bourgeoisie as the market-based ruling class and the Soviet rulers as a ruling class based on a form of capitalist money which is fundamentally bureaucratic. The question as to whether the two layers within the Soviet ruling class should themselves be termed 'classes' is not crucial to an understanding of the nature of Soviet society. (See above, Chapter 6, pp.243-46). The distinction between the two layers, however, is.

       The world proletariat, meanwhile — that is, the class dominated by capital and absolutely dispossessed of the means of production — contains not only workers and those seeking work, but also people who for long periods of time derive their means of subsistence from the social wage, or who are starving. It is not especially important whether or not the long-term unemployed or the starving are described as being in the working class. What is important is to recognise that the fundamental division in world capitalist society is between capital and its controllers on one side and the proletarian dispossessed on the other; that these two forces are global; and that an understanding of their antagonism (the fundamental class struggle) is necessary to a full understanding of their nature. On this basis consideration can be given to the unfolding of this class antagonism at a local level, and the related 'composition' of its two sides. (See above, Chapter 1, Note 9).

21   Doubtless the use by Ticktin and Filtzer of the idea of 'negative' workers' control appears to have a certain radicality with respect to both the traditional Trotskyist support for Soviet production relations and the various critiques of the 'all-powerful' Soviet regime made by other Leninists such as Cliff. (And it is evidently more radical than the use of the term by Connor, who does not endeavour to make a critique of the overall mode of production). But it must be criticised nonetheless as a product of an exaggerated conceptual separation of the category of the 'labour process' from the broader categories of a political economy founded upon the generalised socialisation of alienated labour. Typically, this has led Filtzer to state that "the price of labour-power has nothing to do with the 'value' of its reproduction." (1986, p.259). In the absence of a discussion of what form actually *is* taken by the reproduction of the socialised worker, and of what relation *does* exist between this reproduction and the price of labour-power, this appears to be little more than an ideological avowal of the belief that Soviet production relations were other than capitalist. Thus it obscures the nature of what in fact was precisely working class struggle against capitalist accumulation — a necessary struggle undermining the efficiency of the exploitation of wage-labour. Once the *Critique* school's work is placed alongside Autonomist Marxist work on the development of working class struggle in the West, it undoubtedly appears highly useful in the formulation of a communist understanding of working class struggle against the needs of capital in the USSR. But at the same time much of its basis can only stand in the way of a unification of a theoretical appraisal of the subversion by workers' power of capitalist strategy in market capitalism with a corresponding appraisal of the subversion by workers' power of capitalist strategy in the USSR.

22   The reforms of 1965 were meant to overcome this latter tendency, but their failure to do so only demonstrated its systemic nature. (Nove 1980b, p.106; Kontorovich 1988).

23   In a discussion of the Soviet academic theory of investment, formulated within the discipline of economics, Giffen concludes that Soviet investment "methodology" has developed "as a result of the immediate and pressing needs to make planning decisions." Moreover, "this has resulted in a multitude of norms and instructions precisely because there is no *a priori* theory, acceptable to the Soviet Union, which allows all expenditures and benefits to be measured on one scale." (1981, p.604). Observing in passing the inherent anti-materialism of the view that the form taken by Soviet decision-making in the area of investment resulted from the absence of a theory which would allow it to be different, we note that Giffen's article does reinforce the view that to be understood in a profound sense Soviet investment must necessarily be grasped in terms of systemic competition of a bureaucratic nature.

24   Only the absence of a theory of the fundamental categories underlying the social production relations can allow Soviet enterprise relations to appear as essentially harmonious, and the conclusion to be reached that the making of what are really concessions suggests that "a suitable term for the typical Soviet factory director is the 'benevolent boss.'" (Andrle 1976, p.86). But since the attempt to fit a concept of surplus appropriation inside a theory founded on "dimensions of social stratification" is premised upon a fairly superficial view of the role of exploitation, it is not surprising that it leads to an ascription of minimal *antagonistic* importance to workers' self-assertion. (pp.158-60).

25   We doubt whether many proletarians are unaware that capitalist exploiters, as long as the horizontal, vertical, or ideological divisions which separate them are not too extreme, not only

recognise and fraternise with each other as those who are 'above' the 'man in the street' — the 'masses,' the 'plebs,' the 'hoi polloi,' the *'prostye liudi'* — in behaviour which might not necessarily be 'networking' but is more broadly described as 'hob-nobbing'; they are also ready, in the interests of their own advancement, to 'do the dirty' on each other, to 'knife each other in the back.' We speak here of profound economic necessities in capitalist society.

26 The categories of the capitalist reproduction of the worker (by which the wage relation is defined) and that of the class struggle (which determines the quantity of resources which the magnitude of the wage represents) are deeper than that of the specific form which the wage takes.

27 Ruble mentions how the supervision of a worker's medical care by enterprise trade union bureaucrats sometimes extended, revealingly, to making sure that he followed the officially prescribed treatment. (1981, p.88).

28 But for a remarkable account of the highly resistant *blatnoi* culture, see Demin 1973. Whilst the importance of the *blatnye*, their autonomy, and their refusal to co-operate, should not be under-estimated, it is significant that there came a point where the culture operated mainly within the confines of the camps.

29 Berliner devotes a whole sub-chapter to the pressure on managers to raise wages in order to keep hold of workers, and their subsequent falsification of wage reporting, as early as 1957. In 1955 Prime Minister Bulganin had already criticised the managerial practice of adjusting norms so as to use up available wage funds. (See Kirsch 1972, p.46).

30 Helgeson notes that between 1959 and 1970 "while there may have been a great deal of movement into and out of Siberia...the net result is nearly insignificant." (1986, p.152).

31 This is a point that Standing, writing for the International Labour Organisation, fails to recognise when he states that "geographical mobility has been restricted by the housing shortage." His further assertion that a massive reduction in the enterprise social wage will enable the Soviet authorities to raise workers' productivity and thereby "combat poverty" (1991, pp.239, 241, 244-48, 250-53) is as typical a statement of bourgeois (or modern Soviet) political ideology as his corresponding 'policy proposal' is of its aims. See Chapman 1991 for a similar view.

32 In relation to problems with maintenance work, Berliner focuses on the 'pressure' to increase output, and on storming. (1957 pp.234-38). That this is an inadequately profound level at which to consider this particular problem for the Soviet system is evident from the fact that the dysfunctional effects of the cycle of storming and slacking would not have been so severe if only workers would have obeyed a simple call to work at a steadier pace.

33 In relation to the class struggle this question is discussed here for the first time.

34 In Table 7.1 we have purposefully avoided giving growth figures in roubles, preferring to cite figures for absolute volume. This is because Soviet money, especially in the producer goods sector, was not based on the rouble. In the argument made, therefore, the problem of relative rouble prices does not arise.

35 S. Smith describes how the introduction of the eight-hour day was a major gain of the 'February Revolution.' (1983, p.119). In the Petrograd area the length of the working day fell from 10.2 hours to 8.4 hours. (p.67). In wartime especially this was a major defeat for the bourgeoisie.

36 The introduction of the 'continuous working week' in 1929-30, which heralded the abolition of the 'universal' day of rest, also caused workers to work four days (in some sectors five) and rest one. This involved an additional reduction in the hours worked per worker. The six-day

working week, with Sunday off for everyone, was reintroduced in 1940. By the end of the 1960s the five-day working week, with two days off, was normal. (Hutchings 1982, p.110).

37   These comments about the length of the working day are of general applicability for most workers. There is, of course, a degree of variation: thus miners, for example, normally work six rather than seven hours a day. But the fall of the official average from 7.96 hours in 1956 to 6.93 hours in 1962 (Brown 1966, pp.304-05) is ample evidence to support the general point being made.

38   See notes 36 and 37 above.

39   There remains the question, of course, of whether in the absence of such a rate of flow of labour into the towns — after, say, 1945 — sufficient growth could have been achieved to satisfy the needs and thirst of Soviet capital within the framework of the prevailing economic system. The fact of productivity growth does not necessarily suggest that this question should be answered in the affirmative, any more than the tendency for 'over-investment' into construction and therefore into new projects (Nove 1980b, pp.163-64) necessarily implies the opposite. After all, we do not know what rate of growth *was* necessary, and the original question is so counter-factual as to be incapable of successful resolution.

For a discussion of the relative importance to Soviet growth of what in Marxist terms are understood as absolute surplus value as against relative surplus value, see Rutland 1985, pp.109-12. Rutland shows, interestingly but without making a critique at a conceptual level, how Soviet economists wrote in classically bourgeois fashion about 'labour productivity' and 'capital productivity.'

40   The merit of Bordiga's work, as is recognised by Camatte (1974) and Goldner (1991), lies in the insistence on the historical importance to Soviet capitalism of the capitalist 'agrarian revolution' associated with Stalin. As noted in Chapter 2 above, however, Bordiga grossly over-estimates the role of the market in the Soviet agricultural sector.

41   On capitalist enclosure more generally, see Midnight Notes 1990.

42   Clearly it would be vain to believe that one could quantify this cheapening in value terms with great precision. Even in regard to food, which is only one wage good of many, it would be impossible to count the number of necessary labour-hours exactly. In addition to work in the countryside, for example, one would also have to account for what was necessary labour in the rest of the agro-industrial complex: not only in fertiliser plants and tractor factories — and tractor repair workshops — but right down to the mines where coal is extracted to make steel to make the lorries which deliver the fertilisers to the villages. Most clerical work for *kolkhozy*, meanwhile, as for the food processing plants, is probably not 'necessary.' One would also have to look at food imports and exports, and indeed at the amount of food consumed by the ruling class. Such an analysis would be of limited usefulness, and in view of the various assumptions which would have to be made it might even be more useful simply to take the official rouble productivity figures straight out of Narod*noe Khoziaistvo*. Here we have endeavoured only to give a broad overview of developments in Soviet agriculture (changes in grain output, sown area, and rural population) in order to show that over the generations there has indeed been a substantial increase in productivity. It remains true that by international standards this sector is highly 'capital intensive' (Dovring 1980): meaning, essentially, that productivity is low and it is not very profitable, or even, if one were somehow able to consider it both in isolation from the rest of the Soviet economy and in terms of an international comparison, actually loss-making. Thus it has its own specific problems which as early as the 1960s led some analysts to refer

to its "permanent crisis." (Laird 1965). But in the present context, which is that of overall social capital and the opposition to it, it is not possible to delve into these problems, nor indeed into those of any other specific sector of the economy.

43   From the present perspective, Chapman's statement that "over the entire period 1928-58 Soviet real wages made no gain while real per capita consumption doubled" (1963a, p.248) is therefore without meaning.

44   No position is expressed here on whether an increased consumption of meat or dairy products involves a 'higher' standard of living in the ethical sense.

45   On housing space see also Matthews 1979, pp.209-14.

46   As above, we are assuming for the sake of simplicity that all constant capital is fixed.

47   See the four volumes of articles published under the collective title *Uskorenie: Aktual'nye Problemy Sotsial'no-Ekonomicheskogo Razvitiia.* (1985-87).

48   A similar analysis is given by Aitov, who writes that one of the principal conditions for the turning of labour into a "prime need" is the "guarantee of order, the reign of organisation [*organizovannost*], the strict control over the observation of labour discipline." (1987, p.95). This is interesting insofar as the context is that of the "change in the relationship to labour" (pp.91-101) which itself is seen as a necessary feature of the "acceleration of scientific-technical progress." Aitov's formulation is couched in more traditional language — it was published by the 'conservative' *Sovetskaia Rossiia* — but overall it differs little from Aganbegian's.

49   Extracts from this document were first made public in Britain. How it reached the West, whether by espionage or though an official leak — or, of course, some combination — was not revealed.

50   In praising the Russian mafia — the "good bad guys" — in the British left-liberal press, Luttwak makes the curious statement that "local mafias act to resist the excessive concentrations of economic power brought about by government corruption." (1995). Referring to the mafia pasts of many of the industrial and financial concerns of present-day Germany, Italy, and Japan, he asserts that the post-1945 recovery would have been much slower had it not been for the criminal 'enterprise' displayed by these concerns after the war. Might this kind of recovery in Russia, though, not be dependent upon as great a dislocation as that which was experienced in these other countries during the war? (It need not, of course, be as great as the dislocation which that war caused in the USSR itself). Luttwak mentions the mafia's role in starting the war in Chechenia but does not draw a connection.

51   See, for example, the role of the mafia in the car factory in Togliatti, which employs 100 000 people. Here, however, we would point to the large profits of the distribution company as set against the losses incurred by the production company. (Scott 1996b).

Bibliography

The notation we have used below is a slightly altered version of the 'Harvard' system. The year given first is the year each work first appeared, either in English or in any other language (e.g. Marx 1939, Debord 1967). If this is different from the year of publication of the edition actually cited, the former appears first in square brackets, and the latter is given at the end of the reference. Where an edition cited has been heavily revised, the first year given is that of the relevant edition's first publication (e.g. Nove 1982); otherwise, such as where a second or later edition differs from the first only in the addition of a new introduction or marginal notes, the first year given is that of the original edition (e.g. James 1950, Thompson 1963).

Abraham, Richard. *See* Kochan and Abraham 1983.

A Communist Effort (London).

A.D. 1985. Cardan's Socialism. *Here and Now* 2 (Summer 1985): 18-19.

Aganbegian, A[bel] G[ezevich]. 1988. *Sovetskaia Ekonomika: Vzgliad v Budushchee.* Moscow: Ekonomika.

Aitov, N. A. 1987. *Sotsial'nye Problemy Uskoreniia Nauchno-Tekhnicheskogo Progressa v SSSR*. Moscow: Sovetskaia Rossiia.

Amann, Ronald. [1978]. Soviet Technological Performance. *Survey* 23, no.2 (103) (Spring 1977-78): 61-72.

Amann, Ronald, and Julian Cooper, eds. 1982. *Industrial Innovation in the Soviet Union.* New Haven: Yale University Press.

_____. 1986. *Technical Progress and Soviet Economic Development*. Oxford: Blackwell.

Amann, Ronald, Julian Cooper, and R. W. Davies, eds. 1977. *The Technological Level of Soviet Industry*. Written with the assistance of Hugh Jenkins. New Haven: Yale University Press.

Andrle, Vladimir. 1976. *Managerial Power in the Soviet Union*. Farnborough: Saxon House.

[Anti-Parliamentary Communist Federation]. 1925a. Communism Suppressed in 'Soviet' Russia. *The Commune,* second series, 1, no.5 (November 1925): 34-35.

_____. 1925b. Communism, Militarism, and 'Sedition.' *The Commune,* second series, 1, no.5 (November 1925): 40-44.

_____. 1926. What is this 'Communism.'? *The Commune,* second series, 1, no.8 (May 1926): 113-18.

APCF. See Anti-Parliamentary Communist Federation.

Appeal of the Workers' Truth Group. [1922]. In *A Documentary History of Communism,*

Vol.1, ed. Robert V. Daniels, rev. ed. (Hanover, New Hampshire: University Press of New England, 1984), 147-48.

Armstrong, John A. 1961. *The Politics of Totalitarianism: The Communist Party of the Soviet Union from 1934 to the Present.* New York: Random House.

Armstrong, Philip, Andrew Glyn, and John Harrison. 1984. *Capitalism Since World War II: The Making and Breakup of the Great Boom.* London: Fontana, 1984.

Arnot, Bob. 1981. Soviet Labour Productivity and the Failure of the Shchekino Experiment. *Critique* 15 (1981): 31-56.

_____. 1988. *Controlling Soviet Labour: Experimental Change from Brezhnev to Gorbachev.* London: Macmillan.

Åslund, Anders. 1989. *Gorbachev's Struggle for Economic Reform: The Soviet Reform Process, 1985-88.* London: Pinter.

Aufheben (Brighton).

Aufheben. 1994. *See* "Decadence: The Theory of Decline or the Decline of Theory? Part 2."

_____. 1995. *See* "Civilization and its Latest Discontents."

Authier, Denis, and Jean Barrot. 1976. *La Gauche Communiste en Allemagne, 1918-21.* Avec des textes de H. Laufenberg, F. Wolffheim, H. Roland-Holst, A. Pannekoek. Critique de la Politique series, ed. Miguel Abensour. Paris: Payot.

Aves, Jonathan. 1992. The Russian Labour Movement, 1989-91: The Mirage of a Russian Solidarnosc. Chap. in Geoffrey A. Hosking, Jonathan Aves, and Peter J. S. Duncan, *The Road to Post-Communism: Independent Political Movements in the Soviet Union, 1985-1991*, pp.138-56. London: Pinter.

Avrich, Paul. 1965. What is 'Makhaevism'? *Soviet Studies* 17, no.1 (July 1965): 66-75.

Bahro, Rudolf. [1977]. *The Alternative in Eastern Europe.* Translated by David Fernbach. London: Verso, 1981.

La Banquise (Paris).

La Banquise. 1983. *See* Le Roman de nos Origines.

_____. 1986. See Sous le Travail, l' Activité.

Baran, Paul A. [1957]. *The Political Economy of Growth.* With an introduction by R. B. Sutcliffe. Harmondsworth: Penguin, 1973.

Baran, Paul A., and Paul M. Sweezy. 1966. *Monopoly Capital: An Essay on the American Economic and Social Order.* New York: Monthly Review Press.

Barbaria, Frank A. 1980. *Modern 'Asiatic' Despotism—Masquerading in Communist Workers' Ideology.* La Mesa, California: Inter-Disciplinary Endeavor to Analyse Societies.

Barker, G. R. [1955]. *Some Problems of Incentives and Labour Productivity in Soviet Industry: A Contribution to the Study of the Planning of Labour in the USSR.* Oxford: Blackwell, [1955].

Barltrop, Robert. 1975. *The Monument: The Story of the Socialist Party of Great Britain.* London: Pluto.

Barrot, Jean. [1972]. Capitalism and Communism. In Barrot and Martin 1972-74, pp.17-53.

_____. [1973]. Leninism and the Ultra-Left. In Barrot and Martin 1972-74, pp.81-108.

_____. 1977. Le 'Rénégat' Kautsky et son Disciple Lénine. Annexe to Karl Kautsky, *Les Trois Sources du Marxisme.* Paris: Spartacus. [English translation published as Jean Barrot, *Leninism or Communism?* Manchester: Wildcat, n.d.]

————. 1978a. *'Bilan': Contre-Révolution en Espagne, 1936-1939*. Paris: Union Générale d'Editions 10/18.

————. [1978b]. *Fascism. Anti-Fascism*. Edmonton, Alberta: Black Cat, 1982.

————. 1979. Critique of the Situationist International. *Red-Eye* 1 (Berkeley): 30-45.

Barrot, Jean and François Martin. [1972-74]. *Eclipse and Re-emergence of the Communist Movement*. Detroit: Black & Red, 1974.

Bauer, Otto. [1920]. *Bolshewismus oder Sozialdemokratie*. Vienna: n.p., 1920. Quoted in Jerome and Buick 1967, 60.

Bauer, Raymond A., Alex Inkeles, and Clyde Kluckhohn. 1956. *How the Soviet System Works: Cultural, Psychological, and Social Themes*. Russian Research Center Studies, no.24. Cambridge, Massachusetts: Harvard University Press.

Bayar, Ali. 1992. La Théorie de Marx et le Mode de Production Partitique. *Revue d'Etudes Comparatives Est-Ouest* (1992), no. 2-3 (June-September): 211-27.

Begg, David, Stanley Fischer, and Rudiger Dornbusch. 1987. *Economics*. 2nd ed. Maidenhead: McGraw-Hill.

Bellis, Paul. 1979. *Marxism and the USSR: The Theory of Proletarian Dictatorship and the Marxist Analysis of Soviet Society*. Atlantic Highlands, New Jersey: Humanities Press.

Belotserkovsky, Vadim. 1979. Workers' Struggles in the USSR in the Early Sixties. *Critique* 10-11 (Winter-Spring 1978-79): 37-50.

Bentwich, Norman. 1946. *From Geneva to San Francisco: An Account of the International Organisation of the New Order*. London: Victor Gollancz.

Bergson, Abram. 1964. T*he Economics of Soviet Planning*. New Haven: Yale University Press.

Bergson, Abram, and Herbert S. Levine, eds. 1983. *The Soviet Economy: Towards the Year 2000*. London: Allen & Unwin.

Berkman, Alexander. [1922]. *The Russian Tragedy*. London: Phoenix, 1986.

————. 1925. *The Bolshevik Myth: Diary 1920-1922*. London: Hutchinson.

Berliner, Joseph S. 1957. *Factory and Manager in the USSR*. Russian Research Center Studies, no.27. Cambridge, Massachusetts: Harvard University Press.

————. 1976. *The Innovation Decision in Soviet Industry*. Cambridge, Massachusetts: Massachusetts Institute of Technology.

————. 1988. Continuities in Management from Stalin to Gorbachev. Chap. in *Soviet Industry from Stalin to Gorbachev: Essays on Management and Innovation*, 261-97. Aldershot: Edward Elgar.

Bettelheim, Charles. [1969]. *On the Transition Between Capitalism and Socialism*. Translated by Fred Ehrenfeld. In Paul M. Sweezy and Charles Bettelheim, *On the Transition to Socialism*. New York: Monthly Review Press, 1971.

————. [1970]. State Property in Social Formations in Transition Between Capitalism and Socialism. Chap. in *Economic Calculation and Forms of Property*. Translated by John Taylor. London: Routledge & Kegan Paul, Routledge Direct Editions, 1976.

————. 1971. *Dictatorship of the Proletariat, Social Classes, and Proletarian Ideology*. Translated by Fred Ehrenfeld. In Paul M. Sweezy and Charles Bettelheim, *On the Transition to Socialism*. New York: Monthly Review Press, 1971.

————. [1974]. *Class Struggles in the USSR. First Period: 1917-1923*. Translated by

Brian Pearce. London: Monthly Review Press, 1976.

_____. [1977]. *Class Struggles in the USSR: Second Period: 1923-1930*. Translated by Brian Pearce. Hassocks, Sussex: Harvester, 1978.

Bienstock, Gregory, Solomon S. Schwarz, and Aron Yugow [Iugov]. 1944. *Management in Russian Industry and Agriculture*, ed. Arthur Feiler and Jacob Marschak. London: Oxford University Press.

Binyon, Michael. 1985. *Life in Russia*. London: Granada, Panther.

Black, Bob. 1985. The Abolition of Work. In *The Abolition of Work and Other Essays* (Port Townsend, Washington: Loompanics, [1985?]), pp.17-33.

Bland, W. B. 1980. *The Restoration of Capitalism in the Soviet Union*. London: Selecteditions.

Blum, William. 1986. *The CIA: A Forgotten History: US Global Interventions Since World War 2*. London: Zed Books.

Bologna, Sergio. 1972. Class Composition and the Theory of the Party at the Origin of the Workers' Councils Movement. *Telos* 13 (Fall 1972): pp. 68-91.

Bordiga, Amedeo. [1918-62]. *Russie et Révolution dans la Théorie Marxiste*. Translated by D[enis] Authier, J[acques] Camatte, and J.Colom. With a preface by J[acques] Camatte. Paris: Spartacus, 1978.

[Bordiga, Amedeo]. [1952]. *Dialogue avec Staline: Questions Essentielles de Théorie Marxiste sur L'Economie Soviétique et sur la Prétendu Socialisme en URSS*. Editions Programmatiques du Parti Communiste Internationale, no.8. Lyons: PCI, 1989.

Bordiga, Amedeo. [1954-55]. *Russie et Révolution dans la Théorie Marxiste*. In Bordiga 1918-62, pp.183-444.

_____. [1956-57]. *Structure Economique et Sociale de la Russie D'Aujourd'hui II: Développement des Rapports de Production après la Révolution Bolchevique*. Translated by Denis Authier, Jacques Camatte, and Jacques Colom. With an introduction by Jacques Camatte. Paris: Editions de l'Oubli, 1975.

_____. [1957]. 7 Novembre 1917-1957: Quarante Ans d'une Estimation Organique des Evènements de Russie dans la Dramatique Développement Social et Historique International. In idem, *Russie et Révolution dans la Théorie Marxiste*.

Borisov, Vadim, Simon Clarke, and Peter Fairbrother. 1994. *See* Clarke, Fairbrother, and Borisov 1994.

Bourrinet, Philippe. 1982. *See* Courant Communiste International. [Philippe Bourrinet]. [1982].

_____. 1992a. *See* Courant Communiste International. [Philippe Bourrinet]. [1992].

_____. 1992b. *Un Itineraire Ambigu: Ante Ciliga, 1898-1992*. Paris: [samizdat].

Bradford, George. 1992. The Triumph of Capital. *Fifth Estate* (Detroit) (Spring 1992): 7-20.

Braverman, Harry. 1974. *Labour and Monopoly Capital: The Degradation of Work in the Twentieth Century*. With a foreword by Paul M. Sweezy. New York: Monthly Review Press.

Brendel, Cajo. 1992. Answer to Dave Douglass. In *Goodbye to the Unions: A Controversy About Autonomous Class Struggle in Great Britain*, 27-36. London: Advocom, for Echanges et Mouvement.

Bricianer, Serge. [1969]. *Pannekoek and the Workers' Councils*. Translated by Malachy Carroll. Introduced by John Gerber. St. Louis: Telos, 1978.

Brinton, Maurice. [Christopher Pallis]. 1970. *The Bolsheviks and Workers' Control*,

1917-1921: The State and Counter-Revolution. London: Solidarity (North London).

Brodersen, Arvid. 1966. *The Soviet Worker: Labor and Government in Soviet Society*. New York: Random House.

Brovkin, Vladimir N. 1987. The Politics of the "New Course." Chap. in *The Mensheviks After October: Socialist Opposition and the Rise of the Bolshevik Dictatorship*, 77-104. Ithaca, New York: Cornell University Press.

Brown, Emily Clark. 1966. *Soviet Trade Unions and Labor Relations*. Cambridge, Massachusetts: Harvard University Press.

Buca, Edward. 1976. *Vorkuta*. London: Constable.

Buick, Adam. 1975. The Myth of the Transitional Society. *Critique* 3 (1975): 59-70.

_____. 1978. Ollman's Vision of Communism. *Critique* 9 (1978): 152.

Buick, A[dam], andW[illiam] Jerome. 1967. *See* Jerome and Buick 1967.

Buick, Adam, and John Crump. 1986. *State Capitalism: The Wages System Under New Management*. London: Macmillan.

Bukharin, Nikolai. [1915]. *Imperialism and World Economy*. With an introduction by V. I. Lenin. London: Merlin, 1972.

_____. [1920]. *The Economics of the Transition Period*. In Nikolai Bukharin, *The Politics and Economics of the Transition Period*, ed. and introd. Kenneth J. Tarbuck. Translated by Oliver Field. London: Routledge & Kegan Paul, 1979.

_____. [1928]. Notes of an Economist (At the Beginning of a New Economic Year). In Nikolai Bukharin, *Selected Writings on the State and the Transition to Socialism*. Translated, edited, and with an introduction by Richard B. Day. With forewords by Stephen F. Cohen and Ken Coates. Armonk, NY: Sharpe, 1982.

[Buonarroti, Philippe-Michel]. [1828]. *Buonarotti's History of Babeuf's Conspiracy for Equality; With the Author's Reflections on the Causes and Character of the French Revolution and His Estimate of the Leading Men and Events of That Epoch. Also His Views of Democratic Government, Community of Property, and Political and Social Equality*. Translated, illustrated, and with original notes by Bronterre O'Brien. London: Hetherington, 1836; repr. New York: Augustus M. Kelley, 1965.

Burawoy, Michael, and Kathryn Hendley. 1992. Between *Perestroika* and Privatisation: Divided Strategies and Political Crisis in a Soviet Enterprise. *Soviet Studies* 44, no.3 (1992): 371-402.

Burawoy, Michael, and Pavel Krotov. 1992. The Soviet Transition from Socialism to Capitalism: Worker Control and Economic Bargaining in the Wood Industry. *American Sociological Review* 57 (February 1992): 16-38.

_____. 1993. The Economic Basis of Russia's Political Crisis. *New Left Review* 198 (March-April 1993): 49-69.

Burnham, James. 1941. *The Managerial Revolution, or What Is Happening in the World Now*. London: Putnam.

Callaghan, John. 1984. The International Socialists. Chap. in *British Trotskyism: Theory and Practice*, 90-121. Oxford: Blackwell.

Camatte, Jacques. [1974]. *Community and Communism in Russia*. Translated from the French. London: David Brown, 1978.

_____. [1980]. *The Echo of Time*. Translated by David Loneragan, with final corrections by Jacqui Goerl. London: Unpopular Books, 1983.

Campeanu, Pavel. 1980. *See* Casals, Felipe Garcia. [Pavel Campeanu]. 1980.

_____. 1988. *The Genesis of the Stalinist Social Order*. Translated by Michael Vale. Armonk, New York: Sharpe.

Capitalism and its Revolutionary Destruction: A Statement by Wildcat. [1986]. Manchester: Wildcat, n.d.

Cardan, Paul. [Cornelius Castoriadis]. [1964]. *Redefining Revolution*. Solidarity pamphlet 44. London: Solidarity (London), n.d.

Carlo, Antonio. [1971]. The Socio-Economic Nature of the USSR. *Telos* 21 (Fall 1974): 2-86.

_____. [1979]. The Crisis of Bureaucratic Collectivism. *Telos* 43 (Spring 1980): 3-31.

_____. [1988-89]. Contradictions of Perestroika. *Telos* 79 (Spring 1989): 29-46.

Carr, E[dward] H[allett]. [1952]. *The Bolshevik Revolution, 1917-23*. Volume 2. Harmondsworth: Penguin, 1966.

_____. [1954]. *The Interregnum, 1923-1924*. London: Macmillan, 1965.

Casals, Felipe García. [Pavel Campeanu]. 1980. *The Syncretic Society*. Translated from the French by Guy Daniels. With a foreword by Alfred G. Meyer. White Plains, New York: Sharpe.

Castoriadis, Cornelius. [1949a]. Socialism or Barbarism. In *Political and Social Writings*, vol. 1, *1946-1955: From the Critique of Bureaucracy to the Positive Content of Socialism*, ed. and trans. David Ames Curtis (Minneapolis: University of Minnesota Press, 1988), 107-58.

_____. [1949b]. The Relations of Production in Russia. In *Political and Social Writings*, vol. 1, 76-106.

_____. [1953]. The Bureaucracy After the Death of Stalin. In *Political and Social Writings*, vol. 1, 242-55.

_____. [1954]. The Situation of Imperialism and Proletarian Perspectives. In *Political and Social Writings*, vol. 1, 256-89.

_____. [1955]. On the Content of Socialism, 1. In *Political and Social Writings*, vol. 1, 290-309.

_____. [1956]. The Proletarian Revolution Against the Bureaucracy. In *Political and Social Writings*, vol. 2, *1955-1960: From the Workers' Struggle Against Bureaucracy to Revolution in the Age of Modern Capitalism*, ed. and trans. David Ames Curtis (Minneapolis: University of Minnesota Press, 1988), 57-89.

_____. [1957]. On the Content of Socialism, 2. In *Political and Social Writings*, vol. 2, 90-154. [Also published as *Workers' Councils and the Economics of a Self-Managed Society*, introd. Peter Dorman (Philadelphia: Wooden Shoe, 1984)].

_____. [1958]. On the Content of Socialism, 3: The Workers' Struggle against the Organization of the Capitalist Enterprise. In *Political and Social Writings*, vol. 2, 155-92.

_____. [1960-61]. Modern Capitalism and Revolution. In *Political and Social Writings*, vol. 2, 226-315.

_____. [1964]. *Redefining Revolution*. See Cardan, Paul. [Cornelius Castoriadis]. [1964]. n.d.

_____. [1964-65]. Marxism and Revolutionary Theory. In *The Imaginary Institution of Society*, trans. Kathleen Blamey, 7-164. Cambridge: Polity Press, 1987.

————. [1973]. General Introduction. In *Political and Social Writings*, vol. 1, 3-36.

————. [1974-91]. *Philosophy, Politics, Autonomy: Essays in Political Philosophy*. Ed. David Ames Curtis. Oxford: Oxford University Press, 1991.

————. [1977]. *Le Régime Social de la Russie*. Paris: Le Vent du Ch'min, 1982. [English translation published as The Social Regime of Russia, *Telos* 38 (Winter 1978-79): 32-47.]

————. 1981a. *Devant la Guerre*. Vol.1. Paris: Fayard. [An English translation of the first chapter was published as Facing the War, trans. Joe Light, *Telos* 46 (Winter 1980-81): 43-61.]

————. [1981b]. The Nature and Value of Equality. In *Philosophy, Politics, Autonomy*, 124-42.

————. 1982a. The Crisis of Western Societies. Translated by David J. Parent. *Telos* 53 (Fall 1982): 17-28.

————. [1982b]. The Greek *Polis* and the Creation of Democracy. In *Philosophy, Politics, Autonomy*. 81-123.

————. 1988. The Gorbachev Interlude. *New Politics* 1, no.4 (new series) (Winter 1988): 60-79.

Castoriadis, Cornelius, C. L. R. James, and Grace Lee. 1958. *Facing Reality*. See James, Lee, and Chaulieu 1958.

Chapman, Janet G. 1963a. Consumption. In *Economic Trends in the Soviet Union*, ed. Abram Bergson and Simon Kuznets (Cambridge, Massachusetts: Harvard University Press, 1963): 235-82.

————. 1963b. *Real Wages in Soviet Russia since 1928*. Cambridge, Massachusetts: Harvard University Press, 1963.

————. 1991. Recent and Prospective Trends in Soviet Wage Determination. In *In Search of Flexibility: The New Soviet Labour Market*, ed. Guy Standing (Geneva: International Labour Organisation), pp.177-98.

Chase-Dunn, Christopher K. 1982. Socialist States in the Capitalist World-Economy. Chap. in Christopher K. Chase-Dunn, ed., *Socialist States in the World-System* (Beverly Hills: Sage), pp.21-55.

Chattopadhyay, Paresh. 1994. *The Marxian Concept of Capital and the Soviet Experience: Essay in the Critique of Political Economy*. Praeger Series in Political Economy, ed. Rodney Green. Westport, Connecticut: Praeger.

Chavance, Bernard. 1980. *Le Capital Socialiste: Histoire Critique de l'Economie Politique de Socialisme (1917-1954)*. Paris: Le Sycomore.

————. 1989. *Le Système Economique Soviétique de Brejnev à Gorbatchev*. Paris: Nathan.

Chen Erjin. [1979]. *China: Crossroads Socialism*. Translated and introduced by Robin Munro. London: Verso, 1984.

Ciliga, Anton. [1938?] The Kronstadt Revolt. *Anarchy* 2 (1971): 13-16.

————. [1938-50]. *The Russian Enigma*. Part 1 [1938, except for Book 3, chap. 9, 1950] translated by Fernand G. Fernier and Anne Cliff; Part 2 [1950] translated by Hugo Dewar and Margaret Dewar. London: Ink Links, 1979.

"Civilization and its Latest Discontents." [Review of *Against His-story, Against Leviathan!*

by Fredy Perlman]. *Aufheben* 4 (Summer 1995): 36-41.

Clarke, Simon. 1990. Crisis of Socialism or Crisis of the State? *Capital & Class* 42 (Winter 1990): 19-29.

_____. 1992. Privatisation and the Development of Capitalism in Russia. *New Left Review* 196 (November-December 1992): 3-41.

_____. 1993a. The Contradictions of 'State Socialism.' Chap. in Simon Clarke, Peter Fairbrother, Michael Burawoy, and Pavel Krotov, *What About the Workers? Workers and the Transition to Capitalism in Russia* (London: Verso), 5-29.

_____. 1993b. The Crisis of the Soviet System. Chap. in Clarke et al., Chap. in *What About the Workers?* 30-55.

_____. 1993c. Privatisation and the Development of Capitalism in Russia. Chap. in Clarke et al., *What About the Workers?* 199-241.

Clarke, Simon, and Peter Fairbrother. 1993a. The Workers' Movement in Russia. *Capital & Class* 49 (Spring 1993): 7-17.

_____. 1993b. Trade Unions and the Working Class. Chap. in Clarke et al., *What About the Workers?* 91-120.

_____. 1993c. The Origins of the Independent Workers' Movement and the 1989 Miners' Strike. Chap. in Clarke et al., *What About the Workers?* 121-44.

_____. 1993d. Beyond the Mines: The Politics of the New Workers' Movement. Chap. in Clarke et al., *What About the Workers?* 145-60.

_____. 1993e. The Strikes of 1991 and the Collapse of the Soviet System. Chap. in Clarke et al., *What About the Workers?* 161-72.

_____. 1993f. After the Coup: The Workers' Movement in the Transition to a Market Economy. Chap. in Clarke et al., *What About the Workers?* 173-98.

Clarke, Simon, Peter Fairbrother, and Vadim Borisov. 1994. The Workers' Movement in Russia, 1987-1992. *Critique* 26 (1994): 55-68.

Cleaver, Harry. 1979. *Reading "Capital" Politically.* Brighton: Harvester.

_____. 1989. Close the IMF, Abolish Debt and End Development: A Class Analysis of the International Debt Crisis. *Capital & Class* 39 (winter 1989): 17-50.

_____. [1997?] Introductory Notes to the Texas Archives of Autonomist Marxism. Worldwide Web address: http://www.eco.utexas.edu/faculty/Cleaver/txarchintro.html.

Cliff, Tony. [1955]. *State Capitalism in Russia.* London: Pluto, 1974.

Cobban, Alfred. 1963. *A History of Modern France. Volume 1: 1715-1799.* 3rd ed. Harmondsworth: Penguin, 1963.

Cohen, Alan. [1990]. *The Decadence of the Shamans, or Shamanism as a Key to the Secrets of Communism.* London: Unpopular Books, 1991.

Cohen, Stephen F. 1985. *Rethinking the Soviet Experience: Politics and History Since 1917.* Oxford: Oxford University Press.

Coleman, Stephen. 1987. Impossibilism. Chap. in Rubel and Crump 1987, 83-103.

Collectif Junius. 1982. *Au-delà du Parti: Evolution du Concept de "Parti" depuis Marx.* Paris: Spartacus.

Comintern. 1919-22. See *Theses, Resolutions and Manifestos of the First Four Congresses of the Third International.* [1919-22].

Communism (Brussels). [Central review in English of the Internationalist Communist Group].

"Communism Against Democracy." 1987. *Communism* 4 (Winter 1987-88) (Brussels): 37-58.

"Communisme: Eléments de Réflection (1)." 1984. *L'Insecurité Sociale*, series 2, 2 (4th quarter, 1984) (Paris). [Somewhat confusingly, the key section "De la Domination de la Marchandise" has been published in English translation [1984?] as "Commodity Production and its Abolition" — along with translations of other texts by the same group — within a French-language cover taken from *L'Insecurité Sociale* 0 [issue zero] (1982)].

Communist Headache. (Sheffield).

Connor, Walter D. 1972. *Deviance in Soviet Society: Crime, Delinquency, and Alcoholism*. London: Columbia University Press.

_____. 1979a. *Socialism, Politics, and Equality: Hierarchy and Change in Eastern Europe and the USSR*. New York: Columbia University Press.

_____. 1979b. Workers, Politics, and Class Consciousness. Chap. in Kahan and Ruble, eds., 1979, 313-32.

_____. 1991. *The Accidental Proletariat: Workers, Politics and Crisis in Gorbachev's Russia*. Princeton: Princeton University Press.

Conquest, Robert. 1986. The Famine Rages. Chap. in *The Harvest of Sorrow: Soviet Collectivization and the Terror-Famine*. London: Hutchinson.

Conquest, Robert, ed. 1967. *Industrial Workers in the USSR*. Soviet Studies Series. London: Bodley Head.

Conradi, Peter, and Mark Franchetti. 1996. See Franchetti and Conradi 1996.

Conyngham, William J. 1973. *Industrial Management in the Soviet Union: The Role of the CPSU in Industrial Decision-Making*. 1917-1970. Hoover Institution Publication 116. Stanford: Hoover Institution Press, Stanford University.

_____. 1982. *The Modernization of Soviet Industrial Management: Socioeconomic Development and the Search for Viability*. Cambridge: Cambridge University Press.

Cook, Linda J. 1993. *The Soviet Social Contract and Why It Failed: Welfare Policy and Workers' Politics from Brezhnev to Yeltsin*. Harvard, Massachusetts: Harvard University Press.

Cooper, Julian. 1982. Innovation for Innovation in Soviet Industry. In Amann and Cooper 1982, 453-513.

Courant Communiste International. [Philippe Bourrinet]. 1982. *La Gauche Communiste d'Italie*. Paris: CCI.

_____. [1992]. *La Gauche Hollandaise: Aux Origines de Courant Communiste International des Conseils*. Paris: CCI.

Crisp, Olga. [1972]. "The Pattern of Industrialisation in Russia, 1700-1914." Chap. in Olga Crisp, *Studies in the Russian Economy Before 1914*. (London: Macmillan, 1976), pp.5-54.

Critique. 1994. [Preamble]. *Critique* 26 (1994): inside front cover.

Crump, John. 1975. *A Contribution to the Critique of Marx*. London: Social Revolution/Solidarity.

_____. 1983. The Development of Capitalism in Japan and the Forming of a Working Class. Chap. in *The Origins of Socialist Thought in Japan*, 3-28. Beckenham: Croom Helm.

_____. [1989]. *The State and Capital in Japan*. Subversion Discussion Paper No. 2. Manchester: Subversion, [1989].

Crump, John, and Maximilen Rubel, eds. 1987. *See* Rubel and Crump 1987.

CWO. [Communist Workers' Organisation]. 1982. *See* "Theories of State Capitalism." 1982.

Dalla Costa, Mariarosa. [1971]. Women and the Subversion of the Community. In *The Power of Women and the Subversion of the Community* (Bristol: Falling Wall Press, 1975), with a foreword by the Power of Women Collective, Britain and the Padua Wages for Housework Committee, and an introduction by Selma James, 21-56.

Dalrymple, Dana G. 1964. The Soviet Famine of 1932-34. *Soviet Studies* 15, no.3 (January 1964): 250-84.

Daniels, Robert Vincent. 1960. *The Conscience of the Revolution: Communist Opposition in Soviet Russia*. London: Oxford University Press.

Darwin, Charles. [1866]. *On the Origin of the Species or the Preservation of Favoured Races in the Struggle for Life*. 6th ed., with additions and corrections. London: John Murray, 1888.

Davies, R. W. 1958. *The Development of the Soviet Budgetary System*. With a foreword by Alexander Baykov. Cambridge: Cambridge University Press, 1958.

————. 1980a. *The Industrialisation of Soviet Russia*, vol.1, *The Collectivisation of Soviet Agriculture, 1929-1930*. London: Macmillan, 1980.

————. 1980b. *The Industrialisation of Soviet Russia*, vol.2, *The Soviet Collective Farm, 1929-1930*. London: Macmillan, 1980.

————. 1986. The Ending of Mass Unemployment in the USSR. Chap. in David Lane, ed., *Labour and Employment in the USSR* (Brighton: Harvester, Wheatsheaf), 21-35.

Davies, R. W., Mark Harrison, and S. G. Wheatcroft, eds. 1994. *The Economic Transformation of the Soviet Union, 1913-1945*. Cambridge: Cambridge University Press.

Davis, Stan, and Bill Davidson. 1991. *2020 Vision: Transform Your Business Today to Succeed in Tomorrow's Economy*. London: Random Century/Business Books, 1991.

Debord, Guy, *Society of the Spectacle*. [1967]. [Revised translation]. Detroit: Black & Red, 1977.

De Brunhoff, Suzanne. *Marx on Money*. [1973]. Translated by Maurice J. Goldbloom, With a preface by Duncan K. Foley. New York: Urizen, 1976.

"Decadence: The Theory of Decline or the Decline of Theory? Part 2." 1994. *Aufheben* 3 (Summer 1994): 24-34.

[Demin, Mikhail]. Mikhaïl Diomine. [1973]. *Le Blatnoï*. Collections "Vécu." Paris: Robert Laffont, 1975.

Deutscher, Isaac. 1950. *Soviet Trade Unions: Their Place in Soviet Labour Policy*. London: Royal Institute of International Affairs.

Dewar, Margaret. 1956. *Labour Policy in the USSR, 1917-1928*. London: Royal Institute of International Affairs, 1956.

Djilas, Milovan. 1957. *The New Class: An Analysis of the Communist System*. London: Atlantic Press, Thames and Hudson.

————. 1969. *The Unperfect Society: Beyond the New Class*. Translated by Dorian Cooke. New York: Harcourt, Brace and World.

————. 1988. The Crisis of Communism. *Telos* 80 (Summer 1989): 117-21.

"Dossier on Class Struggle and Social Conditions in Russia and Ex-USSR." [1993-95]. *Echanges* 78/79, no. 4/94-1/95 (1995): 4-64.

Dovring, Folke. 1980. Capital Intensity in Soviet Agriculture. In *Agricultural Policies in the USSR and Eastern Europe*, ed. Ronald A. Francisco, Betty A Laird, and Roy D. Laird, Westview Special Studies on the Soviet Union and Estern Europe (Boulder, Colarodo: Westview), pp.5-26.

Dunayevskaya, Raya. [1942-43]. See Forest, F. [Raya Dunayevskaya]. 1942-43.

————. [1946-47]. *See* Forest, F. [Raya Dunayevskaya]. 1946-47.

————. [1958]. *Marxism and Freedom: From 1776 Until Today*. 4th ed. With a preface by Harry McShane, and an original preface by Herbert Marcuse. London: Pluto, 1975.

————. [1958-72]. *For the Record: The Johnson-Forest Tendency, or Theory of State Capitalism, 1941-51: Its Vicissitudes and Ramifications*. Detroit: News and Letters, 1972.

————. [1963]. Introduction to the Second Edition of *Marxism and Freedom*. Included with Dunayevskaya 1958, pp.16-20.

————. [1982]. Andropov's Ascendancy Reflects Final Stage of State-Capitalism's Degeneracy. In *The Marxist-Humanist Theory of State-Capitalism: Selected Writings by Raya Dunayevskaya*, with an introduction by Peter Hudis (Chicago: News and Letters, 1992), 143-48.

Dyker, David A. 1983. *The Process of Investment in the Soviet Union*. Cambridge: Cambridge University Press.

Dziewanowski, M. K. 1989. *A History of Soviet Russia*. Third ed. Englewood Cliffs, New Jersey: Prentice Hall, 1989.

Echanges (London and Paris).

Echanges et Mouvement. 1977. See *In Chile Tanks. In Europe Unions*.

————. 1979. *The Refusal of Work: Facts and Discussions*. London: Echanges et Mouvement.

————. [1993-95]. *See* "Dossier on Class Struggle and Social Conditions in Russia and Ex-USSR."

Ellman, Michael. 1975. Did the Agricultural Surplus Provide the Resources for the Increase in Investment during the First Five Year Plan? *The Economic Journal* 85 (December 1975): 844-64.

————. 1982. Did Soviet Economic Growth End in 1978? In *Crisis in the East European Economy: The Spread of the Polish Disease*, ed. Jan Drewmowski (London: Croom Helm), pp. 131-42.

————. 1989. *Socialist Planning*. Second edition. Cambridge: Cambridge University Press.

Engels, Friedrich. [1877-78]. *Anti-Dühring: Herr Eugen Dühring's Revolution in Science*. Beijing: Foreign Languages Press, 1976.

————. [1896-1925]. *Dialectics of Nature*. Second revised edition. Moscow: Progress, 1954.

Fakiolas, R. 1962. Problems of Labour Mobility in the USSR. *Soviet Studies* 14 (July 1962): pp.16-40.

Fantham, John, and Moshe Machover. 1979. *The Century of the Unexpected: A New Analysis of Soviet Type Societies*. London: Big Flame.

Fehér, Ferenc. 1983. The Functioning of the System: Conflicts and Perspectives. In Fehér,

Heller, and Márkus 1983, pp. 219-99.

Fehér, Ferenc, Agnes Heller, and György Márkus. 1983. *Dictatorship Over Needs*. Oxford: Blackwell.

Ferment Ouvrier Révolutionnaire. [FOR]. 1965. *Pour un Second Manifeste Communiste*. Paris: Losfeld.

[Fernandez, Neil]. 1984. The Progression of the Movement. *A Communist Effort* 1 (March 1984): 14-20.

_____. [1985]. Russia 1917: In Defence of Council Communism. *A Communist Effort* 4 [1985]: 4-11.

_____. [1989a]. *Capitalism and Class Struggle in the USSR*. Subversion Discussion Paper No.1. Manchester: Subversion, [1989].

_____. 1989b. *Notes on Class Struggle in the USSR*. Subversion Discussion Paper No.4. Manchester: Subversion.

Filtzer, Donald. 1986. *Soviet Workers and Stalinist Industrialization: The Formation of Modern Soviet Production Relations, 1928-1941*. London: Pluto.

_____. 1991. The Contradictions of the Marketless Market: Self-financing in the Soviet Industrial Enterprise, 1986-90. *Soviet Studies* 43, no. 6 (1991): 989-1009.

_____. 1992a. Economic Reforms and Production Relations in Soviet Industry, 1986-90. Chap. in *Labour in Transition: The Labour Process in Eastern Europe and China*, ed. Chris Smith and Paul Thompson. London: Routledge.

_____. 1992b. *Soviet Workers and De-Stalinization: The Consolidation of the Modern System of Soviet Production Relations, 1953-1964*. Cambridge: Cambridge University Press.

FOR. *See* Ferment Ouvrier Révolutionnaire.

Forest, F. [Raya Dunayevskaya]. 1942-43. An Analysis of Russian Economy. [Published in three parts]. *The New International* (New York). December 1942, pp.327-32; January 1943, pp.17-22; February 1943, pp.52-57.

_____. 1946-47. The Nature of the Russian Economy: A Contribution on the Discussion on Russia. [Published in two parts]. *The New International*. (New York). December 1946, pp.313-17; January 1947, pp.27-30.

Franchetti, Mark, and Peter Conradi. 1996. Europe's Roaring Trade in Sex Slaves. *The Sunday Times*, 9 June 1996.

Frank, Peter, and Ronald J. Hill. 1986. *See* Hill and Frank 1986.

Friedgut, Theodore, and Lewis Siegelbaum. 1990. Perestroika from Below: The Soviet Miners' Strike and its Aftermath. *New Left Review*, no. 181 (May-June 1990): 5-32.

Friedrich, Carl J., and Zbigniew K. Brzezinski. 1961. *Totalitarian Dictatorship and Autocracy*. London: Praeger.

Füredi, Frank. 1986. *The Soviet Union Demystified: A Materialist Analysis*. London: Junius.

Galbraith, John Kenneth. 1972. *The New Industrial State*. Harmondsworth: Penguin.

_____. 1974. *Economics and the Public Purpose*. London: André Deutsch.

Gerber, John. [1978?]. The Formation of Pannekoek's Marxism. Preface to Bricianer [1969]. 1978.

Gerschenkron, Alexander, ed. 1962. *Economic Backwardness in Historical Perspective*. Cambridge, Massachusetts: Harvard University Press.

Gidwitz, Betsy. 1982. Labor Unrest in the Soviet Union. *Problems of Communism* 31, no.6 (November-December 1982): 25-42.

Giffen, Janice. 1981. The Allocation of Investment in the Soviet Union: Criteria for the Efficiency of Investment. *Soviet Studies* 33, no.4 (October 1981): pp.593-609.

GIK. *See* Group of International Communists of Holland.

Gluschenko, Irina. 1993. "Russian Health Care: The Collapse Continues." *Russian Labour Review* 2 (1993): 42.

GOC. *See* Groupes Ouvriers Communistes.

Godson, Joseph. 1981. "The Role of the Trade Unions." Chap. in Schapiro and Godson, eds., 1981, pp.106-29.

Goldman, Emma. 1925. *My Disillusionment in Russia.* New York: Crowell, 1970.

_____. 1931. *Living My Life.* Vol. 2. New York: Dover.

Goldman, Marshall I. 1963. *Soviet Marketing: Distribution in a Controlled Economy.* London: Macmillan, Free Press of Glencoe.

Goldner, Loren. 1991. Amadeo Bordiga, the Agrarian Question and the International Revolutionary Movement. *Critique* 23 (1991): 73-100.

Gombin, Richard. 1978. Council Communism. Chap. in *The Radical Tradition: A Study in Modern Revolutionary Thought* (London: Methuen), pp.81-118.

Gomulka, Stanislaw. 1986. The Incompatibility of Socialism and Rapid Innovation. Chap. in *Growth, Innovation and Reform in Eastern Europe* (Brighton: Harvester, Wheatsheaf), 42-61.

Gorbachev, Mikhail. 1985a. Kursom Edinstva i Splochennnosti. Speech to a meeting of electors in the Kievskii ward of the city of Moscow in the elections to the RSFSR Supreme Soviet, 20 February 1985. In *Izbrannye Rechi i Stat'i*, tome 2, ed. CPSU Central Committee, Institute of Marxism-Leninism (Moscow: Izdatel'stvo Politicheskoi Literatury, 1987),

_____. 1985b. Rech' na Vneocherednom Plenume TsK KPSS [Speech to the Extraordinary Plenum of the CPSU Central Committee], 11 March 1985. In *Izbrannye Rechi i Stat'i,* tome 2, pp.129-33.

_____. 1985c. *Korennoi Vopros Ekonomicheskoi Politiki Partii.* Report to the Conference of the CPSU Central Committee on Issues Concerning the Acceleration of Scientific-Technical Progress, 11 June 1985. In *Izbrannye Rechi i Stat'i*, pp.251-78.

_____. 1986. *Politicheskii Doklad Tsentral'nogo Komiteta KPSS XXVII S'ezdu Kommunisticheskoi Partii Sovetskogo Soiuza.* [Political Report of the Central Committee to the 27th Congress of the CPSU], 25 February 1986. Moscow: Izdatel'stvo Politicheskoi Literatury, 1986.

_____. 1987. *Perestroika: New Thinking for Our Country and and the World.* London: Collins.

Gorlin, Alice C. 1985. The Power of Soviet Industrial Ministries in the 1980s. *Soviet Studies* 27, no.3 (July 1985): 353-70.

Gorman, David. 1990. The Myth of Working Class Passivity: Commodity Fetishism, Class Formation and Proletarian Self-Emancipation. *Radical Chains* 2 (Winter 1990-91): 4-10.

Gorter, Herman. [1920]. *Open Letter to Comrade Lenin: A Reply to "'Left-Wing Communism':*

an Infantile Disorder." London: Wildcat, 1989.

_____. [1921]. *Manifesto of the Fourth Communist International.* [Samizdat edition]. [Newcastle-under-Lyme: Careless Talk Collective, 1985?]. [Also in *Workers' Dreadnought* (London), 8 October - 10 December 1921].

_____. [1923]. *The Communist Workers' International.* [Samizdat edition.] [Newcastle-under-Lyme: Careless Talk Collective, 1985?].

[Gramsci, Antonio]. [1929-35]. The Intellectuals. In *Selections from the "Prison Notebooks" of Antonio Gramsci*, ed. and trans. Quintin Hoare and Geoffrey Nowell Smith (London: Lawrence and Wishart, 1971), pp.5-23.

Grancelli, Bruno. 1988. *Soviet Management and Labor Relations.* London: Allen & Unwin.

Granick, David. 1961. *The Red Executive: A Study of the Organization Man in Russian Industry.* New York: Doubleday, Anchor.

_____. 1987. *Job Rights in the Soviet Union: Their Consequences.* Cambridge: Cambridge University Press.

Gregory, Paul R., and Robert C. Stuart. 1981. *Soviet Economic Performance.* Second ed. New York: Harper & Row.

Grossman, Gregory. 1977. The 'Second Economy' of the USSR. *Problems of Communism* 26, no. 5 (September-October 1977): 25-40.

Group of International Communists of Holland. [1930]. *The Fundamental Principles of Communist Production and Distribution.* Translated, edited, and with a foreword and postscript, by Mike Baker. London: Movement for Workers' Councils, 1990.

[Group of International Communists of Holland]. [1934]. *The Bourgeois Role of Bolshevism.* Glasgow: Glasgow People's Press, n.d. [English translation originally entitled *Theses on Bolshevism*].

Groupes Ouvriers Communistes. [1929]. "L'Ouvrier Communiste et les Syndicats." In *L'Ouvrier Communiste Contre les Syndicats*, supplement to *Jeune Taupe* 35 (1981) (Paris), 1-8. [Originally published in serialised form as "Faut-Il Conquérir les Syndicats ou les Détruire?" in *L'Ouvrier Communiste*, 1-5 (1929)].

Guattari, Félix, and Toni [Antonio] Negri. [1985]. *Communists Like Us: New Spaces of Liberty, New Lines of Alliance.* With a postscript by Toni Negri. Translated by Michael Ryan. Semiotext(e) Foreign Agents Series. New York: Semiotext(e), 1990.

Guerre Sociale. [1977]. Psychedelic Bordiguism: Invariance and Fictive Capital. Translated from the French. In *Ruins of Glamour, Glamour of Ruins* (London: Unpopular Books, 1986), 22-30.

Hambro, Hilde. 1992. Commodity Fetishism: Foundations, Functions and Historical Specificity. M. Phil. thesis, University of Glasgow.

Hanson, Philip. 1981. *Trade and Technology in Soviet-Western Relations.* London: Macmillan.

_____. 1986. The Serendipitous Soviet Achievement of Full Employment: Labour Shortage and Labour Hoarding in the Soviet Economy. In David Lane, ed., *Labour and Employment in the USSR* (Brighton: Harvester, Wheatsheaf), 83-111.

Harman, Chris. [1971]. *The Nature of Stalinist Russia and the Eastern Bloc.* In Peter Binns, Tony Cliff, and Chris Harman, *Russia: From Workers' State to State Capitalism*, 37-72. London: Bookmarks, 1987.

_____. 1990. The Storm Breaks. *International Socialism* 46 (Spring 1990): 3-93.

Haynes, Viktor, and Olga Semyonova. 1979. *Workers Against the Gulag: The New Opposition in the Soviet Union*. London: Pluto Press.

Helgeson, Ann. 1986. Geographical Mobility: Its Implications for Employment. Chap. in David Lane, ed., *Labour and Employment in the USSR* (Brighton: Harvester, Wheatsheaf), 145-75.

Heller, Agnes. [1974]. *The Theory of Need in Marx*. London: Allison & Busby, in association with Spokesman Books, 1976.

_____. 1983. Political Domination and its Consequences. Part 2 in Fehér, Heller, and Márkus 1983, pp.137-217.

Hewett, Ed A. 1988. *Reforming the Soviet Economy: Equality versus Efficiency*. Washington D.C.: Brookings Institution.

Hilferding, Rudolf. [1910]. *Finance Capital: A Study of the Latest Phase of Capitalist Development*. Ed. with an introduction by Tom Bottomore, from translations by Morris Watnick and Sam Gordon. London: Routledge & Kegan Paul, 1981.

_____. [1940]. State Capitalism or Totalitarian State Economy. In C. Wright Mills, ed., *The Marxists* (Harmondsworth: Penguin, 1963), 323-28.

Hill, Ronald J., and Peter Frank. 1986. *The Soviet Communist Party*. Third edition. London: Unwin Hyman.

Hobsbawm, E. J. [1968]. *Industry and Empire*. Pelican Economic History of Britain Series, vol.3, *From 1750 to the Present Day*. Harmondsworth: Penguin, 1969.

Holubenko, M. 1975. The Soviet Working Class: Discontent and Opposition. *Critique* 5 (1975): 5-25.

Horner, Karl. [Anton Pannekoek]. [1919?] *Sozialdemokratie und Kommunismus*. Hamburg: publisher unknown, n.d. Quoted at length in English translation in "Social Democracy and Communism," chap. 6 of Bricianer 1969.

Horvat, Branko. 1982. *The Political Economy of Socialism: A Marxist Social Theory*. New York: Sharpe.

Hosking, Geoffrey. 1985. *A History of the Soviet Union*. London: Collins, Fontana.

Hough, Jerry F. 1972. The Soviet System: Petrification or Pluralism? *Problems of Communism* 21, no.2 (March-April 1972): 25-45.

_____. 1976. Political Participation in the Soviet Union. *Soviet Studies* 28, no.1 (January 1976): 3-20.

_____. 1979. Policy-Making and the Worker. In Kahan and Ruble 1979, 367-96.

Hubbard, Leonard E. 1942. *Soviet Labour and Industry*. London: Macmillan.

"The Hunt for Red October: Ten Days That Didn't Overthrow Capitalism." 1991. *Wildcat* (London) 15 (Autumn 1991): 17-22.

Hutchings, Raymond. 1982. *Soviet Economic Development*. Second edition. Oxford: Blackwell.

ICG. [Internationalist Communist Group]. 1987. *See* "Communism Against Democracy." 1987.

ICP. 1991. *See* International Communist Party. 1991.

IMF. 1991. *See* International Monetary Fund et al. 1991.

IMF. 1992. *See* International Monetary Fund 1992.

In Chile Tanks. In Europe Unions. 1977. *Echanges et Mouvement* 11 (1977).

Inkeles, Alex. 1968. *Social Change in Soviet Russia*. Cambridge, Massachusetts: Harvard University Press.

Inkeles, Alex, and Raymond A. Bauer. 1959. *The Soviet Citizen: Daily Life in a Totalitarian Society*. Written with the assistance of David Gleicher and Irving Rosow. Russian Research Center Studies, no.35. Cambridge, Massachusetts/London: Harvard University Press/ Oxford University Press.

L'Insecurité Sociale (Paris).

L'Insecurité Sociale. 1982. *See* "Les Branches d'Octobre." 1982.

————. 1984. *See* "Communisme: Eléments de Réflection (1)." 1984.

Insurrezione. 1984. *Prolétaires, Si Vous Saviez: Italie, 77-80*. Paris: Ombre Hérétique.

Institute of Economics, Academy of Sciences of the USSR. 1957. *Political Economy* [A Textbook]. 2nd ed. English trans. ed. C. P. Dutt and Andrew Rothstein. London: Lawrence and Wishart.

International Communist Party. 1991. *Revolution and Counter-Revolution in Russia*. Texts of the Communist Left, no.5. Liverpool: International Communist Party.

International Monetary Fund. 1992. *World Economic Output, October 1992*. Washington DC: International Monetary Fund.

International Monetary Fund, the World Bank, the Organisation for Economic Co-operation and Development, and the European Bank for Reconstruction and Development. 1991. Energy. Chap. in *A Study of the Soviet Economy*, vol.3 (Paris: OECD), 181-227.

Internationale Situationniste, 1958-69. 1975. Paris: Champ Libre. [A complete collection of all issues of the journal *Internationale Situationniste*].

[Iugov.] Yugoff, A[ron]. [1929]. *Economic Trends in Soviet Russia*. Trans. Eden Paul and Cedar Paul. London: George Allen & Unwin, 1930.

————. 1931. *Piatiletka*. Berlin: Sotsialisticheskii Vestnik.

[Iurevskii.] Yourievsky, I. [1932]. From Lenin to Stalin. In Joseph Shaplen and David Shub, *Socialism, Fascism, Communism* (New York: American League for Democratic Socialism, 1934), 123-73.

James, C. L. R. [1950]. *State Capitalism and World Revolution*. Written in collaboration with Raya Dunayevskaya and Grace Lee. New ed. With an introduction by Paul Buhle. Chicago: Charles H. Kerr, 1986.

————. [1963]. Lenin and the Vanguard Party. In *The C. L. R. James Reader*, ed. Anna Grimshaw, with an introduction by the editor (Oxford: Blackwell, 1992), 327-30.

James, C. L. R., Grace C. Lee, and Pierre Chaulieu [Cornelius Castoriadis]. [1958]. *Facing Reality*. Detroit: Bewick, 1974.

James, C. L. R., et al. 1956. *See* Johnson, Christianson, Chaulieu, Brendel, Massen, and Hughes 1956.

Jerome, W[illiam], and A[dam] Buick. 1967. Soviet State Capitalism? The History of an Idea. *Survey* 62 (January 1967): 58-71.

Jeune Taupe (Paris).

Johnson [C. L. R. James], Christianson, Chaulieu [Cornelius Castoriadis], [Cajo] Brendel, [Theo] Massen, and Hughes. [1956]. Preface to the Second Edition of James 1950. Included with the 1986 edition, pp.xxix-xxxiv.

[Jones, R. M.] 1984. *The Experience of the Factory Committees in the Russian Revolution*.

Council Communist Pamphlet No.2. Cardiff: Scorcher.

Kahan, Arcadius. [1962]. "Labour Turnover in the Soviet Union." Reprinted in Arcadius Kahan, *Studies and Essays on the Soviet and East European Economies*, vol.1, *Published Works on the Soviet Economy*, ed. Peter B. Brown (Newtonville, Massachusetts: Oriental Research Partners, 1991).

————. 1979. Some Problems of the Industrial Worker. In Kahan and Ruble 1979, 283-312.

Kahan, Arcadius, and Blair A. Ruble. 1979. *Industrial Labor in the USSR*. A Special Study of the Kennan Institute for Advanced Russian Studies, The Wilson Center, No. 1; Pergamon Policy Study, No. 20. New York: Pergamon.

Kaser, Michael. 1970. *Soviet Economics*. London: Weidenfeld and Nicholson, World University Library.

Katsenelinboigen, A. Coloured Markets in the Soviet Union. 1977. *Soviet Studies* 29, no.1 (January 1977): 62-85.

Kautsky, Karl. [1919]. *Terrorism and Communism: A Contribution to the Natural History of Revolution*. Translated by W. H. Kerridge. London: National Labour Press, 1920.

————. [1930]. *Bolshevism at a Deadlock*. Translated by B. Pritchard. London: George Allen & Unwin, 1931.

————. [1933]. Marxism and Bolshevism — Democracy and Dictatorship. In Joseph Shaplen and David Shub, eds., *Socialism, Fascism, Communism* (New York: American League for Democratic Socialism, 1934), 174-215.

Kay, Geoffrey. 1975. *Development and Underdevelopment: A Marxist Analysis*. London: Macmillan.

————. 1976. The Falling Rate of Profit, Unemployment, and Crisis. *Critique* 6 (1976): 55-75.

————. 1979a. *The Economic Theory of the Working Class*. London: Macmillan.

————. 1979b. Why Labour is the Starting-Point of Capital. In *Value: The Representation of Labour in Capitalism*. Essays ed. by Diane Elson (London: CSE Books), 46-66.

Kay, Geoffrey, and James Mott. 1982. *Political Order and the Law of Labour*. London: Macmillan.

Kelly, Kevin D. Capitalism, Socialism, Barbarism: Marxist Conceptions of the Soviet Union. 1985. *Review of Radical Political Economics* 17, no.4 (Winter 1985): 51-71.

Kennedy, Paul. [1988]. *The Rise and Fall of the Great Powers: Economic Change and Military Conflict from 1500 to 2000*. London: Collins/Fontana, 1989.

Keynes, John Maynard. [1936]. *The General Theory of Employment, Interest and Money*. Vol. 7 of *The Collected Writings of John Maynard Keynes*. London: Macmillan, for the Royal Economic Society, 1973.

[Khayati, Mustapha]. 1969. Reform and Counterreform in Bureaucratic Power. In *Situationist International Anthology*, pp.256-65.

Kirsch, Leonard Joel. 1972. *Soviet Wages: Changes in Structure and Administration since 1956*. Cambridge, Massachusetts: Massachusetts Institute of Technology.

Kochan, Lionel, and Richard Abraham. 1983. *The Making of Modern Russia*. Second edition. Harmondsworth: Penguin.

Kollontai, Alexandra. [1921]. *The Workers' Opposition*. Solidarity (London) Pamphlet 7. London: Solidarity (London), n.d. [early 1970s?].

Konrad, George, and Ivan Szelenyi. 1979. *The Intellectuals on the Road to Class Power*. Translated by Andrew Arato and Richard E. Allen. Brighton: Harvester.

Kontorovich, Vladimir. 1988. Lessons of the 1965 Soviet Economic Reform. *Soviet Studies* 11, no.2 (April 1988): 308-16.

Kornai, Janos. [1979]. "The Reproduction of Shortage." In Janos Kornai, *Contradictions and Dilemmas: Studies on the Socialist Economy and Society* (Cambridge, Massachusetts: MIT Press, 1985), pp.6-32.

————. 1980a. *Economics of Shortage*. 2 vols. Contributions to Economic Analysis series, gen. eds. D. W. Jorgenson and J. Waelbroeck. Amsterdam: North Holland Publishing Company.

————. [1980b]. "'Hard' and 'Soft' Budget Restraint." In *Contradictions and Dilemmas*, pp. 33-51.

————. 1992. *The Socialist System: The Political Economy of Socialism*. Oxford: Clarendon.

Korsch, Karl. [1938]. The Marxist Ideology in Russia. In *Karl Korsch: Revolutionary Theory*, ed. Douglas Kellner (London: University of Texas Press, 1977), 158-64.

Kravchenko, Bohdan. 1975. *See* Holubenko, M. [Bohdan Kravchenko]. 1975.

Kuron, Jacek, and Karol Modzelewski. [1965]. *Solidarnosc: The Missing Link? A New Edition of Poland's Classic Revolutionary Socialist Manifesto, Kuron and Modzelewksi's Open Letter to the Party*. With an introduction by Colin Barker. London: Bookmarks, 1982.

Laird, Roy. D., ed. 1965. *Soviet Agriculture: The Permanent Crisis*. Associate ed. Edward L. Crowley. New York: Praeger.

Lampert, Nick. 1986. Job Security and the Law in the USSR. In David Lane, ed., *Labour and Employment in the USSR* (Brighton: Harvester, Wheatsheaf), 256-77.

Lane, David. 1971. *The End of Inequality? Stratification Under State Socialism*. Penguin Modern Sociology Monographs, gen. ed. Tom Burns, Social Stratification series, ed. David Lockwood. Harmondsworth: Penguin.

————. 1972. Dissent and Consent Under State Socialism. *Archives Européennes de Sociologie* [now the *European Journal of Sociology*] 13, no.1 (1972): 37-44.

————. 1976. *The Socialist Industrial State: Towards a Political Sociology of State Socialism*. London: George Allen & Unwin.

————. 1985a. *Soviet Economy and Society*. Oxford: Blackwell.

————. 1985b. *State and Politics in the USSR*. Oxford: Blackwell.

————. 1987. *Soviet Labour and the Ethics of Communism: Full Employment and the Labour Process in the USSR*. Brighton: Harvester, Wheatsheaf.

————. 1991. *The End of Social Inequality? Class, Status and Power Under State Socialism*. London: George Allen & Unwin.

————. 1992. The Changing Social Structure. Chap. in *Soviet Society Under Perestroika*, completely revised edition, 147-84. London: Routledge.

Lane, David, and Felicity O'Dell. 1978. *The Soviet Industrial Worker: Social Class, Education and Control*. Oxford: Martin Robertson, 1978.

Laqueur, Walter. 1967. *The Fate of the Revolution: Interpretations of Soviet History*. London:

Weidenfeld & Nicholson.

Lebowitz, Michael A. 1992. *Beyond "Capital": Marx's Political Economy of the Working Class*. London: Macmillan.

Lefebvre, Henri. 1977. *De l'Etat: 3: Le Mode de Production Etatique*. Paris: Union Générale d'Editions.

Lenin, V[ladimir] I[l'ich]. [V. I. Ul'ianov]. [1902]. *What is to be Done? Burning Questions of Our Movement*. Beijing: Foreign Languages Press, 1975.

_____. [1915]. On the Slogan for a United States of Europe. In *The Lenin Anthology*, ed. Robert C. Tucker (New York: W. W. Norton, 1975), 200-03.

_____. [1917a]. *The Impending Catastrophe and How to Combat It*. In *Collected Works*, vol. 25 (June-September 1917) (London: Lawrence and Wishart), 319-65.

_____. [1917b]. *The State and Revolution: The Marxist Theory of the State and the Tasks of the Proletariat in the Revolution*. Moscow: Progress, 1977.

_____. [1918a]. *The Immediate Tasks of the Soviet Government: Six Theses on the Immediate Tasks of the Soviet Government*. Moscow: Progress, 1951.

_____. [1918b]. *"Left-Wing" Childishness and the Petty-Bourgeois Mentality*. Moscow: Progress, 1968.

_____. [1918-23]. *On State Capitalism During the Transition to Socialism*. Moscow: Progress, 1983. [A collection].

_____. [1920]. *Left-Wing Communism, An Infantile Disorder*. Beijing: Foreign Languages Press, 1975.

[Leontiev, L. A., M. B. Mitin, P. N. Fedosiev, V. Z. Kruzhkov, L. A. Orbeli, V. P. Potemkin, P. F. Iudin, S. I. Vavilov, M. P. Tolcherov, and M. N. Korneiev, eds.]. [1943]. Teaching of Economics in the Soviet Union. Translated by Raya Dunayevskaya. *American Economic Review* 34, no.3 (September 1944): 501-30. [Original article unsigned; authors given here are editors of the Soviet source journal, as conventionally cited].

"Les Branches d'Octobre." 1982. *L'Insecurité Sociale* 3 (4th quarter 1982) (Paris).

Levine, Norman. 1975. *The Tragic Deception: Marx Contra Engels*. Twentieth Century Series, no. 8. Oxford: Clio.

Lipsey, Richard G. 1989. *An Introduction to Positive Economics*. 7th ed. London: Weidenfeld & Nicholson.

Littlejohn, Gary. 1984. *A Sociology of the Soviet Union*. New York: St. Martin's Press.

Loginov, V. P. 1989. Ispol´zovanie Trudovogo Potentsiala. Chap. in V. P. Loginov, *Rezervy Ekonomicheskogo Rosta*. Editor-in-chief L. I. Abalkin. Moscow: Nauka.

Lorimer, Frank. 1946. *The Population of the Soviet Union: History and Prospects*. Geneva: League of Nations, Economic, Financial and Transit Department, 1946.

Lowit, Thomas. 1971. *Le Syndicalisme de Type Soviétique: L'URSS et les Pays de l'Est Européen*. Paris: Librairie Armand Colin.

Luttwak, Edward. 1995. "The Good Bad Guys." *The Guardian*, 31 July 1995.

[Maksimov]. Maximoff, G[regorii] P[etrovich]. 1940. *The Guillotine at Work: Twenty Years of Terror in Russia*. Chicago: Chicago Society of the Alexander Berkman Fund.

Mandel, David. 1988. Economic Reform and Democracy in the Soviet Union. *Socialist Register* (1988): 132-53.

_____. [1989]. 'Revolutionary Reform' in Soviet Factories: Restructuring Relations

Between Workers and Managers. In D. Mandel 1991b, 7-41.

_____. [1990a]. The Rebirth of the Soviet Labour Movement: The Coalminers' Strike of July 1989. In D. Mandel 1991b, 51-78.

_____. [1990b]. 'A Market Without Thorns': The Ideological Struggle for the Soviet Working Class. In D. Mandel 1991b, 91-116.

_____. [1990c]. 'Destatization' and the Struggle for Power in the Soviet Economy: A New Phase in the Labour Movement. In D. Mandel 1991b, 117-53.

_____. [1991a]. The Strike Wave of March-April 1991. In D. Mandel 1991b, 155-207.

_____. 1991b. *Perestroika and the Soviet People: Rebirth of the Labour Movement*. Montreal: Black Rose Books.

Mandel, Ernest. 1968. The Soviet Economy. Chap. in *Marxist Economic Theory*, trans. Brian Pearce (London: Merlin), 548-604.

_____. 1974. Ten Theses on the Social and Economic Laws Governing the Society Transitional Between Capitalism and Socialism. *Critique* 3 (Autumn 1974): 5-21.

_____. 1976. Introduction to Marx [1867]. 1976.

_____. 1979. Once Again on the Trotskyist Definition of the Social Nature of the Soviet Union. *Critique* 12 (Autumn-Winter 1979-80): 117-26.

_____. 1989. *Beyond Perestroika: The Future of Gorbachev's USSR*. Translated by Gus Fagan. London: Verso.

_____. 1991. The Roots of the Present Crisis in the Soviet Economy. *Socialist Register* (1991): 194-210.

Manifeste du Groupe Ouvrier du Parti Communiste Russe (Bolchévik). [1923]. *Invariance*, ser. 2, 6 (2nd quarter 1975) (Paris): 44-64.

Marcuse, Herbert. [1958]. *Soviet Marxism: A Critical Analysis*. Harmondsworth: Penguin, 1971.

Márkus, György. 1983. Economic and Social Structure. Part 1 in Fehér, Heller, and Márkus 1983, pp.1-133.

Marnie, Sheila. 1990. *Labour Market Reform in the USSR: Fact or Fiction?* EUI Working Paper ECO No. 90/24. Badia Fiesolana, Italy: European University Institute.

Marx, Karl. [1843a]. *Critique of Hegel's Doctrine of the State*. In Karl Marx, *Early Writings*, translated by Rodney Livingstone and Gregor Benton, introduced by Lucio Colletti, 57-198. Harmondsworth: Penguin, 1975.

_____. [1843b]. *On the Jewish Question*. In *Early Writings*, 211-41.

_____. [1844]. Critique of Hegel's Philosophy of Right. Introduction. In *Early Writings*, 243-57.

_____. [1845]. [Theses on Feuerbach]. Concerning Feuerbach. In *Early Writings*, 421-23.

_____. [1847]. *Wage Labour and Capital*. Beijing: Foreign Languages Press, 1978.

_____. [1850]. *The Class Struggles in France: 1848-50*. In Karl Marx, *Political Writings*, vol. 2, *Surveys from Exile*, edited and introduced by David Fernbach, 35-142. Harmondsworth: Penguin, 1973.

_____. [1852a]. *The Eighteenth Brumaire of Louis Bonaparte*. In *Political Writings*, vol. 2, *Surveys from Exile*, 143-249.

_____. [1852b]. *Letter to Joseph Weydemeyer*. In Karl Marx and Frederick Engels, *Selected Correspondence*. Moscow: Progress, 1975.

_____. [1856a]. *Revelations of the Diplomatic History of the 18th Century*. In Karl Marx and Frederick Engels, *Collected Works*, vol. 15, 25-96. London: Lawrence and Wishart, 1986. [Later given the title *Secret Diplomatic History of the 18th Century*, as in *The Unknown Marx: Documents Concerning Karl Marx*, ed. with an introduction by Robert Payne (New York: New York University Press, 1971), 225-323.]

_____. [1856b]. Speech at the Anniversary of the *People's Paper*. In *Political Writings*, vol.2, *Surveys from Exile*, 299-300. Harmondsworth: Penguin, 1973.

_____. [1859]. *A Contribution to the Critique of Political Economy*. Translated by S. W. Ryazanskaya. With an introduction by Maurice Dobb. Moscow: Progress, 1970.

_____. [1867]. *Capital: A Critique of Political Economy*. Vol.1. Translated by Ben Fowkes. With an introduction by Ernest Mandel. Harmondsworth: Penguin, 1976.

_____. [1871]. *The Civil War in France*. Address of the General Council of the International Workingmen's Association. Presented on 30th May 1871. In Karl Marx, *Political Writings*, vol.3, *The First International and After*, edited and introduced by David Fernbach, 187-236. Harmondsworth: Penguin, 1974. [See also Marx 1934].

_____. [1873]. Postface to the second edition of Volume 1 of *Capital*. In Marx 1867, 94-103.

_____. [1875]. *Critique of the Gotha Programme*. In *Political Writings*, vol.3, *The First International and After*, 339-59.

_____. [1885]. *Capital: A Critique of Political Economy*. Vol.2. Translated by David Fernbach. With an introduction by Ernest Mandel. Harmondsworth: Penguin, 1978.

_____. [1894]. *Capital: A Critique of Political Economy*. Vol.3. Translated by David Fernbach. With an introduction by Ernest Mandel. Harmondsworth: Penguin, 1981.

_____. [1903]. "Introduction" to *A Contribution to the Critique of Political Economy*. Published as an appendix to the cited 1970 edition of the latter work (Marx [1859], pp.188-217) and as an introduction to the cited 1973 edition of the *Grundrisse* (Marx [1939], pp.83-111). [Page references are given to the translation published in the latter edition, which is considered to be superior; but for the sake of accuracy the first publication date is given as that of the specific shorter text.]

_____. [1905-10]. *Theories of Surplus Value. Part 2*. Trans. S. Ryazanskaya. London: Lawrence and Wishart, 1969.

_____. [1932]. *Economic and Philosophical Manuscripts of 1844*. 5th revised ed. London: Lawrence and Wishart, 1973.

_____. [1933]. "Results of the Immediate Process of Production." Published as an appendix to the cited 1976 edition of the Volume 1 of *Capital* (Marx [1867], pp.948-1084).

_____. [1934]. First Draft of "The Civil War in France." [Extract]. In *Political Writings*, vol.3, *The First International and After*, 236-68.

_____. [1939]. *Grundrisse: Foundations of the Critique of Political Economy (Rough Draft)*. Translated with a foreword by Martin Nicolaus. Harmondsworth: Penguin, 1973.

Marx, Karl, and Frederick Engels. [1843-95]. *Pre-Capitalist Socio-Economic Formations: A Collection*. Moscow: Progress, 1979.

_____. [1846]. *The German Ideology*. London: Lawrence and Wishart, 1965.

_____. [1848]. *Manifesto of the Communist Party*. In Karl Marx, *Political Writings*, vol.1, *The Revolutions of 1848*, edited and introduced by David Fernbach, 67-98. Harmondsworth: Penguin, 1973.

Matthews, Mervyn. 1972. *Class and Society in the USSR*. London: Allen Lane, Penguin.

_____. 1979. The Soviet Worker at Home. In Kahan and Ruble, eds. 1979, pp. 209-31.

_____. 1986. *Poverty in the Soviet Union: The Life-Styles of the Underprivileged in Recent Years*. Cambridge: Cambridge University Press.

_____. 1989. *Patterns of Deprivation in the Soviet Union Under Brezhnev and Gorbachev*. Stanford: Hoover Institution Press, Stanford University.

Mattick, Paul. [1939-67]. *Anti-Bolshevik Communism*. London: Merlin, 1978.

_____. 1969. *Marx and Keynes: The Limits of the Mixed Economy*. Boston: Porter Sargent, Extending Horizons Books.

McAuley, Alastair. 1979. *Economic Welfare in the Soviet Union: Poverty, Living-Standards, and Inequality*. Hemel Hempstead: George Allen and Unwin.

_____. 1981. Welfare and Social Security. Chap in Schapiro and Godson, eds. 1981, pp.194-230. London: Macmillan.

McAuley, Mary. 1969. *Labour Disputes in Soviet Russia, 1957-65*. Oxford: Clarendon.

_____. 1977. *Politics and the Soviet Union: An Introductory Analysis*. Harmondsworth: Penguin.

McCauley, Martin. 1981. *The Soviet Union Since 1917*. Longman History of Russia Series, gen. ed. Harold Shukman. London: Longman.

McLellan, David. [1973]. *Karl Marx: His Life and Thought*. London: Granada, 1976.

Medvedev, Roy. [1971]. *Let History Judge: The Origins and Consequences of Stalinism*. London: Macmillan, 1972.

_____. 1979. *On Stalin and Stalinism*. Translated by Ellen de Kadt. Oxford: Oxford University Press.

Medvedev, Zhores A. 1987. *Soviet Agriculture*. London: Norton.

Meek, James. 1996a. Yeltsin Calls a Round for the Vodka Vote. *The Guardian*, 17 February 1996.

_____. 1996b. The Vodka Scourge Crippling Russia. *The Guardian*, 24 February 1996.

Melotti, Umberto. [1972]. *Marx and the Third World*. Translated by Pat Ransford. Edited with a foreword by Malcolm Caldwell. London: Macmillan, 1977.

Men, L. L. 1986. The Capitalist Nature of the 'Socialist' Countries: A Politico-Economic Analysis. In L. L. Men, *Two Texts for Defining the Nature of the Communist Programme* (Hong Kong: International Correspondence, 1986), pp.1-75.

Mészáros, István. 1977. Political Power and Dissent in Postrevolutionary Societies. In Mészáros 1995, pp. 898-916.

_____. 1985. The Division of Labour and the Postcapitalist State. In Mészáros 1995, pp. 917-36.

_____. 1990. 'Socialism Hoy Dia.' In Mészáros 1995, pp.965-76.

_____. 1995. *Beyond Capital: Towards a Theory of Transition*. London: Merlin.

Meyer, Alfred G. 1961. "USSR, Incorporated." *Slavic Review* 20, no.3 (October 1961): pp.369-76.

Midnight Notes (New York).

Midnight Notes. 1990. New Enclosures. *Midnight Notes* 10 (Fall 1990): 1-100.

Mihill, Chris. Vodka Cuts Russian Life Expectancy. *The Guardian*, 10 March 1995.

Mill, John Stuart. [1848]. *Principles of Political Economy, with Some of Their Applications to Social Philosophy*. In two volumes. London: Longmans, Green & Co., 1886.

Millar, James R. 1970. Soviet Rapid Development and the Agricultural Surplus Hypothesis. *Soviet Studies* 22, no.1 (July 1970): 77-93.

_____. 1974. Mass Collectivization and the Contribution of Soviet Agriculture to the First Five-Year Plan: A Review Article. *Slavic Review* 33, no.4 (December 1974): 750-66.

Millman, Gregory J. 1995. The Golden Vanity. Chap. in *Around the World on a Trillion Dollars a Day: How Rebel Currency Traders Destroy Banks and Defy Governments*, rev. ed. (London: Bantam, 1995), pp.65-94.

Milward, Alan S., and S. B. Saul. 1977. The Economic Development of Russia, 1861-1914. Chap. in *The Development of the Economies of Continental Europe, 1850-1914* (London: George Allen & Unwin), pp.365-426.

Molyneux, John. 1987. The Ambiguities of Hillel Ticktin. *Critique* 20-21 (1987): 131-34.

Munis, G. [Manuel Fernandez Grandizo]. 1946. *Les Révolutionnaires Devant la Russie et le Stalinisme Mondial*. Mexico: Editorial Revolución.

_____. [1960]. *Unions Against Revolution*. In G. Munis and J[ohn] Zerzan, *Unions Against Revolution: Two Essays* (Detroit: Black & Red, 1975), 5-38.

_____. 1975. *Parti-Etat: Stalinisme: Révolution*. Paris: Spartacus.

Munting, Roger. 1982. *The Economic Development of the USSR*. London: Croom Helm.

[*Narodnoe Khoziaistvo*, 1958.] *See* USSR Council of Ministers, Central Statistical Administration. 1959.

[*Narodnoe Khoziaistvo*, 1961.] *See* USSR Council of Ministers, Central Statistical Administration. 1962.

[*Narodnoe Khoziaistvo*, 1962.] *See* USSR Council of Ministers, Central Statistical Administration. 1963.

[*Narodnoe Khoziaistvo*, 1965.] *See* USSR Council of Ministers, Central Statistical Administration. 1966.

[*Narodnoe Khoziaistvo*, 1967.] *See* USSR Council of Ministers, Central Statistical Administration. 1968.

[*Narodnoe Khoziaistvo*, 1968.] *See* USSR Council of Ministers, Central Statistical Administration. 1969.

[*Narodnoe Khoziaistvo*, 1970.] *See* USSR Council of Ministers, Central Statistical Administration. 1971a.

[*Narodnoe Khoziaistvo*, 1922-72.] *See* USSR Central Statistical Administration. 1972.

[*Narodnoe Khoziaistvo*, 1975.] *See* USSR Council of Ministers, Central Statistical Administration. 1976.

[*Narodnoe Khoziaistvo*, 1917-77.] *See* USSR Council of Ministers, Central Statistical Administration. 1977.

[*Narodnoe Khoziaistvo*, 1978.] *See* USSR Central Statistical Administration. 1979.

[*Narodnoe Khoziaistvo*, 1922-82.] *See* USSR Central Statistical Administration. 1982.

[*Narodnoe Khoziaistvo*, 1987.] *See* USSR State Committee on Statistics. 1988.

[*Narodnoe Khoziaistvo*, 1988.] *See* USSR State Committee on Statistics. 1989.

[*Narodnoe Khoziaistvo*, 1989.] *See* USSR State Committee on Statistics. 1990.

[*Narodnoe Khoziaistvo*, 1990]. *See* USSR State Committee on Statistics. 1991.

[*Narodnoe Khoziaistvo*, 1991]. *See* USSR State Committee on Statistics. 1992.

[*Naselenie SSSR*, 1973]. *See* USSR Council of Ministers, Central Statistical Administration, 1975.

Negation. [1974?] *LIP and the Self-Managed Counterrevolution*. Detroit: Black & Red, 1975.

Negri, Toni [Antonio]. [1967-83]. *Revolution Retrieved: Writings on Marx, Keynes, Capitalist Crisis and New Social Subjects, 1967-83*. With a preface by John Merrington. Vol.1 of the Red Notes Italy Archive. London: Red Notes, 1988.

—————. [1968]. Keynes and the Capitalist Theory of the State Post-1929. In *Revolution Retrieved*, 5-42.

—————. [1971]. Crisis of the Planner-State: Communism and Revolutionary Organisation. In *Revolution Retrieved*, 91-148.

—————. [1973-74]. Reformism and Restructuration: Terrorism of the State-as-Factory-Command. In *Working Class Autonomy and the Crisis: Italian Marxist Texts of the Theory and Practice of a Class Movement*, ed. Red Notes (London: Red Notes/Conference of Socialist Economists, 1979), 33-37.

—————. 1977. La Forma Stato: Per la Critica dell'Economia Politica della Costituzione. Milan: Feltrinelli. Referred to in Ryan 1991, pp.207-14.

—————. [1978]. Capitalist Domination and Working Class Sabotage. In *Working Class Autonomy and the Crisis*, 93-137.

—————. [1979]. *Marx Beyond Marx: Lessons on the Grundrisse*. New ed. Translated by Hary Cleaver, Michael Ryan, and Maurizio Viano. Ed. Jim Fleming. New York/London: Autonomedia/Red Notes, 1991. With a full bibliography of Autonomist writings, ed. Harry Cleaver, Jim Fleming and Conrad Herold.

—————. [1982]. Archaeology and Project: The Mass Worker and the Social Worker, in *Revolution Retrieved*, 199-228.

—————. 1984. Review of *La Dynamique du Capitalisme au XXe Siècle*, by Pierre Souyri. *Classes Dangéreuses* 4 (Autumn 1984): 56-58.

—————. [1986]. State and Class in the Phase of Real Subsumption. In *The Politics of Subversion: A Manifesto for the Twenty-First Century*, trans. James Newell, with an introduction by Yann Moulier, itself trans. Philippa Hurd (Oxford: Polity, 1989), pp.177-90.

—————. 1990. Postscript, 1990. Translated by Jared Becker. Appended to Félix Guattari and Toni Negri, *Communists Like Us: New Spaces of Liberty, New Lines of Alliance*, trans. Michael Ryan, Semiotext(e) Foreign Agents Series, ed. Jim Fleming and Sylvère Lotringer (New York: Semiotext(e)), 149-73.

Nove, Alec. [1958a]. "The Problem of 'Success Indicators' in Soviet Industry." In Nove 1964, pp.83-98.

—————. [1958b]. "The Politics of Economic Rationality: Observations in the Soviet Economy." In Nove 1964, pp.51-66.

—————. [1962]. "Was Stalin Really Necessary?" In Nove 1964, pp.17-39.

—————. 1964. *Was Stalin Really Necessary? Some Problems of Political Economy*.

London: Allen & Unwin.

_____. 1971. The Agricultural Hypothesis: A Comment on James R. Millar's Article. *Soviet Studies* 22, no.3 (January 1971): 394-401.

_____. 1975. Is There a Ruling Class in the USSR? *Soviet Studies* 27, no.4 (October 1975): 615-38.

_____. [1978]. "Some Observations on Criteria for the Study of the Soviet Union." In Nove, *Political Economy and Soviet Socialism* (London: Allen & Unwin, 1979), 219-39.

_____. 1980a. Socialism, Planning and the One-Party State. In T. H. Rigby, Archie Brown, and Peter Reddaway, ed., *Authority, Power and Policy in the USSR: Essays Dedicated to Leonard Schapiro* (London: Macmillan), 77-97.

_____. 1980b. *The Soviet Economic System.* Second edition. London: Allen & Unwin.

_____. [1982]. *An Economic History of the USSR.* [Revised ed.] Harmondsworth: Penguin.

O'Hearn, Dennis. 1981. The Second Economy in Consumer Goods and Services. *Critique* 15: 93-109.

Orwell, George. [Eric Blair]. [1937]. *The Road to Wigan Pier.* Harmondsworth: Penguin, 1962.

_____. [1949]. *Nineteen Eighty-Four.* With an introduction by Ben Pimlott, and a Note on the Text by Peter Davison. Harmondsworth: Penguin, 1989.

Osinskii, V. V. 1918. O Stroitel'stve Sotsializme. *Kommunist* 2 (April 1918), p.5.

Outside and Against the Unions: A Communist Response to Dave Douglass' [sic] Text "Refracted Perspective." [1992]. London: Wildcat.

Oxenstierna, Susanne. 1990. *From Labour Shortage to Unemployment? The Soviet Labour Market in the 1980s.* Stockholm: University of Stockholm, Swedish Institute for Social Research.

Packard, Vance. [1960]. *The Waste Makers.* London: Longman, 1961.

Pannekoek, Anton. [1911-12]. Massenaktion und Revolution. *Neue Zeit* 30. Cited in English translation in The Kautsky-Pannekoek Controversy, chap. 3 in Bricianer 1969, p.126.

_____. [1912]. Marxist Theory and Revolutionary Tactics. In *Pannekoek and Gorter's Marxism*, edited and introduced by D.A.Smart, 50-73. London: Pluto, 1978.

_____. [1919?]. *See* Horner, Karl. [Anton Pannekoek]. [1919?]

_____. [1920]. *World Revolution and Communist Tactics.* In *Pannekoek and Gorter's Marxism*, edited and introduced by D.A.Smart, 93-141. London: Pluto, 1978.

_____. [1934]. The Theory of the Collapse of Capitalism. Translated and introduced by Adam Buick. *Capital & Class* 1 (Spring 1977): 59-81.

_____. [1938]. *Lenin as Philospher: A Critical Examination of the Philosphical Basis of Leninism.* Translated from German by the author. New York: New Essays, 1948.

_____. [1947-49]. *Workers' Councils.* [Reprinted in four parts]. London: Echanges et Mouvement, 1984. [The first three sections were written in 1941-42, the fourth and fifth in 1944 and 1947].

Parkin, Frank. [1971]. *Class, Inequality, and Political Order: Social Stratification in Capitalist and Communist Societies.* London: Granada, 1972.

Parry, Albert. 1966. Underground Capitalism. Chapter in *The New Class Divided: Science and Technology Versus Communism*, 178-96. London: Macmillan.

Perlman, Fredy. [1968]. Introduction: Commodity Fetishism. Introduction to Rubin [1928]. 1972.

_____. [1969]. *The Reproduction of Daily Life*. Detroit: Black & Red, 1972.

_____. 1983. *Against His-story, Against Leviathan! An Essay*. With illustrations borrowed from William Blake. Detroit: Black & Red.

Pipes, Richard. 1984. *Survival Is Not Enough: Soviet Realities and America's Future*. New York: Simon and Schuster.

Platform of the Forty-Six. [1923]. [15/10/1923]. In Carr 1954, pp.367-73.

Platform of the Left Opposition. [1927]. London: New Park, 1963.

Pollock, Friedrich. [1941]. State Capitalism: Its Possibilities and Limitations. In *The Essential Frankfurt School Reader*, ed. Andrew Arato and Eike Gebhart, with an introduction by Paul Picconbe (Oxford: Blackwell, 1978), 71-94.

Ponton, Geoffrey. 1994. *The Soviet Era: Soviet Politics from Lenin to Yeltsin*. Oxford: Blackwell.

Pravda. Vstrecha Sovetskogo Rukovodstva Zhurnalistami, 20 August 1991, p.2.

Pravda, Alex. 1979a. Spontaneous Workers' Activities in the Soviet Union. In Kahan and Ruble 1979, 333-66.

_____. 1979b. Industrial Workers: Patterns of Dissent, Opposition and Accommodation. In *Opposition in Eastern Europe*, ed. Rudolf L. Tókés, 209-62. London: Macmillan.

_____. 1981a. East-West Interdependence and the Social Compact in Eastern Europe. In *East-West Relations and the Future of Eastern Europe: Politics and Economics*, ed. Morris Bornstein, Zvi Gitelman, and William Zimmerman, 162-87. London: Allen & Unwin.

_____. 1981b. Political Attitudes and Activity. In *Blue-Collar Workers in Eastern Europe*, ed. Jan F. Triska and Charles Gati, 43-67. London: Allen & Unwin.

_____. 1982. Is There a Soviet Working Class? *Problems of Communism* 31, no.6 (November-December 1982).

Pye, Lucian W. 1990. Political Science and the Crisis of Authoritarianism. *American Political Science Review* 84, no.1 (March 1990): 3-19.

Radical Chains (London).

Rakovski, Marc [Gyorgy Bence and Janos Kis]. 1978. *Towards an East European Marxism*. London: Allison & Busby.

Ralis, Max. 1981. Workers' Social Perceptions. Chap. in Schapiro and Godson, eds., 1981, 231-50. London: Macmillan.

Red Notes, ed. 1979. *Working Class Autonomy and the Crisis: Italian Marxist Texts of the Theory and Practice of a Class Movement: 1964-79*. London: Red Notes/CSE Books.

_____. 1981. *Italy 1980-81—After Marx, Jail! The Attempted Destruction of a Commuist Movement*. London: Red Notes.

Remember Kronstadt. 1991. *Wildcat* (London) 15 (Autumn 1991): 23-30.

Révolution Sociale (Paris).

Ricardo, David. [1817]. *On the Principles of Political Economy and Taxation*. In *The Works and Correspondence of David Ricardo*, ed. Piero Sraffa, with the collaboration of M. H. Dobb, vol. 1 (Cambridge: Cambridge University Press, 1951).

Riesel, René. 1969. Preliminaries on the Councils and Councilist Organisation. In *Situationist International Anthology* (q.v): 270-82.

Rittersporn, Gabor T. 1993. Buying Intellectual Pre-Fabs. *Telos* 96 (Summer 1993): 53-60.

Rizzi, Bruno. [1939]. *The Bureaucratization of the World: The USSR: Bureaucratic Collectivism*. Translated and with an introduction by Adam Westoby. Tavistock Studies in Sociology, ed. Frank Parkin. London: Tavistock, 1985. [A translation of the part of a longer work which deals specifically with the USSR.]

Roberts, B. C., and Maria Feingold. 1958. *Trade Unions and Industrial Relations in the Soviet Union*. London: Workers' Educational Association.

Rogger, Hans. 1983. *Russia in the Age of Modernisation and Revolution, 1881-1917*. Longman History of Russia Series. London: Longman.

Roland, Gérard. 1989. *Economie Politique du Système Soviétique*. With a preface by Alec Nove. Socialisms Collection, gen. ed Bernard Chavance, Marcel Drach, and Gérard Roland. Pubd. with co-operation of the Belgian Ministry of National Education. Paris: L'Harmattan, 1989.

"Le Roman de nos Origines." 1983. *La Banquise* 2 (2nd quarter, 1983) (Paris): 3-58. [A detailed history of much of the communist tendency.]

Romanenkova, Gortenziya. 1991. Rural-Urban Migration in the USSR: Its Role in Redistributing Population and Labour Resources. In *In Search of Flexibility: The New Soviet Labour Market*, ed. Guy Standing (Geneva: International Labour Organisation), pp.165-75.

Rosdolsky, Roman. [1968]. *The Making of Marx's "Capital."* Vol.1. 2nd pbk ed. Translated by Pete Burgess. London: Pluto, 1989.

Rose, R.B. 1978. *Gracchus Babeuf: The First Revolutionary Communist*. London: Edward Arnold.

Rubel, Maximilien. [1973]. The Plan and Method of the "Economics." In *Rubel on Karl Marx: Five Essays*, ed. Joseph O'Malley and Keith Algozin (Cambridge: Cambridge University Press, 1981), pp.190-229.

Rubel, Maximilien, and John Crump, eds. 1987. *Non-Market Socialism in the Nineteenth and Twentieth Centuries*. London: Macmillan.

Rubin, Isaak Illich. [1928]. *Essays on Marx's Theory of Value*. Trans. Milos Samardzija and Fredy Perlman. Detroit: Black and Red, 1972.

Ruble, Blair A. 1981. *Soviet Trade Unions: Their Development in the 1970s*. Cambridge: Cambridge University Press.

Rühle, Otto. [1920]. *Report from Moscow*. Republished on floppy disc. London: Wildcat, 1994.

_____. [1924]. *From the Bourgeois to the Proletarian Revolution*. London/Glasgow: Socialist Reproduction/Revolutionary Perspectives, 1974.

_____. [1931]. *See* Steuermann, Carl. [Otto Rühle]. [1931]. 1932.

_____. [1939]. *The Struggle Against Fascism Begins With the Struggle Against Bolshevism*. English ed. With an introduction by Alfredo M. Bonanno. London: Bratach Dubh Editions, 1981. [Originally appeared in *Living Marxism* (Chicago) 4, no.8, 1939.]

_____. [1940]. Weltkrieg, Weltfaschismus, Weltrevolution. In Otto Rühle, *Schriften* (Hamburg: Rowohlt, 1971). Cited in Bourrinet [1992], pp.216-17.

"Russian Workers' Opposition Joins Fourth International." 1922. *Workers' Dreadnought* (London) (17/6/1922).

Rutland, Peter. 1985. *The Myth of the Plan: Lessons of Soviet Planning Experience*. London: Hutchinson.

_____. 1990. Labor Unrest and Movements in 1989 and 1990. *Soviet Economy* 6, no.4 (October-December 1990): 345-84.

Ryan, Michael. 1991. Epilogue to Negri [1979].

Sabatier, Guy. 1977. *Traité de Brest-Litovsk, 1918: Coup d'Arret à la Révolution*. Paris: Spartacus.

Salvadori, Massimo. [1976]. *Karl Kautsky and the Socialist Revolution, 1880-1938*. Trans. Jon Rothschild. London: NLB, 1979.

Samuelson, Paul A. 1967. *Economics: An Introductory Analysis*. 7th ed. New York: McGraw Hill.

Sapir, Jacques. 1980. *Pays de l'Est: Vers La Crise Généralisée?* Lyons: Fédérop.

_____. 1984. *Travail et Travailleurs en URSS*. Paris: La Découverte.

_____. 1989. *Les Fluctuations Economiques en URSS, 1941-1985*. Paris: Ecole des Hautes Etudes en Sciences Sociales.

_____. 1990. *L'Economie Mobilisée: Essai sur les Economies de Type Soviétique*. Paris: La Découverte.

_____. 1992. Au Travail... S'il en Reste. Chap. in *Feu le Système Soviétique? Permanences Politiques, Mirages Economiques, Enjeux Stratégiques* (Paris: La Découverte), pp.92-101.

Schapiro, Leonard. 1955. *The Origin of the Communist Autocracy: Political Opposition in the Soviet State: First Phase: 1917-1922*. London: Bell & Sons, 1955.

_____. 1960. Preface to the First Edition of *The Communist Party of the Soviet Union*, pp.ix-xvi. [Included with second edition, 1970].

_____. 1967. *The Government and Politics of the Soviet Union*. Second ed. London: Hutchinson.

_____. 1970. *The Communist Party of the Soviet Union*. Second ed. London: Methuen.

_____. [1971]. "Totalitarianism in the Doghouse." In *Political Opposition in One-Party States*, ed. L. Schapiro (London: Macmillan, 1972), 268-76.

_____. 1981. The End of an Illusion. In Schapiro and Godson, eds., 1981, 1-14.

Schapiro, Leonard, and Joseph Godson, eds. 1981. *The Soviet Worker: Illusions and Realities*. London: Macmillan.

Scholem, G[ershom]. 1971a. Kabbalah. *Encyclopaedia Judaica*, vol.10, 489-653. Jerusalem: Keter Publishing House.

_____. 1971b. Sefirot. *Encyclopaedia Judaica*, vol.14, 1104-5. Jerusalem: Keter Publishing House.

Schroeder, Gertrude E. 1991. *Perestroyka* in the Aftermath of 1990. *Soviet Economy* 7, no.1 (January-March 1991): 3-13.

Schwarz, Harry. 1951. *Russia's Soviet Economy*. London: Jonathon Cape.

Scott, Carey. 1996a. Oblivion? Russia Will Vote for That. *The Sunday Times*, 10 March 1996.

_____. 1996b. Russia Asks: Would You Buy a Used Lada from this Man? *The*

Sunday Times 4 October 1996.

————. 1996c. Moscow Aghast at Kremlin Killers. *The Sunday Times*, 13 October 1996.

Seeger, Murray. 1981. Eye-Witness to Failure. Chap. in Schapiro and Godson, eds., 1981, pp.76-105.

Seidman, Michael. 1988. *Towards a History of Workers' Resistance to Work: Paris and Barcelona during the French Popular Front and the Spanish Revolution, 1936-38.* London: News from Everywhere. [A reprint from the *Journal of Contemporary History* (London) 23 (1988): 191-220].

[*Sel'skoe Khoziaistvo*, 1971]. *See* USSR Council of Ministers, Central Statistical Administration, 1971b.

Service, Robert. 1979. *The Bolshevik Party in Revolution: A Study in Organisational Change, 1917-1923.* London: Macmillan.

Shachtman, Max. [1940-61]. *The Bureaucratic Revolution.* New York: Donald Press, 1962.

Shanin, Teodor, ed. 1983. *Late Marx and the Russian Road: Marx and 'the Peripheries of Capitalism.'* History Workshop Series. London: Routledge & Kegan Paul.

Shatz, Marshall. 1967. Jan Waclaw Machajski: The Conspiracy of the Intellectuals. *Survey* 62 (January 1967): 45-57.

————. 1989. *Jan Waclaw Machajski: A Radical Critic of the Russian Intelligentsia and Socialism.* Pittsburgh: University of Pittsburgh Press.

Shipler, David K. [1983]. *Russia: Broken Idols, Solemn Dreams.* Macdonald, Futura, 1985.

Shipway, Mark. 1987. Council Communism. Chap. in Rubel and Crump, eds., *Non-Market Socialism*, pp.104-26.

————. 1988. *Anti-Parliamentary Communism: The Movement for Workers' Councils in Britain, 1918-45.* London: Macmillan.

Shortall, Felton C. 1994. *The Incomplete Marx.* Aldershot: Avebury.

SI. *See* Situationist International.

Siegelbaum, Lewis H. 1983. *The Politics of Industrial Mobilization in Russia, 1914-1917.* London: Macmillan.

————. 1988. *Stakhanovism and the Politics of Productivity in the USSR, 1935-1941.* Pbk. ed. Cambridge: Cambridge University Press, 1990.

Simon, Henri. [1982]. *Poland: 1980-82: Class Struggle and the Crisis of Capital.* Translated by Lorraine Perlman. Black & Red, 1985.

Simis, Konstantin M. 1982. *USSR: Secrets of a Corrupt Society.* Translated by Jacqueline Edwards and Mitchell Schneider. London: J. M. Dent & Sons.

Situationist International. [1961]. Instructions for Taking Up Arms. In *Situationist International Anthology*, 63-65.

————. [1963]. Ideologies, Classes and the Domination of Nature. In *Situationist International Anthology*, 101-09.

————. [1967]. The Explosion Point of Ideology in China. In *Situationist International Anthology*, 185-94.

————. [1969]. Reform and Counterreform in Bureaucratic Power. In *Situationist International Anthology*, 256-65.

Situationist International Anthology. [1953-71]. Edited and translated by Ken Knabb. With a preface by the editor. Berkeley: Bureau of Public Secrets, 1981.

Skilling, H. Gordon. [1966]. Interest Groups in Soviet Politics: An Introduction. In H. Gordon Skilling and Franklyn Griffiths, eds., *Interest Groups in Soviet Politics*, pp.3-45.

Skilling, H. Gordon, and Franklyn Griffiths, eds. 1971. *Interest Groups in Soviet Politics*. Princeton: Princeton University Press.

Skurski, Roger Ben. 1970. The Distribution of Consumer Goods in the Soviet Union. Ph.D. diss., University of Wisconsin.

Smith, Adam. [1776]. *The Wealth of Nations. Books 1-3.* With an introduction by Andrew Skinner. Harmondsworth: Penguin, 1979.

Smith, Alan H. 1983. *The Planned Economies of Eastern Europe.* London: Croom Helm.

Smith, Alex Duval. 1996. Foreign Bodies. *The Guardian,* 13 June 1996.

Smith, Gordon B. 1992. *Soviet Politics: Struggling with Change.* London: Macmillan.

Smith, Hedrick. 1976. *The Russians.* London: Sphere.

Smith, S. A. [1983]. *Red Petrograd: Revolution in the Factories, 1917-1918.* Pbk. ed. Cambridge: Cambridge University Press, 1985.

Socialism or Barbarism. [1961]. Solidarity pamphlet 11. London: Solidarity, 1969.

Socialist Party of Canada. [SPC]. 1948. *The Russian Revolution: Its Origin and Outcome.* Winnipeg: SPC.

Socialist Party of Great Britain. [SPGB]. [1915-48]. *Russia Since 1917: Socialist Views of Bolshevik Policy.* London: SPGB, 1948.

_____. [1918]. The Revolution in Russia: Where It Fails. In SPGB 1915-48, 9-18.

_____. [1920]. A Socialist View of Bolshevik Policy. In SPGB 1915-48, 18-23.

_____. [1924]. The Passing of Lenin. In SPGB 1915-48, 27-36.

_____. [1928]. Trotsky States His Case. In SPGB 1915-48, 36-41.

_____. [1930]. Russia: Land of High Profits. In SPGB 1915-48, 42-46.

_____. [1943]. Is Russia Socialist? In SPGB 1915-48, 83-91.

_____. [1946]. Russia and Democracy. In SPGB 1915-48, 96-101.

_____. 1967. *Russia 1917-1967: A Socialist Analysis.* London: SPGB.

Socialist Reproduction/Revolutionary Perspectives. 1974. *On the Origins and Infancy of Proletarian Revolutionary Politics: An Introduction to Left Communism in Germany From 1914 to 1923.* Introduction to Rühle 1924.

[Solidarity.] 1961. *See Socialism or Barbarism.* 1961.

Solzhenitsyn, Alexander. [1973]. *The Gulag Archipelago.* [Vol.1]. Trans. Thomas P. Whitney. [London]: Collins/Fontana, 1974.

"Sous le Travail, l'Activité." 1986. *La Banquise* 4 (Summer 1986): 9-24.

Soviet Academy of Sciences. 1957. *See* Institute of Economics, Academy of Sciences of the USSR 1957.

SPC. *See* Socialist Party of Canada.

SPGB. *See* Socialist Party of Great Britain.

Stalin, J[oseph]. [J. Dzhugashvili]. [1952]. *Economic Problems of Socialism in the USSR.* Moscow: Foreign Languages Publishing House.

Standing, Guy. 1991. Wages and Work Motivation in the Soviet Labour Market: Why a "BIP" and not a "TIP", is Required. *International Labour Review* 130 , no.2 (1991): 237-53.

Steuermann, Carl. [Otto Rühle]. [1931]. *La Crise Mondiale, ou Vers le Capitalisme d'Etat.*

Translated from the German. Paris: NRF, 1932.

Sutton, Antony C. 1968. *Western Technology and Soviet Economic Development, 1917 to 1930*. Stanford, California: Hoover Institution on War, Revolution, and Peace.

Sweezy, Paul M. [1942]. *The Theory of Capitalist Development: Principles of Marxian Political Economy*. New York: Monthly Review Press, Modern Reader paperback edition, 1966.

Szelenyi, Ivan. 1979. The Position of the Intelligentsia in the Class Structure of State Socialist Societies. *Critique* 10-11 (1979): 51-76.

Temkina, Anna A. 1992. The Workers' Movement in Leningrad, 1986-91. *Soviet Studies* 44, no.2 (April 1992): 209-36.

"Theories of State Capitalism." [1982?]. *Revolutionary Perspectives* 19: 8-31.

[*Theses of the Democratic Centralists*]. 1921. Ocherednye Zadachi Partii. *Pravda*. 22/1/1921.

Theses of the Left Communists. [1918]. [Originally entitled "On the Current Situation"]. Glasgow: Critique, 1977.

Theses, Resolutions and Manifestos of the First Four Congresses of the Third International. [1919-22]. Edited by Alan Adler. Translated by Alix Holt and Barbara Holland. With an introduction by Bertie Hessel and a glossary compiled by the editor. London: Ink Links/ Pluto, 1983.

Thompson, E[dward] P. [1963]. *The Making of the English Working Class*. Revised edition. Harmondsworth: Penguin, 1968.

Ticktin, Hillel. 1973a. Towards a Political Economy of the USSR. *Critique* 1: 20-41.

_____. 1973b. Political Economy of the Soviet Intellectual. *Critique* 2: 5-21.

_____. 1976. The Contradictions of Soviet Society and Professor Bettelheim. *Critique* 6: 17-44.

_____. 1977. The USSR: The Beginning of the End? *Critique* 7 (1976): 88-93.

_____. 1978. The Class Structure of the USSR and the Elite. *Critique* 9 (1978): 37-61.

_____. 1979. Is Market-Socialism Possible or Necessary? Transcript (slightly revised) of a contribution to the Critique conference, 12-13/10/1979. *Critique* 14: 13-21 and 35-39.

_____. 1983a. The Transitional Epoch, Finance Capital and Britain: Part 1: The Political Economy of Declining Capitalism. *Critique* 16 (1983): 23-42.

_____. 1983b. Andropov: Disintegration and Discipline. *Critique* 16 (1983): 111-22.

_____. 1986a. Towards a Theory of Finance Capital: Part 2: The Origins and Nature of Finance Capital. *Critique* 17 (1986): 1-16.

_____. 1986b. The Year after the Three General Secretaries: Change Without Change. *Critique* 17 (1986): 113-35.

_____. 1987a. The Political Economy of Class in the Transitional Epoch. *Critique* 20/21 (1987): 7-25.

_____. 1987b. The USSR after Chernobyl. *Critique* 20/21 (1987): 195-96.

_____. 1988. The Contradictions of Gorbachev. *Journal of Communist Studies* 4, no. 4 (December 1988): 83-99.

_____. 1990. Mikhail Gorbachev and Mrs. Thatcher: Allies in Crisis. *Critique* 22

(1990): 92-104.

_____. 1990-92. What Is a Socialist Society? In *Unmasking Reality: Lectures Given to the John Maclean Society, 1990-92*, ed. Paul B. Smith ([Glasgow]: [John Maclean Society], [1992]), 14-32.

_____. 1991a. The Decline of Capitalism. *Critique* 23 (1991): 153-58.

_____. 1991b. The International Road to Chaos. *Critique* 23 (1991): 9-32.

_____. 1991c. *The Origins of the Crisis in the USSR: Essays on the Political Economy of a Disintegrating System*. New York: Sharpe.

_____. 1991d. The Politics of Race: Discrimination in South Africa. *Critique* 24 (1991): 1-115.

_____. 1992a. Permanent Chaos Without a Market: The Non-Latinamericanization of the USSR. *Studies in Comparative Communism* 25, no.3 (September 1992): 242-56.

_____. 1992b. Trotsky's Political Economy of Capitalism. Chap. in *The Trotsky Reappraisal*, ed. Terry Brotherstone and Paul Dukes (Edinburgh: Edinburgh University Press), 216-32.

_____. 1993. The Growth of an Impossible Capitalism. *Critique* 25 (1993): 119-32.

_____. 1994a. The Nature of an Epoch of Declining Capitalism. *Critique* 26 (1994): 69-93.

_____. 1994b. The State of Soviet Studies in the Post-War Period: A View from the Left. In *Contemporary Political Studies 1994*, vol.1, ed. Patrick Dunleavy and Jeffrey Stanyer (London: Political Science Association), 45-58.

Tillium, Ian. 1994. Technological Despotism. *Here and Now* 15 (1994): 11-21.

_____. 1997. "Thinking Up Reasons" in the Scottish Highlands: Grant Allocation, Control over Labour, and the Making of Concessions. Unpublished manuscript made available to the author.

Trotsky, Leon. [Lev Bronstein]. [1920]. *Terrorism and Communism: A Reply to Karl Kautsky*. New York: New Park Publications, 1975.

_____. [1936]. *The Revolution Betrayed: What is the Soviet Union and Where Is It Going?* Translated by Max Eastman. London: Faber & Faber, 1937.

_____. [1939a]. The USSR in War. In *In Defence of Marxism (Against the Petty Bourgeois Opposition)*, 3-26. London: New Park, 1971. [September 1939].

_____. [1939b]. Again and Once More Again on the Nature of the USSR. In *In Defence of Marxism*, pp.29-39. [October 1939].

_____. [1940]. Letter to the Workers of the USSR. In *The Age of Permanent Revolution: A Trotsky Anthology*, ed. and introduced by Isaac Deutscher, with the assistance of George Novack, 281-84. New York: Dell Publishing Co., 1964. [May 1940].

United Nations. 1993. *Statistical Yearbook 1991*. New York: United Nations, Department of Economic and Social Information and Policy Analysis (DESIPA).

Uskorenie: Aktual'nye Problemy Sotsial'no-Ekonomicheskogo Razvitiia. 1985-87. 4 vols. Editor-in-chief D. Valovoi. Moscow: CPSU Central Committee, "Pravda," 1985, 1986 (2 vols.), and 1987.

USSR Central Statistical Administration. 1972. *Narodnoe Khoziaistvo SSSR 1922-1972gg: Iubileinyi Statisticheskii Ezhegodnik*. Moscow: Statistika.

_____. 1979. *Narodnoe Khoziaistvo v 1978 godu: Statisticheskii Ezhegodnik.* Moscow: Finansy i Statistika.

_____. 1982. *Narodnoe Khoziaistvo za 60 Let: Iubileinyi Statisticheskii Ezhegodnik.* Moscow: Finansy i Statistika.

USSR Council of Ministers, Central Statistical Administration. 1959. *Narodnoe Khoziaistvo v 1958 godu: Statisticheskii Ezhegodnik.* Moscow: Gosudarstvennoe Statisticheskoe Izdatel´stvo.

_____. 1962. *Narodnoe Khoziaistvo v 1961 godu: Statisticheskii Ezhegodnik.* Moscow: Gosstatizdat.

_____. 1963. *Narodnoe Khoziaistvo v 1962 godu: Statisticheskii Ezhegodnik.* Moscow: Gosstatizdat.

_____. 1966. *Narodnoe Khoziaistvo v 1965 godu: Statisticheskii Ezhegodnik.* Moscow: Statistika.

_____. 1968. *Narodnoe Khoziaistvo v 1967 godu: Statisticheskii Ezhegodnik.* Moscow: Statistika.

_____. 1969. *Narodnoe Khoziaistvo v 1968 godu: Statisticheskii Ezhegodnik.* Moscow: Statistika.

_____. 1971a.*Narodnoe Khoziaistvo v 1970 godu: Statisticheskii Ezhegodnik.* Moscow: Statistika.

_____. 1971b. *Sel´skoe Khoziaistvo SSSR: Statisticheskii Sbornik.* Moscow: Statistika, 1971.

_____. 1975. *Naselenie SSSR: Chislennost´, Sostav i Dvizhenie Naseleniia, 1973: Statisticheskii Ezhegodnik.* Moscow: Statistika.

_____. 1976. *Narodnoe Khoziaistvo v 1975 godu: Statisticheskii Ezhegodnik.* Moscow: Statistika.

_____. 1977. *Narodnoe Khoziaistvo za 60 Let: Iubileinyi Statisticheskii Ezhegodnik.* Moscow: Statistika.

USSR State Committee on Statistics, Information Pubication Centre. 1988. *Narodnoe Khoziaistvo SSSR v 1987 godu: Statisticheskii Ezhegodnik.* Moscow: Finansy i Statistika.

_____. 1989. *Narodnoe Khoziaistvo SSSR v 1988 godu.* Moscow: Finansy i Statistika.

_____. 1990. *Narodnoe Khoziaistvo SSSR v 1989 godu.* Moscow: Finansy i Statistika.

_____. 1991. *Narodnoe Khoziaistvo SSSR v 1990 godu.* Moscow: Finansy i Statistika.

_____. 1992. *Narodnoe Khoziaistvo SSSR v 1991 godu.* Moscow: Finansy i Statistika.

Van der Post, Laurens. [1964]. *Journey Into Russia.* Harmondsworth: Penguin, 1985.

Vaneigem, Raoul. 1962. Basic Banalities. [Part 1]. In *Situationist International Anthology*, pp. 89-100.

_____. 1967. *The Revolution of Everyday Life.* Translated by Donald Nicholson-Smith. With a preface by the translator. London: Left Bank Books/Rebel Press, 1983.

Voline [Vsevolod Eichenbaum]. [1947]. *The Unknown Revolution.* With a foreword by Rudolf Rocker. Montreal: Black Rose Books, 1975.

Voslensky, Michael. [1980]. *Nomenklatura: Anatomy of the Soviet Ruling Class.* Translated by Eric Mossbacher. London: Bodley Head, 1984.

Walker, Martin. [1986]. *The Waking Giant: The Soviet Union Under Gorbachev.* London:

Sphere, 1987.

Wallerstein, Immanuel. [1975]. Old Problems and New Syntheses: The Relation of Revolutionary Ideas and Practices. Chap. in *The Capitalist World-Economy* (Cambridge: Cambridge University Press, 1979), pp. 231-49.

_____. [1982]. Socialist States: Mercantilist Strategies and Revolutionary Objectives. Chap. in *The Politics of the World-Economy: The States, the Movements, and the Civilizations* (Cambridge: Cambridge University Press, 1984), pp.86-96.

_____. [1990]. Marx, Marxism-Leninism, and Socialist Experiences in the Modern World System. Chap. in *Geopolitics and Geoculture: Essays on the Changing World-System* (Cambridge: Cambridge University Press, 1991), pp. 84-97.

Weitzman, Martin L. 1984. *The Share Economy: Conquering Stagflation.* Cambridge, Massachusetts: Harvard University Press.

West, Nigel. [Rupert Allason]. [1981]. MI5 and the CPGB. Chap. in *MI5: British Security Service Operations, 1909-1945*, pp. 58-95. London: Triad/Panther, 1983.

Wheatcroft, S. G. 1981. On Assessing the Size of Forced Concentration Camp Labour in the Soviet Union, 1929-56. *Soviet Studies* 23, no.2 (April 1981): 265-95.

Wilczynski, J. 1982. *The Economics of Socialism: Principles Governing the Operation of Centrally Planned Economies Under the New System.* Studies in Economics Series, ed. Charles Carter. Fourth ed. London: Allen & Unwin.

Wildcat (Karlsruhe).

Wildcat (London).

Wildcat. [1986]. *See Capitalism and its Revolutionary Destruction: A Statement by Wildcat.*

_____. [1991]. *See* "The Hunt for Red October: Ten Days That Didn't Overthrow Capitalism."

_____. [1992]. *See Outside and Against the Unions: A Communist Response to Dave Douglass' [sic] Text "Refracted Perspective."*

Wildt, Andreas. 1979. Totalitarian State Capitalism: On the Structure and Historical Function of Soviet-Type Societies. Translated by David J. Parent. *Telos* 41 (Fall 1979): 33-57.

Wiles, P. J. D. 1962. *The Political Economy of Communism.* Oxford: Blackwell.

_____. 1977. *Economic Institutions Compared.* Oxford: Blackwell.

Wilhelm, John Howard. 1979. Does the Soviet Union Have a Planned Economy? A Comment on 'From the Achieved Level.' *Soviet Studies* 31, no. 2 (April 1979): 268-74.

_____. 1985. The Soviet Union Has an Administered, Not a Planned, Economy. *Soviet Studies* 37, no.1 (January 1985): 118-30.

Witheford, Nick. 1994. Autonomist Marxism and the Information Society. *Capital & Class* 52 (Spring 1994): 85-125.

Wittfogel, Karl. [1957]. *Oriental Despotism: A Comparative Study in Total Power.* With a new foreword by the author. New York: Random House, Vintage Books, 1981.

Wolin, Simon. 1974. The Mensheviks Under the NEP and in Emigration. Part 3 of *The Mensheviks: From the Revolution of 1917 to the Second World War*, 241-348. With contributions by David Dallin, George Denicke, Leo Lande, Boris Sapir, and Simon Wolin. Hoover Institution Publication No. 117. Translated by Gertrude Vakar. Chicago: University of Chicago Press.

[Workers' Dreadnought.] 1922a. *See* "The Workers' Opposition in Russia." 1922.

_____. 1922b. *See* "Russian Workers' Opposition Joins Fourth International." 1922.

[Workers' Group.] [1923.] See *Manifeste du Groupe Ouvrier du Parti Communiste Russe* (Bolchévik). [1923.]

"The Workers' Opposition in Russia." 1922. *Workers' Dreadnought* (London) vol. 9, 12 (3/6/1922).

[Workers' Truth]. [1922]. See Appeal of the Workers' *Truth Group*. [1922].

Yanowitch, Murray. 1977. *Social and Economic Inequality in the Soviet Union: Six Studies*. London: Martin Robertson.

_____, ed. 1979. *Soviet Work Attitudes: The Issue of Participation in Management*. Oxford: Martin Robertson.

_____. 1985. *Work in the Soviet Union: Attitudes and Issues*. London: Sharpe.

Yugoff, A[ron]. *See* [Iugov], A[ron].

Zaslavskaia, Tat´iana. [1983]. "The Novosibirsk Report." [Report on the Necessity in the USSR of a Deeper Study into the Social Mechanism of Economic Development.] Trans. Teresa Cherfas. *Survey* 28, no.1 (Spring 1984): 88-108.

_____. 1986a. Reshaiushchee Uslovie Uskoreniia Sotsial´no-Ekonomicheskogo Razvitiia. *EKO (Ekonomika i Organizatsiia Promyshlennogo Proizvodstva)* 141 (March 1986): 3-25.

_____. 1986b. Chelovecheskii Faktor Razvitiia Ekonomiki i Sotsial´naia Spravedlivost´. *Kommunist* (1293), no. 13 (September 1986): 61-73.

Zaslavsky, Victor. [1979-80]. The Regime and the Working Class. Chap. in *The Neo-Stalinist State: Class, Ethnicity, and Consensus in Soviet Society*, 44-65. Brighton: Harvester, 1982.

_____. [1980]. Socioeconomic Inequality and Changes in Soviet Ideology. Chap. in *The Neo-Stalinist State*, 66-90.

_____. [1982]. Closed Cities and the Organized Consensus. Chap. in *The Neo-Stalinist State*, 130-64.

_____. [1987]. Three Years of *Perestroika*. *Telos* 74 (Winter 1987-88): 31-41.

_____. 1993. Russia and the Problem of Democratic Transition. *Telos* 96 (Summer 1993): 26-52.

[Zerowork]. 1975. Introduction. *Zerowork* 1 (December 1975) (New York): 1-6.

Zerowork (New York).

Zerzan, John. 1974. Organized Labor Versus the 'Revolt Against Work': The Critical Contest. *Telos* 21 (Fall 1974): 194-206. [Also in G[randizo] Munis and J[ohn] Zerzan, *Unions Against Revolution: Two Essays* (Detroit: Black & Red, 1975), 47-62.]

Zimin, A. 1977. On the Question of the Place in History of the Social Structure of the Soviet Union (An Historical Parallel and a Sociological Hypothesis). Translated by Brian Pearce. In *Samizdat Register 1: Voices of the Socialist Opposition in the Soviet Union*, ed. Roy Medvedev, 116-47. London: Merlin.

Zinoviev, G[rigorii] I[evseevich]. [1925]. *Le Léninisme: Introduction à l'Etude du Léninisme*. Paris: Bureau d'Editions de Diffusion et de Publicité, 1926.

Zukin, Sharon. 1978. The Problem of Social Class under Socialism. *Theory and Society* 6: 391-427.